Public Economics

Public Economics

Theory and Policy

Essays in Honor of Amaresh Bagchi

Edited by

M. Govinda Rao

Mihir Rakshit

SAGE www.sagepublications.com
Los Angeles • London • New Delhi • Singapore • Washington DC

Jointly published in 2011 by

SAGE Publications India Pvt Ltd
B1/I-1 Mohan Cooperative
Industrial Area   and
Mathura Road,
New Delhi 110 044, India
www.sagepub.in

**National Institute of
Public Finance and Policy**
18/2 Satsang Vihar Marg
Special Institutional Area
New Delhi 110 067, India

SAGE Publications Inc
2455 Teller Road
Thousand Oaks, California 91320, USA

SAGE Publications Ltd
1 Oliver's Yard, 55 City Road
London EC1Y 1SP, United Kingdom

SAGE Publications Asia-Pacific Pte Ltd
33 Pekin Street
#02-01 Far East Square
Singapore 048763

Published by Vivek Mehra for SAGE Publications India Pvt Ltd, Phototypeset in 10.5/12.5 Joanna MT by Tantla Composition Pvt Ltd, Chandigarh and printed at Chaman Enterprises, New Delhi.

Library of Congress Cataloging-in-Publication Data

Public economics: theory and policy: essays in honor of Dr. Amaresh Bagchi/ edited by M. Govinda Rao, Mihir Rakshit.
    p. cm.
  Includes bibliographical references and index.
  1. Fiscal policy.   2. Finance, Public.   I. Govinda Rao, M.
II. Rakshit, Mihir.   III. Bagchi, A. (Amaresh)

HJ192.5.P797   336—dc22   2010   2010038413

ISBN: 978-81-321-0502-2 (HB)

The SAGE Team: Elina Majumdar, Sushmita Banerjee, Amrita Saha and
              Deepti Saxena

Contents

—— • ✦ • ——

Contents

Reminiscences

List of Tables and Figures

———— • ✦ • ————

List of Tables

List of Figures

List of Abbreviations

———— • ✦ • ————

BBLR	Broad Based Low Rate
CBD	Convention on Bio-diversity
CENVAT	Central Value Added Tax
CGF	Credit Guarantee Finance
CSO	Central Statistical Organization
DCRF	Debt Consolidation and Relief Facility
EPAP	Eleventh Plan Approach Paper
FD	Fiscal Deficit
GDP	Gross Domestic Product
GEF	Global Environment Fund
GHG	Green House Gas
GPF	General Provident Fund
GPG	Global Public Goods
HRD	Human Resources Development
HSN	Harmonized System of Nomenclature
HST	Harmonized Sales Tax
ICOR	Incremental Capital Output Ratio
IIP	Index of Industrial Production
IT	Income Tax
MDG	Millennium Development Goals
MRP	Maximum Retail Price
NAIRU	Non-Accounting Inflation Rate of Unemployment
NDP	Net Development Product
NHDP	National Highway Development Project

OECD	Organization for Economic Cooperation and Development
PAN	Permanent Account Number
PDS	Public Distribution System
PPP	Public-private Partnership
PVAT	Prepaid Value Added Tax
QST	Quebec Sales Tax
RD	Rural Development
RNR	Revenue Neutral Rate
SDG	School Development Grant
SEEA	Settled System of Environmental Economic Accounting
SNA	System of National Accounts
SSA	Sarva Shiksha Abhiyan
TFC	Twelfth Finance Commission
TLM	Teaching and Learning Material
UNCTAD	United Nations Conference on Trade and Development
UNICEF	United Nations Children's Fund
WTO	World Trade Organization

जय हिन्द

डॉ. सी. रंगराजन
Dr. C. RANGARAJAN

अध्यक्ष
प्रधानमंत्री की आर्थिक सलाहकार परिषद्
विज्ञान भवन सौंध 'ई' हाल
मौलाना आज़ाद रोड
नई दिल्ली-110 011
CHAIRMAN
Economic Advisory Council to the Prime Minister
Vigyan Bhavan Annexe, 'E' Hall
Maulana Azad Road
New Delhi-110 011

Foreword

———— • ✦ • ————

It is an honor to write the Foreword to this volume, which is a collection of essays in honor of Dr Amaresh Bagchi who passed away in February 2008. I had known Dr Bagchi intimately for the last three decades. We had served together in one or two committees.

Dr Bagchi was an outstanding economist who gave shape to the discipline of public finance in our country. He came to the academic field a bit late. He joined the academia after about two decades of working in the income tax department of Government of India. His essays were models of logic and precision. They were marked by analytical rigor and clarity. His writings covered all aspects of public finance—direct and indirect taxes, tax administration, fiscal deficit and public debt, fiscal decentralization and public expenditure. On the question of fiscal deficit, we shared a common interest. While he approached it from the angle of fiscal policy, I looked at it from the angle of monetary policy. We agreed that fiscal deficits must be kept under control, while there were differences on the modalities of monitoring it.

The death of Dr Bagchi has left a deep void in the arena of public finance in India. The essays included in the volume cover a wide range. This volume is a fitting tribute to one who had spent his entire life working on different facets of public finance. I must thank all the authors for their excellent contributions. This volume is an important addition to the literature on public economics in our country.

C. Rangarajan

(C. Rangarajan)

दूरभाष 011-23022311, 23022313 फैक्स 011-23022318 ई-मेल c.rangarajan@nic.in
Telephone : 011-23022311, 23022313 Fax : 011-23022318 e-mail : c.rangarajan@nic.in

Acknowledgments

———— • ✦ • ————

Working on this book in honor of Dr Amaresh Bagchi has been a great pleasure. It is due to the popularity of Dr Bagchi that his friends and colleagues were very forthcoming in contributing to the volume and attending to the several queries in spite of their extreme demand on time. The family members of Dr Bagchi, particularly his wife, Mrs Ratna Bagchi, daughter, Dr Uttara Chatterjee, and son, Dr Kaushik Bagchi were very forthcoming in sharing with the authors the various aspects of his life and works. We would also like to thank SAGE Publications, particularly Ms Elina Majumdar for the keen interest shown in publishing this collection of essays. Thanks are also due to Mr N. Natarajan who attended to the logistics of getting the editorial queries answered by various authors and for looking after various aspects of publication.

Introduction

————— • ✦ • —————

This volume is a tribute to Amaresh Bagchi, a pre-eminent scholar in public finance who passed away in February 2008. Amaresh Bagchi was a keen researcher who relentlessly undertook policy research and advocacy in public economics, in an academic career spanning over three and a half decades preceded by almost two decades of experience in tax and economic administration in Government of India. The chapters included in the volume have been contributed by his close friends and colleagues and deal with both theoretical and applied topics in public economics. Most of the topics dealt with in the collection were dear to Amareshda and it is hoped that the volume will be a fitting tribute to the scholar who had unparalleled passion for both theory and empirical research in public economics.

Much of Amaresh Bagchi's research was in applied public economics, but he had tremendous love for theory and never missed an opportunity to studiously learn, admire, and get excited about nuances in theoretical developments. Amaresh Bagchi was a late entrant to a full-time academic profession; he spent the first two decades of his career in tax and economic policy administration in the Ministry of Finance. He put the knowledge gained from his experience of policy administration to great advantage by combining rigor with relevance in his research studies. Amaresh Bagchi made significant contributions in several areas, including tax policy and administration and fiscal federalism. His love for theory is best evidenced in the review article of a book which put together the outcome of a week-long symposium organized by the Centre for Economic Studies at the University of Munich. The symposium involved two great stalwarts in public finance and public choice—Richard Musgrave and James Buchanan, the former firmly rooted his analysis on the assumption of a benevolent state and the latter approached the subject from the perspective of public choice, in which the state was assumed to be a problem rather than a solution. Amaresh Bagchi was also concerned about the poor quality of teaching and research in public economics in India and went on to edit a volume that contained basic contributions to theory and applied public economics for the benefit of the students (Bagchi, 2005). Unpretentious and affable, Amaresh Bagchi was very concerned with poverty and deprivation and firmly believed that the end of all policies should be to usher in a just society. Indeed, he was the bridge between the left and the right, often torn between them, but nevertheless was equally at home across ideological spectrums.

Amaresh Bagchi's scholarship, unpretentious character, and humility earned him a large number of friends and admirers. Some of us who worked closely with him decided to put together this volume in memory of our association with him and as a tribute to his scholarship. All the contributors to this volume were close friends and colleagues of Amaresh Bagchi and all of us benefited immensely from close professional associations with him. The volume has 10 papers besides two tributes, one from Professor Tapas Majumdar who, in fact was Amaresh Bagchi's teacher, and another by Shankar Acharya, who was his close friend and colleague initially at National Institute of Public Finance and Policy (NIPFP) and later in the Ministry of Finance.

The first paper in the volume by Sudipto Mundle highlights the life and works of Amaresh Bagchi. Mundle traces his journey from his birth in Malda in 1930 to his education at the Presidency College, Kolkata. It is here he developed friendship and professional association with the likes of Dr D.N. Ghosh and Professor Mihir Rakshit which lasted his entire professional journey. Mundle records Bagchi's tenacious pursuit of tax cases of high profile political personalities as an Indian Revenue Service Officer. His entry into scholarly pursuits such as economics research, though late, was helped by his experience with institutional realities. As an official of the Ministry of Finance, he was called upon to provide background research to the policy on bank nationalization. He also assisted the K.N. Raj Committee on "Taxation of Agricultural Wealth and Incomes". These are just two examples of the many that left an imprint on his scholarship on policy making. Joining the NIPFP as Reserve Bank of India (RBI) Chair Professor and later as its Director led him to make significant contributions in fiscal policy research, advocacy, and capacity building.

As an expert in fiscal policy, Amaresh Bagchi was very concerned about persistence of large deficits but was not in favor of the mechanical way in which the fiscal consolidation targets were set. Mihir Rakshit's paper in this volume questions the very logic of the targets on revenue and fiscal deficits, and their phasing under the Fiscal Responsibility and Budget Management (FRBM) Act, 2003, as well as the fiscal restructuring plan recommended by the Twelfth Finance Commission. Although the FRBM Act, 2003 was forced to be abandoned in 2008 due to the global financial crisis, Rakshit points out that the Act itself was a veritable source of discord among the three policy making bodies in India, namely, the Finance Ministry, the Planning Commission, and the Reserve Bank of India. While the Planning Commission questions the definition of revenue deficit, it does not really have a fundamental objection to the FRBM Rules. Of course, it wants to extend the fiscal deficit target to be achieved by two years. In contrast, Rakshit has fundamental objections to the nature as well as phasing of the fiscal deficit targets required for achieving socio-economic goals. It contends that static targets for revenue and fiscal deficits are clearly inappropriate when the economy is faced with business or agricultural cycles. In fact, fiscal policy will have to take a pro-cyclical stance when such cycles are in vogue. Rakshit argues that the targets set by the fiscal structuring plan of the Twelfth Finance Commission are clearly sub-optimal from the long-term developmental perspective. Although it has a broadly consistent macroeconomic exercise, it is devoid of cost benefit calculations of borrowing.

Reforming the tax system was at the heart of Amaresh Bagchi's research, and while he was fascinated by the nuances of optimal tax theory, he saw that actual tax reforms will have to follow the best practice approach of broadening the base, lowering rates, and reducing differentiation in tax rates to evolve a simple and administrable tax system. Richard M. Bird's paper on "broadening base, lowering rate" approach to tax reforms in developing countries, makes a critical appraisal on the applicability of the best practice approach to tax reform. The essence of this approach is to broaden the tax base so that equivalent revenue can be realized at a lower tax rate. Levying the tax at lower rates is necessary to minimize the distortions because the distortion is equivalent to square of the tax rate. Bird discusses the broad contours of broad-based low-rate approach and more specifically, the desirability of developing countries relying on (*a*) consumption *versus* income tax; (*b*) broader base versus narrower base; (*c*) policy to reduce the size of the informal economy; and (*d*) the usefulness of tax incentives. He argues that the growth-oriented tax system should minimize the three costs in taxation—the cost of collection, the compliance cost, and the cost of economy in terms of distortions. In his scheme, a growth-oriented tax system should have low and stable taxation of profits, some taxation of agricultural and informal sectors of the economy, and major reliance on broad-based consumption tax. He also cautions against tax incentives and that tax policy and reforms should not become a hostage to profits, and economic considerations should rule it.

Amaresh Bagchi was one of the pioneers of consumption tax reform in the country. The Expert Committee Report on the Reform of Trade Taxes in India in 1995 headed by Amaresh*da*, characterized the Indian consumption tax system in the mid-1990s as "archaic, irrational, and complex, and according to notable experts the most complex in the world". Although the introduction of Value Added Tax (VAT) has improved the structure of consumption tax in significant ways from what was described here, much remains to be done and Goods and Services Tax (GST) reform is the way forward. Ehtisham Ahmad and Satya Poddar in their paper on the "GST Reforms and Intergovernmental Considerations in India" comprehensively deal with various constitutional, structural, and operational issues relating to the introduction of GST in India. They examine the design issues pertaining to GST in the country to replace the prevailing multiple consumption taxes. Combining taxes on goods and services in a unified manner is necessary to eliminate cascading. GST reform at the central level will help to broaden the base to cover stages subsequent to manufacturing. Similarly, at the state level, the VAT, at present, is levied only on goods and needs to be extended to services, not only to minimize cascading but also to expand the base of the tax. The chapter discusses alternative models of GST, including concurrent dual GST, the national GST, state GSTs, and non-concurrent dual GSTs, and underlines the formidable challenges of center-state coordination and harmonization, whichever option is chosen. The authors discuss various other design aspects such as measuring the revenue neutral rates, the issues of taxing food items, and hard-to-tax areas such as land and real properties, non-profit sector, and financial services. The difficulties in taxing services of interstate nature at the state level, and the need for harmonizing law and administration in different states too are pointed out in the chapter.

Fiscal federalism was another area which fascinated Amaresh Bagchi and he himself did considerable work on intergovernmental fiscal issues. Notable among his contributions on fiscal federalism was the Kale Memorial Lecture he delivered at the Gokhale Institute of Politics and Economics, Pune. The normative framework on fiscal federalism or what has come to be known as the first-generation theories of fiscal federalism has been developed with the assumption of a benevolent state and keeping in view the advanced market economies. The implementable rules derived from this framework cannot be applied uncritically to developing country situations, particularly those in transition from plan to market. The policy responsiveness to regional resource allocations depends on the nature of policies and institutions and even as centralized planning strategy is no more relevant to resource allocation, the legacy left by adopting the plan strategy has continued. These include controls on prices and outputs, and impediments placed on the mobility of factors as well as products with significant implications for regional pattern of resource allocation. Govinda Rao's paper attempts to identify important institutional features of these economies that make the modifications in the normative propositions necessary. These include impact of planning in distorting the budgetary systems, overhang of public enterprises and its inhibiting influence on the development of the market, controls over prices and output and the distortions and invisible regional transfers they create, physical barriers to mobility and trade across different regions, need to replace public enterprise profits with taxes and variety of instruments used to establish regional equity under planning, and the problems that can get created in a market economy.

Public goods and externalities are at the core of public finance. Much of the literature in this area focuses on public goods within countries. The large gains from international peace, trade, and environment have led to considerable interest in these global public goods. In his paper, U. Sankar reviews the different definitions of global public goods and chooses the definition and framework provided by Kaul, Conceicau, Goulven, and Mendoza for evaluating the provision of global public goods. He considers different ways of classifying global public goods. Using the above framework, particularly the concept of triangle of public-ness, the chapter assesses the working of three global regimes, namely, the World Trade Organization, the United Nations Framework Convention on Climate Change, and the Convention on Biological Diversity. It discusses issues such as subsidiary principle, incentives and delivery systems in the provision of global public goods. It concludes that in the three existing global institutions there are no built-in measures for achieving dynamic efficiency and that development concerns get low priority.

Ehtisham Ahmad and Nicholas Stern were the pioneers in applying modern public finance methods to the reform of indirect taxes in the early 1980s and NIPFP under Raja Chelliah and Amaresh Bagchi provided them the intellectual environment to initiate studies on India. In their chapter "Effective Carbon Taxes and Public Policy Options", they extend the methodology to the issues relating to the design and implementation of environmental taxes. Designing such a tax involves varying tax rates, according to the carbon content of different goods.

An important issue in carbon taxation concerns the assignment of the function to different levels of government, the allocation of carbon quotas to industries and trading in them and compensation to the poorest household that may be affected by the tax. For both administrative and political economy considerations, it is desirable to design carbon taxes uniformly across states, and this could be achieved by a central tax or harmonized state level taxes. In the Indian context, they recommend central excise as the most appropriate instrument for carbon taxation because, at the state level, levying state VAT at different rates would not be desirable. The authors also introduce a cap-and-trade scheme in which trading can take place between enterprises, if prior quotas are assigned to key upstream industries, and revenues can be generated by auctioning of the quotas. The carbon tax or quota-trading scheme must be accompanied by measures to compensate the poorest households that might be affected. These could be administered by state governments, and partially financed by the revenues from carbon tax or auctioning of quotas. The revenues from these instruments can also be used to finance any required restructuring of manufacturing or other activities.

Keeping in view the deep interest Amaresh Bagchi had on the sustainability of the development process, Ramprasad Sengupta in his chapter, "Sustainable Economic Growth and Modeling for Resource and Income Accounting", focuses on the conceptual and methodological issues. The chapter begins by examining the basic feasibility of the long run steady-state growth while maintaining the ecosystems of the natural environment. He argues that in the growth model, capital should include knowledge capital as well. The human capital often embodies technological progress. This has warranted the use of the concept of weak sustainability in the literature to answer the questions relating to the feasibility of steady growth. The paper identifies the conditions of sustainable growth defined in a framework of weak sustainability and endogenous growth as driven by research and development (R&D) and human innovations of various kinds. This brings out the need for the development of a more comprehensive macroeconomic accounting system with the additional coverage and its reclassification for treating explicitly natural, human, and knowledge capital formations for characterizing economic changes and calibrating development policies.

In order to operationalize the concept of sustainable development in the accounting context, the paper further develops a theoretical approach of resource and income accounting using an input-output framework. The model depicts the environment-economy interaction along with the material balances. From this interaction model the estimates for the environmentally adjusted indicators of macroeconomic development like GDP, NDP, and savings are derived. The chapter highlights the importance of the interaction of environmental and economic accounting for sustainable development policies.

Amaresh Bagchi had tremendous interest in the economics of education, mainly as a humanist economist and also due to his close association with his teacher and friend, Professor Tapas Majumdar. Keeping this in view, Arnab and Anjan Mukherjee in their chapter, "Do Public Funds Increase Days of Instruction in Primary Schools?", investigate the role of public funds in ensuring a certain minimum number of instructional days in primary schools. Using data on primary schools from three districts, the chapter first documents that the distribution of instructional days may reasonably be thought of as a binary variable where a school is either functional (i.e., with more than 201 instructional days) or is not (i.e., has less than 201 instructional days). Second, it is shown that receiving any public funds is important for the schools to be functional; however, the marginal effect of volume of public funding diminishes with larger amounts of funding. Finally, monitoring schools in terms of the number of academic visits by Block Resource Centre (BRC) and Cluster Resource Centre (CRC) coordinators as well as the presence of head teachers are important in ensuring that primary schools are functional in the sense that we have defined. These findings emphasize the important ways to improve the quality of primary schooling in India.

Amaresh Bagchi had considerable concern on the quality and content of teaching of public economics courses in universities. Keeping this in view, Arindam Das-Gupta, in the last chapter, identifies important gaps in the coverage of typical public economics courses, if they are to remain relevant given the rapidly changing scope of the public sector in the past 50 years. The chapter takes as its starting point topics not covered or inadequately covered in leading undergraduate public finance and public economics textbooks. Of the various topics identified, three topics discussed in detail are economic principles of the government budget, non-tax revenues, and the global fiscal commons. The discussion in each case focuses on definitions and principles—both theoretical and applied—rather than real-world examples. Other topics identified but not discussed in detail include the choice between modes of intervention for public service delivery, the role of government in the information sector, and public financial management and administration.

We hope these chapters do justice to the enormous appetite for knowledge that Amaresh Bagchi had. In this volume the readers would find that some chapters are theoretical and while others discuss policy matters. This has been done in order to commemorate Amaresh Bagchi's enormous love for both theoretical and applied subjects in public economics. In producing this volume we hope, we have tried to give this noble scholar something in return for his contributions.

M. Govinda Rao
Mihir Rakshit

Reference

Bagchi, Amaresh (ed.). 2005. *Readings in Public Finance*. New Delhi: Oxford University Press.

1

Amaresh Bagchi: His Life and Work

Sudipto Mundle

—— • ✦ • ——

I Introduction

This piece is a homage to an exceptional human being who has had a
great influence on the trajectory of my career. I hope, therefore, that
the reader will forgive me for starting this on a personal note, sharing
with you the particularly poignant circumstances in which I write it.
I first met Amaresh Bagchi in the summer of 1985, when he invited
me to join the NIPFP as RBI Chair Professor. My impression from that
first meeting, which I carry to this day, was the exceptional simplicity
and humanity of this man. A few minutes into the conversation, I could
tell that he belonged to that rare breed of people who combine in
themselves the wisdom of scholarship with long years of experience in
the practical business of designing and implementing policies, a true
mandarin. We worked together for the next nine years, with occasional
gaps when I went on secondment to the government and he went on
an assignment to the World Bank, until I left for a job with the Asian
Development Bank (ADB) in 1994. We met infrequently after that on
my visits to India, and it struck me that he seemed to be aging quite
rapidly. I did not know at the time that he was suffering from an ailment
that was progressively debilitating him. Yet, this was a highly productive
period in his life. Today I write this piece sitting in the same room in
which he worked for the last few years of his life, and at the same desk

at which he sat till the day on which he was hospitalized, two days before he died. Some of his old papers are still on the shelves, some frequently used documents saved on the desktop of the computer, bits of stationery and some personal knick-knacks are still in the drawers. It is a very moving experience.

II Early Life

Amaresh Bagchi was born in Malda in West Bengal in 1930. His parents, Karunamoy and Bimala Bagchi, had three children—Amaresh, his brother Pashupathinath, and sister Bijoli. Amaresh Bagchi studied in the Malda Zilla School where his father was a teacher and also the headmaster. Even as a young boy, he excelled in his studies. He passed the matriculation final school examination, with sixth rank in undivided Bengal (today's Bangladesh plus West Bengal), in 1945. This fetched him a merit scholarship to study in Presidency College in Kolkata, one of India's most outstanding institutions. Perhaps no other college in India has produced so many brilliant scholars generation after generation in so many different fields. Many of these students came from modest *mofussil* backgrounds, with merit scholarships providing them the passage to Kolkata's vibrant intellectual life and the wider world beyond. Bagchi could not have hoped for a better place to launch him on his future career that straddled the worlds of scholarship and government.

It was in Presidency that Bagchi developed his deepest values, his interest in macroeconomics, and some of his strong friendships. As a student living in Hindu Hostel he witnessed, first hand, the horror of a communal riot: human beings slaughtering other human beings even as they begged for mercy. This is what made him passionately pacifist and secular in his outlook, with a deep empathy for the underdog. It was also during this period that Bagchi developed his special interest in macroeconomics. It was this interest that drew him to two of his closet friends, D.N. Ghosh and Mihir Rakshit.

Like Bagchi, D.N. Ghosh was also a *mofusssil* boy who had come to study in Presidency. They were taught by legendary teachers like Bhabatosh Datta in Presidency and Panchanan Chakraborty in Calcutta University. Ghosh was a year ahead of Bagchi and had started attending lectures on Keynes delivered by Chakraborty for 5th year students. He recalls that Bagchi, who was still in his 4th year, sought special permission to attend these lectures because of his interest in the subject. They would also frequently meet in Chakarborty's house to listen to the latter's encyclopedic knowledge about the linkage between economic theory and economic history. Towards the end of this period Bagchi met Mihir Rakshit, who later went on to become one of India's most distinguished macroeconomic theorists. Rakshit recalls that he was traveling by bus no. 3B, his daily commuting route, with a copy of Kalecki's *Economic Dynamics* in his hand. A person sitting nearby reached out to him and asked if he could take a look. That was Bagchi and it was the beginning of their lifelong friendship.

There is a particular episode during this period, related by his wife Ratna and also his close friends, which was quite characteristic of Bagchi's humility, his tendency to worry, and his strong risk aversion. In his M.A. examination, after he had completed several papers Bagchi felt that he had not written his answers well and decided to drop out, losing a year. It turned out later that in all the papers for which he had taken the examination, he had secured first class marks.

III His Career

Bagchi joined the Indian Revenue Service in 1954 and was posted in Kolkata for the next four years. It was here that he met the woman who would be his partner for the rest of his life. Ratna Bagchi was raised in Kolkata. She studied at the Gokhale School, one of Kolkata's leading institutions for women's education, and went on to graduate from Gokhale College. They married in 1957 and were blessed with two children. Their son Kaushik is now a professor in Baltimore, and their daughter Uttara is a doctor in Kolkata.

Bagchi was subsequently posted to Jalpaiguri in 1958, followed by Cuttack in 1962, and Patna in 1965. He acquired a formidable reputation as an income tax officer. In a particularly high profile case he doggedly pursued a leading politician of the region, traveling to some of the remotest villages in search of evidence of unreported income. Rumor has it that even till his last days the politician remembered Bagchi and spoke of his tenacity. Bagchi's dedication to the revenue service notwithstanding, he was clearly missing the intellectual excitement that had originally drawn him to the world of scholarship. In 1967 he took a year's leave from the revenue service and went back to Presidency College as a Senior Fellow in Economic Studies.

The following year he went back to the Revenue Department in the Ministry of Finance in New Delhi. Here, he re-connected with his old friend D.N. Ghosh who was by now a Deputy Secretary in the Banking Division that later became the Banking Department. The Banking Division was responsible for preparing the policy on bank nationalization and for its implementation. However, the division had virtually no officers other than Ghosh. He wanted Bagchi's help in drafting the bank nationalization legislation and later implementing the policy. Bagchi was then in the prestigious Tax Policy Unit and reluctant to move. After much persuasion over several lunch sessions he finally agreed. It is a tribute to Bagchi that a senior officer, who initially opposed Bagchi's transfer to the Banking Department, later came to regard him as one of the department's "*ratnas*" (jewels) and strongly endorsed Bagchi's penchant for academic rigor even in his bureaucratic work.

The nationalization of banks was a controversial move, associated with the imposition of emergency. It became one of the main symbols of the inefficient *dirigiste* regime that existed prior to the 1991 reforms and which is blamed for stunting India's growth potential. However, it was also a measure that directed credit for the first time to poor farmers, who had till then been entirely dependent on rapacious rural moneylenders. No doubt this sat well with Bagchi's egalitarian values and his concern for the underdog. It also has to be said that in the recent global financial crisis, when some of the world's biggest banks collapsed or had to be bailed out, India's public sector banks, in particular, have stood out for their robust performance. This is due in large measure to the high level of capitalization of the public sector banks, their prudent lending practices, and their strict compliance with RBI regulations. This too would have pleased Bagchi enormously had he been around today.

Another important task Bagchi undertook at this time was to assist the Raj Committee on Taxation of Agricultural Wealth and Income as an Adviser. His research on presumptive taxation laid the foundation for one of the key proposals of the Committee, the Agricultural

Holdings Tax. This was perhaps the first serious effort in modern India to directly tax the agricultural sector. Alas, this recommendation was politically unpalatable in a country where two-thirds of the vote bank is dependent on agricultural incomes. It did not get beyond the report of the committee. Exclusion of this sector remains one of the most iniquitous features of India's tax system even to this day.

It often happens in life that what initially appears as a set back, later turns out to be a blessing in disguise. An event of this kind in the Banking Department shifted Bagchi's career on to a different and vastly more rewarding path. He was up for promotion as Deputy Secretary in the department and well qualified because of his experience in the department. However, he was pushed aside in favor of another candidate from a higher service cadre who reportedly knew very little about banking. Those familiar with the episode say that Bagchi was quite disappointed, and this triggered his decision to once again take leave from the government and re-engage with the academic world. He was offered a fellowship by the Indian Council of Social Science Research to pursue his research at the economics department of Jawaharlal Nehru University. He was later awarded a Ph.D. for his thesis on "The Concept of Income in Taxation", which remains an important contribution to the literature on this subject to this day.

Bagchi returned to the Ministry of Finance as Director of the Fiscal Policy Unit in the Economic Division in 1975. His Ph.D. thesis and other research, his work on presumptive taxation for the Raj committee, and contributions to several other committees and working groups had by now established him as an expert in the field of fiscal policy. He was, therefore, able to put his distinct stamp on the work of the division at this time. Though a full blown reform of India's tax system would not get underway for another decade or so, Bagchi attempted to nudge the system in a more rational direction. This was also the time when he began interacting with a small but remarkable group of scholar-bureaucrats who would later lead the reforms that transformed India from a *dirigiste*, autarkic, slow growing economy to a liberal open economy that is now one of the fastest growing economies in the world. Among others, this group included Manmohan Singh, Bimal Jalan, Montek Singh Ahluwalia, Shankar Acharya, and Raja Chelliah, probably India's best known public finance expert. Chelliah, who had just returned from the International Monetary Fund (IMF) and was associated with the Ministry of Finance as a Senior Adviser, was at the time laying the foundation for a research

5

institute specializing in public finance and policy work: the National Institute of Public Finance and Policy (NIPFP). Once the Institute was established with Chelliah as its director, he invited Bagchi to join the institute as the first Reserve Bank of India Chair Professor. They continued to collaborate closely, along with others, in setting the terms of debate on reform of India's tax system.

Bagchi returned to the Ministry of Finance for the last time as Officer on Special Duty (Economic Affairs) in 1984 and after a year he was back to NIPFP as its Director on Chelliah's retirement in 1985. This was another turning point in Bagchi's career. By now the call for tax reform had gathered considerable momentum as part of the overall push towards market-oriented reforms in India, and NIPFP became the institutional hub for much of the research on fiscal reforms. Building on the foundations laid by Chelliah, Bagchi oversaw a period of dynamic growth in the institute over the next 10 years. In addition to traditional areas of research in direct taxes, indirect taxes, public expenditure, state finances and state taxes, municipal finances, and fiscal federalism, the institute now extended its research into other areas of public policy such as macroeconomic policy, environment policy, urban development policy, and so on. Many departments of the Central government as well as states, municipalities, and the succession of Finance Commissions came to see the institute as a major resource centre for their policy work. Bagchi also laid great emphasis on attracting scholars of repute from within India and abroad to spend time at the institute and in building links with academic institutions and universities. He also initiated a scholarship program to send young researchers from within and outside the institute to some of the best universities in the world for higher studies.

Apart from these initiatives in building NIPFP, Bagchi continued to play an active role in the ongoing process of economic reforms, serving on several important Commissions, Committees, and working groups. He came to be seen as a person who recognized areas of government failure and the need for reforms, while at the same time recognizing areas of market failure and the need for sound regulation, that is, a reformer who was also mindful of the limits of liberalization. Today, the world is struggling to reign in the excesses of free market fundamentalism, especially de-regulated financial markets that have run amok. Bagchi would have been pleased to see that his "middle path" has now become the mainstream view.

Bagchi retired as Director of NIPFP in 1995, but continued his research as an honorary Emeritus Professor in the institute, a position he held till the end. He remained remarkably active during this last phase of his career. He was a member of the Eleventh Finance Commission from 1998–2000 and a member of the Prime Minister's Economic Advisory Council from 1998–2004, a member of the Planning Commission's Steering Committee on Resources for the 11th Five Year Plan, and a member of the Commission on Center-state Relations at the time of his death. He was also on the Academic Council of the Jawaharlal Nehru University and on the Board of Management of the Indira Gandhi Institute of Development Research. He was very productive in his research and writing during this phase, producing a number of papers and articles on various topics in public finance. It is quite typical of the man that he was still working at his desk at NIPFP until just a few hours before he was hospitalized on 18 February 2008.

IV His Contribution

Bagchi's contributions were to the world of ideas as well as to the world of action, the two worlds that Bagchi straddled through his long career. However, as Keynes once observed, it is not commonly understood how far the actions of practical men are guided by theories of one kind or another emanating from the world of ideas. The organizing theme of Bagchi's career was indeed to make explicit his ideas through research papers and articles in the world of scholarship and let those ideas guide his work in the world of action, initially as an officer in the Ministry of Finance, and later as an authoritative adviser on fiscal policy in the various policy making committees and commissions on which he served.

Bagchi's academic contributions covered a wide range of topics in the field of public finance, but it would be fair to say that his main contributions were in the fields of tax policy and fiscal federalism.[1] Broadly Bagchi's work can be divided into two phases: before and after 2000. In the first phase, Bagchi focused on tax policy. His early research was on income taxation. Starting with his work on presumptive taxation in agriculture, based on agricultural holdings, for the Raj Committee on Taxation of Agricultural Wealth and Income, he went on make a major contribution on the concept of income for taxation in his Ph.D. thesis. Later he extended his coverage to property tax, sales tax and, especially, the value added tax. The underlying theme of all of this work was rationalization and reform of a highly distorted tax system, particularly the system of domestic trade taxes. As such, he came to be recognized as one of the architects of tax reforms in India, along with Raja Chelliah and others. What is distinctive about Bagchi's contribution to tax reform is that his work was not only always informed by theory but also firmly grounded in reality, thanks to his experience as a tax administrator. Also, his reform proposals always sought to correct for government failure without losing sight of the problems arising from market failure.

Though Bagchi continued to write on tax policy and other aspects of public finance, his main contribution after 2000 was in the field of fiscal federalism and intergovernmental finances. As always, his research work was designed to feed into his work in the world of action, and was well reflected in the positions he took in official platforms like the 11th Finance Commission, the 11th Plan Steering Committee on Resources, and finally the Commission on Center-state Relations. Bagchi was unhappy with the increasing centralization of economic power in India, and the intrusion of the central government into areas that constitutionally belonged to the states. He was equally unhappy about the multiplicity of channels for transferring resources from the central authorities to the states, which is again an intrusion into the constitutional role of the Finance Commission, and other distortions in the transfer system that violate the principles of incentive compatibility. In short, Bagchi found it disturbing that intergovernmental fiscal relations were being driven by ad hoc decisions and political economy factors, rather than sound principles of fiscal federalism. The two places where he dealt with this whole class of issues are his Note of Dissent to the Report of 11th Finance Commission and in his Kale Memorial Lecture delivered at the Gokhale Institute of Economics and Politics in 2001.

Apart from his writings on tax policy and fiscal federalism, three other pieces of work should be mentioned in particular. His study on tax administration, an important but neglected topic, undertaken jointly with Richard Bird and A. Das-Gupta; his joint paper with Pulin Nayak on "Theory of Public Finance and the Planning Process: The Indian Experience", which remains a major contribution on the subject, and his edited volume on "Readings in Public Finance", which covered the entire field from public choice theory and public goods to tax theory, macro aspects of fiscal policy and fiscal federalism (Bagchi et al., 1995; Bagchi and Nayak, 1994; Bagchi, 2005). Particularly interesting in the last collection is Bagchi's own article reviewing the papers of the "Symposium on Fifty Years of Public Finance from Richard Musgrave to James Buchanan". Between Musgrave's conception of a benevolent, interventionist state rescuing capitalism from failures of the market and Buchanan's conception of the state as a self-serving leviathan, we have the boundaries of public finance laid out for us by these two great economists.

Lying in the intersection between Bagchi as a scholar and Bagchi as a practitioner, we have Bagchi, the institution builder. He collaborated with Chelliah from the outset as the latter laid the ground work for establishing the NIPFP, which Bagchi joined as RBI Professor. Later, as director of the Institute, Bagchi built on the foundations laid by Chelliah to develop NIPFP as a leading center for research in public finance and economic policy making. It is a great loss to the Institute and to the field of public finance in India that just over a year after Bagchi's death, Chelliah too has passed away—two great pillars of the profession have left us.

V Amaresh Bagchi: The Man

Amaresh Bagchi was an outstanding student, a distinguished scholar, and a recognized authority among practitioners in the field of public finance. But above all, he was a simple, honest and hardworking person. Reminiscing about him, his wife Ratna speaks mainly about his deep commitment to work. His books and papers literally stretched from his office to his dining table at home, symbolizing his attitude to work as the single most important mission in his life. This perhaps reflects the embodiment of his moral compass in Gandhian values rather than the Protestant ethic, because Bagchi was also a very secular humanitarian. He spoke loudly against all injustice or violation of human rights and was in favor of an egalitarian society. He incorporated them in his writings. Bagchi's belief in the Gandhian dictum of simple living and high thinking did not prevent Bagchi from enjoying the simple pleasures of life. He loved a hearty meal as much as good music. His favorites were *Rabindra sangeet* and Western classical music as well as music from the Caribbean. His journalist brother-in-law Gautam Adhikari, who fondly recalls their endless debates on the virtues of a liberal society, also recalls the many family picnics when Bagchi would let his hair down and sing *Rabindra sangeet*.

Bagchi was also a very loving father who doted on his children. Here are some vignettes from his daughter Uttara:

> As a child, I remember my father going a lot on tours, all over the country. I always waited eagerly for him to come back, as he never came back without a present. The presents ranged from coloring pencils, books, colorful bangles, and trinkets to local sweets from that place. I always had a share of these, even if the tour was only for a day.
>
> As I grew up and got more involved with my school curriculum, I decided to study medicine. He was very happy with my decision. I went on a hot summer day, in the month of June, in Delhi to take the medical school entrance exams. The exam was not easy. He accompanied me into the examination hall, till I found my seat, next to one of the two windows in the room. About ten minutes after starting, one of the invigilators announced that an anxious father, waiting outside, wanted to know if his daughter was bothered by the strong sunlight streaming in through the window. There was a boy next to the other window. Everyone looked at me. I pretended not to hear. A month later I came to know that I had passed the exam.
>
> Many years later, as I moved to Kolkata, I sometimes made trips to Delhi to meet my parents. From the time the aircraft landed on the tarmac, till I reached his house, I would receive at least half a dozen phone calls from my father, enquiring each time about my exact location. I miss those phone calls now.

Bagchi was also exceptionally loyal to his friends. Here are some thoughts from two of his closet friends. Mihir Rakshit confides that he shared everything he wrote with Bagchi before publication, and always received his candid comments. Though Rakshit originally established himself as a theorist, today he is also widely appreciated for his extremely insightful applications of theory to macroeconomic policy in India. Rakshit says that it was Bagchi who persuaded him to move beyond theory to its practical applications in the Indian context and is immensely grateful to Bagchi for this. On a similar note Bagchi's other great friend, D.N. Ghosh, speaks of the many ways in which Bagchi helped him. He recalls that when he was at a crossroads in his career, it was Bagchi who persuaded him to take a break in academia as an ICSSR scholar in JNU, much like Bagchi himself had done. It was again Bagchi who persuaded Ghosh to write regularly for *Economic and Political Weekly* (EPW), which led to Ghosh's close association with this remarkable journal, his contribution of regular columns to the newspapers, and eventually the publication of his book on governance and accountability.

Amaresh Bagchi, the scholar bureaucrat who so impressed me with his simplicity and humility when we first met nearly 25 years ago, is not with us any more. Had he been here, perhaps nothing would have made him happier than to listen to these affectionate reminiscences of his family and friends.

Note

1   This section draws considerably on an excellent obituary piece by M. Govinda Rao, with whom Bagchi collaborated for many years (see, Rao 2008).

References

Bagchi, Amaresh (ed.). 2005. *Readings in Public Finance*. New Delhi: Oxford University Press.
Bagchi, Amaresh and Pulin Nayak. 1994. "Public Finance and the Planning Process: The Indian Experience", in A. Bagchi and N. Stern (eds), *Tax Policy and Planning in Developing Countries*. New Delhi: Oxford University Press.
Bagchi, Amaresh, Richard Bird and Arindam Das-Gupta. 1995. "An Economic Approach to Tax Administration Reform", Discussion paper no. 3, International Centre for Tax Studies, Faculty of Management, University of Toronto, Canada.
Rao, M. Govinda 2008. "Amaresh Bagchi: Public Finance Economist Par Excellence", *Economic and Political Weekly*, 43 (10, 8–14 March): 10–13.

2

Budgetary Rules and Plan Financing: Revisiting the Fiscal Responsibility Act

Mihir Rakshit

———— •✦• ————

Good sense, sir, and rightmindedness
Have little need to speak by rule.
And if your mind on urgent truth is set,
Need you go hunting for an epithet?

— Goethe, 2005

I Introduction

Many of the issues addressed in this chapter were discussed earlier (Rakshit, 2001, 2005a, 2005b) when I had had the benefit of Amareshda's invaluable comments and suggestions—something I sorely missed this time. The issues, however, have remained as live as ever. Apart from the fact that the global economic crisis forced the Government of India, in late 2008, to abandon (albeit temporarily) its targets for reducing fiscal and revenue deficits as per the Fiscal Responsibility and Budget Management Act (FRBMA), 2003, the targets have proved a veritable source of discord among the three main policy making bodies in India, namely, the Ministry of Finance (MF), the Planning Commission (PC), and the Reserve Bank of India (RBI). While PC, keeping the developmental goals in view, has often mooted proposals for bypassing the budgetary targets set under the FRBMA, until recently the other two policy makers as also the Twelfth Finance Commission (GoI, 2004) were wholly in favor of adhering to the targets through thick and thin.[1] In 2004, the PC strongly urged that USD 10 billion worth of the RBI's foreign exchange reserves be used over the next two years for augmenting infrastructural investment.[2] The response to the proposal on the part of FM was far from enthusiastic.[3] In 2006, the Commission went further and made a strong case for revising the fiscal targets set under the FRBMA for purposes of stepping up development expenditure, but the suggestions were given a quiet burial.

The erstwhile budgetary targets have no doubt been abandoned in the face of the global and the domestic downturn. But apart from the fact that the targets were anyway unattainable under the prevailing conditions, it is far from clear how far the ministry has now come to appreciate the basic issues in this regard, or whether it has been swayed by the examples set by the US and other countries and by the endorsement of such fiscal expansionism by international financial institutions. Be that as it may, there appears to prevail widespread misperception among Indian commentators concerning the short- and long-run budgetary policies required for ironing out cycles, promoting developmental objectives, and keeping inflation range-bound. In this context, revisiting these policy issues on the present occasion would, I believe, be a fitting tribute on my part to the memory of someone who not only studied India's fiscal problems with a missionary zeal throughout his life, but was also instrumental in kindling my interest in the subject.

The point of departure of this chapter is the 2006 Planning Commission proposal mooted in the Eleventh Plan Approach Paper (EPAP) for revising the targets for revenue and fiscal deficits set under the Fiscal Responsibility and Budget Management Act (FRBMA). In view of the fact that under the prevailing accounting practices, government grants for building tangible assets are treated as revenue, not capital expenditures, EPAP toys with the idea of redefining revenue deficit to make it economically meaningful, but ultimately favors retaining the current definition and suggests that the government should abandon "revenue deficit" altogether as a budgetary target and focus only on "the fiscal deficit and the primary deficit as the relevant control variables" (GoI, 2006). Second, the Paper recommends modification of the FRBMA rules so that targets for fiscal deficits are adjusted for cyclical variations in GDP.[4] Third, the FRBMA targets for fiscal deficits, it is suggested, may be shifted "further out by say two years" in order to have an improved time profile of the Eleventh Plan expenditure.

The suggestions relate primarily to financing the Eleventh Plan and its phasing, but they involve more fundamental issues concerning the nature and phasing of fiscal targets appropriate for attaining basic social and economic goals. The main questions that need to be addressed in this connection are the following:

1. How far are the revenue deficit, fiscal deficit, and primary deficit suitable as control/target variables?
2. On what basis should the quantitative dimensions of the targets be fixed?
3. Is there any optimum debt-GDP ratio and if so, what is its relation to targets for deficits?
4. Should the targets be adjusted for cyclical or other shocks?

Many of the conceptual and policy issues that arise while seeking answers to these questions are of a general nature, but their resolution in the context of the structure and working of the Indian economy often require going beyond the conventional fiscal wisdom.

II Budget Deficits and Their Targeting

Budget Deficit: Accounting Convention and Economic Significance

In economic theory, receipts and expenses of an economic agent during a year are treated as capital or current in accordance with whether they entail any change in the agent's asset/liability position or stream of future receipts or payments. A surplus (deficit) in current account then reflects saving (dissaving) or addition to (fall in) the agent's net asset.[5] Since all expenses have to be met from current or capital receipts,[6] saving (or revenue surplus) of the agent must necessarily equal net deficit on capital account.[7] The counterpart of government's fiscal deficit is gross borrowing of the agent which may be different from surplus in capital account, due to non-debt creating capital account transactions.

The above definitions suggest that if one is interested in tracing temporal changes in the net worth position of an economic agent, the behavior of revenue balance rather than that of variations in *gross* indebtedness is of crucial significance. Indeed, debt financing of investment is often essential for prosperity of business enterprises, though they need to keep a close watch on the cost of borrowing and the (risk-adjusted) return on investment. Even revenue deficits may not necessarily be a bad thing: a household can improve its (inter-temporal) utility through borrowing for purposes of consumption smoothing. Thus, running revenue deficits or piling up debt need not testify profligacy or myopia, but may be optimal for maximizing the agent's objective function.

The foregoing observations are not without relevance for government deficits either. The only caveat is that unlike that of private economic agents, the government's objective function is intertemporal *social* welfare, involving the well-being of both present and future generations. Hence, the significance of budget deficits lies in their welfare consequences arising through changes in the *economy's* consumption, saving, investment, or other relevant variables. It is from this perspective that one has to evaluate the optimality of various fiscal targets.

Revenue Deficit: Some Social Cost-benefit Calculus

Assume that (*a*) the measures of revenue deficit figuring in government budgets conform to economic principles and (*b*) the economy operates close to the full employment level. What then are the costs and benefits of revenue deficit?

The negative impact of revenue deficit operates through three routes. First, since the deficit reflects dissaving due to budgetary operations,[8] there is a fall in capital accumulation and growth.[9] Second, internally held public debt does not, to be sure, represent the economy's liability in the usual sense of the term; but since a larger debt involves higher deadweight loss of taxes required for its servicing, revenue deficits entail a diminution of future GDP. Third, though there is no capital stock against public debt due to revenue deficits, it is treated as wealth by private agents[10] and hence leads to a lowering of investment and saving ratios. In order to correct for this distortion in private saving, the government needs to raise taxes,[11] but these in their turn involve some deadweight loss for the economy.

Quite clearly, a cutback in revenue deficit raises future GDP and hence, (future) social welfare through an increase in private and public consumption or through an improvement in income distribution via taxes and transfers.[12]

What about the cost of reducing revenue deficit? Since the composition of a given revenue deficit and the mode of its cutback by a specified amount can vary enormously, it is necessary to have some benchmark for purposes of comparison. It is natural in this connection to assume that given the (full employment) GDP and interest payments on outstanding debt, the levels of public consumption, redistributive expenditure, and taxes are so chosen that the current social welfare is maximized. Under these conditions, the decline in current social welfare due to a reduction in revenue deficit equals at the margin the loss on account of a rise in tax collections or of a fall in public consumption, or redistributive expenditure.[13] For assessing the desirability of the cutback in revenue deficit, it is this loss of current social welfare that needs to be compared with the (maximum potential) increase in social well-being in the future arising from additional capital accumulation and lowering of the debt-GDP ratio. If this trade-off between current and future well-being is larger (smaller) than the society's time preference, maximization of intertemporal social welfare requires revenue deficit to be reduced (raised).

Given the above perspective, what is the rationale of targeting zero revenue deficit, as suggested under the golden rule? Since government saving under this rule is zero, it subsumes that private saving is socially optimal, or that social time preference is the same as that of private agents. There are several reasons why the rule may in fact violate optimality. Government policies, let us recall, is supposed to maximize intergenerational welfare, not welfare of only the present generation. Hence, not only may the optimum revenue deficit in any period be positive or negative, but it is also likely to vary over time. In a growing economy,[14] it may be welfare-promoting to reduce (potential) consumption of the relatively wealthy posterity and for alleviating acute deprivation of the present generation. Again, since the marginal cost of raising tax revenue tends to go down with economic advancement, debt financing of a part of current government consumption and redistributive expenditure need not be reprehensible. Alternatively, the government may target a revenue surplus for supplementing private saving if the society as a whole values highly the international standing associated with rapid GDP growth,[15] or people are collectively prepared to undergo privation for enriching the posterity.[16] Be that as it may, both revenue deficit and its components form important control variables and require meticulous cost-benefit analysis for their targeting over time.

The targeting of revenue deficit considered above is for an economy without any output gap. Economists of all hues (including those subscribing to the golden rule) agree that the target (applicable for a full employment economy) is to be attained on an average over a trade cycle, with below average deficits during booms and above average ones in times of depression. Such pro-cyclical adjustment of revenue balances promotes welfare through consumption smoothing and moderation of the cycle itself. Similar departures from the (full employment) deficit target are optimal in the case of agricultural cycles in countries like India. Finally, if the government finds itself saddled with large interest payments on account of public debt, the optimal provisioning of public goods and redistributive expenditure may involve a huge deadweight loss if the revenue deficit target is to be met at one go. Alternatively, there would be a substantial cut in private consumption or serious worsening of income distribution. In such cases, a gradual rather than big-bang adjustment of revenue deficit (through a series of cutbacks in primary revenue deficit) towards its target level would minimize the loss of social welfare.

Fiscal Deficit and Public Debt

Fiscal deficit represents addition to public debt without any reference to what the borrowing is used for.[17] This makes it difficult to relate the deficit to saving, capital accumulation, and changes in the net asset position of the government and the economy. Hence arises the need for specifying the components of the deficit, especially the extent to which it represents debt financing of revenue or capital expenditure.[18] Since we have already discussed the policy issues pertaining to revenue

17

deficit, the rest of the section is devoted to an examination of fiscal
deficit incurred for meeting capital expenditure alone.

Note first that borrowing for asset creation does not entail the
costs discussed in connection with revenue deficit: it may cause some
crowding out of private investment, but aggregate saving and investment
of the economy tend to go up;[19] public debt, as in the case of financial
liabilities of the business sector, is matched by assets;[20] increased revenue
from publicly-funded capital stock can obviate the need for raising
the tax-GDP ratio.[21] Does this mean, as the FM's interpretation of the
golden rule seems to suggest (*Financial Express*, 2006), that any amount
of fiscal deficit is OK so long as it finances capital expenditure? Since
not only the FM's, but also the Twelfth Finance Commission's (TFC's)[22]
and RBI's observations on the economic rationale behind the targets
for fiscal deficit are far from illuminating, a few clarificatory words on
the matter appear to be in order.

Optimum Deficit and Debt in a Neoclassical Economy

The golden rule bars government borrowing for revenue expenditure,
but does not suggest that any amount of debt-financed public investment
is good for the economy. Here also we require a cost-benefit calculus
for estimating the optimal levels of fiscal deficit[23] and the debt-GDP
ratio(s) associated with them. Let us first consider the determinants of
optimum deficits and debt in a neoclassical full employment economy
assuming that (*a*) private and social rates of time preferences are the same
and (*b*) there are no costs of taxation. While assumption (*a*) implies the
golden rule and rules out debt financing of current expenditure,[24] the
implication of (*b*) is somewhat more complex and would be taken up
when we examine how its relaxation affects the optimal fiscal policy
rules.

Under assumptions (*a*) and (*b*) the optimal levels of fiscal deficit and
of government's capital expenditure are the same. For examining their
determinants it is useful to start with a neoclassical aggregate production
function where human capital (K_h), infrastructural capital (K_i), and other
capital (K_2) enter as separate arguments. For any given supply of labor
and capital (K), or given the aggregate capital-labor ratio $k\ (=K/L)$, there

is an optimum combination of k_h $(=K_h/L)$, k_1 $(=K_1/L)$ and k_2 $(=K_2/L)$ at which GDP[25] (per head) is maximum. Let the optimal k_i's be $k_i^*(i = h, 1, 2)$. Since the three capital stocks are non-fungible (in the short run), from an initial, suboptimum composition of K, k_i's can be adjusted to their optimum values only through differential rates of growth of K_i's. When investment in a sector does not involve rising marginal cost of adjustment,[26] under an efficient program the entire capital formation should take place in the sector[27] i where the shortfall of k_i from k_i^* is the largest or the marginal productivity of K_i is the highest. Only after the composition of capital stock has become optimum, is it optimal to allocate investment such that all K_i's grow at the same rate. With rising marginal cost, investment may be positive in all sectors during the adjustment process, but even so the highest share should generally go to the sector where the shortfall of the capital stock from its optimum is the largest.

What has the optimum investment program suggested above got to do with policies concerning fiscal deficit and public debt? The clue to the answer lies in the (differential) gaps between social and private returns[28] in different sectors and the consequent suboptimality of the scale of investment, as well as the composition of capital stock. The most glaring manifestation of this suboptimality is to be found in the huge shortfall of infrastructure and human capital in developing countries. In order to correct the distortions, the government can invest directly in these sectors, or support private investment through subsidies, viability grants, or alternative forms of private-public partnerships (PPPs). While the best way of effecting the required increase in investment is a matter of detail and varies from sector to sector[29] and over time, some of the important characteristics of the optimum time profile of government's capital expenditure or fiscal deficit as a ratio of GDP[30] are not too difficult to discern.

Consider first the targeted ratio of fiscal deficit (f), f_n, *when the* composition of capital stock is optimum.[31] The value of f_n is given by:

$$f_n = \frac{I_g}{Y} = \frac{I_g}{I} \cdot \frac{I}{Y} = s \cdot \frac{1}{k}\left[\lambda_h \cdot k_h^* + \lambda_1 k_1^* + \lambda_2 k_2^*\right] = s.\lambda \qquad (1)$$

Where I_g = capital expenditure of the government; Y = GDP; I = investment; s = optimum saving (and investment) ratio; λ_i = optimum share of the government's capital expenditure in the ith sector; and λ = optimal share of government investment in total investment.

Relation (1) suggests that the greater the (overall) gap between the social and private returns, the higher should be the value of λ for ensuring the optimal saving ratio; otherwise the return on foregone consumption will be lower and the saving ratio (driven by private preferences) less than its optimum. Again, since the gap between the social and private returns tends to be larger in social and infrastructural sectors, λ_h and λ_l should be higher than λ_2 under the optimum program. It is, thus, obvious that the larger the optimum saving ratio and greater the shares of k_h^* and k_l^* in k, the higher should be the value of f_n.

Second, during the early phase of the government's debt-financed investment program, f should be larger, the greater the shortfall of initial k_h and k_l from their optimum values, the larger the aggregate saving ratio and smaller the adjustment costs of sectoral investments.

Third, the targeted f under the optimal budgetary program should initially be higher than f_n. Over time f falls and approaches f_n when (social) returns on the three types of capital have become equal. In case adjustment costs tend to fall over time,[32] the time profile of optimal fiscal deficit will be inverted U-shaped, rising over a period of time and then falling (to f_n), as the composition of K moves towards its most efficient configuration.

What about the optimum time trajectory of public debt? It is useful to consider first the steady state debt-GDP ratio, d_n, under the optimal fiscal program, remembering that public debt by itself does not impose any cost when (*a*) there is no deadweight loss on account of taxation and (*b*) the outstanding amount of debt reflects accumulated capital financed by the government. Since the steady state is characterized by optimum composition of capital stock:

$$d_n = \left(\lambda_h \cdot \frac{K_h}{K} + \lambda_l \cdot \frac{K_l}{K} + \lambda_2 \frac{K_2}{K} \right) \cdot \frac{K}{Y}$$
$$= (\lambda_h \alpha_h + \lambda_l \alpha_l + \lambda_2 \alpha_2) \, v$$
$$= \lambda v \tag{2}$$

Where α_i = ratio of capital stock of sector i to total capital stock;
$\qquad$ v = (overall) capital-output ratio.[33]

Quite clearly, the larger the values of λ and v, the higher will be the long-run, optimum debt-GDP ratio. Thus, if λ and v are one-third and 4.5 respectively (not outlandish values by any reckoning), the optimum debt-GDP ratio would be 150 percent! Since v is positively impacted by saving and the importance of knowledge-based activities requiring a whole host of infrastructural services tends to raise the optimum value of λ, a 150 percent value of d_n is likely to be an underestimate.

Given some debt-GDP ratio d_0 to begin with, its behavior over time is determined by the optimum time profile of fiscal deficit and the GDP growth associated therewith.[34] During the adjustment of k_h and k_l (and of k) towards their optimum levels, the growth rate of government investment exceeds that of GDP, but the gap between the two rates tends to disappear over time. The implication is that under the optimal program of fiscal deficit, the debt-GDP ratio rises over time[35] and approaches d_n.

Cost of Taxation

Since a part, often a major part, of benefit from publicly funded investment in social and infrastructural sectors does not directly accrue to the exchequer and all taxes (and transfers) involve some deadweight loss, it is important to consider how costs of taxation affect the aforementioned results relating to debt financing of government's capital expenditure. The most important effect of these deadweight losses is to reduce the social return on investments which require raising tax for purposes of debt servicing. The additional tax often remains significant even after allowing for the automatic increase in tax revenue (with little extra cost) as GDP rises[36] with public investment. Let us see how the resulting, optimal fiscal deficit program differs from the one considered in the previous paragraphs.

First and perhaps the most neglected in the on-going discussion on debt and deficit, seignorage[37] now becomes a preferred mode of financing government investment. In the absence of any cost of taxation it does not matter whether the government borrows from the central bank or the public for purposes of capital expenditure so long as its social return exceeds the opportunity cost, that is, return on private investment:[38] the net gain to the economy is the same in both cases. But when deadweight losses are large, substitution of borrowing from the public by seignorage tends up to a point to raise economic welfare, given the level and composition of the government's capital expenditure.

However, as we have discussed elsewhere (Rakshit, 2005b), there is a limit beyond which relying on seignorage becomes counterproductive. Even so, this source of funding can be quite significant: the optimum seignorage[39] as a ratio of GDP is around 2 percent under a 6 percent growth rate and can be more than 3 percent if a well designed public investment program pushes growth rate to 8.5 percent or above.[40]

Second, costs of taxation tilt the balance in favor of commercially viable investment projects and against those which are characterized by large positive externalities and high social returns, but do not directly yield commensurate revenue to the government. Some of the social sector investment may thus become suboptimal due to collection-cum-distortionary costs of raising tax revenue.

Third, costs of taxation reduce the (maximum attainable) social welfare, but can raise the need for debt financed government investment. The reason is that (a) some projects which directly raise the supply of public goods or improve income distribution on an enduring basis now tend to turn optimal and (b) in many a public-private partnership project government financing becomes superior to private funding, given the differential between the two borrowing rates. One or two illustrations may help clarifying the points.

Consider the optimum way of meeting the housing needs of government departments. Under the first best program the government may rent the required service from the market and meet the cost from tax revenue, remembering that there is little difference between social and private returns in respect of housing. However, when costs of taxation are significant, the government can improve social welfare through financing construction of its buildings, taking advantage of its relatively low borrowing rate. In many PPPs, while harnessing the managerial and operational efficiency of private entrepreneurs, the government should remain responsible for providing the bulk of finance on grounds of optimality (Rakshit, 2006): the widely prevalent view that reduction of fiscal deficit constitutes the *raison d'etre* of PPP is thus totally wrong. Or consider a project in some backward area which raises incomes of the indigent, but the additional output is somewhat lower than what would be generated by private sector investment of similar magnitude. The project should not be publicly funded under the first best situation—through taxes-and-transfers the indigent could then be made better off—but forms part of the government's optimum fiscal program when costs associated with taxes-and-transfers are factored in.

Fiscal Deficit under Business Cycles

We have already considered how targets for revenue deficits (under full employment) require anti-cyclical adjustments in the course of a business cycle. Such adjustments in revenue deficits automatically entail anti-cyclical fiscal deficit. There are also other factors because of which it is welfare-promoting to adjust fiscal deficit over trade cycles.

First, the government should in general try to implement its (optimal) investment program without any reference to trade cycles: starting new investment projects when there is a slack and slowing down completion of on-going projects for cooling the economy are inefficient and wasteful.[41] Since cyclical variations are most pronounced for private investment, strictly time bound fiscal sop for fixed capital expenditure in times of unemployment would help attainment of the optimum balance between private and public investment.

Second, monetized financing of government expenditure should be anti-cyclical, with temporal variations in borrowings from the central bank matching that in fiscal deficit. This would be in tune with keeping (full employment) seignorage at its optimum level.

Finally, cycles originating in supply-side shocks, for example, variations in monsoon or oil prices, are often more important in developing countries than text-book cycles. This makes higher fiscal deficit, or providing larger support to investments that make the economy more resilient to such shocks, optimal as a long-term strategy. So far as the cyclical components of fiscal deficit are concerned, they would involve variations in external borrowing for smoothening domestic absorption—something which is not necessary when the cycles are demand driven. The reason is that an adverse supply-side shock of a random nature temporarily reduces the full-employment output, but not the country's average Non-Accelerating Inflation Rate of Employment (NAIRU) national income. Hence, borrowing from abroad in times of the fall in the (short-term) full-employment income and paying back the debt when income is above the NAIRU level improves intertemporal social welfare.[42]

II Planning Commission and Its Critics

In light of our discussion in the previous section, we now address the issues and questions posed in connection with the EPAP proposals. These issues, let us recall, relate to redefinition of revenue deficits; focusing only on fiscal and primary deficits as control variables; adjustment of deficits for output gaps; and compatibility of targets for debt and deficits with the Plan expenditure and its phasing.

Revenue Deficit: Definition and Uses

The conventional measure of revenue deficit is marred by two major deficiencies. Government expenditures routed through various agencies for creation of productive assets (as EPAP has noted) are treated as current, not capital; and so are all outgoes on human resource development (HRD). In view of the importance of these two categories of expenditure, the current definition of revenue deficit is quite inappropriate for examining the impact of the budget or framing policies. The solution, our earlier analysis suggests, lies not in abandoning revenue deficit altogether as a target variable, but in having an estimate that conforms to economic logic: recall the crucial importance of (properly defined) revenue deficit as a tool of promoting intertemporal social welfare. The usual objections against such redefinition—on the grounds of (*a*) violation of long established, constitutionally recognized practices[43] and (*b*) loss of credibility of the government[44]—do not appear well grounded. There is nothing sacrosanct about accounting practices that are seriously misleading. "Deficit financing" or government budget deficit,[45] long considered the most important source of inflation, has ceased to figure in budget documents since the late 1980s. Again, only since 1991 has the government started providing estimates of fiscal and primary deficits. Our suggestion is that (despite these precedents) let the budget, if the government so desires, continue to present conventional estimates of revenue deficit (RD) under the head RD_0, but provide along with that two other measures of revenue deficit,[46] RD_1 and RD_2, defined as follows:

$RD_1 = RD_0$ – Government "revenue" expenditure for creation of tangible assets;

$RD_2 = RD_1$ – Government expenditure for human resource development.

Retention of RD_0 would satisfy the official penchant for not abandoning long-standing practices[47] and be of no harm, so long as it is not used for economic analysis or as a policy target. RD_1 reflects government "dis-saving" as defined in the System of National Accounts (SNA), and forms part[48] of Central Statistical Organization (CSO) estimates of domestic saving. RD_1, being comparable with other types of saving under SNA, is not irrelevant for analytical and policy purposes, especially if the focus is on accumulation of physical capital in a full employment economy. However, RD_1 includes government expenditures on education and health, which practically all economists interested in analyzing the sources of growth have come to regard as (human) capital formation, not current consumption. Hence, for an analysis of how far budgetary operations subtract from (or add to) the pool of domestic resources used for raising productive capacity of the economy, RD_2 is obviously superior to RD_1. For the same reason RD_2 must constitute an important fiscal target for attaining the optimum intertemporal consumption profile.

III Targeting Debts and Deficits for the Indian Economy

Before suggesting the modalities for setting the likely dimensions of deficits and debt in the Indian context, it is instructive to consider the official including the TFC (Twelfth Finance Commission) approach to the budgetary exercise under the FRBMA. While the Central Government's revenue and fiscal deficit targets under FRBMA, as originally scheduled to be attained by 2008–09,[49] are zero and 3.0 percent, respectively, TFC stipulations are more wide ranging and are for both the Centre and states:[50] between 2004–05 and 2009–10 the combined revenue, fiscal, and primary deficits, and the debt-GDP ratio are slated to be reduced from 4.5, 8.9, 2.8 and 80.8 to zero, 6.0, 1.5 and 74.5 percent respectively. The main instruments for attaining the TFC targets are: (a) an increase in the tax-GDP ratio by 2 percentage points; (b) freezing the primary expenditure-GDP ratio at the 2004–05 level; and (c) a step-up in the ratio of government investment to GDP by 1 percentage point. Moreover, in order to induce the states to attain the stipulated targets, following the TFC recommendations, the Union Government has introduced a scheme for consolidation of states' debt and lighten their debt burden considerably,[51] provided they enact a fiscal responsibility legislation and adhere to the debt consolidation and relief facility (DCRF) guidelines (as laid down by the Union Government).[52]

The first point to be noted, in connection with these budgetary targets is that they are annual, and set for specific years without any reference to the possibilities of business or agricultural cycles occurring in those years. As already argued, since cyclical factors often make the actual output deviate significantly from the economy's full-employment growth path, sticking to prestipulated fiscal targets is liable to be grossly suboptimal under these conditions. Hence, even while the *average* target over the medium run may be adhered to, both the revenue and fiscal deficit targets for particular years are required to be adjusted for closing the output gap and smoothening domestic absorption.

We have documented elsewhere (Rakshit, 2004, 2007a) how the near-exclusive focus on reducing fiscal deficit irrespective of the state of the macro-economy proved seriously counterproductive during 1996–2003. No less glaring has been the growth-debilitating impact of the budgetary policies during Q_2, 2007–Q_4, 2009. The Indian economy has clearly been on a decelerating growth trajectory from as early as March 2007, six months before the outbreak of the US sub-prime crisis and the onset of the global financial turmoil (Rakshit, 2009). GDP growth came down from 10.3 percent in Q_1, 2007 to 9.3 percent in the next quarter, further to 7.8 percent in Q_2, 2008, and was projected to grow by at least 2 percentage point less during 2007–08 by practically all forecasters. Unmistakable signals of significant growth slowdown were also evident from the monthly data for the Index of Industrial Production (IIP): industrial growth came down from 14.8 percent in March, 2007 to 11.3 percent in April, 2007 and showed a steeply negative trend thereafter, declining to 5.5 percent in March, 2008 and averaging a dismal 2.1 percent over the four-month period.

However, despite the darkening domestic and international economic scenario and the widely held perception that the global economy was heading towards its worst crisis since the Great Depression, in the 2008–09 budget not only was there no program for tackling the prospective economic slide, but the Union and the state governments taken together proposed to cut back revenue deficit by 0.4 and fiscal deficit by 0.7 percentage points. It was only in the first week of December, 2008, when no remission of the prolonged and growing demand deficiency was in sight and practically all developed and developing countries (including China) had already initiated expansionary measures on a large scale, did the Government of India deem it necessary to abandon the FRBMA targets for the time being[53] and announced a fiscal stimulus package. It took nearly two more months for the Central government to announce (on January 29, 2009) relaxation of the revenue and fiscal deficit targets set for the states under the DCRF guidelines. Remembering that for effectiveness of anti-cyclical measures, their timeliness is of the essence, the government inaction and dithering over a period of no less than seven quarters underscores the baleful effect of laying down a rigid timeframe relating to targets for debts and deficits.

Of much greater consequence for the country's long-term development prospects is the glaring suboptimality of the targets set under the FRMBA—something which has prompted the Planning Commission to suggest changes, in both the nature of the targets and their phasing. The targets, let us recall, have been set as per the TFC recommendations, keeping the FRBMA provisions in view. The TFC's is indeed an elaborate and fairly consistent macro-economic exercise, but is devoid of the cost-benefit calculus of the type suggested in the previous section. To see how, consider the most glaring deficiency of the targets in this regard.[54] According to a World Bank report (2006), loss of manufacturing output on account of power shortage is 8.5 percent in India, compared with less than 2 percent in China and Brazil. Bottlenecks in transport, ports, and infrastructure are also estimated to cause significant losses in output, especially in export-oriented manufacturing units. The report goes on to suggest: the current gap between infrastructural stocks between China and India[55] "is so large that for India to catch up only to China's *present levels of stocks per capita*, it would have to invest 12.5 percent of GDP per year through 2015" (italics added). No less yawning is India's HRD gap in the context of her much higher infant mortality, malnutrition among the children, illiteracy, and the shortfall in educational attainments compared with that of East Asian and many other emerging market economies. Hence, arises the need for an optimality exercise for setting a time profile of fiscal targets in consonance with the country's developmental goals.

Our analysis in the previous section suggests that instead of fixing (as TFC does) the targets for deficits and debts on the basis of some projected GDP growth[56] one should start with the short-term, full-employment GDP and the historically given debt obligations, and work out the welfare implications of alternative levels of the government's primary expenditures (consisting of public consumption, subsidies, and government investments) and modes of meeting these expenditures and interest payments. Their welfare implications, as already noted, arise through the impact of the *primary fiscal instruments* on the current and (potential) future levels of public and private consumption and investment, their composition, and distribution of income. Since the future (full employment) GDP and public debt are affected by current fiscal measures, the optimality exercise involves working out the time profile of the targeted sets of fiscal variables, including revenue deficit, fiscal deficit, primary deficit, and public debt *as ratios of full employment GDP*.

In light of the modalities of fiscal programing outlined earlier, it is not difficult to appreciate how seriously marred the TFC exercise is. The Planning Commission's approach in this regard (GoI, 2006) is much more sensible. Apart from recognizing the need for adjustment of budgetary targets in response to cyclical swings, the Commission considers alternative GDP growth trajectories, their implications for investment, saving and current account balance, and the fiscal targets required under each trajectory. Indeed, the Commission goes further and notes how (*a*) public infrastructural investment creates a congenial economic environment for crowding in private capital formation; and (*b*) the magnitude as also the phasing of the revenue and fiscal deficit targets (originally) set by the Ministry of Finance would stand in the way of promoting "inclusive growth", as visualized by the government. It is also noteworthy that the Commission's approach, unlike that of other official bodies,[57] starts from relatively basic considerations and is not hidebound by a purely legalistic policy framework irrespective of its economic rationale under the prevailing circumstances. However, the approach, our earlier discussion suggests, nevertheless requires modifications in some crucial respects.

The hallmark of the EPAP approach consists in working out the investment ratios along with the government's revenue and fiscal balances corresponding to alternative GDP growth scenarios. However, the underlying incremental capital-output ratios (ICORs) used for the growth projections appear to be derived from the past data, not from an optimality exercise. The absence of a well-designed social cost-benefit calculus is also apparent, in respect of the projected allocation of aggregate investment among different lines of economic activities, and between the private and the public sector. The estimates for private capital formation are based on its past behavior and shortfall of such investment, if any, is to be made up by the public sector—something which cannot but be grossly inefficient—remembering that the comparative advantage of the two sectors in undertaking investment varies widely across industries or economic activities.[58] So far as infrastructural investment in concerned, the EPAP envisages an increase in its ratio to GDP from 4.5 percent in the Tenth Plan "to an average of around 7.5 percent" (GoI, 2006). Not only is the ratio significantly short of what is warranted in the context of the country's yawning infrastructural gap, but "public resources being limited", the major part of these investments is projected to be undertaken by private entrepreneurs, with partial financial support from the government in some cases, through public-private partnership (PPP). The interesting point to note in this connection is that the perceived shortage of "public resources" for undertaking investment in crucial sectors is basically due to the EPAP's acceptance of the FRBMA targets for the *average* levels of revenue and fiscal deficits over the five-year period (though not for each year separately). It is this consideration which seems to have constrained the Commission to limit its targets for public capital formation at 10.2 percent, even though aggregate investment is projected to reach 35.1 percent of GDP.

Elsewhere (Rakshit, 2006), we have discussed in some detail why (*a*) private businessmen will find most infrastructural investment projects unattractive; and (*b*) the government support under PPP to private investors through upfront or viability grants[59] is both costly and counterproductive. The reasons lie in the lumpiness-cum-long durability of most of these investment projects; their large externalities that private entrepreneurs cannot internalize; the dominance of fixed over marginal costs in production of infrastructural goods and services; extremely high risk, that is, difficult to disperse or manage by private investors; and hence the astronomical discount factor due to their (own) high risk premium, as well as the huge spread of the borrowing cost over the rate on government securities.[60] In view of the operation of these factors, private instead of public financing of infrastructural projects yielding high social returns is generally suboptimal.

The above is amply illustrated by the experience of the National Highway Development Programme (NHDP) for inducing large scale private investment in highway projects through provision of upfront grants and tolling right to the concessionaire. After the initial phase characterized by private entrepreneurs' cherry-picking of the port and other connectivity projects, where the overwhelming part of the facilities had already been set up by the government and high density of traffic was assured, the program has gone completely awry over the last two years, with very few bids forthcoming for the remaining projects, especially the greenfield ones. This is apart from the deadweight loss of tolling and the large potential revenue foregone by the government in the projects granted under PPP.[61] While for both highway and other infrastructural projects[62] the prevailing system of PPPs requires drastic redesigning in several aspects,[63] so far as financing is concerned, it cannot be overemphasized that reliance on private funds for making the fiscal deficits conform to the FRBMA stipulations would not only result in a grossly suboptimal scale and composition of total capital outlay, but is likely to be seriously counter-productive, from the viewpoint of the medium- and long-term budgetary viability. For purposes of harnessing the operational efficiency of private entrepreneurs, it is much more cost effective for the government, as under the UK scheme of Credit Guarantee Finance (CGF), to borrow and make the major part of the funds available to private builders at market rates of interest[64] with adequate guarantee and safeguard against moral hazard. Let us take stock of the most important budgetary implication of this line of reasoning, taking into account our earlier discussion of the modalities of an optimal development program and its financing for the Indian economy.

First, in the context of country's infrastructural-cum-human resources gap, a public investment of 10.2 percent of GDP out of a total of 35.1 percent, as proposed by the EPAP, appears abysmally small. Even allowing for the adjustment cost of a sharp rise in investment in a particular sector within a short timeframe, a target of raising aggregate public sector capital formation to 16–17 per cent of GDP over a three-year period is both feasible and desirable, remembering that (a) blueprints of a number of infrastructural including the highway projects have already been finalized; and (b) private entrepreneurs have been extremely chary of funding them. In fact, private capital accumulation in India had already been decelerating long before the global economy faced a financial upheaval (Rakshit, 2009). Growth of private investment came down from 20.4 percent in 2005–06 to 14.8 percent in 2006–07 and further to 5.9 percent in 2007–08 (GoI, 2008, 2009). No less significant was the slowdown in growth of corporate capital formation from a peak of 36.1 percent in 2005–06 to 20.4 percent and 16.8 percent, respectively in the next two years.[65] In this context, the public sector investment target suggested by us may perhaps be considered too conservative! Indeed, our discussion of the optimal time profile of the scale and composition of aggregate investment suggests that over the subsequent six–seven years, public sector investment needs to go up to perhaps 20–22 percent for dealing with the imbalance in the composition of the country's capital stock in a cost effective manner.

Second and related to the first, implementation of the investment program suggested earlier would involve an immediate jump in fiscal deficit as also a rising trajectory of the targeted deficit over the next decade,[66] contrary to the time-profile set by all official bodies. While estimating the projected deficit we need to recognize that as of now there is scope for an increase in the government's revenue balance by 3 to 4 percentage points through elimination of distortionary subsidies, like those on petroleum products, fertilizer, irrigation, and other inputs; extension and rationalization of the value added tax; and bringing company dividends, capital gains, inheritance, and all export earnings[67] under the tax net. But the need for a significant step-up in HRD expenditure[68] on top of the enlarged infrastructural investment would still entail about 14–15 percent fiscal deficit in the initial years.[69] However, over the 10-year period, the increasing scope for seignorage revenue[70] and for taxation of the incremental value of land and real estates (driven by improvement in infrastructural facilities) would make the growth of fiscal deficit lag behind that of public investment.

Third, given the fact that the investment program is for a full-employment economy, the increase in fiscal deficit would no doubt involve a diminution of private investment. But such crowding out is precisely what is required for attaining the basic goals of developmental planning: one should not be unduly worried when a step-up in some highly productive, publicly-funded investment crowds out relatively low-productivity private capital formation.

Finally, the need for a substantial rise in infrastructural-cum-social sector investment in times of demand deficiency can hardly be overemphasized. What is no less important to recognize is that under these conditions, additional public investments entail zero opportunity cost and their financing through seignorage, apart from enlarging the crowding-in effect, also helps in lightening the future debt burden of the government. Unfortunately, though the on-going crisis has dealt a blow to the deeply entrenched fiscal orthodoxy in India, the steps taken and pronouncements made so far[71] continue to betray quite inadequate appreciation in official circles of the role of budgetary instruments for furthering basic economic and social goals.

Notes

1 Note that slippages did occur, but they were not due to lack of effort on the part of the Ministry of Finance.
2 Since the expenditure was to be through a special purpose vehicle (SPV)—an off-balance-sheet entity of the government—it would be in conformity with the letter, though not the spirit of the FRBMA.
3 Indeed, the proposal received flak from practically all sections of Indian economists (see Rakhsit, 2009 for a somewhat contrarian view). For its part the government after much dithering adopted a similar scheme in 2007, by which time the country's infrastructural gap had widened considerably, and the project costs went up sharply.
4 In fact, this was one of our suggestions made in 2001 while commenting on the Fiscal Responsibility and Budget Management Bill (Rakshit, 2001).
5 Taking depreciation as part of current expenses, even when there is no actual expenditure on this count.
6 Or drawing down cash balances or sale of assets.
7 The reason is that all capital account expenses must then *exceed* aggregate capital receipts by the agent's net saving during the period.
8 Ignoring the indirect effects of these operations on private sector saving.
9 Though the fall in aggregate saving and capital accumulation is generally less than the revenue deficit.
10 Unless the Ricardian equivalence holds (Barro, 1974), which is not generally the case, especially in developing economies with large capital market imperfections (Rakshit, 2005b).
11 The increase in tax is over and above what is required to meet interest payments, remembering that tax financed interest payments leave the private disposable income unchanged and hence do not correct for the distortion in private saving.
12 Remembering that their distortionary costs tend to be moderate at relatively high GDP.

13 Since the marginal impact of the three fiscal variables on current social welfare is the same.

14 Especially when growth is primarily due to disembodied technological progress of the Solovian variety (Solow, 1956).

15 Which means that such standing enters as an argument in the social welfare function.

16 In these cases there is an externality in the individual propensity to save: an individual is prepared to consume less for attaining the social goal, provided others are also doing so. Hence, the role of the government in stepping up aggregate saving. For further details see Rakshit (2001).

17 Or, what is the scale and composition of capital receipts. Thus the borrowing may be used for meeting current or capital expenditure. Alternatively, given the level of the government's current and capital expenditure, a reduction in tax revenue matched by an equivalent amount of increase in non-debt creating capital receipts (for example, recovery of loans or disinvestment proceeds) leaves fiscal deficit unchanged. Hence the problem.

18 Ignoring non-debt creating capital receipts of the government. See Rakshit (2000) for a discussion of some economic and policy implications of these receipts.

19 This comes about through a rise in interest rate under the neoclassical mechanism: the associated increase in saving prevents a one-to-one crowding out.

20 So that the effects of public debt on the economy's saving and investment are no different from that of the accumulated stock of the business sector's financial liabilities.

21 We shall presently consider the case where this may not be so.

22 See Government of India, 2004.

23 What RBI calls "neutral" fiscal deficit may at first appear akin to this "optimal" fiscal deficit. But apart from the fact that RBI makes no mention of the short- and long-term costs of debt financing, the concept (as in the case of "neutral monetary policy") seems to refer to that level of deficit whose impact on aggregate demand is neutral, that is, neither expansionary, nor contractionary. The problem, as we have noted elsewhere (Rakshit, 2005b), is that fiscal deficit is often a poor measure of the expansionary impact of a budget: a deficit (surplus) can in fact be contractionary (expansionary) depending upon the scale and composition of government expenditure.

24 Alternatively, the socially optimum rate of saving is the same as the private rate of saving.

25 Though strictly speaking we should consider NDP rather than GDP.

26 In general, the marginal cost rises since if a given addition to installed capacity is to be accomplished within a shorter period, both the acquisition and installation costs of capital tend to be higher. Implementing agencies often also require time to build up their capacity for handling large-scale investment. In some cases adjustment costs become prohibitive beyond a point: even if resources are available, construction of a new highway or a port (say) within a year is not feasible (that is, entails infinite cost).

27 If $k_i < k_i^*$ in (say) h and 1, k_i is automatically larger than k_2^*.

28 The most important reasons for the gap are indivisibility of investment projects (especially in infrastructure), positive externality, high cost (private or social) of charging the beneficiaries, the higher risk for an individual than for the economy as a whole, and gross imperfection of the capital market. The gap is yawning in the case of roads, communications, and marketing facilities which reduce chronic underutilization of resources, both human and physical (Rakshit, 2006).

29 For an analysis of the optimum mode of investment in highways, see Rakshit (2006).

33

30 Remembering that given the time profile of labor supply, technology, and adjustment costs of sectoral investments, an optimum combination of k_h, k_1, and k_2 imply some corresponding combination of investment-GDP ratios in the three sectors.

31 Under this condition investment in the ith sector as a ratio of total investment would equal k_i^*, so that the composition of capital stock remains unchanged.

32 With learning and experience.

33 When α_i's are optimal.

34 Recall that (a) all interest payments are financed through taxes and (b) fiscal deficit itself affects GDP through improvement in allocative efficiency and saving (due to higher return on capital). The latter effect does not, however, obtain in the steady state.

35 Assuming that the initial, historically given level of d does not exceed d_n. We have already noted why d_0 is likely to be significantly less than d_n unless the government has been indulging in large scale, debt financed current expenditure for a considerable period.

36 Note that it is the additional income over what would have taken place in the absence of public investment (that is, with no crowding out of private investment) that is relevant here.

37 That is, printing money or borrowing from the central bank.

38 Note that seignorage reflects addition to private asset in the form of reserve money. Hence, under the golden rule it (seignorage) should be used only for purposes of investment.

39 Which, given the demand for real balances, depends on GDP growth and the social cost of inflation (Rakshit, 2005b).

40 In the official writings on deficit and debt, seignorage is conspicuous by its absence and clubbed with borrowing from the public even though there is grave concern on rising interest payments on public debt. Particularly curious is the TFC report (GoI, 2004) which despite its extensive discussion of the need for reducing debt and deficit, makes no mention of the composition of debt and significance of seignorage for the debt burden.

41 Only when the economy is caught in a liquidity trap, as Japan was during the 1990s, may large scale public investment even with some wastage be justified.

42 However, allowing for foreign borrowing and lending changes the optimum time profile of the country's domestic consumption, investment and its composition, current account balance as also the revenue, and the fiscal deficit—something which we do not go into on the present occasion.

43 Thus the Planning Commission (GOI, 2006) does not ultimately favor its own redefinition of revenue deficit on these grounds.

44 The problem of credibility is hammered by FM and RBI, not PC.

45 Reflecting the amount of government expenditure met through issue of Treasury Bills.

46 Following the practice of providing alternative measures of money supply that help greatly in analyzing the behavior of the macroeconomy and formulating monetary policies.

47 Unless they have long been given up by governments in advanced Western economies.

48 With a negative sign.

49 Until the global economic crisis made all plans for containing budgetary deficits go haywire.

50 The TFC stipulations for the center are however the same (or consistent with) those set by the Union Government and hence are in accord with the FRBMA in this regard.

51 Under this scheme all outstanding state loans from the Center at end march, 2005 are consolidated. The consolidated amount carries an interest rate of 7.5 percent and is to be repaid over a 20-year period.

52 Under the DCRF guidelines, the states' revenue and fiscal deficit targets as also their annual market borrowing ceilings are set as per the TFC projections. One of the major TFC recommendations is that, henceforth, the states are to borrow from the market (not the Union government) for financing their deficits.

53 The first official announcement that the government would miss the fiscal targets for 2008–09 came from the deputy Chairman of the Planning Commission on October 30, 2008; but the reason for the slippage lay in enlarged oil and fertilizer subsidies—the deleterious impact of which can hardly be overemphasized (Rakshit, 2007b)—not in proactive policies for boosting aggregate demand.

54 For a more comprehensive assessment of the TFC program, see Rakshit (2005a).

55 Though in 1980 "India had higher infrastructural stocks" than China.

56 Which the TFC takes to be 7 percent per annum over the five-year period, 2005–10.

57 For example, the Ministry of Finance, the Reserve Bank and TFC.

58 This is apart from the budgetary problems such a scheme would tend to create.

59 For example, the minimum financial support from the government that would make private investment in the project viable.

60 Of similar maturity.

61 Because of its faulty design—something we have elaborated in Rakshit (2006).

62 Especially those characterized by large externality, high risk, etc.

63 See Rakshit (2006).

64 Since the private entrepreneurs would be responsible for timely completion of projects and maintenance of infrastructural facilities against a stream of guaranteed payments (with a suitable escalator clause), the risk of the project turning non-viable is borne primarily by the government.

65 The Indian economy, let us recall, was yet to feel any significant impact of the crisis threatening the advanced countries like USA and together with China and a few other emerging economies was deemed to be largely 'de-coupled'.

66 The investment program, it may be noted, refers to public sector outlay, including funding of projects under PPPs. This is what is relevant for government deficit and debt.

67 Remembering that export subsidies on selected sectors are also grossly distortionary.

68 Conventionally included in revenue expenditure.

69 Note that the figures refer to the ratio of aggregate deficit to full-employment, *not actual*, GDP.

70 Though the revenue by itself does not reduce the conventionally measured fiscal deficit, substitution of seignorage for market borrowing, as emphasized in the section on budget deficits, causes a cutback in the government's interest obligations over time and helps reducing the deadweight loss due to taxes and transfers.

71 Up to mid February, 2009.

References

Barro, Robert J. 1974. "Are Government Bonds Net Wealth?", *Journal of Political Economy*, 82 (6): 1095–1117.

Goethe, Johann Wolfgang von. 2005. *Faust*, Part I. London: Penguin Classics.

Government of India. 2004. *Report of the Twelfth Finance Commission (2005–10)*, New Delhi.

———. 2008. *National Accounts Statistics*, Central Statistical Organization (CSO). Available online at http://www.mospi.gov.in/mospi_cso_rept_pubn.htm. (downloaded in February 2009).

———. 2009. *Quick Estimates of National Consumption Expenditure, Saving and Capital Formation 2007–08*, CSO. Available online at http://www.mospi.gov.in/mospi_press_releases.htm (downloaded in February 2009).

Financial Express. 2006. "Adhering to Deficit Targets Vital for Economic Stability", August 28.

Planning Commission, Government of India. 2006. *Towards Faster and More Inclusive Growth: An Approach to the 11th Five Year Plan*, New Delhi.

Rakshit, Mihir. 2000. "On Correcting Fiscal Imbalances in the Indian Economy: Some Perspectives", *Money & Finance*, 2 (2): 19–58; reprinted in Mihir Rakshit (2009), *Money and Finance in the Indian Economy*, pp. 96–141. New Delhi: Oxford University Press.

———. 2001. "Restoring Fiscal Balance through Legislative Fiat: The Indian Experiment", *Economic and Political Weekly*, 36 (23): 2053–62; reprinted in Mihir Rakshit (2009), *Money and Finance in the Indian Economy*, pp. 35–60. New Delhi: Oxford University Press.

———. 2004. "Some Macroeconomics of India's Reform Experience', in Kaushik Basu (ed.), *India's Emerging Economy: Performance and Prospects in the 1990s and Beyond*, pp. 83–114. MIT Press, Cambridge, Massachusetts.

———. 2005a. "Some Analytics and Empirics of Fiscal Restructuring in India", *Economic and Political Weekly*, 40 (31): 3440–49; reprinted in Mihir Rakshit (2009), *Money and Finance in the Indian Economy*, pp. 142–66. New Delhi: Oxford University Press.

———. 2005b. "Budget Deficit: Sustainability, Solvency and Optimality", in A. Bagchi (ed.), *Readings in Public Finance*, pp. 339–80. New Delhi: Oxford University Press.

———. 2006. "Issues in Infrastructural Investment: National Highway Development Programme", *Money & Finance*, 2 (24–25): 49–80; reprinted in Mihir Rakshit, 2009. *Macroeconomics of Post-Reform India*, pp. 235–63. New Delhi: Oxford University Press.

———.2007a. "Some Puzzles of India's Macroeconomy", in K.L. Krishna and A.Vaidyanathan (eds), *Essays in Honour of Prof. K.N. Raj*, pp. 70–92. New Delhi: Oxford University Press.

———. 2007b. "Inflation in a Developing Economy: Theory and Policy", *Money & Finance*, 3 (2): 89–138; reprinted in Mihir Rakshit (2009), *Macroeconomics of Post-Reform India*, pp. 182–231. New Delhi: Oxford University Press.

———. 2009. "India Amidst the Global Crisis", *Economic and Political Weekly*, 44 (March 28–April 3): 94–106.

Solow, Robert M. 1956. "A Contribution to the Theory of Economic Growth", *Quarterly Journal of Economics*, 70 (1): 65–94.

World Bank. 2006. *India—Inclusive Growth and Service Delivery: Building on India's Success*, Report No. 34580-IN.

3

The BBLR Approach to Tax Reform in Emerging Countries

Richard M. Bird

———— • ✦ • ————

As I recall, I first met Amaresh Bagchi in 1986 when I was a visitor at the National Institute for Public Finance and Policy, shortly after he had become the Director. It was immediately apparent that he was not only a serious public finance scholar but that he was also something even rarer, a good man. Our frequent interchanges over the next two decades reinforced these initial impressions and added to them a better understanding on my part of how deeply Amaresh cared about improving India's fiscal system. Particularly fruitful in this respect were two brief periods when we were both in Washington and had the opportunity for many personal as well as professional discussions. He was a friend whose company I enjoyed, whose work I read with care and appreciated, and with whom I had many great exchanges on professional matters even when we were, as usual, continents apart physically though seldom professionally.

The first time we were together in Washington was, by coincidence (I hope!), more or less the time at which the World Bank, in effect, decided to get out of the tax policy business. As I was told at the time by a senior Bank official, it had been decided that taxation in developing countries was not a subject that required any additional research by the Bank. The final word on the subject so far as the bank was concerned at the time was contained in a document issued in 1991 under the title *Lessons of Tax Reform*. To sum up that document—not quite fairly—it essentially argues that the correct approach to designing tax systems in developing countries may be summed up in four words: Broad Bases, Low Rates: the BBLR approach. I have recently had occasion to consider how well this advice has held up over the years, and it seems appropriate to put forth some of these thoughts on the present occasion, in honor of Amaresh Bagchi. I hope he would have agreed with much of what I say, but I suspect he would have told me, as he often did, that I tend to put forth my ideas rather more strongly than their substance warrants. He will be missed.

I Broadening Tax Bases[1]

No one likes taxes. People do not like to pay them. Governments do not like to impose them. Unfortunately, taxes are necessary both to finance desired public spending in a non-inflationary way and to ensure that the burden of paying for such spending is fairly distributed. Since even necessary taxes impose real costs on society, good tax policy seeks to minimize those costs. However, tax policy is not just about economics. It is also about justice and hence, reflects such political factors as the degree of concern about fairness. In many countries, the increased economic growth of recent years has increased disparities between the rich and the poor. How people see the distributive effects of tax systems matters. In the end, however, no matter what any country may *want* to do with its tax system—or what it *should* do from one perspective or another (ethical, political, or developmental)—in reality what it *does* do is always constrained by what it *can* do. A country's economic structure and its administrative capacity as well as its political institutions all tend to reduce the tax policy options available. Nonetheless, some options almost always exist. The holy trinity of options proposed by most fiscal experts are broader bases, lower rates, and better administration. I begin the review of these options by considering what gets taxed—the tax base.

Developing countries face many difficult challenges in designing and implementing suitable tax systems. Many countries (like India) have large traditional agriculture sectors that are difficult to tax. Other significant components of the potential tax base lurk in other equally "hard-to-tax" sectors ranging from small business and the informal economy to cross-border investments. The traditional tax base afforded by international trade has also become increasingly hard to exploit in the face of pressures for trade liberalization. On the other hand, economic growth generally expands tax bases and such growth is often encouraged by (and usually results in) closer involvement with the international economy.

As countries develop, the mass modern production and consumption activities on which the tax systems of developed countries rest—taxes on wages and personal income, on corporate profits, on consumption —expand. This base needs to be reached without either overstraining administrative capacity or unduly discouraging the expansion of such activities. However, the leading edge of growth—outward-oriented development—may become the bleeding edge of the fiscal system as it becomes more and more difficult to levy taxes effectively on capital income, thus potentially exacerbating internal inequalities and political pressures on the tax system. Life is not easy for tax people in developing countries, and it is not becoming any easier.

As World Bank (1991) argues, one important aspect of good tax policy is to minimize unnecessary costs of taxation and one important way to do so is to make tax bases as broad as possible. A broad-based consumption tax, for example, will still discourage work effort, but such a tax will minimize distortions in the consumption of goods if all or most goods and services are subject to tax.[2] It has also been long argued that the tax base for income tax should also be as broad as possible, treating all incomes, no matter from what source, as uniformly as possible, although some recent discussion is beginning to cast increasing doubt on this once conventional piece of wisdom.[3]

II Growing Tax Bases

Much discussion of taxation in developing countries seems to assume, as it were, that "unto each a base (or bases) is given". If the tax base is indeed "given", then the only policy issue to be addressed is how it can be best exploited—for example, by reducing exemptions and by bringing non-payers into the tax net. In reality, however, tax bases are not simply "given": they can be "grown"—or destroyed—through the manner in which a given tax burden is collected. Taxes may, for example, discourage or encourage the "formalization" of the economy, they may foster or discourage the growth of such "tax handles" as imports, or they may be used to shape and direct economic growth into particular channels in a variety of ways and for a variety of purposes. As Emran and Stiglitz (2005) have recently reminded us, in the long run the manner in which (and from whom) taxes are collected may affect not only growth and distribution, but also the future level and mix of revenues itself.[4] The long-run "fiscal impact" (or "revenue productivity") effect of tax policy and administration decisions needs careful attention.

Consider, for example, four questions often raised with respect to the challenges facing tax policy in developing countries:

1. Should more reliance be put on consumption than on income taxes?
2. Are broader tax bases always better than narrower bases?
3. Should tax policy be designed to reduce the size of the "informal economy"?
4. What should be done with tax incentives?

Until recently, the answers of most fiscal experts to these questions were more or less that: (*a*) consumption taxes are better; (*b*) so are broader bases; (*c*) every effort should be made to tax the informal sector; and (*d*) finally, tax incentives are almost always a bad idea. How do these answers hold up in light of recent analysis and experience?

III Taxes and Growth

Over the past 50 years, there have been many policy prescriptions for economic growth (Easterly, 2002). Policy advisors have (in rough chronological order) urged increased capital investment, improvements in education, population control, reduction of government controls on market activities, and loan forgiveness programs as "silver bullets" that would result in improved economic performance in developing countries. Unfortunately, none of these cures has worked as advertised. Similarly, there is no magic tax strategy to encourage economic growth. Some countries with high tax burdens have high growth rates and some countries with low tax burdens have low growth rates. Looking at the relationship between growth rates and tax rates in the United States over the last 50 years, for instance, reveals that the US had its greatest periods of economic growth during those years where the tax rates were the highest (Slemrod and Bakija, 1996). This does not mean that high tax rates are the key to economic growth, since growth rates might have been even higher in those years with high tax rates, if the rates had been lower. But it does suggest that there is still much that we do not understand about the relation between taxes and growth.

Nonetheless, if one tried to visualize a purely growth-oriented tax system, it might perhaps be one with a relatively low and stable tax on profits and some taxation of the traditional agricultural and informal sectors, but with major fiscal reliance being placed on a broad-based consumption tax, which makes some allowance for necessary consumption. What would likely be conspicuously missing in any such design is any explicit concern for fairness in taxation. I return to this point later.

Consumption or Income

Even from a growth perspective, however, some modifications to the conventional answers summarized above seem required. First, should taxation focus more on consumption than income? In general, yes. But there is not all that much difference between the two in the context of most developing countries, and some "consumption" in national accounting terms is really "investment" from the growth perspective and hence, should not be taxed.[5] Moreover, even though many emerging countries get little or no revenue from taxing capital income, their tax systems may nonetheless have high adverse effects on investment and growth, owing to the high effective tax rates imposed at the margin (Mintz, 2006). Nonetheless, as discussed below, income taxes also have a distinctive role to play in a "good" tax mix.

Broader Base

Should bases be broader rather than narrower? Often the answer is again, yes. Sometimes, however, as in the productive consumption case and perhaps also in the capital income case, broader may be worse.[6] If people lack food to eat or basic clothing and shelter, and they are not sufficiently healthy and educated to engage in productive work, they are unlikely to be economically productive. For example, sometimes excluding items that constitute a significant fraction of the consumption of poor people from the VAT base may be a perfectly sensible growth-facilitating policy, although developing and implementing a finely nuanced VAT structure along these lines is a tricky exercise (as Bird and Gendron, 2007 discuss in some detail).

Growth in the sense of enhancing the productivity of the labor force and equity in the sense of not taxing the poor may thus sometimes be fully compatible objectives. In addition, from a broader perspective societal disaffection with the inequities accompanying growth may sometimes require a degree of visible fiscal correction in order to make growth-facilitating policies politically feasible. Poverty alleviation is more a task for expenditures than for taxes. At the very least, however, heavy taxes on items that constitute major consumption expenditures for the poor should be avoided.

Tax Informality

Should taxes be used to punish the informal economy? Yes, but again great care is needed in both design and administration. While even a bad tax on a good base may sometimes be a good idea (Auriol and Warlters, 2005), care must be taken to ensure that the "good" does not become the enemy of the better, as Sally Wallace and I have elsewhere discussed in detail (Bird and Wallace, 2004). An easier task than taxing those in the informal sector is to remove the many barriers created by tax and regulatory systems discouraging people from entering the formal sector. A recent World Bank and International Finance Corporation (2008) publication, for example, places India near the bottom of the list with respect to the costs to formal business of complying with the tax system: this is obviously not conducive to economic growth.

Tax Incentives

What should be done with tax incentives? In this case, there is no reason to add a "but" to the conventional answer: eliminate them. Despite their continuing popularity, the evidence is—as these things go in the social sciences—virtually overwhelming: tax incentives are usually redundant and ineffective. They reduce revenue and complicate the fiscal system, without achieving their stated objectives efficiently or effectively. Excessive use of tax incentives complicates administration, facilitating evasion and corruption. Once created, concessions usually prove hard to remove and are often enlarged at the initiative of taxpayers who lobby for more concessions or simply redefine existing concessions in unforeseen and presumably undesired ways.

Elsewhere (Bird, 2000) I have suggested that to maximize the likelihood of beneficial results from tax concessions and to reduce the damage that may be caused by poorly-designed and implemented incentives, countries should at the very least stick to three simple rules:

1. Keep it simple: incentives should be as few in number and as simple in structure as possible.
2. Keep records on who receives what concessions and at what cost in revenue forgone and also, if the incentive is intended to achieve some particular objective, on the measurable results. In the absence of such information, government is simply throwing money away.
3. Evaluate the numbers at regular intervals to determine whether the incentive is achieving results worth its estimated cost and, if it is not, eliminate it.

Unfortunately, almost no country follows these simple prescriptions, presumably because the political advantages of ambiguity outweigh the potential social gains from transparency. Developing countries cannot waste public money like this.[7] Much more needs to be done to assess and evaluate tax incentives on the basis of evidence instead of relying on the largely unwarranted faith in their efficacy evidenced by their proliferation around the world.

IV Lowering Tax Rates

Countries can increase revenues in only three ways: raise rates, expand bases, and improve administration. Raising rates within the existing system is the most obvious approach. It is also often the most politically acceptable approach. On the other hand, it is generally the least economically desirable solution. Raising rates when traditional tax bases are not expanding, when new bases can shift abroad, and when administration is weak, is unlikely to increase much revenue. Even if revenues do increase, so may inequity and inefficiency. Distortions associated with taxation increase (broadly) with the square of the tax rate, so inefficiency increases with rate increases, especially those affecting economically mobile sectors such as foreign investors. Horizontal inequity may also increase because only those few unfortunates trapped within the tax system bear the burden. When those who comply are penalized and those who cheat escape, a country is not on the path to building a sustainable state revenue system. Moreover, if, as seems often to be the case, it turns out to be most expedient to increase taxes on the politically weaker segments of society, vertical inequity may also be exacerbated.

While, as noted earlier, statutory rates do not necessarily tell the tale—effective rates are what matters for many purposes—the experience of recent years suggests that many countries have been listening to the conventional BBLR advice or, more likely, emulating the neighbors. Statutory income tax rates have in general declined strikingly around the world in recent decades. Although in most countries VAT revenues have replaced declining trade taxes (and excises) and not income taxes, concern has been expressed over this trend by those who view income taxes as the only flag under which tax progressivity sails.

I have some sympathy with this proposition. Historically, reliance on the income tax has indeed been seen as "a mirror of democracy"

(Webber and Wildavsky, 1986: 526). However, I do not agree that the reduction of nominal income tax rates is always or necessarily a politically and socially retrogressive move. Taxes impose real costs on society as a whole. Developing countries (in which resources are by definition scarce) should strive to keep such costs as low as possible in order to free resources for socially desired objectives.

V The Costs of Taxes

Of course, taxes are not themselves a cost but simply a means of transferring resources from private to public use. Economic costs arise only when total resources available for society's use, whether for public or private purposes, are reduced by taxes. There are several ways taxes can reduce the size of the economic pot from which all must draw.

Administrative Costs

To begin with, it obviously costs something to collect taxes. The actual cost of collecting taxes in developed countries is (very) roughly 1 percent of tax revenues. In developing countries, the costs of tax collection may be substantially higher: Gallagher (2004) reports administrative costs ranging from 0.9 to 3.9 percent for six developing countries; Warlters and Auriol (2005) report results for an additional nine countries in the range of 1.1 to 3.6 percent.

Compliance Costs

Taxpayers also incur compliance costs, over and above the actual payment of tax. Third parties also incur compliance costs. One of the few reported studies of compliance costs in developing countries (by Chattopadhyay and Das-Gupta, 2002 for the Indian personal income tax) found compliance costs to be more than 10 times higher than in developed countries. Similarly, Shekidele (1999) found compliance costs for excises in Tanzania to be more than 15 times higher than similar costs in more developed countries. Costs of paying taxes are generally considerably higher in poor than in rich countries for several reasons. One reason for this is the sheer complexity of their tax structures and the cumbersome administrative methods employed. Another reason is because compliance costs are sensitive to the stability of tax legislation as well as to such changes in the external environment as inflation, and such factors are more prominent in developing countries.[8]

Efficiency Costs

Finally—and the major concern of most economists—taxes impose "deadweight" (distortionary) costs that alter decisions made by businesses and individuals, as the relative prices they confront are changed. In most circumstances, the resulting changes in behavior reduce the efficiency with which resources are used and hence, lower output and potential well-being.[9]

Virtually all taxes affect resource decisions at the margin. Consumption taxes, such as the value-added tax, may discourage the consumption of taxed as opposed to untaxed goods (for example, housing). Taxes on gasoline, alcohol, and cigarettes may reduce the consumption of these items.[10] Income taxes, because they tax the return to savings, may alter the amount of savings or the form in which savings are held. Failure to tax capital gains, until they are realized (when the asset is sold), encourages the holding of assets (lock-in effect). Taxes may also affect investment, and such effects may be especially important when economies are more open to trade and investment. Foreign investors may choose to locate their activities in a particular country for many reasons— the relative costs of production, access to markets, and sound infrastructure—but taxes may also influence their choice. When taxes lower the after-tax return on investments, the level of investment and hence, growth is lower than it would otherwise be. Corporate income taxes may also influence the decision to incorporate the composition of a firm's capital structure (use of debt or equity financing) and dividend policy.

The importance of such tax effects is a matter of considerable debate, but the current consensus is that they are much more important than was earlier thought. Efficiency costs of taxation in developed countries are usually estimated to be some multiple of the administrative and compliance costs mentioned above. The lowest estimates of the efficiency costs of taxes for developed countries are at least 20–30 percent of revenues collected, and much higher estimates (ranging well over 100 percent) are common in the literature (Auerbach and Hines, 2002).

Such estimates are both hard to make and controversial. Nonetheless, unless public expenditures produce social benefits at least equal to the "marginal cost of public funds" (MCF), they are by definition, not worth what they cost. A recent study found the average MCF in 38 African countries to be close to those found in a number of developed countries, namely, around 1.2 (Warlters and Auriol, 2005).[11] This implies that the last (marginal) dollar spent by the public sector would have to yield at least USD1.20 in public benefits—more if compliance costs were taken into account—in order to be worthwhile.

Whatever their size, efficiency losses from taxation are real. However, they are not directly visible: they arise essentially because something does not happen, some activity did not occur or occurred in some other form than it would have in the absence of the distortionary tax. Output that is not produced is nonetheless output (and potential welfare) lost, so poor countries need to design taxes to minimize such possible adverse consequences. Unfortunately, the absence of visible concrete evidence means that there is seldom much political weight behind this concern.

One way to reduce the costs of taxation is to shift to consumption taxes (VAT) instead of income taxes, since this will reduce the extent to which taxes affect the location of businesses, alter production techniques, or change the forms in which business is conducted. However, as I will emphasize shortly, personal income taxes are often politically essential as the primary indicator of the importance governments attach to fairness. Moreover, countries with personal income taxes need to tax corporate income also to prevent tax avoidance by individuals as well as to collect taxes from foreign-owned firms.

To the extent that efficiency costs of taxation result from rational policy decisions (for example, to redistribute income through the fiscal system), they may be worth incurring. A key question is, thus, whether the income tax is in fact an effective re-distributor. If it is, the efficiency cost of taxation may be worth paying, though one should of course still strive to reduce administrative and compliance costs. But if progressive income taxes do not do much for distribution, and are unlikely to do so except by incurring very high costs, then presumably countries can reduce rates to reduce their marginal distortionary effect at little cost in terms of distribution.

VI Progressivity and Fairness

Fairness is a key issue in designing any tax regime. Indeed, from one perspective, taxes exist primarily to secure equity. National governments do not need taxes to secure funds: they can simply print the money required to fund operations. The tax system may be viewed as a mechanism designed to take money away from the private sector in as efficient, equitable, and administratively inexpensive ways as possible. Of course, what is considered equitable or fair by one person may differ from the conceptions held by others. Some may stress horizontal over vertical equity, for example, as Organization for Economic Co-operation and Development (OECD, 2006) argues is increasingly true in developed countries. Others may tilt the balance the other way, as "progressive" thinkers have long done.

Broadly, *horizontal equity* requires those in similar circumstances to pay the same amount of taxes, while *vertical equity* requires appropriate differences among taxpayers in different economic circumstances. Those who have the same ability to pay should of course bear the same tax liability; equally, fairness would seem to require those taxpayers with greater ability to pay relatively higher taxes. Both concepts have appeal. Unfortunately, neither is very useful in actually setting up a tax system.

I consider here only the question of whether "growing" governments in developing countries on the basis of VATs rather than income tax is an inherently bad idea.[12] First, I ask whether even progressive income taxes in developing countries are very redistributive; the answer is, not much. Second, I then ask whether VATs in such countries are regressive; the answer is, not necessarily. And finally, I ask whether in some circumstances a "good" VAT may not be better than a "bad" income tax; the answer is, of course it may, depending upon the details of both the country and the two taxes.

Are Income Taxes Progressive?

Chu, Davoodi, and Gupta (2000) surveyed 36 studies of tax incidence in 19 different developing countries: 13 found the tax system progressive, and seven each found the tax system proportional and regressive; the others had mixed findings or insignificant effects. Most of the reported progressivity came from income taxes. So the answer to the first question is that income taxes in most developing countries are likely somewhat progressive. Indeed, to the extent income taxes do not impinge on the poorest—those outside the market sector—they are bound to be progressive. Even within the sector that is subject to the income tax, progressive rates mean that the impact of the tax is progressive, at least within the group of those who must pay tax on all (most) of their income, for example, because they receive it in the form of wages from a public sector employer. In most developing countries, however, little if any tax is collected from either capital income or self-employment (mixed) income and that little is most unlikely to be distributed very progressively.

Income taxes may thus help share the burden of government a bit more fairly, but they are unlikely to have any significant influence on distributional outcomes (Harberger, 2006). As Lindert (2003) shows, it was not by taxing the rich but by taxing the growing middle class that developed countries "grew" large states. Big states may—if those who control them wish to do so—help the poor more than small states, but they do so through expenditures much more than through taxes. In fact, such well-known "welfare states" as Sweden have been very careful not to kill the golden goose of private investment that largely (if indirectly) finances their big public sectors.

Is VAT Regressive?

Three types of taxes are levied on consumption in most developing countries: import taxes, excise taxes, and VATs. For the most part, the growth in VAT replaced the other two types of consumption tax. This change has almost certainly made the tax system more progressive (Gemmell and Morrissey, 2003) for a number of reasons. First, the impact of trade taxes (especially including the "burden" imposed by their protective effect) is likely to be regressive, in the context of most developing countries. Second, excise taxes (even those justified by good economic arguments such as external effects) are also generally—with the notable exception of those affecting motor transport—regressive. Third, VAT in most developing countries is not particularly regressive and may indeed in some be slightly progressive.[13]

Can a Good VAT be Better Than a Bad Income Tax?

In some circumstances it can, even if one sets aside the more favorable "tax-base" effects discussed earlier. Consider the case of a country with a large shadow economy. Income taxes do not reach this sector, and indeed appear to be associated with its expansion (Schneider and Klingmaier, 2004). On the other hand, to some extent, a VAT functions like a presumptive tax on the informal sector since credits are available only to registered firms, and those earning income in the shadow sector are taxed when they purchase formal-sector commodities (Glenday and Hollinrake, 2005). Increasing income tax rates in such countries generally impinges primarily on two limited groups. The first consists of government employees, who often soon receive counterbalancing wage increases that eat up any revenue gains. The second are employees of large, formal market firms, which tends to discourage the expansion of the formal sector. Increasing VAT may, on the other hand, to some extent tend to make life in the formal sector relatively more attractive. Such a substitution is not only preferable in terms of growth but may even in some cases increase the horizontal equity of the tax system by imposing more tax on the informal sector. Indeed, if a VAT is combined with, say, increased excises on such important higher-income consumption goods as motor vehicles, then increasing indirect taxes in some countries may be significantly more progressive than just raising the rate of a personal income tax that affects only a limited group of formal sector wage earners.

Of course, there are also good reasons for keeping direct taxes on both income and property, in the tax mix as well. Corporate income taxes are needed to buttress personal income taxes, to ensure an equitable share of the returns on cross-border investment, and to tap economic rents to some extent (Bird, 2002). Moreover, to maintain and grow the state, the tax system must tap into those sectors that grow and since growth usually results in the growth of the employed middle class, a mildly progressive personal income tax (like a VAT) can be an important way to ensure that state revenues share in the prosperity. Perhaps, most importantly, only by visibly taxing the better-off through both income and property taxes can countries use the tax system as a "state-building" tool.[14] Similarly, since sustainable tax policy needs to be accepted as fair by those affected, and automobiles and big houses are much more visible than income, the more taxation can effectively be imposed on such items, the better.

VII Improving Tax Administration

To this point, I have generally supported, in a qualified way, both prongs of the tax reform fork—BB and LR—set out in the World Bank (1991) study, that I took as my starting point. However, an important lesson that has been learned time and again in the last few decades is that to get reform not only under way, but to do so in a sustainable fashion, a third horse needs to be harnessed to the BBLR chariot, that is better tax administration. This "third horseman" of tax reform has received much less attention from analysts than it warrants.[15] Reaping revenues from tax rate changes (in any direction) requires effective tax administration. Raising revenues through base expansion requires even better tax administration. New taxpayers must be identified and brought into the tax net and new collection techniques developed. Such changes take time to implement. The best tax policy in the world is worth little, if it cannot be implemented effectively. Tax policy design must take into account the administrative dimension of taxation. What can be done to a considerable extent inevitably determines what is done.

The importance of good administration has long been as obvious to all concerned with tax policy in developing countries as its absence in practice. One cannot assume that whatever policy designers can think up can be done or that any administrative problems encountered can be easily and quickly remedied. How a tax system is administered affects its yield, its incidence, and its efficiency. Administration that is unfair and capricious may bring the tax system into disrepute and weaken the legitimacy of state actions.

VIII Assessing Tax Administration

Tax administration is a difficult task even at the best of time and in the best of places, and conditions in few emerging countries match these specifications. Revenue outcomes are not always the most appropriate basis for assessing administrative performance.[16] How revenue is raised—the effect of revenue-generation effort on equity, the political fortunes of the government, and the level of economic welfare—may be equally (or more) important as *how much* revenue is raised. Private as well as public costs of tax administration must be taken into account, and due attention must be paid to the extent to which revenue is attributable to enforcement (the active intervention of the administration) rather than compliance (the relatively passive role of the administration as the recipient of revenues generated by other features of the system).[17] Assessing the relation between administrative effort and revenue outcome is by no means a simple task. Neither is improving administrative efforts and outcomes.

It is useful to think of the problem of tax administration at three levels—architecture, engineering, and management (Shoup, 1991). The first level concerns the design of the general legal framework—not only the substance of the tax laws to be administered but also a wide range of important procedural features. Once the general architectural design has been determined, the engineer takes over and sets up the specific organizational structure and operating rules for the tax administration. Finally, once the critical institutional infrastructure has been erected, the tax managers charged with actually administering the tax system can do their jobs. One cannot assess how well a tax administration is functioning, let alone suggest how to improve it, without taking into account not only the environment in which it has to function but also the laws it is supposed to administer and the institutional infrastructure with which it has been equipped.

To appraise the efficiency or effectiveness of tax administration, one thus needs to take into account both the degree of complexity of the tax structure and the extent to which that structure remains stable over time. Complexity and its implications for tax administration has long been a concern even in the most developed countries. Even the most sophisticated tax administration can easily be overloaded with impossible tasks (Hood, 1976). Such concerns are obviously critical in countries in which less well-equipped administrators are asked to tackle inherently complex tasks in a generally hostile and often information-poor environment. The life of the tax administrator is made even more complicated by the propensity of many governments, reflecting in part the unstable political and economic environment, to alter tax legislation annually, or even more frequently. Both the complexity of the tax structure and its stability are thus important factors to be weighed in assessing tax administration.

Dis-aggregation of the "black box" of tax administration along such lines is particularly important since the main ways to improve administrative outcomes are either to alter the tasks with which the administration is charged or to strengthen the tools with which it is equipped. Simple exhortations to "do better" are of little use to resource-strapped administrators faced with impossible tasks. Experience around the world demonstrates that the single most important ingredient for effective tax administration is clear recognition at high political levels of the importance of the task and willingness to support good administrative practices even if political friends are hurt. Few developing countries have been able to leap this initial hurdle.[18] The widespread reluctance to collect taxes efficiently and effectively without fear or favor may be understandable in countries which are fragile politically, but without such efforts no viable long-term tax system can possibly be put into place. If the political will is there, the techniques needed for effective tax administration are not a secret.

IX How to Fix Tax Administration

Indeed, the basic recipe for effective tax administration has only three ingredients: political will to administer the tax system effectively, a clear strategy for achieving this goal, and adequate resources for the task. It helps, of course, if the tax system is well designed, appropriate for the country in question, and relatively simple. But even the best designed tax system will not be properly implemented unless these three conditions are fulfilled.

If the political will exists, the blueprint for effective tax administration is relatively straightforward. The tax administration should be given an appropriate institutional form, adequately staffed with trained officials, and properly organized, which usually means an organizational structure based on function or client groups. Computerization and appropriate use of modern information technology are important (Bird and Zolt, 2008), but technology alone is not sufficient and must be carefully integrated into the tax administration. Putting all this into place takes time, resources, direction, and effort. But it can be done, as countries from Singapore to Chile have shown.

In addition to giving the administration simpler and more enforceable laws to administer, experience suggests that the best approach to improving tax administration begins by assuming that the taxpayer is a client (albeit probably not a willing one) to be served, and not a thief to be caught. Studies on taxpayer behavior around the world suggest that services to taxpayers that facilitate reporting, filing and paying taxes, or that impart education or information among citizens about their obligations under the tax laws, are often as or more cost-effective in securing compliance than measures (auditing, penalties) more directly designed to counter non-compliance.

Improving tax compliance is not the same as discouraging non-compliance (Slemrod, 1992). Low compliance may to some extent be a function of high compliance costs, as well as of more basic problems such as lack of state legitimacy, inadequate connection between taxes and benefits, and perceptions of tax fairness. As a rule, in most countries some taxpayers always pay (often because they have no choice), some always cheat, and some cheat when they think they can get away with it. An important task of tax administration is to prevent the mix from tipping in the direction of pervasive non-compliance. To do so, life must not only be made more difficult for non-compliers but also easier for compliers (Torgler, 2007). It is thus important to simplify procedures for taxpayers, for example, by eliminating demands for superfluous information in tax returns and consolidating return and payment forms. Once procedures are simplified, the tax administration can then concentrate on its main tasks: facilitating compliance, monitoring and enforcing compliance, and controlling corruption.

Facilitating Compliance

The first task of any tax administration is to facilitate compliance—to make sure that those who should be in the system are in the system and that they comply with the rules. To do so:

1. Taxpayers must be found. If they are required to register, the registration process should be as easy as possible. Systems must be in place to identify those who do not register voluntarily. An appropriate unique taxpayer identification system is needed to facilitate compliance and enforcement.[19]
2. The administration needs a process to determine tax liabilities. This may be done administratively (as with most property taxes) or by some self-assessment procedure (as with most income taxes and VATs).
3. Taxes must be collected. In many countries, this is best done through the banking system. It is seldom appropriate for tax administration officials to handle money directly.

   The authorities should provide adequate taxpayer service in the form of information, pamphlets, forms, advice agencies, payment facilities, telephone and electronic filing, and so on, to make taxpayer compliance with the system as easy as possible. There should also be a clear and functioning system of review and appeal.

Monitoring and Enforcing Compliance

Since some taxpayers are not honest, a second important task is to enforce compliance and reduce tax evasion. To do so, the administration needs to understand the extent and nature of the potential tax base in order to estimate the "tax gap". Without some knowledge of the unreported base, and its determinants, no administration can properly allocate its resources to improve tax collection and ensure everyone bears at least a roughly fair share of the tax burden. Close attention must also be paid to ensuring that those who are in the system file on time and pay the amounts due. Adequate interest charges must be imposed on late payments to ensure that non-payment of taxes does not become a cheap source of finance. Similarly, an adequate penalty structure is needed to ensure that those who should register do so, that those who should file do so, and that those who underreport their tax bases are sufficiently penalized to increase the costs of evading tax. All in all, as Harberger (1989) once noted, good tax administration is not rocket science: it's more like being a good accountant. Unfortunately, in many countries good accountants are scarce—not least in the tax department.

Controlling Corruption

A third major task is to keep not just taxpayers but tax collectors honest. Corruption undermines confidence in the tax system, affects willingness to pay taxes, and reduces a country's capacity to finance government expenditures (Fjeldstad, 2005). No government can expect taxpayers to comply willingly if taxpayers believe the tax structure is unfair or that the revenue collected is not effectively used. But even sound tax structure and sound expenditure policy can be vitiated by capricious and corrupt tax administration. Developed countries took centuries to develop, and implement systems to prevent dishonest tax officials from corrupt practices (Webber and Wildavsky, 1986). Tax officials must be adequately compensated so that they do not need to steal to live. Ideally, they should be professionally trained, promoted on the basis of merit, and judged by their adherence to the strictest standards of legality and morality. Temptation should be reduced by reducing direct contacts between officials and taxpayers, and reducing discretion (and increasing supervision) when they do have such contact. Developing countries trying to sustain relatively large governments on precarious fiscal foundations find it hard to deal with such problems.

There is no single prescription—no secret recipe—that, once adopted, will ensure improved tax administration in any country. Countries exhibit a wide variety of tax compliance levels, reflecting not only the effectiveness of their tax administrations but also taxpayer attitudes towards taxation and towards government in general. Attitudes affect intentions and intentions affect behavior. Attitudes are formed in a social context by such factors as the perceived level of evasion, the perceived fairness of the tax structure, its complexity and stability, how it is administered, the value attached to government activities, and the legitimacy of government. Government policies affecting any of these factors may influence taxpayer attitudes and hence the observed level of taxpayer compliance. Measures sometimes advisable in countries with very low compliance levels, such as the massive application of administrative penalties may be inappropriate and may even have perverse effects in countries with higher compliance levels.

X The Resource Problem

The scarcity of tax administration resources is a constant in most countries. Despite the high potential pay-off, in terms of increased revenue, it is usually difficult, and often impossible, for tax departments to obtain and retain qualified staff or even to meet such basic material needs as office space and computers. Tax administrators are civil servants and hence, subject to all the constraints affecting civil services. Reform strategies that require substantial additional administrative resources—particularly staff—are, hence, usually doomed to failure, because the needed resources will not materialize fully or in a timely fashion.[20] Good administrative reform strategies are usually based more on the better allocation of available resources than on accretions of major additional resources.

One important improvement may simply be to reduce unproductive tasks such as processing reams of information of which no uses is made. Another may be to create specialized offices to deal with particular groups of taxpayers (for example, by size or industry). Yet another approach in some countries has been to privatize certain tax administration activities traditionally performed by government. For example, tax collection can be outsourced to banks, which are specialized in the handling and control of payments. Of course, simply entrusting banks with the task of receiving payments or returns (and even, in some countries, processing returns) does not assure success. Proper systems must be designed, the tax department must exercise adequate supervision, and the remuneration paid to the banks must be appropriate. Much time and effort has been spent on such matters in countries in which collection through the banking system operates successfully.

Most recent attempts to reform tax administration center on information technology (IT). No modern tax administration can perform its tasks efficiently without using IT, but in some countries, the expectation of greater effectiveness from computerization has not materialized. Successful modernization efforts do not simply computerize antiquated processes but re-engineer the whole system; for example, consolidating return and payment forms, eliminating unnecessary and unused information required from taxpayers, and so on. Successful computerization requires a fundamental reorganization in both systems and procedures; it is not a way to side-step such reforms. Moreover, even the best computerized system will not produce useful results, unless there are real incentives for tax administrators to utilize the system properly.

Still, the large-scale information processing and coordination problems facing tax administrations usually require the adoption of effective computerized processes in even the poorest countries in such areas as: (a) taxpayer records and tax collection (taxpayer compliance); (b) internal management and control over resources; (c) legal structure and procedures; and (d) systems to lower taxpayer compliance costs. Another reason why tax administrations need IT expertise is simply because some of their most important clients—multinational companies and, increasingly, large domestic firms—employ sophisticated computer systems, which are beyond the investigative capacity of technologically backward tax administrations. IT is thus in a sense a "double-edged" tool: in the hands of taxpayers, it may make tax administration more difficult (especially in an open economy), but in the hands of the administration it may enable a more robust response to such challenges (Bird and Zolt, 2008).

XI Conclusion

In the end, as I have recently argued elsewhere (Bird, 2008), what countries do to reform their tax systems and how successful they are generally depends less on the economics of taxation than on the politics of taxation. Nonetheless, what we have learned from 50 years of experience and reflection on fiscal issues in developing countries is that what might be called the "Washington fiscal consensus" discussed in this paper—broader bases and lower rates—holds up fairly well. Of course, as Alfred Marshall once said, "every short sentence about economics is inherently false".[21] In the spirit of trying to get a bit closer to what may be true, I have therefore, noted some qualifications to and questions about the basic BBLR approach. In addition, I have emphasized the fundamental importance of understanding and improving tax administration. No one can work in this field without recognizing the importance of the administrative dimension of tax reform; too often, however, inadequate attention has been paid to this critical aspect of the problem when thinking about tax policy in emerging countries. This is not a mistake that Amaresh Bagchi ever made. We should learn from his example.

Notes

1 Some of the ideas contained in this paper were also discussed in my recent NIPFP lecture (Bird, 2008), although the focus of that lecture on the political economy aspects of the process of tax reform was very different from the more substantive focus of the present paper.
2 In theory, in order to minimize efficiency losses different tax rates should be imposed on each commodity, with higher rates imposed on those goods and services where the changes in behavior are the smallest. To do so, however, requires much more information about how taxes alter behavior than is available in most countries. Moreover, this approach does not take administrative and equity concerns into account. For these reasons, in practice it seems generally advisable to impose a uniform tax rate to the extent possible. A few items, such as gasoline, tobacco products, and alcohol, may be taxed at relatively higher rates, either because of regulatory reasons or because the demand for these products is relatively unresponsive to taxation; such taxes can be designed to avoid excessive regressivity.
3 See, for example, Boadway (2005) and Barreix and Roca (2008). This question is explored in more detail in Bird and Zolt (2010).
4 Much the same inference can be drawn from such other recent papers as Auriol and Warlters (2005) and Gordon and Li (2009). For a slightly different take on this issue, see the recent survey by Bahl and Bird (2008).
5 The careful early work of Shoup (1965) on this subject deserves more attention than it has received.
6 There is also a strong case for heavy narrow excise taxes on a small range of products both in economic and revenue terms. Essentially, a good excise tax system is one that (a) taxes few products, (b) taxes those products correctly, and (c) is administered well. Most excise systems in developing countries fall well short of this standard. Excises are imposed on too many products; the rate structure is not logical; and administration leaves much to

be desired. The result is all too often a complex structure that produces less revenue and more distortions than it should and is not well administered (see Cnossen, 2006).

7 Of course, in some instances as Bates (2007) emphasizes, such ways of putting public money into private pockets may be a pay-off required to keep the current politicians in power so from their point of view it may not be a waste of money—it is not their money, after all. But it is still a social waste.

8 Compliance and administrative costs may sometimes be substitutes to some extent—for example, when taxpayers are required to provide more information, thus increasing their costs while presumably reducing the administrative costs that would otherwise be incurred to secure that information. On the other hand, administrative and compliance costs may also be complementary, as when a more sophisticated administration both requires more information and then increases administrative costs by using the new information to undertake more audits and other enforcement actions.

9 There are exceptions. First, when taxes are "lump sum"—that is, the tax burden is the same regardless of behavioral responses—there are no distortionary effects. But such taxes are of no importance in the real world. Second, to the extent that taxes fall on economic rents— payments to factors above those needed to induce them into the activity concerned— they may not affect economic activity. Well-designed taxes on natural resources and land, for example, may thus to some extent produce revenue without economic distortion. Finally, some taxes may not only create no distortions in economic behavior but may even induce desirable behavior. Certain environmental levies, for example (even such crude proxies such as taxes on fuel), may to some extent have such effects. "Good" taxes—those with no bad economic effects—should, of course, be exploited as fully as possible, but most revenue needed to finance government inevitably gives rise to efficiency costs.

10 As noted earlier, not all such effects need be bad: for instance, if tobacco consumption falls, people may live longer, healthier, and more productive lives.

11 Auriol and Warlters (2005) do not take compliance costs explicitly into account. They suggest that the similarity observed between developed and developing countries may result from two offsetting factors. First, developed countries tend to have higher taxes and heavier reliance on income taxes, both of which are associated with higher MCFs; second, developing countries tend to have higher administrative costs and larger informal sectors, both of which are again associated with higher MCFs. An additional factor, which also cannot easily be taken into account in the CGE framework used for MCF estimates, is that, as Shah and Whalley (1990) argue, since economic rents are more prevalent in the fragmented economies of developing countries, many taxes that might in more integrated market systems impact economic margins may fall on such rents and hence create less distortion.

12 For further discussion of a few of the many complex points touched on (or skipped over) in this section, see Bird and Zolt (2005).

13 The evidence for this conclusion is reviewed in Bird and Gendron (2007).

14 The case for property taxes is developed at length in Bird and Slack (2004). On taxation and state-building in general, see Brautigam, Fjeldstad, and Moore (2007).

15 Not so incidentally, much of what I have learned about tax administration I learned from Amaresh Bagchi and Arindam Das-Gupta when I had the pleasure of working with them some years ago on a paper reviewing the then scanty literature on the subject (Bagchi, Bird, and Das-Gupta, 1995).

16 For example, even if it costs only USD 1 to collect USD 100, it does not follow that to get another USD 100 in revenue one simply needs to spend an additional dollar on tax administration. Not only are such figures sensitive to tax rates but the marginal revenue yield

equals the average only under very special circumstances (Vazquez-Caro et al., 1992). More importantly, as Slemrod and Yitzhaki (2002) show, the optimal size of a tax administration is likely to be where marginal revenue exceeds marginal cost, perhaps by a wide margin.

17 In one of the few books on how tax administrations actually function in developing countries, Radian (1980) stresses the extent to which officials tend to be passive recipients of funds rather than active collectors of them.

18 See, for instance, the telling comparison in Bergman (2003) of Argentina, which conspicuously has not leaped the hurdle, and Chile, which has. As IDB (2006) notes, there is still much we do not understand about why Chile has been able to do so much: however, as Bergman (2003) shows, the willingness of Chile's leaders—of very different political persuasions—to support effective administration stands out.

19 Manglik (2008) suggests that India's PAN system falls short in this respect.

20 Salvation through reorganization is not likely to solve the problem. For example, setting up more independent revenue authorities that are to some extent freed from civil service restrictions on hiring and pay may sometimes help, but on the whole the evidence seems to suggest that any country that has the will, strategy, and resources to reform tax administration probably does not need an independent revenue authority—and a country in which these critical ingredients are lacking is unlikely to be successful even if it creates such an authority.

21 The Marshall sentence—which, it should be noted, is itself short—is cited in Gardner (2006: 7).

References

Auerbach, A.J. and J.R. Hines, Jr. 2002. "Taxation and Economic Efficiency", in A.J. Auerbach and M. Feldstein, (eds), *Handbook of Public Economics*, Vol. 3, pp. 1251–92. Amsterdam: Elsevier.

Auriol, E. and M. Warlters. 2005. "Taxation Base in Developing Countries", *Journal of Public Economics*, 89 (4): 625–46.

Bagchi, A., R.M. Bird, and A. Das-Gupta. 1995. "An Economic Approach to Tax Administration Reform", Discussion Paper No. 3, International Centre for Tax Studies, University of Toronto.

Bahl, R.W. and R.M. Bird. 2008. "Tax Policy in Developing Countries: Looking Back and Forward", *National Tax Journal*, 61 (2): 279–301.

Barreix, A. and J. Roca. 2008. "Strengthening a Fiscal Pillar: The Uruguayan Dual Income Tax", *CEPAL Review*, 92 (August): 121–40.

Bates, R.H. 2007. *When Things Fell Apart: State Failure in Late-century Africa*. Cambridge, UK: Cambridge University Press.

Bergman, Marcelo. 2003. "Tax Reforms and Tax Compliance: The Divergent Paths of Chile and Argentina", *Journal of Latin American Studies*, 35(3): 593–624.

Bird, R.M. 2000. "Tax Incentives for Investment in Developing Countries", in G. Perry, J. Whalley, and G. McMahon (eds), *Fiscal Reform and Structural Change in Developing Countries* (2 vols.), Vol. 1, pp. 201–21. London: Macmillan for International Development Research Centre.

———. 2002. "Why Tax Corporations?" *Bulletin for International Fiscal Documentation*, 56 (5): 194–203.

Richard M. Bird

Bird, R.M. 2008. "Tax Challenges Facing Developing Countries", Inaugural Lecture of the Annual Public Lecture Series of the National Institute of Public Finance and Policy, New Delhi, March.

Bird, R.M. and E. Slack. 2004. International Handbook of Land and Property Taxation. Cheltenham, UK and Northampton, MA: Edward Elgar.

Bird, R.M. and E.M. Zolt. 2005. "Redistribution via Taxation: The Limited Role of the Personal Income Tax in Developing Countries", UCLA Law Review, 52 (6): 1627–95.

———. 2008. "Technology and Taxation in Developing Countries: From Hand to Mouse", National Tax Journal 61 (4): 791–821.

———. 2010. "Dual Income Taxation and Developing Countries", Columbia Journal of Tax Law, 1 (2): 174–217.

Bird, R.M. and P.P. Gendron. 2007. The VAT in Developing and Transitional Countries. Cambridge: Cambridge University Press.

Bird, R.M. and S. Wallace. 2004. "Is It Really so Hard to Tax the Hard-to-Tax? The Context and Role of Presumptive Taxes", in J. Alm, J. Martinez-Vazquez and S. Wallace (eds), Taxing the Hard-to-Tax: Lessons from Theory and Practice, pp. 121–58. Amsterdam: North-Holland

Boadway, R.W. 2005. "Income Tax Reform for a Globalized World: The Case for a Dual Income Tax", Journal of Asian Economics, 16 (6): 910–27.

Brautigam, D., O. Fjeldstad, and M. Moore. 2007. Taxation and State-Building in Developing Countries Cambridge. UK: Cambridge University Press.

Chattopadhyay, S. and A. Das-Gupta. 2002. "The Compliance Cost of the Personal Income Tax and its Determinants", Available online at http://planningcommission.nic.in:80/reports/sereport/ser/stdy_prsnltax.pdf (downloaded on August 16, 2010).

Chu, K., H. Davoodi, and S. Gupta. 2000. "Income Distribution and Tax and Government Social Spending Policies in Developing Countries", Working Papers No. 214, UNU/WIDER.

Cnossen, S. 2006. (ed.) Excise Tax Policy and Administration. Pretoria: UNISA Press.

Easterly, W. 2002. The Elusive Quest for Growth. Cambridge MA: MIT Press.

Emran, M.S. and J.E. Stiglitz. 2005. "On Selective Indirect Tax Reform in Developing Countries", Journal of Public Economics, 89 (4): 599–623.

Fjeldstad, O-H. 2005. "Corruption in Tax Administration: Lessons from Institutional Reforms in Uganda", Working Paper No.10, CMI, Bergen.

Gallagher, M. 2004. "Benchmarking Tax Systems", Public Administration and Development, 25: 125–44.

Gardner, M. 2006. Aha! A Two Volume Collection: Aha! Gotcha. Aha! Insight. Washington DC: Mathematical Association of America.

Gemmell, N. and O. Morrissey. 2003. "Tax Structure and the Incidence on the Poor in Developing Countries", Research paper No. 03/18, Centre for Research on Economic Development and International Trade, University of Nottingham.

Glenday, G. and D. Hollinrake. 2005. "Assessment of the Current State of VAT Implementation in SADC Member States". Report prepared for the SADC Trade, Industry, Finance and Investment (TIFI) Directorate; Report presented at Southern African Development Community Workshop on VAT Study to fourteen Member States of SADC, Kopanong Hotel, Benoni, South Africa, Nov 23–25, 2005. Available online at http://fds.duke.edu/db?attachment-34—1654-view-829 (downloaded on August 16, 2010).

Gordon, R. and W. Li. 2009. "Tax Structure in Developing Countries: Many Puzzles and A Possible Explanation", Journal of Public Economics, 93 (7–8): 855–66.

Harberger, A.C. 1989. "Lessons of Tax Reform from the Experiences of Uruguay, Indonesia, and Chile", in M. Gillis (ed.), Tax Reform in Developing Countries, pp. 27–43. Durham NC: Duke University Press.

Harberger, A.C. 2006. "Taxation and Income Distribution: Myths and Realities", in J. Alm, J. Martinez-Vazquez and M.Rider (eds), *The Challenges of Tax Reform in a Global Economy*, pp. 13–37. New York: Springer.

Hood, C. 1976. *The Limits of Administration*. New York: Wiley.

Inter-American Development Bank (IDB). 2006. *The Politics of Policies: Economic and Social Progress in Latin America, 2006 Report*. Washington: Inter-American Development Bank.

Lindert, P.H. 2003. *Growing Public: Social Spending and Economic Growth Since the Eighteenth Century*. Cambridge: Cambridge University Press.

Manglik, G. 2008. "Using Technology to Reduce Income Tax Evasion in India", *Tax Notes International*, 50 (8): 705–14.

Mintz, Jack M. 2006. *The 2006 Tax Competitiveness Report: Proposals for Pro-Growth Tax Reform*. Toronto: C.D. Howe Institute.

OECD (Organisation for Economic Co-operation and Development). 2006. "Reforming Personal Income Tax", Policy Brief, March. Available online at http://www.oecd.org/dataoecd/43/21/36346567.pdf (downloaded on August 16, 2010).

Radian, A. 1980. *Resource Mobilization in Poor Countries: Implementing Tax Reform*. New Brunswick NJ: Transaction Books.

Schneider, F. and R. Klinglmair. 2004. "Shadow Economies Around the World: What Do We Know?" Working Paper No. 0408, Department of Economics, Johannes Kepler University of Linz.

Shah, A. and J. Whalley. 1990. "Tax Incidence Analysis of Developing Countries: An Alternative View", *World Bank Economic Review*, 5 (3): 535–52.

Shekidele, C. 1999. "Measuring the Compliance Cost of Taxation. Excise Duties 1995–96", *African Journal of Finance and Management*, 7 (2): 72–84.

Shoup, C.S. 1965. "Production from Consumption", *Public Finance*, 20 (2): 175–202.

———. 1991. "Melding Architecture and Engineering: A Personal Retrospective on Designing Tax Systems", in Lorraine Eden (ed.), *Retrospectives on Public Finance*, pp. 19–30. Durham, NC: Duke University Press.

Slemrod, J. 1992. *Why People Pay Taxes*. Ann Arbor: University of Michigan Press.

Slemrod, J. and E. Bakija. 1996. *Taxing Ourselves: A Citizen's Guide to the Great Debate on Tax Reform*. Cambridge MA: MIT Press.

Slemrod, J. and S. Yitzhaki. 2002. "Tax Avoidance, Evasion, and Administration", in Alan J. Auerbach and Martin Feldstein (eds), *Handbook of Public Economics*, Vol. 3, pp. 1423–70. New York: Elsevier Science.

Torgler, B. 2007. *Tax Compliance and Tax Morale: A Theoretical and Empirical Analysis*. Cheltenham, UK and Northampton MA: Edward Elgar.

Vazquez-Caro, J., G. Reid and R.M. Bird. 1992. *Tax Administration Assessment in Latin America*. Latin America and Caribbean Technical Department, Regional Studies Program, Report No. 13. Washington: World Bank.

Warlters, Michael and Emmanuelle Auriol. 2005. "The Marginal Cost of Public Funds in Africa", Research Working Paper No. 3679, World Bank.

Webber, C. and A. Wildavsky.1986. *A History of Taxation and Expenditure in the Western World*. New York: Simon and Shuster.

World Bank. 1991. *Lessons of Tax Reform*. Washington: World Bank.

World Bank and International Finance Corporation. 2008. *Paying Taxes 2008*. Washington, DC: World Bank.

4

GST Reforms and Intergovernmental Considerations in India

Satya Poddar and Ehtisham Ahmad

I Introduction

The replacement of the state sales taxes by the VAT in 2005 marked a significant step forward in the reform of domestic trade taxes in India. Implemented under the leadership of Dr Asim Dasgupta, Chairman, Empowered Committee of State Finance Ministers, it addressed the distortions and complexities associated with the levy of tax at the first point of sale under the erstwhile system and resulted in a major simplification of the rate structure and broadening of the tax base. The state VAT design is based largely on the blueprint recommended in a 1994 report of the National Institute of Public Finance and Policy, prepared by a team led by late Dr Amaresh Bagchi (hereinafter, the "Bagchi Report") (see Bagchi et al., 1994). In recommending a state VAT, the Bagchi Report clearly recognized that it would not be the perfect or first best solution to the problems of the domestic trade tax regime in a multi-government framework. However, the team felt that this was the only feasible option within the existing framework of the Constitution and would lay the foundation for an even more rational regime in the future.

Buoyed by the success of the state VAT, the Center and the states are now embarked on the design and implementation of the perfect solution, alluded to in the Bagchi Report. As announced by the Empowered Committee of state finance ministers in November 2007, the solution is to take the form of a "Dual" Goods and Services Tax (GST), to be levied concurrently by both levels of government.

The essential details of the Dual GST are still not known. Will it necessitate a change in the constitutional division of taxation powers between the Center and the states? Will the taxes imposed by the Center and the states be harmonized, and, if so, how? What will be treatment of food, housing, and interstate services such as transportation and telecommunication? Which of the existing Center and state taxes would be subsumed into the new tax? What will be the administrative infrastructure for the collection and enforcement of the tax? These are issues which ultimately define the political, social, and economic character of the tax and its impact on different sectors of the economy, and households in different social and economic strata.

It is some of these aspects of the proposed GST that are the subject matter of this paper. We focus on the essential questions relating to the Dual GST design, and first discuss the need for, and the objectives of GST reform. We then describe alternatives to the Dual GST already endorsed by the Empowered Committee, not because they are superior in any way to the Dual GST, but to allow a fuller discussion of the trade-offs involved in the choice among them. Subsequent sections consider the question of tax base and rate, and proper treatment of various components of the tax base (for example, food, housing, and financial services) in light of international best practices. The last section provides a discussion of the issues that arise in the taxation of cross-border transactions, both interstate and international. An important question in this regard is the feasibility of, and the rules for, taxation of interstate supplies of services.

II The Current Taxes and Their Shortcomings

The principal broad-based consumption taxes that the GST would replace are the Central Value Added Tax (CENVAT) and the service tax levied by the Center, and the VAT levied by the states. All these are multi-stage value-added taxes. The structure of these taxes today is much better than the system that prevailed a few years ago, which was described in the Bagchi Report as "archaic, irrational, and complex—according to knowledgeable experts, the most complex in the world". Over the past several years, significant progress has been made to improve their structure, broaden the base, and rationalize the rates. Notable among the improvements made are:

1. the replacement of the single-point state sales taxes by the VAT in all of the states and union territories;
2. reduction in the central sales tax rate to 2 percent, from 4 percent, as part of a complete phase out of the tax;
3. the introduction of the service tax by the Center, and a substantial expansion of its base over the years; and
4. rationalization of the CENVAT rates by reducing their multiplicity and replacing many of the specific rates by ad valorem rates based on the maximum retail price (MRP) of the products.

These changes have yielded significant dividends in economic efficiency of the tax system, ease of compliance, and growth in revenues.

The State VAT eliminated all of the complexities associated with the application of sales taxes at the first point of sale. The consensus reached among the states for uniformity in the VAT rates has brought an end to the harmful tax competition among them. It has also lessened the cascading of tax.

The application of CENVAT at fewer rates and the new system of CENVAT credits has likewise resulted in fewer classification disputes, reduced tax cascading, and greater neutrality of the tax. The introduction of the service tax has been a mixed blessing. While it has broadened the tax base, its structure is complex. The tax is levied on specified services, classified into 100 categories. This approach has spawned many disputes about the scope of each category. Unlike goods, services are malleable, and can and are often packaged into composite bundles that include taxable as well as non-taxable elements. Also, there is no standardized nomenclature for services, such as the Harmonized System of Nomenclature (HSN) for goods.

The design of the CENVAT and state VATs was dictated by the constraints imposed by the Constitution, which allows neither the Center nor the states to levy taxes on a comprehensive base of all goods and services and at all points in their supply chain. The Center is constrained from levying the tax on goods beyond the point of manufacturing, and the states in extending the tax to services. This division of tax powers makes both the CENVAT and the state VATs partial in nature and contributes to their inefficiency and complexity. The principal deficiencies of the current system, which need to be the primary focus of the next level of reforms, are discussed in the following pages.

Taxation at Manufacturing Level

The CENVAT is levied on goods manufactured or produced in India. This gives rise to definitional issues as to what constitutes manufacturing, and valuation issues for determining the value on which the tax is to be levied.[1] While these concepts have evolved through judicial rulings, it is recognized that limiting the tax to the point of manufacturing is a severe impediment to an efficient and neutral application of tax. Manufacturing itself forms a narrow base.

Moreover, the effective burden of tax becomes dependent on the supply chain, that is, the taxable value at the point of manufacturing relative to the value added beyond this point.[2] It is for this reason that virtually all countries have abandoned this form of taxation and replaced it by multi-point taxation system extending to the retail level.[3]

Australia is the most recent example of an industrialized country which replaced a tax at the manufacturing or wholesale level by the GST and extended it to the retail level. The previous tax was found to be unworkable, in spite of the high degree of sophistication in administration in Australia. It simply could not deal with the variety of supply chain arrangements in a satisfactory manner.

Exclusion of Services

The states are precluded from taxing services. This arrangement has posed difficulties in taxation of goods supplied as part of a composite works contract involving a supply of both goods and services, and under leasing contracts, which entail a transfer of the right to use goods without any transfer of their ownership. While these problems have been addressed by amending the Constitution to bring such transactions within the ambit of the State taxation[4] (by deeming a tax on them to be a tax on the sale or purchase of goods), services per se remain outside the scope of state taxation powers. This limitation is unsatisfactory from two perspectives.

First, the advancements in information technology and digitization have blurred the distinction between goods and services. Under Indian jurisprudence, goods are defined to include intangibles, for example, copyright, and software, bringing them within the purview of state taxation. However, intangibles are often supplied under arrangements which have the appearance of a service contract. For example, software upgrades (which are goods) can be supplied as part of a contract for software repair and maintenance services. Software development contracts could take the character of contracts for manufacturing and sale of software goods or for rendering software development services, depending on the roles and responsibilities of the parties. The so-called value-added services (VAS) provided as part of telecommunication services include supplies (for example, wallpaper for mobile phones, ring tones, jokes, cricket scores, and weather reports), some of which could be considered goods. An online subscription to newspapers could be viewed as a service, but online purchase and download of a magazine or a book could constitute a purchase of goods. This blurring also clouds the application of tax to transactions relating to tangible property. For example, disputes have arisen whether leasing of equipment without transfer of possession and control to the lessee would be taxable as a service or as a deemed sale of goods.

The traditional distinctions between goods and services (and for other items such as land and property, entertainment, and luxuries) found in the Indian Constitution have become archaic. In markets today, goods, services, and other types of supplies are being packaged as composite bundles and offered for sale to consumers under a variety of supply chain arrangements. Under the current division of taxation powers, neither the Center nor the states can apply the tax to such bundles in a seamless manner. Each can tax only parts of the bundle, creating the possibility of gaps or overlaps in taxation.

The second major concern with the exclusion of services from the state taxation powers is its negative impact on the buoyancy of state tax revenues. With the growth in per capita incomes, services account for a growing fraction of the total consumer basket, which the states cannot tax. With no powers to levy tax on incomes or the fastest growing components of consumer expenditures, the states have to rely almost exclusively on compliance improvements or rate increases for any buoyancy in their own-source revenues. Alternatives to assigning the taxation of services to the states include assigning to the states a share of the central VAT (including the tax from services), as per the Australian model.

Tax Cascading

Tax cascading occurs under both Center and state taxes. The most significant contributing factor to tax cascading is the partial coverage of Central and state taxes. Oil and gas production and mining, agriculture, wholesale and retail trade, real estate construction, and range of services remain outside the ambit of the CENVAT and the service tax levied by the Center. The exempt sectors are not allowed to claim any credit for the CENVAT or the service tax paid on their inputs.

Similarly, under the state VAT, no credits are allowed for the inputs of the exempt sectors, which include the entire service sector, real property sector, agriculture, oil and gas production, and mining. Another major contributing factor to tax cascading is the Central Sales Tax (CST) on interstate sales, collected by the origin state and for which no credit is allowed by any level of government.

While no recent estimates are available for the extent of tax cascading under the Indian tax system (see Ahmad and Stern [1984, 1991], and Bagchi et al. [1994] for earlier work), it is likely to be significant, judging by the experience of other countries which had a similar tax structure. For example, under the Canadian manufacturers' sales tax, which was similar to the CENVAT, the non-creditable tax on business inputs and machinery and equipment accounted for approximately one-third of total revenues from the tax. The extent of cascading under the provincial retail sales taxes in Canada, which are similar to the state VAT, is estimated to be 35–40 percent of total revenue collections.

A priori, one would expect the magnitude of cascading under the CENVAT, service tax, and the state VAT to be even higher, given the more restricted input credits and wider exemptions under these taxes.[5] The service tax falls predominantly on business to business (B2B) services and is, thus, highly cascading in nature.

Tax cascading remains the most serious flaw of the current system. It increases the cost of production, and puts Indian suppliers at a competitive disadvantage in the international markets. It creates a bias in favor of imports, which do not bear the hidden burden of taxes on production inputs. It also detracts from a neutral application of tax to competing products. Even if the statutory rate is uniform, the effective tax rate (which consists of the statutory rate on finished products and the implicit or hidden tax on production inputs) can vary from product to product depending on the magnitude of the hidden tax on inputs used in their production and distribution. The intended impact of government policy towards sectors or households may be negated by the indirect or hidden taxation in a cascading system of taxes.

Complexity

In spite of the improvements made in the tax design and administration over the past few years, the systems at both Central and state levels remain complex. Their administration leaves a lot to be desired. They are subject to disputes and court challenges, and the process for resolution of disputes is slow and expensive. At the same time, the systems suffer from substantial compliance gaps, except in the highly organized sectors of the economy. There are several factors contributing to this unsatisfactory state of affairs.

The most significant cause of complexity is, of course, policy-related and is due to the existence of exemptions and multiple rates, and the irrational structure of the levies. These deficiencies are the most glaring in the case of the CENVAT and the service tax.

The starting base for the CENVAT is narrow, and is being further eroded by a variety of area-specific, and conditional and unconditional exemptions. A few years ago, the government attempted to rationalize the CENVAT rates by reducing their multiplicity, but has not adhered to this policy and has reintroduced concessions for several sectors/ products.

The key problem with the service tax is the basic approach of levying it on specified services, each of which generates an extensive debate as to what is included in the base. Ideally, the tax base should be defined to include all services, with a limited list of exclusions (the so-called "negative list").[6] The Government has been reluctant to adopt this approach for the fear that it could bring into the tax net many services that are politically sensitive.

The complexities under the state VAT relate primarily to classification of goods to different tax rate schedules. Theoretically, one might expect that the lower tax rates would be applied to basic necessities that are consumed largely by the poor. This is not the case under the state VAT. The lowest rate of 1 percent applies to precious metals and jewelry, and related products—hardly likely to be ranked highly from the distributional perspective. The middle rate of 4 percent applies to selected basic necessities and also a range of industrial inputs and IT products. In fact, basic necessities fall into three categories—exempted from tax, taxable at 4 percent, and taxable at the standard rate of 12.5 percent. The classification would appear to be arbitrary, with no well-accepted theoretical underpinning. Whatever the political merits of this approach, it is not conducive to lower compliance costs. Most retailers find it difficult to determine the tax rate applicable to a given item without referring to the legislative schedules. Consumers are even less aware of the tax applicable to various items. This gives rise to leakages and rent seeking.

Another source of complexity under the state VAT is determining whether a particular transaction constitutes a sale of goods. This problem is most acute in the case of software products, and intangibles such as the right to distribute/exhibit movies or time slots for broadcasting advertisements.

Compounding the structural or design deficiencies of each of the taxes is the poor or archaic infrastructure for their administration. Tax-payer services, which are a lynchpin of a successful self-assessment system, are virtually non-existent or grossly inadequate under both Central and state administrations. Many of the administrative processes are still manual, not benefiting from the efficiencies of automation. All this not only increase the costs of compliance but also undermines revenue collection.

III Objectives of Tax Reform

Basic Objectives

The basic objective of tax reform would be to address the problems of the current system discussed previously. It should establish a tax system that is economically efficient, neutral in its application, distributionally attractive, and simple to administer.

As argued in Ahmad and Stern (1991), distributional or sectoral concerns have been at the heart of the excessive differentiation of the Indian tax system, but the objectives are negated by the cascading effects of the taxes. While an optimal design of the consumption tax system, taking into account both production efficiency and distributional concerns, would not imply uniformity of the overall tax structure, the desired structure can be achieved by a combination of taxes and transfers.

Ahmad and Stern (1991) analyze the optimal pattern of tax rates, implied by a given degree of aversion to poverty and concern for the poor. At high levels of concern for the poor, one would reduce the tax on cereals (but not dairy products) and increase the taxes on non-food items (durables). Thus, a differentiated overall structure appears desirable for a country in which the government has consistently expressed a concern for the poor.

However, individual taxes should not be highly differentiated, as that complicates administration, and makes it difficult to evaluate the overall effects of the tax design. This applies particularly to value-added type of taxes. In principle, a single rate (or at the most two-rate) VAT, together with excises and spending measures could achieve the desired distributional effects, for reasonable degrees of inequality aversion of policy makers.

In particular, it is important from an administrative perspective that close substitutes should not be taxed at very different rates so as to avoid leakages and distortions. Revenue considerations suggest that the tax base should be broad and comprise all items in the consumer basket, including goods, services, as well as real property.

The neutrality principle would suggest that:

1. the tax be a uniform percentage of the final retail price of a product, regardless of the supply-chain arrangements for its manufacturing and distribution;
2. the tax on inputs be fully creditable to avoid tax cascading; and
3. the tax be levied on the basis of the destination principle, with all of the tax on a given product/service accruing in the jurisdiction of its final consumption.

Multiple VAT rates become a source of complexity, and disputes, for example, over borderlines, add to the costs of tax administration and compliance. It is for this reason that countries like New Zealand, Singapore, and Japan have chosen to apply the tax at a low and uniform rate, and address any concerns about vertical equity through other fiscal instruments, including spending programs targeted at lower-income households.[7]

Another important objective of tax reform is simplification of tax administration and compliance, which is dependent on three factors. The first determining factor for simplicity is the tax design itself. Generally, the more rational and neutral the tax design, the simpler it would be to administer and encourage compliance. If the tax is levied on a broad base at a single rate, there would be few classification disputes and the tax-specific record keeping requirements for vendors would be minimal. The tax return for such a system can be as short as the size of a postcard. It would simplify enforcement and encourage voluntary compliance.

The second factor is the infrastructure for tax administration, including the design of tax forms, data requirements, system of tax rulings and interpretations, and the procedures for registration, filing, and processing of tax returns, tax payments and refunds, audits, and appeals. A modern tax administration focuses on providing services to taxpayers to facilitate compliance. It harnesses information technology to enhance the quality of services and to ensure greater transparency in administration and enforcement.

The third factor, in a federation such as India, is the degree of harmonization among the taxes levied by the Center and the states. The Empowered Committee has already indicated a preference for a dual

GST, consisting of a Center GST and a state GST. Under this model, harmonization of the Center and state GSTs would be critical to keep the overall compliance burden low. Equally important is harmonization of GSTs across the states.

Fiscal Autonomy and Harmonization

An important consideration in the design of reform options is the degree of fiscal autonomy of the Center and the states. It goes without saying that the power to govern and to raise revenues goes together. The Constitution of India lays down a clear division of powers between the Center and the states, including the power to levy taxes. Should the Center and the states then have complete autonomy in levying and collecting the taxes within the parameters specified in the Constitution, or should they voluntarily or otherwise conform to certain common principles or constraints? Should they collectively agree to have their individual taxes consolidated into a single national tax, the revenues from which get shared in some agreed manner among the constituent units? Such a system would have much to commend itself from the perspectives of economic efficiency, and the establishment of a common market within India. Indeed, such political economy compromises have been adopted by China and Australia. China moved to a centralized VAT with revenue sharing with the provinces, ensuring that provinces got as much revenues as under the prior arrangements, plus a share of the increment. In Australia, the GST is a single national levy and all the GST revenues collected by the Center are returned to the state. However, such a compromise is unlikely to find much favor with the states in India, as is already revealed in their preference for the Dual GST.

To give political substance to the federal structure in India, the states (as well as the Center) are likely to insist that they have certain autonomy in exercise of their taxation powers. Full autonomy would mean that:

1. retain the power to enact the tax;
2. enjoy the risks and rewards of "ownership" of the tax (that is, not be insulated from fluctuations in revenue collections);
3. be accountable to their constituents; and
4. be able to use the tax as an instrument of social or economic policy.

Notwithstanding the above, there is a clear recognition of the need for harmonization of the Center and state taxes. Fiscal autonomy is important to allow the Center and the states to set the tax rates according to their revenue needs. Harmonization of tax laws and administrative procedures is needed to simplify compliance and enforcement. It is also necessary to ensure that interstate differences in policies and procedures do not generate additional economic distortions. An important question then is about the desired degree of harmonization and the mechanism for achieving it.

The elements of harmonization can be divided into three broad sets: tax rates, tax base, and tax infrastructure, that is, the administration and compliance system. The first two elements could be viewed as important levers on which states would want to have some degree of control to achieve their social, economic, and fiscal policy objectives. However, the experience of other countries as well as their sub-national governments suggests that changes to the GST base are not a suitable instrument for social and economic policy (as discussed in greater detail in a later section in considering the treatment of food). While the tax base is a subject of intense debates at the time the tax is introduced, changes in the base after its introduction have been infrequent. This has especially been the case where the tax was initially levied on a broad and comprehensive base. Where the tax was initially levied on a narrow base, subsequent changes in the base have then been felt necessary to minimize anomalies, distortions, and revenue leakages created by the narrow base. Achieving such changes once the tax has been brought in, however logical, is invariably politically contentious because of vested interests. It is, thus, important to get the structure right at the outset, as the base (and quite often the rate) cannot be easily changed, ex post facto.

The VAT in the European Union is an example reflecting these policy considerations. The base for the EU VAT is uniform, as codified in the EU Directive,[8] which is binding in all member states. There are important variations in the base, but these are essentially in the form of derogations granted for the arrangements existing at the time of introduction of the tax, and were intended to be temporary (though this has not always been the case). The tax rates are specified as floor rates (with some provision for reduced rates and maximum rates), below which member states cannot set their rates.

Administration and compliance is an area where the need for harmonization is the greatest, and where Center-State or interstate variations are unlikely to serve any social or economic policy objective. This includes items such as the taxpayer registration system, taxpayer identification numbers, tax forms, tax reporting periods and procedures, invoice requirements, cross-border trade information systems, and IT systems. Harmonization of these elements would result in significant savings in costs of implementing the GST (by avoiding duplication of effort in each government), as well as recurring savings in compliance costs. Harmonization would also permit sharing of information among governments, which is essential for effective monitoring of cross-border transactions. A common set of tax identifier numbers across states and the Central government is a key element in the efficient exchange of information.

Harmonization of tax laws is also critical. Variation in the wording and structure of tax provisions can be an unnecessary source of confusion and complexity, which can be avoided by having the Center and the states adopt a common GST law. An alternative is to agree on the key common elements, if separate laws are chosen. Some of the critical elements for harmonization include common time and place of supply rules, as well as common rules for recovery of input tax, valuation of supplies, and invoicing requirements. There would then be merit in harmonizing the system of tax interpretations and rulings as well (for example, about classification of goods and services, determination of what constitutes taxable consideration, and definition of export and import).

These considerations suggest that harmonization of virtually all major areas of GST law and administration would be desirable. There is merit in keeping even the GST rate(s) uniform, at least during the initial years, until the infrastructure for the new system is fully developed (see Ahmad et al., 2008 for the GCC proposals). Harmonized laws would mean lower compliance costs for taxpayers, and may also improve the efficiency of fiscal controls.

The Central Sales Tax (CST) in India provides a very useful model for such harmonization. The CST is a state-level tax, applied to interstate sales of goods, based on the origin principle. The tax law (including the base, rates, and the procedures) is enacted by Parliament, but the states collect and keep the tax. It is a perfect example of absolute harmonization, with the State enjoying the risks and rewards of ownership of the tax.

It is worth emphasizing that harmonization should not be viewed as constraining the fiscal autonomy of the Center or the state. Rather, this is a framework that facilitates more efficient exercise of taxation powers, and all jurisdictions would be worse off without harmonization. This was the case under the previous state sales tax system, under which interstate tax rate wars became a race to the bottom. Even today, they all suffer because of lack of harmonization of information and technology architectures, as a result of which they are unable to share information on interstate trade. Harmonization should allow greater exploitation of the benefits of a common market.

Center and State Taxation Powers

As noted earlier, the current division of taxation of powers under the Constitution is constraining for both the Center and the states. Neither is able to design a comprehensive and neutral tax on goods and services of the type found in modern tax systems. The Constitution divides taxation powers between the Center and the states by sector (for example, agriculture, manufacturing, and land and property) or type of taxes (for example, luxury tax, tax on the sale or purchase of goods, and excise duty). A notable feature of the current division is that the two levels of government have no area of concurrent jurisdiction, with the exception of stamp duties. This approach, while it may have served the country well in the past, is no longer optimal for modern economies where the traditional dividing lines between sectors are blurred, and new social, environmental, and economic issues emerge which require new forms of taxation instruments. The need for a substantial realignment of taxation powers is also emphasized by Rao (2008):

Paradigm shift in tax policy is necessary to recognise that tax bases of central and state governments are interdependent. The principle of separation of tax bases followed in the Constitutional assignment does not recognise the interdependence. It is therefore desirable to provide concurrent tax powers to Centre and States in respect of both income and domestic consumption taxes. In the case of personal income tax, separation of tax powers between the centre and states based on whether the income is from agricultural or non-agricultural sector has been a major source of tax evasion. As agriculture is transformed into a business it is important to levy the tax on incomes received from all the sources both for reasons of neutrality and to minimise tax evasion. At the same time, both centre and states could be allowed to levy the tax with the latter piggybacking the levy on the central tax subject to a ceiling rate. Similarly, it is important to unify multiple indirect taxes levied by the central and state governments into a single goods and services tax (GST) preferably with states piggybacking on the central levy with clearly defined tax rooms for the two levels of government. The transition to such a concurrent tax system requires integrating the existing CENVAT and service taxes and extending the tax to the retail level which would, inter alia, entail amendment of the Constitution. The states could piggyback on the levy.

Thus, the current search for options for tax reform warrants a review of the existing Constitutional arrangements, which may well require a substantial realignment. For example, the Dual GST would require giving the Center and the states concurrent indirect taxation powers, subject to prohibition on extra-territorial taxation, that is, the incidence of tax be restricted to consumption within the territory of the taxing jurisdiction.[9]

While such a review is beyond the scope of this paper, our discussion of alternative options in the next section proceeds with the assumption that suitable constitutional amendments would be made to enable the implementation of the chosen option.

IV Options for the Center and State GSTs

In defining options for reform, the starting point is the basic structure of the tax. For purposes of this discussion, we start with the assumption that any replacement of the current taxes would be in the form of a classical VAT, which is consumption type (allowing full and immediate credit for both current and capital inputs attributable to taxable supplies) and destination based (that is, the tax levied on the basis of the place of consumption of the goods and services, not the place of production). Under this system, credits for input taxes are allowed on the basis of invoices issued by the vendors registered for the tax. This is the most common type of structure adopted around the world. Its superiority over other forms of consumption taxes is well accepted in India, as well as other countries.

The choices that remain then relate essentially to the assignment of powers to levy the tax to the Center and the states, and the tax base and rates. In the remainder of this section, we deal with the question of assignment, and then turn to the question of tax base and rates in the next section. The main options for the VAT assignments include:

1. Concurrent Dual GST
2. National GST
3. State GSTs

All these options require an amendment to the Constitution. For the sake of completeness of discussion, we also consider an additional option, Non-concurrent Dual VAT, that does not require an amendment to the Constitution. We now discuss each of these options in turn in the following sections.[10]

Concurrent Dual GST

Under this model, the tax is levied concurrently by the Center as well as the states. Both the Central Government and the Empowered Committee appear to favor this model.

While full details of the model are still awaited, two variants have been identified in public discussions so far. The initial variant, discussed in November, 2007, entailed both the Center and the states levying concurrently the GST on goods, but most of the services (except services of a local nature) remaining subject to the Center GST only. The Central GST would thus apply to both goods and services, extending to the entire supply chain, including wholesale and retail trade. The state GSTs would largely be confined to goods only, with minor changes from the current state VATs.

Under the more recent variant (Empowered Committee of State Finance Ministers, 2008), both goods and services would be subject to concurrent taxation by the Center and the states. This variant is closer to the model recommended by the Kelkar Committee in 2002 (Kelkar et al., 2004).

The main difference between the two variants is in the treatment of services, reflecting apprehensions about the feasibility of defining the place of supply (that is, destination) of interstate services. Even the more recent variant recognizes that there would be a set of interstate services for which the place of destination would be difficult to determine. The state tax on these services would be collected by the Center, and then apportioned among the states in some manner.

Other notable features of this variant are as follows:

1. There would a single registration or taxpayer identification number, based on the Permanent Account Number (PAN) for direct taxation. Three additional digits would be added to the current PAN to identify registration for the Center and State GSTs.
2. States would collect the state GST from all of the registered dealers. To minimize the need for additional administrative resources at the Center, states would also assume the responsibility for administering the Central GST for dealers with gross turnover below the current registration threshold of Rs. 1.5 crores under the CENVAT. They would collect the Central GST from such dealers on behalf of the Center and transfer the funds to the Center.
3. Procedures for collection of Central and state GSTs would be uniform. There would be one common tax return for both taxes, with one copy given to the Central authority and the other to the relevant state authority.
4. Other indirect taxes levied by the Center, states, or local authorities at any point in the supply chain would be subsumed under the Central or the state GST, as long as they are in the nature of taxes on consumption of goods and services.

At a broad conceptual level, this model has a lot to commend for itself. It strikes a good balance between fiscal autonomy of the Center and states, and the need for harmonization. It empowers both levels of government to apply the tax to a comprehensive base of goods and services, at all points in the supply chain. It also eliminates tax cascading, which occurs because of truncated or partial application of the Center and state taxes.

The apprehension about feasibility of application of state GST to interstate services is understandable, given the complete absence of any framework in India for determining their place of supply. However, the task of developing such a framework is not insurmountable. In fact, such frameworks do already exist for application of national VAT to international cross-border services, which could be adapted for inter-state services. Canada has developed such a framework for application of provincial sales taxes or GST to services.

Another point to note is that interstate services are provided predominantly by the organized sector (for example, telecom and transportation services), which is generally tax compliant. Once the rules are framed, they would program their accounting and invoicing systems to collect and remit the tax accordingly.

Admittedly, there are interstate services which have no unique place of supply. Take, for example, the supply of group health insurance to a corporation with employees throughout India, or auditing or business consulting services provided to a corporation or conglomerate with business establishments in several states. The determination of place of supply of such services is going to be somewhat arbitrary. However, such services are almost entirely B2B supplies, the tax on which is fully creditable to the recipient under a comprehensive taxation model. The arbitrariness in the rules would thus have no impact on the final tax collections of the Center or the states.

The Empowered Committee proposal is silent on the treatment of land and real property transactions in the description of this option. Assuming this omission is deliberate, it is a major drawback of the option. As discussed further in the next section, modern VATs apply to all supplies, including supplies of land and real property. The service tax has already been extended to rentals of commercial property and construction services. There are no compelling social or economic policy reasons for excluding these services from the scope of the GST.

National GST

Under this option, the two levels of government would combine their levies in the form of a single national GST, with appropriate revenue sharing arrangements among them. The tax could be controlled and administered by the Center, states, or a separate agency reporting to them. There are several models for such a tax. Australia is the most recent example of a national GST, which is levied and collected by the Center, but the proceeds of which are allocated entirely to the states.[10]

In China, the VAT law and administration is centralized, but the revenues are shared with the provinces. In going with this model, the Center had assured the provinces that they would continue to get what they did under the previous arrangement and changes in revenue shares would be phased, in over an extended period of 15 years (See Ahmad, 2008).

Under the Canadian model of the Harmonized Sales Tax (HST), the tax is levied at a combined federal and provincial rate of 13 percent (5 percent federal rate, 8 percent provincial rate) in the three participating provinces. Tax design and collection are controlled by the Center, but the provinces have some flexibility to vary their tax rate. The revenues from the tax are shared among the participating provinces, on the basis of consumer expenditure data for the participating provinces.

In Austria and Germany, the tax design is controlled by the Center, but states collect the taxes. This has led to incentive problems, as some of the Länders have begun to use tax administration measures to achieve tax policy goals. In Mexico, the establishment of a VAT at the Center replaced state sales taxes, but had to be part of a political economy compromise that assured the state an automatic share of the revenues generated from all federal taxes.

A single national VAT has great appeal from the perspective of establishment and promotion of a common market in India. However, the states may worry about the loss of control over the tax design and rates. Indeed, some control over tax rates is a critical issue in achieving accountable, sub-national governance, and hard budget constraints (Ambrosiano and Bordignon, 2006). The states may also be apprehensive that the revenue sharing arrangements would over time become subject to social and political considerations, deviating from the benchmark distribution based on the place of final consumption. The Bagchi Report also did not favor this option for the fear that it would lead to too much centralization of taxation powers.

These concerns can be addressed partially through suitable administrative arrangements and Center-State agreements. The tax design could be made subject to joint control of the Center and the states. The states would necessarily lose the flexibility of interstate variation in tax design, but that is also the perceived strength of this option. Given that the Center does not have the machinery for the administration of such a tax, the states would presumably play a significant role in its administration. The revenue sharing formula could also be mandated to be based on the destination principle, as under the Canadian HST.

The key concerns about this option would thus, be political. Notwithstanding the economic merits of a national GST, will it have a damaging impact on the vitality of Indian federalism? With no other major own-source revenues, will individual states become too dependent on collective choices and feel disempowered to act on their priorities? Will it be possible for the governments with such diverse political interests and philosophies to reach a consensus and adhere to it?

While one can have a healthy debate on each of these issues, international experience suggests that discretionary use of broad-based consumption taxes for social, political, or economic policy purposes tends to be limited. The dominant consideration in their design is their neutrality and efficiency in raising revenues. This is also reflected in the design of the state VATs in India. In spite of vast political and economic differences among them, the states have been able to forge a consensus on a common VAT design. A national GST would extend this consensus to the Center. But participation of the Center could fundamentally alter the delicate balance of interests that currently prevails in the Empowered Committee and make the consensus harder to achieve.

State GSTs

Under this option, the GST would be levied by the states only. The Center would withdraw from the field of general consumption taxation. It would continue to levy income taxes, customs duties, and excise duties on selected products such as motor fuels to address specific environmental or other policy objectives. The loss to the Center from vacating this tax field could be offset by a suitable compensating reduction, in fiscal transfers to the states. This would significantly enhance the revenue capacity of the states and reduce their dependence on the Center. The US is the most notable example of these arrangements, where the general sales taxes are relegated to the states.

There would be significant hurdles in adopting this option in India. First, it would seriously impair the Center's revenues. The reduction in fiscal transfers to the states would offset this loss, but still the Center would want to have access to this revenue source for future needs. Second, the option may not be revenue neutral for individual states. The incremental revenues from the transfer of the Center's tax room would benefit the higher-income states, while a reduction in fiscal transfers would impact disproportionately the lower-income states. Thus, the reform would be inequality enhancing, and against the traditions of successive governments in India (of all political shades). Third, a complete withdrawal of the Center from the taxation of inter-state supplies of goods and services could undermine the states' ability to levy their own taxes on such supplies in a harmonized manner. In particular, it would be impractical to bring interstate services within the ambit of the state GST without a significant coordinating support from the Center.

Non-concurrent Dual VATs

Under the concurrent Dual GSTs, the Center and state taxes apply concurrently to supplies of all goods and services. It poses two challenges. First, it requires a constitutional amendment. Second, a framework is needed for defining the place of supply of interstate services and for the application of state GST to them. Both of these hurdles can be circumvented if the GST on goods were to be levied by the states only and on services by the Center only. The states already have the power to levy the tax on the sale and purchase of goods (and also on immovable property), and the Center for taxation of services. No special effort would be needed for levying a unified Central tax on interstate services.

This option would not address any of the deficiencies of the current system, identified in a previous section, if the taxes on goods and services were to be levied in an uncoordinated manner, as two separate partial taxes. It would perpetuate the difficulties in delineating supplies of goods and services, and compound tax cascading.

The main appeal of this option is as a variant of the state GST option, discussed previously. In levying the VAT on services, the Center would essentially play the coordinating role needed for the application and monitoring of tax on interstate services. The Center would withdraw from the taxation of goods. Even the revenues collected from the taxation of services could be transferred back to the states, partially or fully.

Within this framework, cascading could be completely eliminated by the states, agreeing to allow an input credit for the tax on services levied by the Center. Likewise, the Center would allow an input credit for the tax on goods levied by the states.

The previous discussion suggests that the design of a GST is going to be a challenge, regardless of the option chosen. All options require significant Center-State coordination and harmonization, and there may be very little room for variance in rate setting by states, at least in the near future. The best option would appear to be a national GST (either through the Constitution or on a voluntary basis), with an appropriate Center-State and interstate revenue sharing arrangement. If a framework for taxation of interstate services can be devised, then the concurrent dual VAT could be the most supportive of the objective of fiscal autonomy. To ensure harmonization of tax base, rules and procedures, it would be desirable to have a single common legislation enacted by Parliament, following the model for the CST. The law would delegate the collection of tax to the Center and states on their respective tax bases, that is, the Center to collect the central GST on supplies of goods and services any where in India, and the states to collect the state GST on supplies within their states (as per the place-of-supply rules specified in the legislation).

V Tax Base and Rates

We turn now to the question of the tax base and rates, within the broad structure of a consumption-type, destination-based, credit-invoice GST. Ideally, the tax should be levied comprehensively on all goods and services at a single rate to achieve the objectives of simplicity and economic neutrality. However, governments often deviate from this ideal either because of concerns about distribution of tax burden (for example, food), or because of administrative and conceptual difficulties in applying the tax to certain sectors of the economy (for example, health care, education, and financial services). These concerns are likely to be paramount at both Center and state levels, and there will be inevitable calls to exempt, or tax at a reduced rate, items of importance to the poor or other particular groups.

As noted earlier, reduced rates or exemptions for basic necessities may not be an efficient way of helping the poor because of a significant spillover of their benefits to the rich. Although the rich spend a smaller proportion of their income on such goods than do the poor because their income is higher they are likely to spend a larger *absolute* amount. As a result, the rich might gain most from applying a reduced tax rate to such goods. The needs of the poor could be more effectively addressed through spending and transfer programs. Distributional concerns should be seen as part of the overall balance of all fiscal instruments and not solely for the GST. Moreover, multiple rates and exemptions increase the costs of administration and compliance. They give rise to classification disputes, necessitate additional record keeping, and create opportunities for tax avoidance and evasion through misclassification of sales.

Notwithstanding the virtues of a single-rate and comprehensive base, debates about the proper treatment of food and a variety of other items are inevitable. In what follows, we discuss some of the most critical aspects this debate, starting with a discussion of the revenue neutral tax rates in the absence of any exemptions or other preferences.

Tax Rates

In discussions on the GST design for India, it has been suggested that the tax would need to be levied at a combined Center-State tax rate of 20 percent, of which 12 percent would go to the Center and 8 percent to the states (vide, for example, the Kelkar Task Force Report, see Kelker et al., 2004). While they fall below the present combined Center and state statutory rate of 26.5 percent (CENVAT of 14 percent and VAT of 12.5 percent), GST at these rates would encounter significant consumer resistance, especially at the retail level, and would give rise to pressures for exemptions and/or lower rates for items of daily consumption. With the notable exception of Scandinavian countries, where the tax is levied at the standard rate of 25 percent, few countries have been successful in levying and sustaining a VAT/GST at such high rates.

Successful GST models adopted by other countries had a very broad base, and a relatively modest tax rate, especially at the time of inception. For example, the New Zealand GST was introduced at the rate of 10 percent, with a base consisting of virtually all goods and services (with the exception of financial services). The Singapore GST was introduced at 3 percent, but the rate has now been raised to 7 percent as inefficient excises and customs duties have been progressively eliminated.

Table 4.1 provides a comparison of the tax base and rates in selected international jurisdictions with "modern" VAT/GST. It provides data on C-efficiency, which is a widely-used measure of the comprehensiveness of the tax base. It is calculated as the ratio of the share of GST revenues in consumption to the standard rate. Any deviation from a 100 percent C-efficiency indicates deviation from a single tax rate on all consumption. Zero-rating of some consumption items would lead to a C-efficiency of less than 100 percent while inclusion of investment or a break in the GST chain could lead to a C-efficiency higher than 100 percent. While a C-efficiency of 100 does not imply a perfect VAT, it can serve as a useful indicator of the productivity of GST revenue, per percentage point of GST rate. The last column in the table shows revenue productivity of GST in these countries, measured as GST revenues per point of the standard rate divided by the GDP (that is, [Aggregate Revenues/Standard Rate]/GDP).

As shown in Table 4.1, the New Zealand GST, which is levied at a single rate on virtually all goods and services, has the highest C-efficiency. The Canadian GST, also levied at a single rate, has low C-efficiency because of zero-rating of food and medicines, and rebates for housing and non-profit sector. Japan and Singapore levy tax at a single rate to a comprehensive base, including food. Yet,

Table 4.1: Comparison of GST Base and Rates, Selected Jurisdictions

Country	Year	Standard Rate %	Consumption % of GDP	C-efficiency	Revenue Productivity
Canada	2005	7	74.8	0.46	0.34
Japan	2004	5	75.5	0.67	0.50
New Zealand	2005	12.5	76.0	0.94	0.73
Singapore	2004	5	54.2	0.70	0.40

Source: Various IMF reports and authors' own estimates.

their C-efficiency is lower than in New Zealand mainly on account of exemptions for supplies by non-profit organizations. The C efficiency of European VATs is generally much lower, in the range of 50 percent, as these taxes are levied at multiple rates, and with exemption for land and housing, financial services, and supplies by public bodies. In general, VATs that have been introduced around the world in the last few years have a higher C-efficiency than the "old" VATs. A low C-efficiency translates into lower revenue productivity of tax, as shown in the last column of the table.

With this background, we turn to an estimation of the size of the GST base in India, and the GST rates that would be required to replace the current indirect tax revenues of the Center and the states.

Poddar and Bagchi's (2007) calculations show that if the GST were to be levied on a comprehensive base, the combined Center-State revenue neutral rate (RNR) need not be more than 12 percent. This rate would apply to all goods and services, with the exception of motor fuels, which would continue to attract a supplementary levy to maintain the total revenue yield at their current levels.

Here are some basic ingredients of the RNR calculations for 2005–06, the latest year for which the necessary data are available. The total excise/service tax/VAT/sales tax revenues of the Center and the states in that year was Rs 134 thousand crore and Rs 139 thousand crore, respectively. Assuming that approximately 40 percent of the central excise revenues and 20 percent of the state VAT/sales tax revenues are from motor fuels, the balance of the revenues from other goods and services that need to be replaced by the GST are Rs 89 thousand crore for the Center and Rs 111 thousand crore for the states, making up a total of Rs 200 thousand crore.

In 2005–06, the total private consumer expenditure on all goods and services was Rs 2,072 thousand crore at current market prices. Making adjustments for sales and excise taxes included in these values and for the private consumption expenditure on motor fuels, the total tax base (at pre-tax prices) for all other goods and services is Rs 1,763 thousand crore.

These values yield a revenue neutral GST rate of approximately 11 percent (200 as percent of 1763 is 11.3 percent). The RNR for the Center is 5 percent and for the states 6.3 percent. Allowing for some leakages, the combined RNR could be in the range of 12 percent. The

Central excise duty rates have been reduced substantially (the standard rate reduced from 16 percent to 10 percent) since 2005. At the current duty rates, the Center RNR is likely to be in the range of 3 percent, bringing the combined RNR to below 10 percent.

These estimates are by no means precise. Even so, they give a broad idea of the levels at which the rate of a national GST could be set, to achieve revenue neutrality for both levels of government. An important question for policy makers is the costs and benefits of deviating from this benchmark of single rate GST. While there would be pressing calls for all kinds of exemptions and lower rates, the economic benefits of a single rate are enormous. The experience of countries like New Zealand, Japan, and Singapore suggests that it is feasible to resist such calls by keeping the tax rate low. There is increasing political support for such an option. It would mark a clean break from the legacy structures, and herald a new era of simple and transparent tax administration.

There is virtue in keeping the GST rate in the 10 percent range, especially at inception. Any revenue shortfall at this rate could be made up by the use of supplementary excises on select demerit goods (for example, tobacco, and alcohol), besides motor fuels. Excises could also be used for select luxury items, which do already attract tax at higher rates. This would help minimize undesirable shifts in the distribution of tax burden (see the discussion in Ahmad and Stern, 1984 and 1991). Clearly, such excises should be limited to a very small list of items which are discrete and not amenable to tax avoidance and evasion.

Food

The main issue in the application of GST to food is the impact it would have on those living at or below subsistence levels. In 2005, food accounted for one-third of total private final consumer expenditures. For those at the bottom of the income scale, it doubtless accounts for an even higher proportion of total expenditures and incomes. Taxing food could thus have a major impact on the poor. By the same token, a complete exemption for food would significantly shrink the tax base.

There are additional considerations that are pertinent to the treatment of food.

1. Food includes a variety of items, including grains and cereals, meat, fish, and poultry, milk and dairy products, fruits and vegetables, candy and confectionary, snacks, prepared meals for home consumption, restaurant meals, and beverages. In most jurisdictions, where reduced rates or exemptions are provided for food, their scope is restricted to basic food items for home consumption. However, the definition of such items is always a challenge, and invariably gives rise to classification disputes. In India, basic food, however defined, would likely constitute the vast bulk of total expenditures on food.

2. In India, while food is generally exempt from the CENVAT, many of the food items, including food grains and cereals, attract the state VAT at the rate of 4 percent. Exemption under the state VAT is restricted to unprocessed food, for example, fresh fruits and vegetables, meat and eggs, and coarse grains. Beverages are generally taxable, with the exception of milk.

3. In the rural sector, the predominant distribution channel for unprocessed food would be either a direct sale by the farmer to final consumers or through small distributors/retailers. Even where food is within the scope of the GST, such sales would largely remain exempt because of the small business registration threshold.

4. Given the large size of farm community in India, which is mostly unorganized, consideration needs to be given to whether it is advisable to exempt (with no right of input tax deduction) all unprocessed farm produce sold by them at the farm gate. In the case of cash crops (produce for further manufacturing or processing, for example, cotton, coffee beans, and oil seeds), it would not be in the interest of the farmers to be exempted from tax. They should, thus, be allowed the option of voluntary registration to pay the tax. It is recognized that an exemption for first sale at the farm gate would be difficult to administer and create inefficiencies in distribution and marketing of farm produce.

These considerations pose some difficult policy issues. Given that food is currently exempt from the CENVAT, the GST under a single-rate, comprehensive-base model would lead to at least a doubling of the tax burden on food (from 4 percent state VAT to a combined GST rate of 10–12 percent). It would call for some tangible measures to offset the impact on the lower-income households. One would be to limit the exemption only to cereals (see Table 4.1) as some of the other food items have lower distributional characteristics.

The alternative of exempting food altogether (or zero rating) would not be any better. First, the revenue neutral rate would jump from 10–12 percent to 18 percent. While the poor would pay less tax on food, they would pay more on other items in their consumption basket. Whether and to what extent they would be better off would depend on the composition of their consumption basket. The higher standard rate would, in turn, lead to pressures for exempting other items (for example, medicines, books, LPG, and kerosene). Third, it could preclude unification of the tax rate on goods with that on services, which are currently taxable at 12.36 percent. Imposition of tax rate at 18 percent on hitherto exempt services (for example, passenger travel, health, and education) would encounter significant political resistance. Fourth, one cannot expect any improvement in taxpayer compliance at such high rates. To the contrary, greater visibility of the Central tax at the retail level could have a negative impact on compliance. Thus, an exemption for food has the potential to totally unravel the simplicity and neutrality of GST.

One could consider a lower rate for food, instead of complete exemption. If the lower rate were to be 5 percent, the revenue neutral standard rate (based on 2005 rate structure) would be pushed up to 16 percent. This may be a reasonable compromise, provided all other goods and services are made taxable at the single standard rate of 16 percent. The risk is that the lower rate for food would become the thin edge of the wedge, which would create irresistible demands for opening the door wider.

An important question is the definition of food that would be eligible for the lower rate. To keep the base broad, and limit the preference to items of consumption by the lower-income households, the lower rate should be confined to "unprocessed" food items (including vegetables, fruit, meat, fish, and poultry). Its scope can be further restricted, by excluding from the preference food pre-packaged for retail sale. This definition would not be without problems, especially where the processing value added is small. For example, if wheat is taxable at 5 percent as unprocessed food, but flour is taxable at 16 percent as processed food, it would encourage consumers to buy wheat and then have it processed into flour.

Overall, the preferred option would appear to be a single-rate, comprehensive-base GST. While no option is perfect, it has the advantage of simplicity and neutrality. As noted earlier, sales of unprocessed food in rural India would largely remain exempt under this option because of the small business exemption. The poor can be further insulated from its impact through direct spending programs, and/or exempt from tax any sales under the Public Distribution System (PDS).

Land and Real Property

Under the "old" VATs (such as those in Europe), land and real property supplies are excluded from the scope of the tax. To minimize the detrimental impact of an exemption under a VAT, business firms are given the option to elect to pay tax on land real property supplies.

Under a modern GST/VAT (for example, in Australia, New Zealand, Canada, and South Africa), housing and construction services are treated like any other commodity. Thus, when a real estate developer builds and sells a home, it is subject to VAT on the full selling price, which would include the cost of land,[11] building materials, and construction services. Commercial buildings and factory sales are also taxable in the same way, as are rental charges for leasing of industrial and commercial buildings. There are only two exceptions: (*a*) resale of used homes and private dwellings, and (*b*) rental of dwellings:

1. A sale of used homes and dwellings is exempted because the tax is already collected at the time of their first purchase, especially for homes acquired after the commencement of the tax. If the sale were to be made taxable, then credit would need to be given for the tax paid on the original purchase, and on any renovations, and additions after the purchase. Except where the prices have gone up, the net incremental tax on resale may not be significant. Theoretically, this system does create a windfall for the existing homes built and acquired prior to the commencement of the tax. In practice, the windfall is not significant as the home construction would have attracted other taxes on construction materials and services that prevailed at that time.

2. Residential rentals are also exempted for the same reason. If rents were to be made taxable, then credit would need to be allowed on the purchase of the dwelling and on repairs and maintenance. Over the life of the dwelling, the present value of tax on the rents would be approximately the same as the tax paid on the purchase of the dwelling and on any renovation, repair, and maintenance costs. In effect (and as with other consumer durables), payment of VAT on the full purchase price at acquisition is a prepayment, of all the VAT due on the consumption services that the house will yield over its full lifetime. A resale of a dwelling is exempted for the same reason: the tax was pre-paid when the dwelling was initially acquired.

3. Many private individuals and families own residential dwellings (including their homes and summer residences) which they may rent to others. They are generally not in the VAT system, so do not get a credit for the VAT paid when they initially acquire their new home. Nor do they claim any credit for any repairs or renovations they may have made to the existing homes. If the rental of such dwelling were subject to tax, owners should also be given a credit for the taxes paid on such costs, which would be complex and difficult to monitor.

Thus, virtually all countries exempt long-term residential rents and resale of used residential dwelling. However, short-term residential accommodation (in hotels, for example) is normally subject to VAT. Any commissions charged by the agents and brokers for the sale or rental of a dwelling are treated as a service separate from the sale or rental of the dwelling and attract tax regardless of whether paid by the buyer or the seller.[12]

Sale or rental of vacant land (which includes rental of car parking spaces, fees for mooring of boats and camping sites) is also taxable under the "modern" VAT system.

It would make sense to incorporate these concepts in the design of GST in India as well.

1. Conceptually, it is appropriate to include land and real property in the GST base. To exclude them would, in fact, lead to economic distortions and invite unnecessary classification disputes as to what constitutes supply of real property.

2. In the case of commercial and industrial land and buildings, their exclusion from the base would lead to tax cascading through blockage of input taxes on construction materials and services. It is for this reason that even under the European system, an option is allowed to VAT registrants to elect to treat such supplies as taxable.
3. Housing expenditures are distributed progressively in relation to income, and their taxation would contribute to the fairness of the GST.
4. The state VAT and the service tax already apply to construction materials and services, respectively, but in a complex manner. For example, there is significant uncertainty whether a pre-construction agreement to sell a new residential dwelling is a works contract and subject to VAT. Where the VAT does apply, disputes arise about the allocation of the sale price to land, goods, and services. While land is the only major element that does not attract tax, the tax rates applicable to goods and services differ, necessitating a precise delineation of the two. Extending the GST to all real property supplies, including construction materials and services, would bring an end to such disputes, simplify the structure, and enhance the overall economic efficiency of the tax.

One potential argument against the levy of GST to land and real property would be that they already attract the stamp duty. This argument can be quickly discarded as the purpose and structure of the stamp duty is quite different from that of the GST. Stamp duty is a cascading tax on each conveyance of title to real property, whereas the GST is a tax on final consumer expenditures. The GST does not impinge on commercial property transactions, after taking into account the benefit of input tax credits. It does not result in tax cascading. Under the model described above, in the case of residential dwellings, GST would apply to the first sale only. Thus, the two taxes cannot be viewed as substitutes. However, the application of GST to real property transactions does warrant a review of the structure and rates of stamp duties and registration fees. The rates should be lowered and the structure rationalized when the GST is introduced.

Non-profit Sector and Public Bodies

Historically, supplies made by governmental bodies and non-profit organizations (including religious institutions, social welfare agencies, and sports and cultural organizations) have been exempted from VAT, on the grounds that such bodies are not engaged in a business and their activities are not commercial in nature. But this is often, and increasingly, not the case. Public enterprises are involved in a wide range of industrial and commercial activities. As deregulation proceeds, the dividing line between public administration and industrial/commercial activities becomes increasingly blurred. For example, postal and telecommunication services were historically viewed as public administration, but this is no longer the case. Government agencies/enterprises provide such services in competition with private firms. The same is true for other activities such as local and intercity transit, operation of airports, radio and television broadcasting, and provision of water, sewer, and sanitation services. Moreover, the public sector in India, as in many other countries, is large and pervasive.

Under the EU VAT Directive, activities of the public sector is divided into three categories: non-taxable, taxable, and exempt. A public body is in principle eligible to claim input tax deductions, only in respect of the VAT paid on inputs acquired for use in making taxable supplies (though a number of member states pay refunds of VAT by matching grant). While this approach may have provided the EU member states with the needed flexibility in dealing with their domestic environment, it falls short of achieving the principal criteria of an efficient VAT system identified earlier. The exempt or non-taxable status of a wide range of supplies by public bodies violates the criterion of economic neutrality. Biases are created in favor of the self-supply of services within the public sector to minimize the amount of non-deductible VAT on inputs. Consumers may be influenced in their purchasing decisions by the fact that the VAT does not apply to certain public sector goods and services. The non-deductible input VAT embedded in the prices of public sector goods and services is passed along to persons in the production-distribution chain who are not final consumers.

The application of a value-added tax requires identification of a supply and the consumer or buyer to whom the supply is made, and valuation of consideration for the supply. Determination of each of these elements gives rise to issues in the public sector due to the nature of the way services are delivered by governments and the manner in which the services are funded. For example, a public body may provide its services for no explicit charge (for example, museum admissions, water, health, and education) and there may not be any identifiable buyer or consumer for certain services provided on a collective basis (for example, sanitation, and police protection). In addition, the political sensitivity to the taxation of certain services and the methods of intergovernmental funding may detract from a neutral application of tax to the public sector activities. As a result, the public sector is subject to special rules in almost all VAT systems currently in place throughout the world.

This is a matter that cannot be dealt with satisfactorily without a systematic review of all of the activities of the governmental bodies and non-profit organizations. However, at this stage it is useful to describe the two broad approaches that other countries have followed.

First, the highly-regarded VAT system in New Zealand (and later Australia)[13] treats all activities of public sector and non-profit bodies as fully taxable.[14] They, thus, collect the VAT on all of their revenues, with the sole exception of revenues from taxes, interest and dividends, and gifts and charitable donations. Under this broad and comprehensive approach, no distinction is made between public administration and commercial/industrial activities of the state or non-profit organizations. By the same token, these bodies are eligible to claim a full credit for their input VAT, in the same manner as private enterprises. This system is conceptually simple, and consequently is in some respects easy to operate. And—by putting public and private sectors on an equal footing—it minimizes potential distortions of competition. In Australia, certain basic medical and educational supplies, and supplies by non-profit organizations below market value (that is, subsidized supplies) are zero-rated.[15] Other supplies are taxable under the standard GST rules, as in New Zealand.

The second is the traditional approach, followed in most other countries. Under this approach, the activities of public and non-profit bodies are divided into two lists: taxable and exempt. There are no simple or mechanical rules for this division, which in practice is based on a variety of economic, social, and practical considerations.

For example, public enterprises engaged in industrial or commercial activities are generally taxable, especially if their revenues from their clients are expected to exceed their costs. Some countries exempt all other fees and charges, while others tax them on a selective basis (including postal charges, airport landing fees, port loading and unloading charges, sale of statistical and other publications, and fees for licenses and permits). Given that not all of the activities of an organization are considered taxable under this approach, an input tax credit is allowed for only those inputs that relate to the taxable activities of the organization.

This latter approach creates difficulties in determining what is taxable and what is exempt, and also in allocating the input taxes between the two (since credit would be given only in respect of taxable activities). It also creates a distortion in the form of a bias against the use of outside contractors by public bodies in their exempt activities. For example, if a municipality used a contractor for construction of a road or a bridge, it would pay the VAT on the contractor's fees and not be eligible to claim a credit for the tax. However, it could avoid the tax if it hired its own employees to do the construction work. As noted earlier, some countries provide a full or partial rebate of the tax related to minimize this "self-supply" bias.

There is little doubt that the New Zealand approach is conceptually superior. It does, however, lead to a larger number of taxpayers, many of whom will be entitled to refunds. Since the management of refunds is an especially problematic aspect of the VAT, particularly in developing countries, the control issues may be a significant drawback.

If governments and public bodies are partially exempted, then one other issue that needs to be considered is the treatment of supplies to governments. This is especially important in a federation. Should one government apply its non-creditable tax to supplies to another government? Or should all governments be immune from taxation as sovereign bodies? In India, CENVAT and state VAT currently apply to government procurement.

Likewise, the GST could be made applicable to supplies to governments with no special rules. However, as noted earlier, this then would create a self-supply bias for public bodies where they buy inputs for an exempt activity.

VI Financial Services

Financial services are exempted from VAT in all countries. The principal reason is that the charge for the services provided by financial intermediaries (such as banks and insurance companies) is generally not explicitly a fee, but is taken as a margin, that is hidden in interest, dividends, annuity payments, or such other financial flows from the transactions. For example, banks provide the service of operating and maintaining deposit accounts for their depositors, for which they charge no explicit fee. The depositors do, however, pay an implicit fee, which is the difference between the pure interest rate (that is, the interest rate which could otherwise be earned in the market without any banking services) and the interest actually received by them from the bank on the deposit balance. The fee is the interest foregone. Similarly, the charge for the services provided by banks to the borrowers is included in the interest charged on the loan. It is the excess of the interest rate on the loan, over the pure rate of interest or cost of funds to the bank for that loan.

It would be straightforward, to levy the tax on this implicit fee, if the reference "pure rate" were easily observable but it is not. The spread between borrowing and lending rates could be measured, and taken as measuring the *total* value added by the intermediary. But in order for the crediting mechanism to work properly, it is necessary to go further and *allocate* this value-added to borrower and lender (with a credit on the tax paid due only to registered taxpayers) which again raises the problem of identifying a reference pure interest rate.[16]

Some financial services are, of course, charged for by a direct and explicit fee, examples being an account charge or foreign exchange commission. Services provided for an explicit charge could be subjected to VAT in the normal way with the taxable recipient having a right of deduction, and a growing number of countries do this. Nevertheless, some countries exempt them all, while others limit the exemption to banking and life insurance. The exemption avoids the need to measure the tax base for financial transactions, but gives rise to other distortions in the financial markets. The denial of credit to the exempt financial institutions, for the VAT charged on their inputs, creates disincentives for them to outsource their business process operations. Where they render services to business clients, the blockage of input tax credits results in tax cascading, adversely affecting their competitive position in the international markets.

Taxing explicit fees for financial services, but treating margin services as exempt, is a possible answer, but it is conceptually flawed (as the same service will be treated differently for VAT purposes depending on how the remuneration for it is taken) and runs the risk that there will be some arbitrage between the two methods of charging to lessen the VAT charge (particularly in the case of supplies to final consumers with no right of deduction).

In China, financial services are taxable under their business tax, which is a tax on turnover with no tax credits allowed on inputs. Because it is a turnover tax, it can be applied to the total spread for margin services, with no need to allocate the spread between borrowers and depositors. Israel and Korea also apply tax in such alternative forms.

Under the service tax, India has followed the approach of bringing virtually all financial services within the ambit of tax, where the consideration for them is in the form of an explicit fee. It has gone beyond this, by bringing selected margin services (where the consideration is the spread between two financial inflows and outflows) within the service tax net. The following are principal examples of such taxable margin services:

1. Merchant discounts on credit/debit card transactions are taxable, as a consideration for credit card services, as are any explicit fees or late payment charges collected from the card member.
2. In foreign currency conversion transactions without an explicit fee, tax applies to a deemed amount of consideration equal to 2 percent of the amount converted.
3. The tax applies to that portion of life insurance premiums that represents a cover for risks.

As there are no compelling economic or social policy reasons for exempting financial services (other than the practical difficulties of defining the consideration for margin services), it would be appropriate to continue this approach under GST. There are, however, certain technical flaws in the measurement of consideration that need to be addressed when switching over to GST. For example, in the case of insurance, the tax applies to the gross amount of risk premium, while a proper measure would be the premiums net of any claims (whether the claim is settled in cash or in kind). This can be accomplished by allowing a credit in respect of any claims paid.

Consideration could also be given to bringing interest margin on non-commercial loans and deposits within the next net on an aggregate basis, as opposed to for each transaction separately.[17] This could be done by computing the aggregate interest margin and apportioning it between the margin from business to business (B2B) and business to consumer (B2C) transactions. The B2B margin could then be zero-rated, and the tax applied to the B2C margin.

In some countries, transactions in gold, silver, and other precious metals are also treated as part of the financial sector, given that these metals are often bought as investments, and not for consumption. They are exempted from tax. However, unlike the approach followed in India of applying a reduced rate of 1 percent to such metals and articles made of such metals, the exemption is confined to only metals of investment-grade purity levels. Jewelry and other articles made of such metals remain taxable at the standard rate.

VII Treatment of Interstate and International Trade

Treatment of interstate and international supplies of goods and services is one of the most crucial elements of the design of a Dual GST. A set of rules is needed to define the jurisdiction in which they would be taxable under the destination principle. Further, a mechanism is needed for enforcing compliance to those rules.

The rules can be relatively straightforward for the application of the Central GST. However, there is a concern that, under a sub-national destination-based VAT, taxation of cross-border transactions could be a significant challenge, in the absence of any interstate fiscal border controls. Even if such border controls were to exist, they would be ineffective for taxation of services, which entail no physical interstate movement. This concern has been a topic of increased discussion over the recent years due to the growth in internet sales and transactions. Cross-border VAT leakage is also a growing concern in the EU because of the removal of border controls between member countries.

In what follows, we first start with the basic framework for defining the place of supply, then look at the policy options for ensuring proper compliance. This discussion draws on Ahmad, et al. (2008) for the GCC Secretariat.

Place of Taxation, International Transactions

In virtually all countries, VAT is levied on the basis of the destination principle. For this purpose, some countries follow the practice of prescribing a set of rules for defining the place of taxation or place of supply. A supply is taxable in a given jurisdiction only if the supply is considered to take place in that jurisdiction. An alternative approach followed by other countries is to first define what supplies are potentially within the scope of the tax, and then provide criteria for determining which of those supplies would be zero-rated as exports. The two approaches yield the same result, even though one excludes exports from the scope of the tax, while the other zero-rates them, having first included them in the scope. The service tax in India follows the second approach.

While the rules and approaches vary from country to country, the basic criteria for defining the place of taxation are as follows (approaches for taxation of services, depicted in Chart 4.1):[18]

1. A sale of goods is taxable if the goods are made available in or delivered/shipped to that jurisdiction (that is, on the basis of place of delivery or shipment to the recipient).
2. A sale of real property is taxable if the property is located in that jurisdiction (that is, on the basis of place of location of the property). Services directly connected with real property are also taxable on this basis (for example, services of estate agents or architects).
3. A supply of other services or intangible property is taxable in that jurisdiction, depending on one or more of the following factors:
   • Place of performance of the service
   • Place of use or enjoyment of the service or intangible property

Chart 4.1
Place of Taxation
(of Supplies other than Goods)

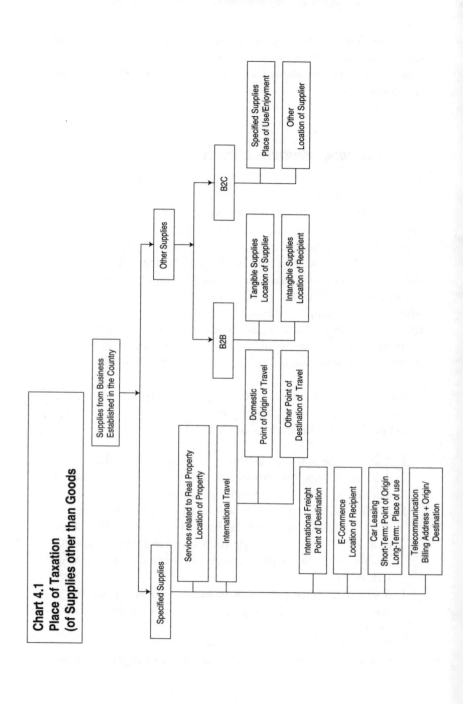

- Place of residence/location of the recipient
- Place of residence/location of the supplier.
4. Special rules apply for certain supplies (also referred to as mobile services) for which there is no fixed place of performance or use/enjoyment, such as:
   - Passenger travel services
   - Freight transportation services
   - Telecommunication services
   - Motor vehicle leases/rentals
   - E-commerce supplies.

In defining the place of taxation of services and intangible property, a distinction is often made between supplies made to businesses (B2B) and final consumers (B2C). B2B supplies are generally defined to be made where the recipient is located or established, regardless of where the services are performed or used. This is particularly the case for the so-called intangible services (for example, advisory or consulting services), for which the place of performance is not important. Thus, all such services rendered to non-residents become zero-rated, and subject to a reverse charge in the country of the recipient, which charge is deductible as long as the recipient is fully taxable. This avoids tax cascading, which would otherwise occur.

By contrast, B2C services are deemed to be made in the jurisdiction where the supplier is located. Many B2C services tend to be tangible or physical in nature, for example, haircuts and admissions to places of amusement, which are used or consumed at the place of their performance. In some countries, B2C intangible services are treated in the same manner as B2B services, that is, they are zero-rated when rendered to non-resident customers.

Special rules apply to the so-called mobile services. For transportation services, the place of supply is defined by reference to the point of origin or destination. In Europe, rail passenger transportation is taxed based on distance traveled in the taxing jurisdiction. For telecommunication, e-commerce, and satellite broadcasting services, the origin rule (taxation in the country of the supplier) can lead to non-taxation, and various solutions have been followed to prevent this. For example, in the EU, e-commerce suppliers to EU final consumers are required to register and account for tax in the country of their customer, using a "one stop shop" registration facility, if they wish. This rule is being extended to intra-EU supplies of telecommunications, e-commerce and satellite broadcasting from January 1, 2015 to present suppliers obtaining an arbitrage advantage by setting up their business in a low-rate, member state. In Canada, a two-out-of-three rule is followed, that is, the supply is made in the jurisdiction if the points of origin and termination are in that jurisdiction, or if one of the points is in the jurisdiction and the supply is billed to an account in the jurisdiction. The rules for e-commerce are varied, but generally follow the rules for telecommunication services. Internet connectivity services are, in fact, telecommunication services. Goods and services bought and sold online are generally taxed on the same manner as those bought offline.

For short-term car rentals, in Europe the place of supply is where the car is first made available to the customer, regardless of the place of its subsequent use. For long-term leases, place of supply could depend on the place of use of the vehicle or the residence of the customer; the EU is adopting such a rule from January 1, 2010 to prevent "rate shopping". Often, similar rules are adopted for leases and rentals of other goods also.

In addition to the above, there are a variety of other complex cross-border transactions for which supplementary rules are required. They relate to global transactions (or master service agreements) for individual supplies to legal entities of a corporate group around the world, triangular transactions, supplies among branches and between branches and head office, and cost reimbursement/allocation arrangements. The complexity of the rules for such transactions has been an issue under discussion, by working groups at the OECD, with a view to developing a framework or guidance for uniformity, and consistency in the treatment of international services and intangibles in different jurisdictions.[19]

It is recognized that under these rules tax could be charged to non-resident business customers on supplies of an intermediate nature (that is, not for final consumption), which would lead to cascading and create competitive distortions. To address this concern, many countries have provisions to provide a rebate of the tax charged to business customers.[20] Such rebates can also be extended to non-business customers, for example, rebates to foreign tourists, for the tax paid on goods bought locally for subsequent export when they return back.

Generally, these rules apply in a symmetrical manner to define exports and imports. Thus, where the supply of, say, consulting services by a domestic supplier is zero-rated because it is supplied to a business located outside the country, the supply of such services by a foreign supplier to a business located in the country would be taxable as an imported service. Imports generally attract tax at the customs border. For services and intangibles, the tax is self-assessed by the recipient under the reverse-charge mechanism.

The combined result of these rules (including the system of rebates for non-resident customers) is to define the place of destination of services and intangibles as follows:

1. For B2B supplies, the place of destination is the place where the recipient is established or located.
2. For B2C supplies of a tangible/physical nature (for example, hair cuts, hotel accommodation, local transportation, and entertainment services), the place of destination is the place where the supplier is established or located, which is generally also the place where the service is performed. For highly mobile B2C supplies of an intangible nature (for example, telecommunication, e-commerce and satellite broadcasting services, for which the place of performance is not linked to the rendering of the service), the place of supply could be the place of residence of the customer (as for B2B supplies), or the place where the services are used or enjoyed. But, because it is wholly impractical to subject final consumers to the reverse charge, in Europe the non-resident supplier is required to register and account for VAT to customer's resident in the European Union.
3. Special rules for specific supplies are generally designed to yield a result similar to that for other supplies. They serve the purpose of providing greater certainty and clarity in situations where the place of location or residence of the supplier or the recipient may not be well-defined or easily ascertainable at the time of the supply.

Place of Taxation, Interstate Transactions

An important question, in the context of the Dual GST, is whether these rules for international cross-border supplies can be adopted for domestic, interstate supplies also. Conceptually, there are no compelling reasons to deviate from them for defining the place of supply at the sub-national level. The only precedent available of a destination-based VAT at the sub-national level is that of Harmonized Sales Tax (HST) in Canada. (The precedent of the EU is different because it is a community of 27 sovereign member states rather than a single nation made up of a union of states in a federation. The EU solution of taxing intra-EU B2B supplies of goods and services by means of zero-rating and then reverse charge accounting in the member state of the taxable recipient may not be the right answer and has led to the problem of carousel fraud.) Surprisingly, Canada deviated from these rules in defining the place of supply in a province in one important respect. In defining the place of supply of services at the provincial level, the primary criterion used in Canada is the place of performance of the service. Thus, if all or substantially all of a service is performed in a province, then the place of supply of the service is considered to be that province, regardless of whether it is a B2B or B2C supply, and where it is used or enjoyed. There appear to be two reasons for it, which are also relevant for the design of the Dual GST in India.

First, it is recognized that the place where the supplier or the recipient is established cannot be defined uniquely at the sub-national level within a common market. A supplier may have establishments/ offices in several states and one or more of them could be involved in rendering the service. At the national level, the country of residence of the counter parties to a transaction needs to be determined for direct tax as well as other regulatory purposes. However, at the sub-national level, such determination is not necessary, especially where there is no direct tax at that level. The basic rules outlined previously, for international supplies cannot be applied in the absence of supplementary rules for defining the place, where the supplier and the recipient are located or established. Take, for example, an HR consulting firm with offices in several states, providing recruitment services to a corporate entity with operations through India. In this case, the basic rule of defining the place of supply of the service to be where the recipient is established cannot be applied as the recipient is established in more than one state.

Second, under the Canadian HST, any input tax paid by a business can be claimed back, as an input credit under the federal GST or the HST regardless of where it is established, as long as the inputs are used in a taxable activity. Thus, there is no adverse consequence of collecting the HST on services, rendered to businesses located in other provinces.

The HST is integrated with the GST to such an extent that it best fits the description of as a national GST, not a Dual GST.

Given these considerations, Canada defines the place of supply of services (other than those subject to special rules) to be the place where they are performed. If they are performed in more than one province, supplementary rules are employed to determine the place of supply. The main supplementary rule defines the place of supply/taxation to be the place to which the employee/officer of the supplier, who had responsibility for negotiating the service contract with the recipient, reports. In effect, under these rules the sub-national tax on services is applied on the basis of the origin principle, that is, where the services are performed.

The Canadian approach does not appear to be suitable for the Dual GST in India, where the Central and state GSTs would be harmonized, but not integrated. It would be desirable to tax B2B supplies of services (and intangibles) in the state of destination, and not of origin.

Given that any tax on B2B supplies would generally be fully creditable, excessive sophistication would not be warranted for defining the place of destination of such supplies. For multi-establishment business entities, the place of destination could be defined simply as the place of predominant use of the service. Where there is no unique place of predominant use, the place of destination could be simply the mailing address of the recipient on the invoice, which would normally be the business address of the contracting party. The risk of misuse of this provision would be minimal, if it is limited to B2B supplies where the tax is fully creditable.

For B2C services, the tax should apply in the state where the supplier is established, which, in turn, could be defined as the place where the services are performed. Where there is no unique place of performance of the service, the place of taxation could be defined to be the state, where the supplier's establishment, most directly in negotiations with the recipient, is located. This would be similar to the Canadian rule.

Taxation of Imports by the States

In most countries, imports attract the VAT/GST at the time of entry into the country. The tax is generally applied on the value of goods declared for customs purposes, including the amount of the customs duty. However, there are no well-established precedents for the application of sub-national taxes to imports. In India, the Center levies an additional duty (called the special additional duty) on imports at the rate of 4 percent, which is meant to be in lieu of the state VAT. This duty is allowed as a credit against the central excise duty on manufacturing, or refunded where the imports are resold and the state VAT is charged on them.

In Canada, the provincial HST is collected by the customs authorities on non-commercial importations of goods. The tax is collected at the time of importation on the basis of place of residence of the person importing the goods. regardless of where the goods enter the country. Commercial importations do not attract the provincial HST because of difficulties in determining their destination within the country. For example, a large consolidated commercial shipment could contain goods that are initially destined to a central warehouse, for subsequent distribution to various parts of the country.

The Canadian system is conceptually appealing and could be considered for the application of state taxes under the Dual GST in India.

Monitoring of Interstate Supplies

We turn now to the design of a suitable mechanism for payment and collection of tax on interstate supplies. As noted earlier, there is a concern that a sub-national destination-based VAT could be subject to substantial leakages in the absence of effective interstate border controls. Many policy prescriptions have been made to deal with the issue, but none implemented so far at the sub-national level.[21]

In our view, these concerns are exaggerated, especially under a dual GST, harmonized between the Center and the state and across the states. It is possible to design suitable mechanisms for proper application of tax on interstate supplies, without resorting to border controls. The current border controls for goods, in the form of interstate check posts, have not been effective in the past. Border controls would not even be feasible for services and intangibles, which involve no physical inter-state movement.

As noted by Bird and Gendron (1998), under a dual GST, the application of the Center GST to all domestic supplies would automatically serve as an audit control for reporting of interstate supplies for purposes of the state GST. The aggregate of the turnovers reported for the state GSTs must equal the total turnover reported for the Center GST. Dealers can misclassify the turnover to different states, but would not be able to suppress the turnover for state GST below the level reported for the Center GST. Where the GST design, rate, and the base is harmonized across the states, the dealers would have little incentive to misclassify the turnover. Under such a system, the focus of the authorities should be on proper reporting of the total turnover, not interstate turnover.

Notwithstanding the above discussion, a mechanism is needed for proper application of sub-national tax on interstate supplies of goods as well as services. For reasons outlined elsewhere (Poddar and Hutten, 2001), zero-rating of interstate supplies is not advisable. Instead, the preferred approach would be to require the vendors to collect the destination state GST on interstate supplies (of goods and services) and remit the tax directly to the destination state.[22] The tax would then be creditable in the destination state under the normal rules, that is, if it relates to inputs for use in making taxable supplies.

This mechanism, referred to as Prepaid VAT (PVAT), is similar to the mechanism of the CST. Under the CST, the tax on interstate sales is charged and remitted to the origin state. Under PVAT, the tax on interstate supplies would be charged and remitted to the destination state. It preserves the destination principle of VAT. Vendors in the origin state collect tax on all of their domestic supplies, whether intra-state or interstate.

The tax collected on interstate supplies would be that of the destination state, and remitted to that state by the vendor. On intra-state supplies, the tax collected would be that of the origin state and paid to that state.

Buyers who are GST registrants (in B2B transactions) would have a strong incentive to ensure that the vendor properly applies the destination tax, which would then be creditable against their output tax in the state of destination. Otherwise, the goods would be subject to the tax of the origin state, which would not be creditable in the state of destination.

Most supplies of services and intangibles to consumers and other exempt buyers (in B2C transactions) would be taxable in the state of origin, without the benefit of zero-rating. However, interstate shipments of goods to consumers would be zero-rated in the state of origin and attract the tax of the destination state (including, for example, mail order supplies of goods). An inducement could be created for consumers also to ensure that the vendor charges the destination state-tax on such shipments. This could be done by imposing a self-assessment requirement, in the destination state on any interstate purchases, on which the vendor has not charged and remitted the destination state tax.

The PVAT mechanism establishes the output-tax-and-input-credit chain, for interstate transactions and, thereby, strengthens the audit trail property of the VAT system. Unlike the system of zero-rating, it creates strong incentives for both the origin and the destination state to monitor compliance, independently of each other, as revenues of both are affected by the zero-rated sales declared by the vendor. This is a unique feature of PVAT, and perhaps it is most significant. Under the traditional system of zero-rating, the quantum of zero-rated sales reported by the vendor affects the revenues of the origin state, but not of the destination state. PVAT creates a simple and effective link between the two.

VIII Harmonization of Laws and Administration

The need for Center-state and interstate harmonization is paramount under the Dual GST. The ultimate goal would be a unified base and one set of rules for the two taxes.

What should be the mechanism for achieving this harmonization? Different options have been adopted in other federations or trading blocks. At one extreme is the example of Australia, where the GST is imposed and administered as a single unified tax levied by the national government. All the revenues from the tax are then distributed to the state. Another such example is that of Harmonized Sales Tax (HST) in Canada, which is levied in three of the ten provinces. The tax is levied and administered under a unified law by the national government, much like the Australian GST. The key difference is in the revenue allocation system. Under the Canadian system, provincial participation in the HST is elective, not mandatory. The tax is levied at the national rate of 7 percent (now reduced to 5 percent), which is increased by 8 percent in those provinces which have elected to participate in it. The revenues attributable to the supplementary rate of 8 percent are then distributed among the participating provinces on the basis of a statistical calculation of the tax base in those provinces (which approximates the revenues they would have collected if they had levied a separate tax of their own). In Australia, there is no state "participation". The tax is a federal tax that is distributed to the states, under a political agreement. The revenues are distributed as grants to the states, taking into account factors such as fiscal capacity and need of individual states. In terms of the operation of the law, the enactment of the law, and the jurisdiction of law, it is exclusively a federal tax.

The system in the Province of Quebec, in Canada, offers another model of harmonization of the national and sub-national taxes. Quebec levies a goods and services tax, called Quebec Sales Tax (QST), the legislation for which follows very closely the model for the federal GST. The two taxes have the same base, definitions, and rules, but levied under two separate statutes. To ensure harmonization of administration, the two governments have entered into a tax collection agreement under which the collection, administration, and enforcement of the federal GST is delegated to the provincial government. The agreement defines the role and responsibilities of the two governments and the policies and procedures to be followed in administering the tax. The federal government retains the power to make any changes in the legislation and to issue rulings, and interpretations, which are adhered to by the province in administering the federal GST. In practice, the province accepts the federal rulings and interpretations for both GST and QST, given the similarities in the two statues.

The EU model is yet another example. This model is quite distinct from the Australian and Canadian models. The focus in the EU model is on minimization of distortions in trade and competition, and not on harmonization of administration. Thus, the VAT base (subject to continuing derogations) is harmonized, as are the basic rules governing the mechanism and application of VAT (time of supply, valuation, place of supply, and so on). The rates are harmonized only within broad bands (for example, the standard rate may not be less than 15 percent) and administration is largely a matter for the member state to decide (but must respect basic principles such as neutrality).

As noted earlier, the CST in India also offers an interesting model of the harmonization mechanism. The CST law is central, but the tax is administered and collected by the states. Indeed, this appears to be most suitable model for India. The GST law for both the Center and the states would be enacted by Parliament under this model. It would define the tax base, place of taxation, and the compliance, enforcement rules and procedures. The rates for the state GST could be specified in the same legislation or delegated to the state legislatures. The legislation would empower the Center and the states to collect their respective tax amounts, as under the CST.

If the governments fail to reach a political compromise on the CST model, the Quebec model would appear to be the next best alternative. It respects fiscal autonomy of the two levels of government, yet facilitates harmonization through the mechanism of binding tax collection agreements between the Center and the state. These agreements would, in turn, encourage adoption of a common GST law.

The Center can play an important role of providing a forum to discuss and develop the common architecture for the harmonized administration of the two taxes. It would have responsibility to develop policies and procedures for GST, in consultation with the Empowered Committee, for example, on the place of supply rules, taxpayer registration and identification numbers, model GST law, design of tax forms and filing procedures, data requirements and computer systems, treatment of specific sectors (for example, financial services, public bodies and governments, housing, and telecommunications), and procedures for collection of tax on cross-border trade, both interstate and international. The proposal made by the Empowered Committee (for delegation of administration of the Center GST for smaller dealers to the states) is very similar, even though the contractual framework for it is yet to be developed.

IX Conclusion

The Empowered Committee describes the GST as "a further significant improvement—the next logical step—towards a comprehensive indirect tax reforms in the country". Indeed, it has the potential to be the single most important initiative in the fiscal history of India. It can pave the way for modernization of tax administration—make it simpler and more transparent—and significant enhancement in voluntary compliance. For example, when the GST was introduced in New Zealand in 1987, it yielded revenues that were 45 percent higher than anticipated, in large part due to improved compliance. It's more neutral and efficient structure could yield significant dividends to the economy in increased output and productivity. The Canadian experience is suggestive of the potential benefits to the Indian economy. The GST in Canada replaced the federal manufacturers' sales tax, which was then levied at the rate of 13 percent and was similar in design and structure as the CENVAT in India. It is estimated that this replacement resulted in an increase in potential GDP by 1.4 percent, consisting of 0.9 percent increase in national income from higher factor productivity and 0.5 percent increase from a larger capital stock (due to elimination of tax cascading).

However, these benefits are critically dependent on a neutral and rational design of the GST. The discussion of selected issues in this paper suggests that there are many challenges that lie ahead in such a design. The issues are not trivial or technical. They would require much research and analysis, deft balancing of conflicting interests of various stakeholders, and full political commitment for a fundamental reform of the system.

Opportunities for a fundamental reform present themselves only infrequently, and thus, need to be pursued vigorously as and when they do become available. As the choices made today would not be reversible in the near future, one needs a long-term perspective. Achieving the correct choice is then a political economy balancing act that takes into account the technical options and the differing needs and constraints of the main partners. Fortunately, there is a very substantial consensus among all stakeholders in the country for a genuine reform. In the circumstances, an incremental or timid response would be neither politically expedient, nor would it serve the needs of India of the 21st century. Experience of countries with modern VATs, such as New Zealand, Singapore, and Japan, suggests that a GST with single-rate and comprehensive base can be a win-win proposition for taxpayers and the fisc alike.

Notes

1 A detailed discussion of the problems can be found in the Bagchi Report.

2 See Ahmad and Stern (1984) for the definition of effective taxes and applications to India. Bagchi et al. (1994) provides estimates of effective excise tax rates, which are shown to vary from less than 1 percent to more than 22 percent.

3 For example, these were precisely the reasons for the replacement of the federal manufacturers' sales tax by the GST in 1991. See Canada Department of Finance (1987) and Poddar and Harley (1989).

4 The Constitution (46th Amendment) Bill 1982 amended Article 366 (29A) of the Constitution to deem a tax on six items to be a tax on the sale or purchase of goods.

5 Kuo et al. (1988) provide estimates of tax cascading under the Canadian federal manufacturers' sales tax and the provincial retail sales taxes.

6 For a detailed discussion of the flaws of the current approach to taxation of services, see Rao (2001), which recommended replacement of taxation of selected services by a general tax on all services (other than excluded services).

7 Canada provides refundable tax credit, GST credit to low-income households through the personal income tax system. The credit is paid in quarterly installments and income-tested for high-income households.

8 The Commission Directive on the Common System of Value Added Tax, which replaced the Sixth Directive.

9 The division of taxation powers between federal and provincial governments in Canada provides an interesting example of such concurrent powers. Under the Canadian Constitutions, the federal government can levy any tax, and the provinces have the power to levy any direct tax within the province. A tax is considered to be a direct tax, if its incidence falls on the person on whom it is levied. Thus, it includes all forms of income and wealth taxes. A sales tax or VAT is also viewed to be direct if it is levied on the buyer/consumer, but not on the vendor. The tax can be collected and remitted by the vendor, acting as an agent of the government, but it has to be levied on the buyer. As a result, the two levels of concurrent powers for all types of taxes, subject to the condition that the provincial taxes can only be levied on persons within the geographical boundary of the provinces.

10 The Australian constitutional situation is that both the states and the Commonwealth (the Federal Government) have power to tax supplies of goods and services. The Constitution prevents laws interfering with interstate trade (including tax laws) and gives the power to collect customs and excise taxes exclusively to the Federal Government. It is forbidden for the Commonwealth to tax state property. To meet this requirement, the GST implementation laws, of which there are six, simply state that they do not impose tax on state properties and the states accept that view, at least at the moment. The GST was introduced on the pretence that it was a state tax being collected by the Commonwealth in order to (a) secure the states' agreements to abolish some of their preexisting transaction taxes, in particular certain stamp duties, financial institutions duties, and so on, and (b) to ensure that the states wouldn't start a round of attempts to challenge the constitutional validity of the law (as was done, unsuccessfully, in the past with income tax, which both states and Commonwealth also have power to collect). The current Government has acknowledged that GST is in fact simply a Federal Tax that it uses to make grants to the states and as a result of this acknowledgement, the Auditor General has, for the first time since 2000, agreed to approve the Commonwealth accounts.

11 Actually, in Australia and New Zealand, this is not always the case. In New Zealand, land (like any other "goods") is the subject of a deemed input tax credit under the "second hand goods" scheme, which has the effect that the tax on a development of land acquired from an unregistered person is the margin of the supplier. This provision affects mainly the land held by individuals outside a business at the commencement of the GST. Such land is permanently sheltered from tax, even where it subsequently enters a commercial supply chain. In Australia, a margin scheme for land is used to work out the taxable value in similar circumstances: the margin scheme operates as a second hand scheme and as a transitional rule to prevent the value of most (but not all) of the value of land as at 1 July 2000 entering into the tax base.

12 Poddar (2009) provides a more detailed discussion of the options for taxation of housing under VAT/GST.

13 The Australian system is structured quite differently from the New Zealand one, even though the net outcome is similar. New Zealand's GST is designed to tax all flows of money, through the Government, whereas Australia's is complicated by the Federal Structure. The Commonwealth does not, in fact, pay GST or claim ITCs—it just does so notionally—whereas the state actually does pay GST and claim ITCs. New Zealand taxes appropriations, whereas Australians says that they are not taxed. In addition, a range of Government-provided services are GST-free or exempt.

14 See Barrand (1991) for a description of the New Zealand system. Aujean et al. (1999) provide an analytical framework for such a system.

15 Zero-rated (called GST-free) supplies are defined as follows:
   1. 38-7 Medical services:
      A supply of a medical service is GST-free.
   2. However, a supply of a medical service is not GST-free under subsection (1) if:
      (a) it is a supply of a professional service rendered in prescribed circumstances within the meaning of regulation 14 of the Health Insurance Regulations made under the Health Insurance Act 1973 (other than the prescribed circumstances set out in regulations 14(2)(ea), (f) and (g)); or
      (b) it is rendered for cosmetic reasons and is not a professional service for which medicare benefit is payable under Part II of the Health Insurance Act 1973.
      [medical services are defined by cross-reference to services covered by a health and health insurance law]
      38-85 Education courses
   A supply is GST-free if it is a supply of:
   (a) an education course; or
      administrative services directly related to the supply of such a course, but only if they are supplied by the supplier of the course. [education course defined as a course leading to a diploma or degree from a primary, secondary or tertiary school with cross-references to recognition by the appropriate state education authority] 38-250 Nominal consideration, etc.
   (1) A supply is GST-free if:
      (a) the supplier is a charitable institution, a trustee of a charitable fund, a gift-deductible entity or a government school; and
      (b) the supply is for consideration that:
         (i) if the supply is a supply of accommodation—is less than 75 percent of the GST inclusive market value of the supply; or
         (ii) if the supply is not a supply of accommodation—is less than 50 percent of the GST inclusive market value of the supply.

115

16 These concepts are discussed in greater detail in Poddar and English (1997) and Poddar (2003).
17 For a more complete discussion of the system in India and how it can be modified and extended, see Poddar (2007).
18 What are discussed in the following pages, are only the basic concepts. The actual rules can be complex, and highly varied from one jurisdiction to the next. For a more rigorous discussion of the approaches being followed in selected international jurisdictions, see Millar (2007).
19 For discussion of the issues and approaches, see OECD (2004).
20 For example, such rebates are provided under Article XXX of the EU VAT Directive.
21 See, for example, McLure (2000), Keen and Smith (2000), and Poddar (1990).
22 The PVAT mechanism, as originally developed by the authors, entailed a prepayment of the destination state VAT, before the goods are shipped. However, under a harmonized Dual GST, such prepayment may not be necessary. There would be enough safeguards in the system to enforce payment of tax on interstate supplies at the same time as on intrastate supplies.

References

Ahmad, Ehtisham. 2008. "Tax Reforms and the Sequencing of Intergovernmental Reforms in China: Preconditions for a Xiaokang Society", in Lou Jiwei and Wang Shuilin (eds), *Fiscal Reforms in China*, pp. 95–128. Washington DC: The World Bank.

Ahmad, E. and N. Stern. 1984. "The Theory of Tax reform and Indian Indirect Taxes", *Journal of Public Economics*, 25 (3): 259–98.

———. 1991. *The Theory and Practice of Tax Reforms in Developing Countries*. Cambridge: Cambridge University Press.

Ahmad, Ehtisham, Satya Poddar, A.M. Abdel-Rahman, Rick Matthews, and Christophe Waerzeggers. 2008. *Indirect Taxes for the Common Market*. Report prepared for the GCC Secretariat.

Ambrosiano, Maria Flavia and Massimo Bordignon. 2006. "Normative Versus Positive Theories of Revenue Assignments", Ehtisham Ahmad and Giorgio Brosio (eds), *Handbook of Fiscal Federalism*, pp. 306–38. UK: Edward Elgar.

Aujean, Michel, Peter Jenkins, and Satya Poddar. 1999. "A New Approach to Public Sector Bodies", *International VAT Monitor* 10 (4): 144–49.

Bagchi, Amaresh, Mahesh C. Purohit, S. Ven Katarama Iyer, O.P. Girhotra, Pawan Aggarwal, and V.L. Narayana. 1994. *Reform of Domestic Trade Taxes in India: Issues and Options*. New Delhi: National Institute of Public Finance and Policy.

Barrand, Peter. 1991. "The Treatment of Non-profit Bodies and Government Entities under the New Zealand GST", *International VAT Monitor* 1.

Bird, Richard and Pierre Gendron. 1998. "Dual VAT's and Cross-border Trade, Two Problems and One Solution", *International Tax and Public Finance*, 5(3): 429–42.

Canada Department of Finance. 1987. *Federal Sales Tax Reform*, Government of Canada Ottawa.

Empowered Committee of State Finance Ministers. 2008. *A Model and Roadmap for Goods and Services Tax in India*, New Delhi: Empowered Committee of State Finance Ministers.

Keen, Michael and Stephen Smith. 2000. "Viva VIVAT!", *International Tax and Public Finance*, 7(6): 741–51.

Kelkar, Vijay, D.C. Gupta, Vineeta Rai, N.S. Sisodia, D. Swarup, and Ashok K. Lahiri. 2004. *Report on Implementation of the Fiscal Responsibility and Budget Management Act, 2003*, Ministry of Finance, Government of India, New Delhi.

Kuo, C.Y., Tom McGirr, and Satya Poddar. 1988. "Measuring the Non-neutralities of Sales and Excise Taxes in Canada", *Canadian Tax Journal*, 38 (3): 655–70.

McLure, Charles. 2000. "Implementing Sub-national VAT's on Internal Trade: The Compensating VAT (CVAT)", *International Trade and Public Finance*, 7 (6): 723–40.

Millar, Rebecca. 2007. "Cross-Border Services—A Survey of the Issues", in Richard Krever and David White (eds), *GST in Retrospect and Prospect*, pp. 317–47. New Zealand: Brookers Ltd.

OECD. 2004. "Report on the Application of Consumption Taxes to the Trade in International Services and Intangibles", Center for Tax Policy and Administration, OECD.

Poddar, Satya. 1990. "Options for VAT at the State Level", in M. Gillis, C.S. Shoup, and G. Sicat, (eds), *Value Added Taxation in Developing Countries*, pp. 104–12. Washington DC: World Bank.

———. 2003. "Consumption Taxes, The Role of the Value Added Tax", in Patrick Honohan (ed.) *Taxation of Financial Intermediation: Theory and Practice In Emerging Economies*, Washington DC: World Bank and the Oxford University Press.

———. 2007. "VAT on Financial Services—Searching for a Workable Compromise", in Richard Krever and David White (eds). *GST in Retrospect and Prospect*, pp. 179–204. New Zealand: Brookers Ltd.

———. 2009. "Treatment of Housing under VAT", mimeograph, presented at the conference on VAT organized by the American Tax Policy Institute, Washington, Feb. 18–19, 2009.

Poddar, Satya and Amaresh Bagchi. 2007. "Revenue-Neutral Rate for GST", *The Economic Times*, New Delhi, November 15, 2007.

Poddar, Satya and Nancy Harley. 1989. "Problems in Moving from a Flawed to a Neutral and Broad-Based Consumption Tax", *Australian Tax Forum*, 6(3).

Poddar, S. and M. English. 1997. "Taxation of Financial Services under a Value-Added Tax: Applying the Cash-Flow Method", *National Tax Journal*, 50 (1): 89–111.

Poddar, Satya, and Eric Hutton. 2001. "Zero-Rating of Inter-State Sales Under a Sub-national VAT: A New Approach", Paper presented at the National Tax Association, 94th Annual Conference on Taxation, Baltimore, November 8–10, 2001.

Rao, M. Govinda. 2001. *Report of the Expert Group on Taxation of Services*. New Delhi: Government of India.

———. 2008. "Unfinished Reform Agendum: Fiscal Consolidation and Reforms—A Comment", in Jagdish Bhagwati and Charles W. Colomiris (eds), *Sustaining India's Growth Miracle*, pp. 104–14. USA: Columbia Business School.

5

Normative Framework of Fiscal Federalism for Economies in Transition

M. Govinda Rao

—— •✦• ——

I Introduction

This chapter deals with the challenges of fiscal federalism in planned economies. The discussion on fiscal federalism in the mainstream literature refers to decentralization and not federalism per se. The benefits attributed to and costs associated with fiscal federalism refer to decentralization.[1] In fact, fiscal federalism is supposed to deal with all multilevel fiscal systems, irrespective of whether the system is federal or unitary. As stated by Oates (1977: 4):

> ...the term federalism for the economist is not to be understood in a narrow constitutional sense. In economic terms, all governmental systems are more or less federal; even in a formally unitary system, for example, there is typically a considerable extent of de facto fiscal discretion at decentralized levels.

Thus, the analysis in this chapter refers to multilevel fiscal systems in all planned economies irrespective of whether they are formally unitary or federal.

The discussion in the chapter relates to planned economies. Of course, centralized planning is negation of federalism. In centrally planned economies, the decisions on prices, outputs, and allocation of resources are taken by the central planner; here, neither the market nor the sub-national governments have any role in resource allocation. The sub-national governments simply implement the functions assigned to them as agents of the central government. However, most of the centrally planned economies have made, and are making a transition from command to market, and in some countries, planned development strategy has historically co-existed with market-determined resource allocation. In economies that followed central planning strategy for a long time, even as they make a transition to the market, the vestiges of planning continue to impact resource allocations, and institutions of market are yet to be developed fully. They impact through controls over prices, outputs, inputs, impediments to free movement of factors and products and above all, lumpiness of past investments persist altering both sectoral and regional resource allocations in ways different from the market or their endowments. In the context, the norms of inter-governmental finance developed in the context of developed market economies need to be modified.

The normative framework on fiscal federalism has two major shortcomings: first, much of the mainstream literature takes a Benthamite view that governments are benevolent despots and do everything to counter market failures. Second, the normative framework in this body of literature has been developed in the context of developed market economies. The normative framework on intergovernmental fiscal arrangements, developed in the context of advanced market economies, will have to be considerably modified to take account of the special characteristics, institutions, and problems of developing and transitional economies.

The objective of the present paper is to identify the salient features of developing and planned economies impacting intergovernmental fiscal arrangements, and to suggest modifications in the policies and institutions. Section II summarizes the normative framework in the existing fiscal federalism literature. Section III brings out the specific characteristics of planned developing economies having an impact on resource allocation. Section IV discusses the impact of planning on interregional resource flows in developing countries and identifies the areas requiring particular attention, reforming fiscal decentralization policies and institutions in these economies. Section V summarizes the major conclusions.

II Fiscal Federalism: The Normative Framework

Fiscal federalism is considered to be an optimal institutional framework for the provision of public services. The idea stems from the observation of Alexis de Tocqueville, more than a century ago, "The federal system was created with the intention of combining the different advantages which result from the magnitude and littleness of nations" (1980, Vol. 1: 163). The critical issue, therefore, is to map the functions with different levels of government to meet diverse preferences of people on the one hand, and reap economies of scale in the provision of the services on the other. The optimality in Tiebout's world is reached, as the footloose consumers "vote on their feet" to choose the bundle of public goods and tax payments (Tiebout, 1956). Even when the consumers do not have footloose mobility and therefore, cannot effectively vote on their feet, optimality is achieved as fiscal differentials are capitalized in terms of market values of properties (Oates, 1969). Alternatively, the median voter exercises his "voice" to choose the public service: tax mix to maximize welfare gains.

The superiority of fiscal federalism, in efficient provision of public services is characterized by the "decentralization theorem". The theorem states:

> ...in the absence of cost savings from the centralized provision of a (local public) good and of inter-jurisdictional externalities, the level of welfare will always be at least as high (and typically higher) if Pareto-efficient levels of consumption are provided in each jurisdiction, than *any single, uniform* level of consumption is maintained across all jurisdictions. (Italics added; Oates, 1972: 54)

Notably, in this formulation, the lower efficiency is due to uniform provision of public services and not due to centralization per se. Nevertheless, ability of the centralized system in meeting diverse preferences is limited by informational and political constraints, and hence, the superiority of fiscal decentralized provision of public services (Oates, 1999).

The assignment system in the normative framework necessarily results in vertical imbalances. For efficiency reasons, all broad-based taxes are assigned to the Center and most expenditure functions are assigned to sub-national levels, and therefore, vertical imbalance is unavoidable, and the intergovernmental transfer system has to resolve the imbalance. This is also because redistribution and stabilization functions are considered to be mainly the functions of Central government, and allocation function is considered to be predominantly in the domain of the sub-national governments. While the matching of revenue and expenditure decisions at the sub-national level, as far as possible is important, the efficient system of assignment envisages that tax powers should be assigned to sub-national levels, to the point where the marginal efficiency loss due to sub-national levy is matched with marginal efficiency gain from fiscal autonomy.

The objective of the transfer system in this framework is to offset the imbalance between the assignment of revenues and expenditures at central and sub-national levels, and interjurisdictional mobility of persons ensures efficiency in the system. The rationale for horizontal transfers in this case is purely for equity reasons, to offset the fiscal disabilities arising from lower-than-stipulated revenue capacity, and higher unit cost of providing public services. Such transfers are also considered to improve efficiency in resource allocation, particularly when interjurisdictional mobility of labor does not equalize the capital-labor ratio, across regions.

Thus, the case for horizontal equalization in intergovernmental transfers rests mainly on equity grounds. Differences in the capacity to raise revenues and unit cost of providing public services among sub-national jurisdictions create different "fiscal residuum" or net fiscal benefits (Buchanan, 1950). The problem is exacerbated when there are origin-based taxes, and similar other factors alter the net fiscal benefits in different sub-national jurisdictions (Boadway and Flatters, 1982). Horizontal equity is established by giving unconditional transfers, so that all sub-national units are enabled to provide a given normative level of public service, at a given tax price.

The debate on the issue of whether the horizontal equalization transfers are efficiency enhancing or involve efficiency cost is an issue that has remained unresolved.[2] In a static sense, if the productivity of investments reflects endowment of resources, the transfers to poor regions reduce the overall productivity and hence, are efficiency reducing. In contrast, if the low productivity in disadvantaged regions is because of the scarcity of public capital (social and physical infrastructure), then we have the case where both equity and efficiency objectives are complementary. In other words, if the public spending from the transfers in fiscally disadvantaged jurisdictions result in generalized externalities and enhance the productivity of capital, the equitable transfers are efficiency enhancing.

The efficiency reason for intergovernmental transfers arises from spillovers. The assignment system, however done, does not match with the geographical boundaries of the jurisdictions, and spillovers have to be resolved thorough the transfer system. Alternatively, some of the functions assigned to the sub-national governments have significant nation-wide externalities and therefore, it is necessary to ensure minimum levels of such services for reasons of efficiency. Open-ended specific purpose transfer with matching requirements is supposed to ensure efficiency on this account.

In the actual design of the transfer system, there are serious operational questions, which cannot be resolved easily. The first has to deal with the proper combination of conditional and unconditional transfers. The second issue has to deal with the extent of horizontal and vertical distribution. There is no unambiguous way to measure the degree of vertical imbalance, and the extent of violation of horizontal equity. With regard to specific purpose transfers it is impossible to measure the degree of externalities to work out optimal cost sharing arrangements or matching ratios. Finally, even if some approximations on fiscal disabilities and matching ratios are made, the actual transfer system in any country would have to take into account the many non-economic objectives, including political objectives. Therefore the actual transfer system, differs from the ideal. Nevertheless, the attempt should be to approach the ideal, both in designing it and in its evaluations.

The departures from the above mentioned normative framework are seen mainly in the political economy approaches, which question the welfare-maximizing objective of governments. These behavioral and institutional approaches have provided new insights and helped in better understanding of the multi-level fiscal systems. Thus, Prodh'omme (1995) questions the superiority of decentralization over centralized provision of public services, but his conclusions are judgmental and not logically argued out. In a more rigorous and meaningful analysis, Bardhan and Mookherjee (2000) show that the fiscal decentralization is gainful, only if the elite capture at local level is less than it is at the central level. As stated by Bardhan (2002: 194), "Even though the extent of relative capture of governments at different levels is crucial in understanding the likely impact of decentralization initiatives, there has been very little work on the subject, either theoretical or empirical". Similarly, Breton (2002) discusses several cases of decentralization failure, which basically arise from behavioral assumptions made in the analysis. These analyses generally bring out the dissatisfaction with the mainstream analysis, in its ability to address the fiscal decentralization issues in the more realistic institutional contexts.

There are a variety of reasons to modify the fiscal federalism analysis available in the mainstream literature before it is applied to the multi-level fiscal systems in developing and transitional countries. This is because developing countries have a predominant primary sector, co-existence of a large traditional sector with low market penetration and a small modern sector, segmented labor markets, low level of savings and investment, imperfect competition with significant trade distortions, and scarcity of foreign exchange. The adoption of planned development strategy in them has further distorted the markets (Newbery, 1987). It is not appropriate to uncritically apply the normative framework of fiscal federalism to address policy issues in such countries. Second, most of these economies have adopted planning in a mixed economy framework. In some, which have chosen to make a transition from centralized planning to market-based resource allocation, the vestiges of planning continue to influence resource allocation outcomes. Developmental planning adopted by developing countries in the past and the vestiges of centralized planning in the economies making a transition from planning to market do influence the fiscal federalism outcomes and therefore, need to be analyzed in greater detail. As stated by Oates (1999: 1145):

> While the existing literature in fiscal federalism can provide some general guidance, ... my sense is that most of us working in the field feel more than a little uneasy when proffering advice on many of the decisions that must be made on vertical fiscal and political structure. We have much to learn.

III Planning and Federalism

The success of the Soviet economy in achieving rapid progress by adopting centralized planning strategy had led many developing countries in the world to adopt planned strategy for investment allocation with heavy reliance on the public sector in the 1950s and the 1960s. While the Soviet Union itself and similar socialist countries adopted centralized planning, many other developing countries such as India and Pakistan adopted a planned development strategy with coexisting private and public sectors. The nature and operation of vertical public sectors in these countries vastly differs from market economies. It is important to understand the salient characteristics of these countries having a bearing on the assignment system as well as interregional resource flows. When many of the instruments of planning create interregional resource transfers which often are invisible, it is difficult to take them into account in the explicit transfer systems. In this section, some important characteristics of the planned economies with implications for assignment of taxes and expenditures, on the one hand, and creating invisible transfers, on the other, are highlighted.

The rapid progress achieved in the initial years after the Bolshevik revolution led many developing countries to adopt the Soviet-style economic planning. These included the countries of the Soviet block and similar other socialist countries, including China and Vietnam. With all investments centrally directed, the sub-national units in these countries were merely de-concentrated implementing agencies of the Center. The absence of property rights rendered the role of taxing properties, incomes, and wealth largely irrelevant in these fiscal systems. With public enterprises taking a pivotal role to generate resources for investment, the location of these enterprises determined the pattern of regional development. Furthermore, often, the difference between government proper and public enterprises in the provision of public services gets blurred in these economies, as many enterprises are directed to provide public services such as schools and hospitals. In general, there is a soft budget constraint, particularly at sub-national levels. The closed nature of these economies takes away the role of competition altogether. In these economies, the advantages arising from the "magnitude" and "littleness" of nations, attributed to federations by Alexis de Tocqueville over a century ago, does not simply accrue. In these economies, there is no meaningful role for the sub-national governments. As stated by Chelliah (1991: 7), "Comprehensive central planning, involving as it does, centralized decision making in relation to production activities and disposal of resources in the 'national interest' is the negation of the principle of true federalism."

The perverse incentives and institutional weaknesses in socialist economies made them inherently unsustainable. It is precisely for this reason that economic federalism fails in centrally planned economies (Inman and Rubinfeld, 1997). The inherent contradictions of the system led to the collapse of the pure centrally planned socialist regimes. There has been a dramatic reform in not only in Central and Eastern Europe, but also in large Asian countries with strong socialist persuasion such as China and Vietnam. The most notable features of reform in these countries are privatization and restoration of the role of markets, opening up of the economies, and decentralization (Bird, Ebel, and Wallich, 1995). The three features are complementary and reinforce each other to make a transition from command to market economy.

Although considerable progress has been made in each of these areas, these economies function in a relatively centralized institutional environment. These countries are in transition, and planning in some form or the other, and continue to coexist with market-based resource allocation. Further, the vestiges of planning and command economy in these economies continue to impact on resource allocation, with important implications for fiscal federalism. These include the continued use of administered prices as an instrument of resource allocation, prevalence of soft budget constraints, contingent liabilities and fiscal risk associated with physical restrictions and impediments to internal trade, restrictions on the mobility of labor and capital, and finally, the historically given spread of physical infrastructure and stock of capital invested in state enterprises.

The transition from command to market economy has impacted on the finances of sub-national governments in a variety of ways. Central governments, in their attempts to contain fiscal imbalances, often push the deficits down. While some countries, notably Vietnam, accomplished almost six percentage point reduction in expenditure-GDP ratio over the period 1990–94 to reduce the inflation rate from a three digit number to a single digit level, the general approach has been to reduce transfer to local governments, while keeping the functional assignment unchanged. This has led to either declining standards in public service provision, as in Russia or in countries with a tradition of soft budget constraints, accumulation of arrears and contingent liabilities as in China (World Bank, 2002) and Hungary (Bird, Ebel, and Wallich, 1995). The Central government continues to play the dominant role in resource allocation, and this is true of countries such as Russia that have adopted formally federal constitutions. Thus, in transitional economies, sub-national governments are yet to acquire a meaningful role in the provision of public services. In particular, no country has assigned any broad-based revenue sources to sub-national governments. Local governments have little autonomy in expenditure decisions.

The second category of economies in which planning has impacted on fiscal federalism are those which have adopted development planning, as a strategy to accelerate growth in a public sector dominated mixed economy framework. The countries such as India and Pakistan fall into this category. The low levels of saving and investment, existence of poor infrastructure and absence of industrial base combined with export pessimism, motivated these countries to channel available savings to priority areas of investment. In a mixed economy, this had to be achieved by assigning "commanding heights" to the public sector, and the private investments had to be channeled into priority areas, through a system of industrial licensing. Elimination of domestic competition was combined with high degree of protection, through a combination of physical restrictions on imports and very high tariffs, to eliminate external competition altogether. As this could lead to large monopolies and highly skewed distribution of incomes and wealth, various legislations to control restrictive trade practices on the one hand and confiscatory levels of taxation on the other were introduced.

Thus, fiscal policy in planned economies, in a mixed economy framework, was designed to (a) finance investment by raising the level of domestic saving, especially public saving; (b) transfer household savings to public investment; (c) reduce inequalities in income and wealth; and (d) aid in social engineering of the volume and direction of economic activity (Bagchi and Nayak, 1994). The way in which fiscal policies were calibrated in these large economies had significant impact on the operation of multi-level fiscal systems. In particular, while the size and diversity of such economies required a significant fiscal decentralization, the adoption of planned development strategy called a high degree of centralization, in both fiscal. and financial systems. In virtually all these economies, economic liberalization in recent years has loosened the grip of planning and has brought in significant changes. However, the legacies of the past policies and structure of institutions continue to impact the operation of the multi-level fiscal system.

The above discussion shows that planning in both centrally planned economies making a transition to the market and those with mixed economy framework has impacted the nature and functioning of fiscal federalism. While, as mentioned earlier, many of the economies have decided to increase fiscal decentralization, alongside making a transition to the market, the reform issues will have to cover many areas not covered in the normative framework, but put forward in the mainstream literature. It is therefore important to understand the implications of planning on fiscal federalism for designing an agenda for reform in these countries.

IV Development Planning and Fiscal Federalism

This section discusses the implications of the adoption of the strategy of investment planning in developing and transitional economies on fiscal federalism, and eventually on the efficiency and equity in the delivery of public services in these economies. As mentioned earlier, despite the progress achieved in fiscal decentralization, privatization and freeing of product and factor markets, the autarchic fiscal system, and the institutions set up to implement the systems continue to impact the functioning of multi-level fiscal operations in these economies in a variety of ways. Some of the important implications of planning on fiscal federalism are discussed in the following sections.

Impact of Planning on Budgeting Systems

The development planning strategy has had important implications on the way in which investment budgets are determined in developing and transitional economies. In India, for example, the process has resulted in the segmentation of both Central and state budgets into "plan" and "non-plan". While in principle, the expenditure on new schemes is supposed be classified as plan, those incurred for the maintenance of the completed schemes is considered non-plan. Thus, spending classified as plan does not necessarily represent investment expenditures. This segmented budgeting practice has prevented a holistic approach to the provision of public services. The emphasis on having larger plans at the state level has resulted in three important outcomes. First, the states have made larger allocations to plans without paying attention to the maintenance of assets such as roads, bridges, and irrigation works, which are in their domain. Second, competing claims for scarce resources and eagerness to take up a large number of schemes have led to spreading the resources thinly with significant cost and time over-runs. Finally, the need to increase the plan size has led to raising resources by the state governments without much regard to their distortionary implications (Rao, 2002).

The most important aspect of the planning process, in a country such as India, is the segmentation of the budget into plan and non-plan categories, and this has led to the separation of the transfer system for plan and non-plan purposes. Both the streams are general purpose transfers intended to offset fiscal disabilities, but are distributed on the basis of different and, often, conflicting criteria. The separate mechanisms employed to determine plan and non-plan transfers have led to the states adopting strategies with adverse incentives to fiscal management, besides inequity and inefficiency in the delivery of public services.[3]

In many of the transitional economies, such as Vietnam, Laos, and China too, the investment budget is determined differently from the recurring budget. The investment budget is determined by a combination of bottom-up and top-down processes, with the Central governments eventually including only a small fraction of the projects demanded by the local governments. The process distorts the prioritization, causes underfunding, and time and cost over-runs. In these countries too, segmented treatment of investment and recurrent expenditures have prevented a holistic view and strategy of their budgets.

In transitional and developing economies, rationalizing the budgeting systems is an important component of reform agenda. As the economies decentralize their fiscal systems further, it is important to have a comparable and uniform system, proper process of determining the budgets, internal and external control mechanisms. Many transitional countries still do not have uniform budget codes and nomenclature. In many of these countries, the accounting system is highly centralized, which does not enable decentralized expenditure management; the treasury control is not effective and external control through independent audit does not exist. Besides being weak, the reporting systems from line ministries and local governments are not standardized. The countries such as Vietnam, Cambodia, and Laos follow the erstwhile French system of budget classification, just as countries such as India, Pakistan, and Bangladesh follow the Anglo-Saxon tradition. In these countries, considerable effort is needed to change over to the GFS classification system. In most socialist countries, budget was traditionally considered a secret document. Reforms in the systems of budgeting and reporting are extremely important as these economies decentralize their fiscal systems further.

Commanding State Enterprises: Implications on the Fiscal Federalism

An important feature of the planned economies is the lead role played by state enterprises in economic activities. In these economies, resource mobilization is done through state enterprise profits. Thus, the volume and pattern of resource mobilization is determined by the way in which public sector prices are administratively determined. With economic liberalization and opening up of the economy, the revenue importance of state enterprises declines. Besides, as taxes replace public enterprise profits, it has different implications for relative prices and allocative efficiency.

The predominance of state enterprises, and its declining role with market-based liberalization, has important implications for fiscal federalism. Mobilizing resources through public enterprise profits rather than taxes has different implications for the assignment of revenue sources to central and sub-national governments. In many planned fiscal systems, sub-national governments derive significant revenues from the state enterprises owned by them, and as the economy is liberalized, the sub-national taxes have to be developed. However, assignment of taxes in most of the planned economies to local governments is meager; though in planned democratic federations such as the Indian state governments collect almost 37 percent of their total revenues from own sources. In many of these economies, realty markets are not well developed, property owners are a powerful elite, and obviously property taxes do not contribute much to the revenues of local governments. Thus, in many of the transitional economies, inability to substitute declining revenues from local state enterprises with local taxes can reduce fiscal autonomy of local governments.

The impact of declining state enterprise revenues on fiscal decentralization is generally seen in both reducing enterprise revenues and reducing transfers to sub-national governments. In most transitional economies, the sub-national governments get significant revenues from state enterprises under their control and vanishing revenues mainly due to the inability of these enterprises to face greater competition in a liberalized open environment increase their fiscal dependence. Reduction in state enterprise revenues, if not compensated by increasing tax revenues, can increase the deficits. One probable result of this is to push the deficits down by transferring expenditure responsibilities to sub-national governments. Thus, in Hungary, the responsibility for welfare expenditures and social safety net was transferred to localities in 1993. In Russia, the central government transferred social expenditures amounting to 6 percent of GDP to localities, and in the next year transferred the responsibility for important national investments to sub-national governments (Bird, Ebel, and Wallich, 1995).

The consequence of pushing down the functions, without adequate devolution of finances in countries such as India, is reduction of the standards of public services or subnational governments or increase in revenues from undesirable revenue sources without any regard for efficiency. The state and local governments in India, for example, are known to raise revenues from residence-based and distortionary taxes, which has created impediments to internal trade, and violated the principle of common market (Rao, 2002). This can also lead to build up of expenditure backlog and arrears in payments as seen in Bulgaria, Romania, Russia, and Ukraine, or undesirable borrowing as in the case of Budapest and Russia's oblasts (Bird, Ebel, and Wallich, 1995: 25).

Public enterprise revenues of sub-national governments can be an important source of distortion and inequity. In the case of commodities, that are relatively inelastic with respect to prices, sales outside the jurisdictions results in the collection of monopoly profits from the non-residents and this is akin to interjurisdictional tax exportation. The subnational governments tend to adopt the strategy of charging low prices to attract diversion of trade in respect of commodities which are price elastic to expand business activities within their jurisdictions, and charge high prices in respect of commodities with low price elasticity, to collect more revenue from non-residents.

An important outcome of the public enterprise activity is the off-budget financing of public services. In many economies, with a strong presence of state enterprises, the enterprises are made to provide many public services such as running of schools, hospitals, housing, and construction of maintenance of roads and bridges. Although with privatization, these activities had to be transferred to sub-national governments, in many countries, enterprises continue to finance public service provision to a considerable extent. The use of extra-budgetary sources to finance public services is particularly significant at local levels. In China, for example, it is estimated that the off-budget financing of expenditures in 1996 was estimated at over 20 percent of GDP. This included uncompensated quasi-fiscal expenditures of enterprises on various public services (World Bank, 2000; Wong, 1999). In Russia, local tax offices permit illegal tax breaks to firms setting up their own kindergartens and providing other social services. Similarly, in Bulgaria, the state enterprises play an important role in health, education, infrastructure, and culture (Jorge, 1995).

Another important implication of the public enterprises is the way they have been used to soften the budget constraints at sub-national levels. In many countries, the local bond market is yet to be developed, and borrowing from the financial system involves considerable contingent liabilities. In India, acute fiscal difficulties by the state governments have led them to use the state enterprises as conduits to undertake additional borrowing and soften the budget constraint (Rao, 2001). Thus, an outcome of the predominant public sector has been to add significant contingent liabilities and fiscal risk to sub-national governments in planned economies.

In most developing and planned economies, government plays an important role in production and distribution activities, through its enterprises. It is generally presumed that when the production and distribution activities are controlled by the government, it is not necessary to put the regulatory system in place, as these enterprises are supposed to be aware of the social responsibilities. As much of the economic activities are run under public monopoly situations, there is no need to have a regulatory system to ensure fair competition. However, as these enterprises are privatized and market discipline is introduced, introducing effective regulatory system becomes imperative.

Developing Sub-national Tax System

An important feature of the plan development strategy seen in both developing and transitional economies is the determination of prices according to the government fiat rather than the market principles. This is a part of the public sector-dominated import substituting strategy. The consequence of this has been that the allocation of resources, both between different industries and regions in these economies, are markedly different if the prices were market determined. These administered prices have important implications for both efficiency and equity in a multilevel fiscal system.

The most important local tax that needs to be developed to strengthen fiscal decentralization is the local property tax in these countries. In order to develop property tax as a significant contributor to local revenues, it is important to establish clear property rights and develop legal and regulatory systems.[4] In many socialist countries, such as Vietnam and China, assignment of property rights and development of a legal system are still in transition. In India, property rights have been assigned and legal institutions exist. But often, the records are not properly maintained and vestiges of planned regime—rent control act, urban land ceiling act—continue to plague rationalization of the property tax system. Also, the property owning class as a pressure group in a local government can be a formidable hindrance to the development of a modern property tax system.

Substituting the administered prices with taxes is a major reform agenda in many planned economies. This changes the revenue assignment system, for, in many transitional economies, the sub-national governments do not have tax powers, and enterprise income has to be substituted by transfers. Some countries such as Romania still assign local enterprise taxes to sub-national governments, and in some others local governments stake "source entitlement" claim. Nevertheless, by and large, the substitution of administered prices with taxes has been to centralize tax collections. On the one hand, the move to decentralize functions has resulted in greater expenditure responsibilities and on the other, substitution of enterprise income with taxes leads to centralization of tax powers. The prime example of this is in China, where after recentralization of tax powers in 1994, the fiscal dependence of the sub-national governments have significantly increased.

Meaningful fiscal decentralization requires significant sub-national taxing powers. Linking tax and expenditure decisions at the margin is critical to ensuring expenditure efficiency and accountability. At present, in most transitional economies, local governments do not have significant tax powers. Even when they are given some tax powers, the sub-national governments have shown general reluctance to raise revenues from the sources assigned to them. In countries such as India, decentralization in tax powers is only up to the state level (Rao, Amar Nath, and Vani, 2004). Even so, the states levy a host of inefficient taxes, including a cascading type sales tax and tax on the interstate sale. Below the state level, even in urban areas, the property tax is not well developed and this has led the local governments to levy inefficient taxes, such as the tax on the entry of goods (octroi) into local areas.

There is much to be done in assigning appropriate tax bases and developing tax administration in these economies. Despite the claim that the local level provides incentive for revenue collections by increasing tax compliance, the experiences of a number of socialist countries such as Russia, China, and Laos have shown that tax compliance will actually decline when the tax collection is decentralized. It is therefore important to pay attention to the design of decentralization in these economies as they make a transition to the market.

Substituting Physical Controls with Market-based Instruments

An important feature, characterizing the three transitional economies, is the prevalence of price and quantity controls. With market-based liberalization and opening up of these economies, price (including interest rate) and quantity controls will have to give way to monetary and fiscal policy instruments. Disbanding command and control systems associated with Soviet style planning, and replacing them with fiscal and regulatory instruments, calls for changes in the decentralization system as well. In most of these economies, some controls over prices have continued, even though most of the commodities are subject to market discipline.

Removal of Impediments to Internal Trade and Mobility

There are a number of other controls and regulations introduced, as a part of planning process. These have created serious impediments to the movement of factors and products within the federation. Thus, a major advantage of fiscal federalism of enabling a nationwide common market while allowing for diversity in preferences is negated. The impediments have been erected to serve the needs of planning, or the rationing, to meet the scarcity situations. These have imposed several hindrances to the movement of factors and products across the country. Thus, there are restrictions on the movement of labor and capital, and restrictions on the movement of products from one region of the country to another. There are also cases where physical barriers are placed on the movement of commodities from one place to another within the country. In many socialist countries, such as China and Vietnam, migration from one region to another and often from rural to urban areas is prohibited, resulting in a large number of illegal migrants without proper access to basic services in fringes of major cities. In many countries, the easiest way to collect revenues is by erecting barriers on highways and arterial roads and collecting (often illegal) taxes. Besides, in countries like India, a poor information base has led to erection of checkpoints at several places to facilitate tax collections. Thus, there are checkpoints for administering sales taxes, state excises on alcoholic products, taxes on motor vehicles, to check the exploitation of forest products, besides police checkpoints. These have been erected not only on state borders but also inside the states. In addition, there are taxes on the entry of goods into local area (Octroi) for which separate checkpoints are erected by the municipalities.

Despite reduced emphasis on the plan and change in scarcity conditions over the years, a number of fiscal and regulatory impediments have continued in most developing and transitional economies. Besides physical controls, there are also fiscal impediments with unintended allocative consequences. Removal of impediments to ensure free movement of factors and products throughout the country is necessary to improve competitiveness, and this will be an important challenge in transitional economies of Asia. An important advantage of federalism is the access to large common markets and in most planned economies, this is not realized.

Balanced Regional Development, Interregional Inequity and Invisible Transfers

In planned economies, there are two explicit ways by which regional allocation of resources is generally brought about. First, the central government's own investment in different regions or regional policy pursued by it determines the level of economic activity and the private sector resource flow. Central investment in infrastructure in different regions determines the flow of private investments. In most planned economies, a variety of policy instruments, such as controls and prices and output, investment patterns, intergovernmental transfers, and Central government's own spending pattern in different regions, alters the resource allocations in unintended ways. Interestingly, often, despite the claims about balanced regional developments, the investment decisions are taken on political considerations, that is, on the basis of bargaining powers and political influence of different regions. In India, for example, despite a lot of emphasis given to regional equity, as on March 2002, four high income states with a population of 29.5 percent and generating state domestic product of 34 percent, accounted for 22.1 percent of investments and

31.6 percent of employment in Central enterprises. In contrast, five low income states with a population of 44.7 percent and generating income of 28.4 percent of the country, accounted for only 26 percent of investments and 42.1 percent of employment. Thus, often, the claims made on balanced regional development are more rhetoric than reality. Interestingly, even as large investments were made in steel plants in the state, with large deposits of manganese and coal in Bihar, Madhya Pradesh, Orissa, and West Bengal, the forward linkages from these large investments were nullified by having "freight equalization policy"—policy of subsidizing freight charges to equalize the prices of steel across the country.

The second explicit method of impacting on regional resource allocation is through intergovernmental transfers. In some socialist planned economies, the expenditure assignment is delegated or de-concentrated, and the transfers are given mainly to carry out these functions. However, in large countries, fiscal decentralization is a reality. However, even in these economies, the determination of the volume and design of the transfer system are important reform issues. In most countries, the transfer system is negotiated. There is no objective mechanism to determine the volume of transfers, nor are there any distribution formulae. In many countries, transfers are determined in the process of determining budgets. This includes Hungary, Poland, and even Vietnam. In the last case, actually, norms are built into the determination of expenditures (Rao, 2003). In Russia until 1994, the ex-post subventions are negotiated between deficit regions and the Ministry of Finance with serious incentive problems. Institution of a rule-based transfer system is an important challenge in these countries.

In India, the Constitution itself provides a mechanism for determining the transfer system. The Finance Commission appointed by the President every five years is supposed to determine the total tax devolution and grants as well as their distribution among various states. The functioning of the Finance Commission, however, has left much to be desired. The Commissions, in effect, follow the 'gap-filling' approach with serious disincentives for fiscal management. In addition, with the emergence of the Planning Commission as an institution determining the resource allocation of the public sector, a parallel transfer system was developed to meet plan expenditure requirements. Both Planning and Finance Commissions give unconditional transfers, and the Planning Commission, in addition, channels Central government loans to state governments. In addition to these agencies, individual ministries give specific purpose transfers.

The most important issue, in both developing planned economies and transitional economies with a strong plan legacy, is that considerable improvements need to be made in the transfer systems. Negotiated transfer system and those with significant disincentives to fiscal management has to be replaced by a formula-based system to offset fiscal disabilities. Further, the institutional mechanism to devolve the transfer system needs to be evolved to make the system objective and transparent.

In addition to regional policies and intergovernmental transfers, there are various sources of implicit interregional transfers, which alter resource allocation across regions. One source of such transfers is various price and quantity controls. Administered determination of prices and quantities determines the profitability of different industries and depending on the resource endowments, different regions. Another important source of implicit transfer is the collection of revenues from origin-based taxes and consequent interregional tax exportation. Origin-based tax system and cascading type of taxes can cause significant interregional resource transfers. These economies are characterized by oligopolistic markets and with mark-up pricing situation; the producing sub-national units collect significant revenues from the consumers in consuming units. In the Indian case, the implicit transfers estimated from subsidized lending to states significantly eroded the progress of explicit transfers in India during the period 1985–95 (Rao, 1997).

Distortions and Inequity

Planned economies through their various policy instruments, to control the resource allocation, introduce several sources of distortion and inequity. Thus, the fiscal federalism in these countries ceases to be efficient institutional arrangement. The distortions are introduced due to the way in which the budgets are formulated, prices are determined through administered mechanisms, and impediments are placed on internal trade and on the movement of commodities and factors of production. Most of the planned economies are making a transition to more market-oriented decentralized systems. However, until the transition is complete, the multi-level fiscal arrangements will have to take these distortions and inequity into account in formulating their federal fiscal policies.

V Concluding Remarks

The chapter argues that the normative framework developed in the mainstream literature on fiscal federalism in the context of advanced market economies needs to be modified to take these special features of developing and transitional economies into account. While there is some literature that considers the more realistic objective function of maximization of returns by individual government agents rather than the usual Benthamite social welfare maximization, and this has provided significant insights, but this chapter does not pretend to provide such an analysis. It merely attempts to examine the special features of planned economies casting shadows on the federal fiscal arrangements and indicate the areas where mainstream literature on fiscal federalism needs modification.

The chapter identifies a number of areas where the planned development strategy can impact on fiscal federalism. Of course, Central planning is the negation of federalism. However, virtually all economies have made a transition from command economy to market-based resource allocation, but vestiges of planning continue to impact resource allocation. Similarly, some countries have adopted planned development strategy within a mixed economy framework. The chapter analyses the impact of planning on the assignment system, overlapping in the assignments, and the implications for intergovernmental transfers arising from the planned development strategy.

There are a variety of ways in which planned development strategy affects the efficiency and equity in multi-level fiscal systems and fiscal federalism can become an optimal institutional arrangement in these countries only when significant reforms are undertaken. These include reforms in planning and budgeting practices, reforms to substitute public enterprise profits with taxes at sub-national levels, developing market-based instruments to substitute physical controls, evolving the transfer system to take into account invisible transfers, and reforms in the fiscal system to reduce distortions.

On the policy side, the scope of reforms in fiscal federalism in developing countries is much more complex and broader than merely looking at the issues in assignment and transfer systems. The reforms in fiscal federalism is inextricably intertwined with privatization, planning and budgeting, reforms in administered price mechanism, various regulations relating to the movement of factors and products, besides the issues discussed in fiscal federalism proper. Any attempt to look at the issues in isolation will make the reforms less potent and ineffective.

Notes

1 Breton (2000) distinguishes federalism from decentralization in terms of the ownership of inextinguishable constitutional powers of the levels of government.
2 In the literature, there has been considerable debate on the issue of efficiency versus equity in the transfer system. In the earlier phase, the discussion between Scott (1950) and Buchanan (1952) remained inconclusive. The controversy was revived again in the 1980s, with Boadway and Fatters (1982) arguing that the equalizing transfers are efficiency enhancing, whereas Courchene (1978) argued that there is a trade-off between equity and efficiency. The issue, however, has remained unresolved.
3 For a detailed analysis of the adverse incentives and efficiency and equity implications of the transfer systems, see Rao and Singh (2005).
4 For a detailed discussion of evolving property tax systems in transitional countries, see Malme and Youngman (2001).

References

Bagchi, Amaresh and Pulin Nayak. 1994. "A Survey of Public Finance and Planning Process", in Amaresh Bagchi and Nicholas Stern (eds), _Tax Policy and Planning in Developing Countries_, pp. 21–87. New Delhi: Oxford University Press.
Bardhan, Pranab. 2002. "Decentralization of Governance and Development", _Journal of Economic Perspectives_, 16(4): 185–205.
Bardhan, Pranab and Dilip Mookherjee. 2000. "Capture of Governance at Local and National Levels", _American Economic Review_, 90 (2): 135–39.
Bird, Richard M., Robert D. Ebel, and Christine I. Wallich (eds). 1995. _Decentralization of the Socialist State_. Washington, DC: World Bank.
Boadway, Robin and Frank Flatters. 1982. _Equalization in a Federal State_, Ottawa: Economic Council of Canada.

Breton, Albert. 1996. *Competitive Governments*. New York and Cambridge: Cambridge University Press.

———. 2000. "Federalism and Decentralization: Ownership Rights and the Superiority of Federalism", *Publius: The Journal of Federalism*, 30 (2):1–16.

———. 2002. "An Introduction to Decentralization Failure", in Ehtisham Ahmad and Giorgio Brosio (eds), *Managing Fiscal Decentralization*, pp. 31. New York and London: Routledge.

Buchanan, James M. 1950. "Federalism and Fiscal Equity", *American Economic Review*, 40 (4): 583–99.

Chelliah, R. J. 1991. *Towards a Decentralised Polity: Outline of a Proposal*, L. K. Jha Memorial Lecture, Fiscal Research Foundation, New Delhi.

Courchene, T. J. 1978. "Avenues for Adjustment: The Transfer System and Regional Disparities", in M. Walker (ed.), *Canadian Confederation at the Crossroads: The Search for Federal—Provincial Balance*, pp. 143–86. Vancouver: The Frazer Institute.

Inman, Robert and Daniel Rubenfeld. 1997. "The Political Economy of Federalism", in Dennis C. Mueller (ed.), *Perspectives on Public Choice: A Handbook*, pp. 73–105. Cambridge, New York: Cambridge University Press.

Jorge, Martinez-Vazquez. 1995. "Intergovernmental Fiscal Relations in Bulgaria", in Bird, Ebel and Wallich (eds) *Decentralization of the Socialist State*, pp. 183–222. Washington DC: World Bank.

Malme J. H. and Joan M. Youngman (eds), 2001. *The Development of Property Taxation in Economies in Transition*. Washington DC: The World Bank.

Oates, W. A. 1969. "The Effects of Property Taxes and Local Public Spending on Property Values: An Empirical Study of Tax Capitalization and Tiebout Hypothesis", *Journal of Political Economy*, 77 (6): 957–71.

———. 1972. *Fiscal Federalism*. New York: Harcourt, Brace and Jovanovich.

———. 1977. 'An Economist's Perspective of Fiscal Federalism' in Wallace E. Oates (ed.), *Political Economy of Fiscal Federalism*, pp. 3–20. Mass: Heath-Lexington.

Oates, Wallace E. 1999. "An Essay on Fiscal Federalism", *Journal of Economic Literature*, XXXVII (3): 1120–49.

Prud'homme, Remy. 1995. "On the Dangers of Decentralization", *World Bank Research Observer*, 10 (2): 201–10.

Rao, M. Govinda. 1997. "Invisible Transfers in Indian Federation", *Public Finance/Finances Publiques*, 52 (3): 299–316.

———. 2001. "State Finances in India", *Economic and Political Weekly*, 37 (31): 3261–71.

———. 2002. "Dynamics of Indian Federalism", paper presented at the Conference on Indian Economic Reforms, Center for Economic Development and Policy Reform, Stanford University, Standford, June 6–7.

———. 2003. "Challenge of Fiscal decentralization in Developing anhd Transitional Economies: An Asian Perspective", in Jorge Maritnez-Vazquez and James Alm (eds) *Public Finance in Developing and Transitional Countries* (Essays in Honhour of Richard Bird), pp. 35–62. Cheltenham and Northanmpton, MA: Edward Elgar.

Rao, M. Govinda, H.K. Amar Nath and B.P. Vani. 2004. "Rural Fiscal Decentralization in Karnataka" in Geetha Sethi (ed.) *Fiscal Decentralization to Local Governments*, 43–84. New Delhi: Oxford University Press for World Bank.

Rao, M. Govinda and Nirvikar Singh. 2005. *Political Economy of Federalism in India*, New Delhi: Oxford University Press.

Scott, A. D. 1950. "A Note on Federal Grants", *Economica*, 17 (68, November): 416–22.

Tocqueville, Alexis de. 1980. *Democracy in America*, New York: Vintage Books. First published by Random House in 1838.

Tiebout, Charles E. 1956. "A Pure Theory of Local Expenditures", *Journal of Political Economy*, 64(5): 416–24.

Wong, Christine. 1999. 'Converting Fees into Taxes: Reform of Extra-budgetary Funds and Inter-governmental Fiscal relations in China, 1999 and Beyond', paper presented at the Association of Asian Studies Meetings, Boston, Massachusetts, March 11–14.

World Bank. 2000. China: Managing Public Expenditures for Better Results, Report No. 20342–CHA, World Bank.

———. 2002. China: National Development and Sub-National Finance, World Bank Report No. 22951–CHA, World Bank.

6

Global Public Goods: Provision, Production, and Benefits

U. Sankar

——— • ✦ • ———

I Introduction

Rapid developments in transport, communication, computer, and information technologies during the last four decades have accelerated the process of globalization and made nations interconnected and interdependent. There are four kinds of developments which are global in nature. These are: (a) increase in world trade in goods and services, capital flows, and technology transfer; (b) global environmental problems such as accumulation of greenhouse gases and loss of bio-diversity; (c) spread of infectious diseases and terrorism across national borders; and (d) UN Millennium Declaration of September 2000 which enabled 189 nations to embrace a vision for a world, in which developed and developing countries would work in partnership, for the betterment of all, particularly the most disadvantaged.

Kaul et al. (2003) note that the existing institutional architecture for global governance exhibits sign of adaptive (dynamic) inefficiency, with institutional changes lagging behind rapidly evolving realities. We see manifestations of the inefficiencies in the stalemate in the WTO Doha Round trade negotiations and tensions in reaching cooperative solutions for achieving greenhouse gas emission reductions. The International Task Force on Global Public Goods, 2006, notes that ours is a world of shared risks and common opportunities, grounded in the world of mutual dependence and growing interconnection.

This chapter reviews alternative approaches to defining global public goods (GPGs) and considers problems in ensuring "public-ness" of their provision, from the perspectives of developing countries. Section II reviews three definitions of GPGs. Section III considers different ways of classifying GPGs, and their implications for provision and financing. Section IV assesses the extent to which the existing international institutional arrangements for global trading regime, climate stabilization, and conservation and sustainable use of biological diversity achieve their goals, and address the concerns of developing counties. Section V contains concluding remarks.

II Definitions of GPG

We review briefly three attempts to define public goods.

Samuelson (1954)

Even though the concept of public good is quite old in economics literature, Samuelson developed the concept in a rigorous manner. According to him, a pure public good must satisfy two features: non-rivalry in consumption and non-excludability. Non-rivalry means that consumption of the good by one person does not decrease its availability to others (for example, knowledge, defense). Non-excludability means that the good is available to all; it is impossible to exclude any one from consuming the good. Samuelson's aim was to determine the optimum mix of public and private goods based on the Pareto criterion of economic efficiency. As the marginal cost of supplying a public good is zero, economic efficiency requires that the good is supplied at zero price. As the good is available free of cost, an individual has no incentive to reveal his true preference for the good. Hence, the free rider problem arises. A limitation of the theory is that it deals only with public provision of public good and does not address the equity issue.

In this framework GPG is defined as a public good whose benefits are available globally.

World Bank, Development Committee (2000)

For the Bank's purposes, global public goods are commodities, resources, and services—and also systems of rules or policy regimes—with substantial cross-border externalities that are important for development and poverty reduction, and that can be produced in sufficient supply only through cooperation and collective action by developed and developing countries. The above definition does not mention features like non-rivalry and non-exclusion, but it is useful for a practitioner interested in funding development projects which aim at poverty reduction.

UNDP, Office of Development Studies

Kaul, Conceicau, Goulven, and Mendoza (2003) provide the following definitions of public goods:

1. Goods have a special potential for being public if they have non-excludable benefits, non-rival benefits, or both.
2. Goods are de facto public if they are non-exclusive and available for all to consume.

The first definition weakens Samuelson's definition as it requires only non-excludability or non-rivalry. The second definition does not require non-rivalry. Hence, a private good can be put in a public domain by public choice (a socially determined process) because it is a merit good, a basic need or a right. See Desai for a historical perspective (2003).

The aim of the authors is to refurbish the concept of GPG. According to them, the need arises because (a) public goods are provided by individuals, communities, nations, and via international cooperation; (b) public participation is essential in the determination of levels of the goods; (c) accrual of benefits depend on capacities and costs of access of different groups; and (d) special problems of developing countries.

They introduce the concept of "triangle of publicness", that is, publicness in consumption, publicness in decision making and publicness in distribution of net benefit. They observe that lack of publicness in decision making can weaken the technical soundness of policy choices, undermine the legitimacy and credibility of organizations, and erode the sense of public ownership, so essential for effective follow-up to international agreements. Developing countries often lack negotiation capacity and face structural adjustment and other difficulties at the implementation stage. This concept of "triangle of publicness", is used to evaluate the structure of international institutions, decision making processes, framing and enforcement of rules, and distribution of net benefits among member nations.

We prefer Samuelson's definition of public goods. However, Kaul et al.'s definition of de facto public goods is relevant, if the global community commits to provision of certain merit goods via collective action. Their concept of triangle of publicness is also useful in designing a fair institutional mechanism for the supply of GPGs.

III Classification of GPGs

GPGs can be classified on the basis of (a) their characteristics, (b) global public choice, (c) stage of production, (d) aggregation technologies, and (e) geographical range.

Characteristics

Pure GPGs satisfy the features of non-rivalry in consumption and non-excludability. Examples of pure GPGs are knowledge, ozone restoration, reduction of green house gases, biological diversity, sound trading regime, stable financial markets, and peace. All persons benefit, may be in varying degrees, depending on their capacities and preferences.

The cost of provision does not increase with the number benefited.

International cooperation and collective action are necessary to solve the free rider problem. Pure global public bads are depletion of ozone layer, accumulation of green house gases, spread of infectious diseases, global financial instability, and terrorism.

Global Choice

Goods are put in the public domain because of global consensus. Examples are poverty eradication, access to safe drinking water, access to sanitation, and compulsory primary education. The goods may be private goods, in the sense that they possess the features of rivalry and excludability, but they are put in the public domain by global community. The rationale for this choice, in individualist tradition, is based on positive externality or being a merit good or simply altruism. From the viewpoint of communitarian (German) tradition, these wants transcend individual likes and dislikes and everyone is entitled to supply of the goods. Unlike the case of pure public good, the cost of provision increases with the number covered. The target group has to be identified and full coverage of members of the target group is necessary to realize the goal.

In the UN Millennium Declaration of September 2000, leaders from 189 nations embraced a vision for the world in which developed and developing countries would work together in partnership for the betterment of all, particularly the most disadvantaged. The Millennium Development Goals (MDGs) are based on the UN Millennium Declaration, 2000. The UN General Assembly approved the goals and targets. It may be seen from Table 6.1 that most of the goods and services needed to achieve the MDGs come under the category GPG by global public choice.

Stage of Production

GPGs may be intermediate goods or final goods. A global trading regime is an intermediate GPG. Most multilateral agreements and rules are intermediate goods. The benefits will accrue to the members only if the last mile problems of access and capacity creation are solved. Universal membership is rare in many multilateral agreements and hence, non-members do not derive the benefits. MDGs such as poverty eradication are final GPGs by global public choice.

Aggregation Technologies

Sandler (2001) refers to the relationship between individual contributions and the aggregate quantity of a public good, as the aggregation technology. Earlier Hirshleifer (1983) made a distinction between weakest link and best shot technologies. Sandler considers four aggregation technologies for public supply aggregation. These technologies are weakest link, best shot, summation, and weighted sum.

1. *Weakest link technology*: In this case, the amount of the GPG consumed by each country depends on the technology of the weakest link. If a country has very poor arrangements to contain contagious diseases, then irrespective of the arrangements made by other countries the latter might suffer in the presence of porous borders delineating countries. Thus, it is essential through a system of financial disincentives and rewards to ensure the compliance of each country with certain minimum health standards. Similarly, in our age of enhanced communication network and free movement of persons across national borders, terrorist activity in one country can easily spread to other countries. Hence, terrorism is viewed as a global public bad.
2. *Best-shot technology*: In the case of this technology, the amount of the public goods received by each region/country depends upon the maximum resource contribution, which is made by a production agent. For example, assume that 10 different production agents in 10 different countries are spending money on research to discover an aids vaccine.

   Given the large monetary and time costs involved in this research, it is only the expenditure of the largest agent that might matter. This has some implications for international cooperation.

Table 6.1: Millennium Development Goals as Global Public Goods

Goal	Type of good
Eradicate extreme poverty and hunger	Merit goods, GPG by global public choice
Achieve universal primary education	Merit good, GPG by global public choice
Combat HIV/AIDS, Malaria, and other diseases	GPG
Promote gender equity and empower women	GPG
Ensure environmental sustainability Integrate the principles of SD in the country policies and reverse the loss of environmental resources Halve by 2015 the proportion of people without sustainable access to safe drinking water	GPG
By 2020 to have achieved a significant improvement in the lives of at least 100 million slum dwellers	Merit good, GPG by global public choice.
Develop a Global Partnership for Development Develop further an open, rule-based, predictable, non-discriminatory trading and financial system	GPG
Includes a commitment to good governance, development, and poverty reduction—both national and internationally	GPG, Equity
Address the special needs of the least developed/land locked countries and small developing states	Equity, GPG by global public choice

Source: Author.

It is very clear that countries must collaborate to form research consortia to tackle the pressing medical and scientific problems in this world. This will help them to gain the maximum social returns from their joint expenditure. If one country succeeds in developing the vaccine, and if it comes under intellectual property rights, then other countries would have to pay monopoly prices or get no access to the medicine. An international organization can facilitate the access on favorable terms to poor countries via compulsory licensing or other means.

3. *Summation technology:* This technology implies that the total supply of a public good is the sum of supplies by all countries. Consumption of the good might be rival or non-rival, excludable or non-excludable. But, if both the characteristics of non-rivalry and non-exclusion are present, then the action of any one country affects the well-being of other countries, and there are bound to

be certain problems of international coordination. Protection of ozone layer and climate stabilization comes under the summation technology.

4. *Weighted sum technology*: In this case, the provision of the public good received by country *i* is the weighted sum of the provisions of the public good by various countries, the weights being the proportions of the good produced by the respective countries, which are consumed by country *i*. Put very simply, the total amount of the good consumed by country *i* is the sum of the quantities provided to it by the various countries. Sulfur emissions received by a country follow this technology.

Geographic Range

Public goods can also be classified according to their geographical range or spillover area. This is the range or area over which their benefits are felt. On the basis of their range, we might classify these goods into local (benefits affecting a small locality), national (pertaining to a nation), regional (relating to groups of nations), and global (pertaining to the entire world). Thus, garbage dumped by a person is a local public bad, as the stench affects only a small locality. The donation made by a rich person to a public park falls under the same category. Defence expenditure leads to a feeling of security, which is a public good for the entire nation. A trade block is a regional good as it benefits a group of nations.

Greenhouse gas emission is a global public bad as it affects people all over the globe. Biodiversity conservation may provide local, national, regional, and global benefits. As this activity takes places at sub-national, national, and global levels there is a strong case for applying the subsidiarity principle to promote decentralization and to eliminate participatory and incentive gaps in the provision of the GPG.

The classification matters both for provision and financing GPGs.

In the case of pure GPG like protection of ozone layer and climate stabilization (summation technology) it is desirable that an international agency determines the achievable global targets based on multilateral consensus. As the capacities for carrying out the commitments vary among countries, the Rio principle of common but differentiated responsibilities is often applied in arriving at national targets/

commitments. In the case of best shot technology, it is desirable that a rich country or group of countries undertake the task in view of their financial and risk bearing capacity, but some collective action is needed to ensure that the technology is accessible to poorer countries on reasonable terms. In the case of weakest link technology, it is essential that "the weakest link" be a member of the agreement.

IV Some Existing Institutional Frameworks

It is worth examining the functioning of the institutional frameworks, in the provision of a few GPGs, through the lens of the GPG framework developed by Kaul et al. (2003) and assess whether or not they ensure global governance and address the concerns of developing countries.

The WTO

The Agreement establishing the WTO states that Parties to this Agreement recognize:

> ...that their relations in the field of trade and economic endeavour should be conducted with a view to raising standards of living, ensuring full employment and a large and steadily growing volume of real income and effective demand, and expanding the production of and trade in goods and services, while allowing for the optimal use of the world's resources in accordance with the objective of sustainable development, seeking both to protect and preserve the environment and to enhance the means for doing so in a manner consistent with their respective needs and concerns at different levels of economic development. (World Trade Organization, 1995)

The agreements and associated legal instrument included in Annexes 1, 2, and 3, called multilateral trade agreements, are integral parts of this Agreement, binding on all members. Annex 1 covers General Agreement on Tariffs and Trade (GATT) 1994 and related agreements, General Agreement on Trade in Services (GATS), and Trade-related Intellectual Property Rights (TRIPS).

GATT 1994 brought within its ambit for the first time agriculture, textiles, and clothing. The Uruguay Round strengthened the existing agreements on safeguards: technical barriers, customs valuation, import licensing, state trading, subsidies, and anti-dumping and countervailing measures. It also includes Agreement on Trade Related Investment Measures. Liberalization of trade in services has just begun under GATS. The TRIPS has established multilateral rules governing intellectual property rights. Annex 2 covers the dispute settlement mechanism and Annex 3 trade policy mechanism. A noteworthy feature is that Annexes 1 to 3 form part of a "single undertaking" approach. Annex 4 contains plurilateral agreements that apply only to members who signed them.

The fundamental principles, which are the foundation of the multilateral trading system, are: (a) most favored-nation (MFN): treating all countries equally; (b) national treatment (NT): treating foreigners and locals equally; and (c) freer trade: reductions in tariffs and removal of non-tariff barriers (NTBs). There are some exceptions to MFN and NT based on developmental and environmental considerations.

The Dispute Settlement System of the WTO is based on clearly-defined rules, with time tables for completing trade disputes. The WTO has 154 members; about two-thirds of members are developing countries. As for the structure of the WTO, the highest authority is the Ministerial Conference. At the second level, there are three bodies: the General Council, the Dispute Settlement Body, and the Trade Policy Review Body. All the three consist of all the WTO members. At the third level, there are Goods Council, Service Council, and TRIPS Council. At the fourth level, there are many committees.

The WTO has a democratic structure. As it is, run by its member governments, all major decisions are made by the membership as a whole. Decisions are generally by consensus; when consensus is not possible, the WTO allows voting on the basis of "one country, one vote". The specific situations are: (a) three-quarters of votes for an interpretation of any of the multilateral agreements and waiver of an obligation imposed on a particular member by any multilateral agreement; (b) approval by all members or by a two-thirds majority, to amend provisions of the multilateral agreements, depending on the nature of the provision concerned; and (c) a two-thirds majority to admit a new member.

The form and structure of the WTO provide a platform for countries in different stages of economic development to articulate their views and concerns. Tariff bindings and gradual elimination of NTBs increase the predictability of market access. The Trade Policy Review mechanism is an open and transparent mechanism for reviewing countries' trade policies and the implementation issues. The Dispute Settlement Mechanism has elements of an international judiciary.

The Agreements incorporate special provisions for developing and least developed countries. The "special and differential treatment" (S&DT) provisions allow developed countries to treat developing countries more favorably than other WTO members. These include non-reciprocity in trade negotiations between developed and developing countries, extra time for developing countries to fulfill their commitments, various means of helping developing countries, and safeguarding the interests of developing countries.

There is a growing awareness among developing country members that the anticipated benefits of trade liberalization have not accrued to most of them. They had reservations about the Agreement on Agriculture and the Agreement on Trade Related Intellectual Properties, but joined the WTO, as all the Agreements come under a single undertaking. Many countries could not seize the trading opportunities because of structural adjustment problems, poor transportation and communication facilities, high cost of compliance with Technical Barriers to Trade and Sanitary and Phyto-sanitary Agreements, and other trade-related costs. The access and participation costs for many small developing countries remain high, both at the negotiating stage and at the implementation stage.

Developing countries perceive that the S&DT provisions have not been implemented effectively. Measures such as capacity building in developing countries, technical assistance and Aid for Trade remain only best endeavor measures and are not mandatory. The world trade in agricultural goods is highly distorted because of high level of subsidies in the European Union, USA, and other developed countries. Many developed countries use non-tariff barriers, such as tighter environmental standards, labor standards, and conformity with process and production methods. These regulations are proliferating, more frequent, stringent, and complex (UNCTAD 2004). There is also asymmetry in trade liberalization. While there is considerable liberalization in flow of goods and capital, there are many barriers to mobility of labor and technology.

The Doha Round of trade negotiations began in 2001 as a Development Round. On most negotiating issues, the agendas are set by developed countries and the participation rates of developing countries in terms of written and oral presentations are poor. Only recently Brazil, China, India, and South Africa made their presence felt in the negotiating forums. Despite seven years of negotiations and hard bargaining, the Doha Round of negotiations is in a stalemate. Mendoza (2003) concludes that WTO is a GPG only in form but not in substance. The challenge is how to make the WTO truly a GPG, addressing the concerns of developing countries.

Climate Change

The United Nations Framework Convention on Climate Change (UNFCC) came into force on March 21, 1994. It has 192 members. It acknowledges that change in the Earth's climate and its adverse effects are common concerns of humankind.

> The ultimate objective of this Convention is stabilization of greenhouse gas concentration in the atmosphere at a level that will prevent dangerous anthropogenic interferences with the climate system. Such a level should be achieved within a time frame sufficient to allow ecosystem to adapt naturally to climate change, to ensure that food production is not threatened and to enable economic development to proceed in a sustainable manner. [Article 2, UNFCC]

Article 3 deals with the principles. It states that:

> Parties should protect the climate system for the benefit of present and future generations of humankind, on the basis of equity and in accordance with their common but differentiated responsibilities and respective capabilities. Accordingly, the developed country Parties should take the lead in combating climate change and the adverse effects thereof. The Parties should take precautionary measures to anticipate, prevent or minimize the causes and mitigate its adverse effects of climate change. Where there are threats of severe or irreversible damage, lack of full scientific certainty should not be used as a reason for postponing such measures. (UNFCCC, 1992)

The UNFCCC takes into account the Rio Principle of common but differentiated responsibilities. It means that that the developed countries have to bear the responsibility "in view of the pressures their societies place on the global environment and of the technologies and financial resources they command" (UNCED, 1992).

The Kyoto Protocol sets binding targets for 37 industrialized countries and the European community for reducing greenhouse gas emissions: an average of 5 percent against 1990 levels over the period 2008–12. It came into force on February 16, 2005. The United States, the largest emitter, has not yet ratified it.

According to the Inter Governmental Panel on Climate Change (2007) fourth assessment report, over the last 100 years (1906–2005) the linear trend in global surface temperature is 0.74°C; rise in global sea level is at an average rate of 1.8 mm per year over 1961–2003. The global average temperature is expected to increase by about 0.2°C per decade over the next two decades. Global average sea level is expected to rise by 18 to 59 cm by the end of the 21st century.

The Stern Review (2006) notes that the scientific evidence for climate change is overwhelming and states that climate change is the greatest and widest-ranging market failure ever seen. The impacts of climate change are not evenly distributed—the poorest countries and people will suffer earliest and most. It estimates the cost of stabilization at 500–550 ppm, CO_2 equivalent at 1 percent of global GDP by 2050, with a range of −2 percent to +5 percent of the GDP. International collective action will be critical in driving an effective, efficient, and equitable response on the scale required. It recommends deeper international cooperation in creating price signals and markets for carbon, technology research development and deployment, and promoting adaptation particularly for developing countries.

Clean Development Mechanism (CDM) is the main formal channel for supporting low-carbon investments in developing countries. There is a huge demand for CDM credit, and hence the market price would have been higher if the United States had ratified the Kyoto Protocol. The United States did not sign the Protocol because of the likely adverse effects on its economy and its competitiveness. Now, it urges that China and India also must make binding commitments on the mitigation. This policy of USA raises two issues on international cooperation. First, when some developed countries have initiated low-carbon policies they fear that their international competitiveness will be eroded. The European Union is pleading for a carbon tax on the US imports. Second, pressing binding commitments on developing countries ignores the Rio principle of common but differentiated responsibilities. It also raises the ethical issue of fair shares in the global commons.

At present, the Global Environment Facility funds are reimbursed to developing countries on the basis of the incremental cost principle. There is no net benefit to developing countries (Ghosh, 2003). A cooperative solution based on individual rationality, coalition rationality, and Pareto optimality would require sharing of net benefits between developed and developing country parties (Sankar, 1995). There is also no compensation mechanism for the past damage. Creation of global tradable permits and its allocation on per capita basis or in relation to past damage will be beneficial to developing countries.

World Bank (2007) identifies four categories of clean energy technologies for reducing tariff and non-tariff barriers. These technologies are: clean coal technologies, wind energy, solar photo-voltaic system, and energy efficient lighting. This technology transfer must be on concessional terms, as recommended in Agenda 21, Chapter 34. Developing countries must remove barriers for adoption of clean energy technologies and promote energy conservation.

As the adverse impact of climate change is more likely on poor countries and poor people, implementation of global commitments, such as the Rio principle of common but differentiated responsibilities and MDGs, necessitates creating climate adaptation funds for the benefit of poor people.

Biological Diversity

Biological diversity is the term given to the variety of life on earth and the natural patterns it forms. It is the fruit of billions of years of evolution, shaped by natural processes and, increasingly, by the influence of humans. It forms the web of life of which we are an integral part and upon which we are so fully dependent. The Preamble to the Convention on Biological Diversity (CBD) refers to the intrinsic value of biological diversity and of the ecological, genetic, social, economic, scientific, educational, cultural, recreational, and aesthetic values of biological diversity and its components. It states that conservation of biological diversity is a concern of humankind (Convention of Biological Diversity, 1992). There are 191 Parties to the CBD.

The CBD has three objectives: (a) conservation of biological diversity; (b) sustainable use of biological resources; and (c) creation of an access and benefit sharing regime for biological resources and the associated traditional knowledge.

Millennium Ecosystem Assessment (2005) notes that, in tropical forests, the impact of the main drivers of change in biodiversity and ecosystems are very high and there is rapid increase in habitat change; high and increasing over exploitation; and low but very rapid increase in climate change, invasive species, and pollution. As for tropical grassland and savannah, the impacts are very high with continuing over-exploitation; moderate but very rapid increase in climate change and pollution; moderate and rapid increase in habitat change; and low but very rapid increase of the impact of invasive species. Hence, the need for early action in tropical areas is obvious.

Biological diversity conservation often results in production of private goods, merit goods, and local, regional, and global public goods. As some of the benefits are not marketed (because markets do not exist or are underdeveloped) or not marketable (because of incommensurable benefits), and as there are spillover effects, the costs of conservation cannot be recovered fully by the conservators. Absence of well-defined property/user rights in forests and other ecosystems, and absence of regulations or/and absence of institutions for management of open-pool common properties, accelerate degradation of biological resources. Therefore, there is under production in conservation activity.

Perrings and Gadgil (2003) note that biological diversity loss imposes two rather different costs. The first results from the loss of genetic information (an intergenerational GPG) caused by the global extinction of species. The second loss results from the reduction, fragmentation, exclusion, or deletion of species from managed ecosystems. They recommend four reforms for stimulating conservation and sustainable use of biological diversity: (a) complementing current large-scale conservation efforts with a decentralized strategy that locates production and conservation areas and puts area management rights and responsibilities in the hands of local authorities; (b) adjusting incentives to reward local communities for the conservation efforts, and holding people who produce negative externalities accountable; (c) extending the Global Environment Fund's (GEF) portfolio and resources to support local conservation efforts that yield global benefits; and (d) consolidating the international institutional architecture, to allow more systematic international trade in global environmental services.

Article 20 of the CBD states that developed country parties shall provide new and additional financial resources to enable developing country parties to meet the agreed full incremental costs to them of implementing measures which fulfill the objectives of the Convention. Developed countries can provide financial support for conservation of biological diversity in the South via increased Overseas Development Assistance, cancellation of debts or/and debt-nature swap, capacity building in taxonomy of flora and fauna, creation of institutional structures for access and benefit sharing regime for biological resources and traditional knowledge, and promoting North-South cooperation.

The CBD wants the developed countries to provide access to biotechnologies on favorable terms to developing countries. Developed countries can also set up joint ventures with developed country partners in commercialization of products based on biological resources and traditional knowledge, and also in setting up the laboratories and training facilities.

At present, the GEF Resource Allocation Framework is built on two key pillars: (a) GEF Benefits Index—a measure of the potential of each country to generate global environmental benefits in the bio-diversity and climate change (only based on mitigation of GHGs) focal areas, and (b) GEF Performance Index—a measure of each country's capacity, policies and practices, relevant to a successful implementation of GEF program and projects. The scope of GEF viewed from the perspective of CBD is narrow. A separate trust fund is needed to cover benefits other than GHG mitigation. Further, measurement of the incremental cost is a difficult exercise because many eco-system services are jointly produced, in fixed or variable proportions, and many diverse agents are involved in the conservation activities. A net benefit sharing formula based on cooperative game theory will make both partners better off.

Most megabiological diversity countries are in the developing world. The biological resources and the associated traditional/indigenous knowledge are either in the public domain, with poor state regulation, or in common property regimes. As a result, the resources and the associated traditional knowledge are viewed as "free goods". The guardians of the resources and the knowledge do not get any benefit when the resources and the knowledge are used for developing new products which come under patents. As a result, bio-piracy occurs on a large scale. Inclusion of country/source of origin, prior informed consent, and access and benefit sharing agreements in applications for patents, based on biological resources and associated traditional knowledge, will prevent biopiracy and benefit owners/guardians of the resources in mega-biodiversity countries in the South, but the TRIPS Council has not accepted the suggestion. Efforts made by megabiological diversity countries to create an international certificate of origin/source which would go along with the resources, and serve as passport for verification by customs authorities and help the patent authorities at the time of registration, have not yet materialized.

Subsidiarity, Incentives, and Delivery System

We assessed the existing global institutional architectures for global trading regime, climate stabilization, and conservation and sustainable use of biological diversity. They have also become GPGs by global public choice since 2000. While the WTO is primarily concerned with trade liberalization in private goods, the regime itself possesses characteristics of GPGs. On the other hand, the UNFCC and the CBD are concerned with common concerns of humankind. Here, international cooperation and partnership between developed and developing countries are more important. In the absence of effective international cooperation there will be underproduction of the GPGs. International cooperation is also essential for both fair access and ensuring publicness in participation, consumption, and distribution of benefits.

Assignment of functions at global, regional, and local levels

In the provision of GPGs, assignment of responsibilities to different stakeholders at global, national, and local levels is necessary. Here, the Subsidiarity Principle is relevant. This Principle assigns decisions and enforcement to the lowest of governments capable of handling it without significant residual externalities. In case of pure GPGs, international cooperation is needed to set priorities, to identify responsibilities of developed and developing countries, to reach binding agreements, to decide financing options, and to reach consensus on enforcement mechanisms. But even in case of pure GPGs, implementation of many decisions has to be at national and regional levels. For example, reduction of GHGs can be achieved by pursuing a variety of policy options, for example, afforestation, switch from coal to natural gas in power generation, substitution of non-conventional energy sources like wind energy and solar energy for thermal energy, and so on. The investment decisions are location-specific. Similarly, in bio-diversity conservation, the conservation measures have to be region/location-specific.

Apart from the assignment function, an incentive structure is needed to reach the goals at the least possible cost. This problem is important in cases where an activity generates private benefits, local public benefits, and global public benefits. In some cases, there may be complementarities between private benefits and public benefits. We need a mechanism to internalize conservation decisions of private individuals and forest department. Effective public participation is needed to ascertain people's preferences regarding the type and level of GPG, peoples' willingness to pay user charges for merit goods, and their involvement in monitoring/enforcement of the delivery systems. Choice of an appropriate institutional framework—public, private, community or public private partnership—should be based on the criteria of least cost service provision, given the goals.

Delivery system

Public responsibility in the provision of GPGs and merit goods does not necessarily imply public production and supply. To avoid leakage in distribution and to ensure adequate supply to the target groups, alternative delivery mechanisms should be explored. One major problem in achieving universal coverage is the "last mile problem". The unit costs of providing many infrastructural services are higher in rural and remote areas than in urban areas. Revenue realization per unit of service is also lower in rural areas. We need innovative, technical, institutional, and management solutions, and subsidies and cross-subsidies to achieve universal coverage. For monitoring and assessing performance, it is desirable to move from input-based measures, such as amount spent, to outcome-based measures. In case of common property resources, creation of self-governing institutions with built-in incentive and penalty structures may be needed to ensure sustainability of the commons (see Ostrom 1990).

V Concluding Remarks

The International Task Force Report on GPGs says that international cooperation is a tool for altruistic purposes, and it serves geopolitical interests. It is also a tool for nations to align their long-term enlightened national interests to achieve common goals. The Rio Declaration of 1992 contains principles for international governance and Agenda 21 gives an action plan. However, despite the establishment of the WTO in 1995, ratification of more than 200 multilateral agreements, and the UN Millennium Declaration, all of them endorsing sustainable development, the intensity of international cooperation has been slow.

Our assessment of the existing global institutional architectures for global trading, climate change, and conservation of biological diversity reveal that (*a*) there are no built-in measures for achieving dynamic efficiency; and (*b*) development concerns get low priority in the implementation of treaties/agreements. We need mechanisms for effective participation by developing countries, both at the rule-making stage and at the implementation stage, to enable them reap the benefits of multilateral agreements.

The factors hindering international cooperation are: (*a*) governments' unwillingness to accept binding international commitments because they restrict their policy spaces; (*b*) political myopia; (*c*) differences in preferences and priorities of governments; (*d*) scientific uncertainty about eco-system functioning and their interaction with the economic system; (*e*) lack of catalytic leadership; (*f*) inadequate funding; and (*g*) difficulties in creating and operating effective institutions for implementation of the shared visions. As noted by Bagchi (2005), the problem lies in the persistent imbalances in decision making in multilateral organizations entrusted with the task of providing GPGs. The challenge for countries is to find ways and means of overcoming the barriers to address the common concerns of mankind in such a way that every nation finds that it is better-off via international cooperation than otherwise.

REFERENCES

Bagchi, A. 2005. "Providing Global Public Goods", *Business Standard*, New Delhi, May 3. Convention on Biological Diversity. 1992. Text of the Convention. Available online at http://www.cbd.int/convention/convention.shtml.

Desai, M. 2003. "Public Goods: A Historical Perspective", in I. Kaul, P. Conceicau, K.L. Goulven and R.U. Mendoza (eds) *Providing Global Public Goods: Managing Globalisation*, pp. 63–77. New York: Oxford University Press.

Ghosh, P. 2003. Issue Note, *Development Policy Forum*, pp. 54–58. Available online at http://www.dse.de/ef/gpg/ghosh.htm (downloaded on June 1, 2008).

Hirshleifer, J. 1983. "From Weakest Link to Best Shot: The Voluntary Provision of Public Goods", *Public Choice*, 41 (3): 371–86.

Intergovernmental Panel on Climate Change. 2007. Fourth Assessment Report, Synthesis Report, Geneva. Available online at http://www.ipcc.ch/pdfassessment-report/ar4/syr/ar4.–syr.pdf (downloaded on April 1, 2009).

International Task Force on Global Public Goods. 2006. *Meeting Global Challenges: International Cooperation in the National Interest*, Final Report, Stockholm, Secretariat of Task Force.

Kaul, I., P. Conceicau, K.L. Goulven, and R.U. Mendoza. 2003. *Providing Global Public Goods: Managing Globalisation*. New York: Oxford University Press.

Mendoza, R.U. 2003. "The Multilateral Trade Regime: A Global Public Good for All?", in I. Kaul, P. Conceicau, K.L. Goulven, and R.U. Mendoza (eds) *Providing Global Public Goods: Managing Globalisation*, pp. 455–83. New York: Oxford University Press.

Millennium Ecosystem Assessment. 2005. *Ecosystem and Human Well-Being: Synthesis*. Washington, DC: Island Press.

Ostrom, M. 1990. *Governing the Commons: The Evolution of Institutions for Collective Action*. Cambridge: Cambridge University Press.

Perrings, C., and M. Gadgil. 2003. "Reconciling Local and Global Public Benefits" in I. Kaul P. Conceicau, K.L. Goulven, and R.U. Mendoza (eds) *Providing Global Public Goods: Managing Globalisation*, pp. 532–55. New York: Oxford University Press.

Samuelson, Paul A. 1954. "The Pure Theory of Public Expenditure", *Review of Economics and Statistics*, 36(4): 387–89.

Sandler, T.M., 2001. "On Financing Global and International Public Goods", World Bank Policy Research Working Paper, No. 263, Washington, DC.

Sankar, U. 1995. "On the Allocation of Joint and Common Costs", in N.S.S. Narayana and A. Sen (eds), *Poverty, Environment and Economic Development*, Festschrift for Kirit S. Parikh, pp. 265–78. Bangalore: Interline Publishing.

Stern, Nicholas. 2007. *The Economics of Climate Change: The Stern Review*. Cambridge: Cambridge University Press. Available online at http://www.hm.treasury.gov.uk/independentreviews/stern_review_economics_climate_change/stern_review_index.cfm. (downloaded on June 20, 2008).

United Nations General Assembly. 2000. Millennium Declaration. Available online at http://www.un.org/millennium/declaration/552e.htm (downloaded on July 1, 2008).

United Nations. 1992. United Nations Framework Convention on Climate Change. Available online at http://unfccc.int/essential_background/convention/background/items/2853.php (downloaded on March 15, 2009).

———. 2005. Millennium Project. Available online at http://www.unmillenniumproject.org/goals/gti.htm (downloaded on March 15, 2009).

United Nations Conference on Environment and Development (UNCED). 1992. Rio Declaration on Environment and Development, Rio de Janeiro, Brazil. Available online at http://www.un.org/documents/ga/conf151/aconf15126-1annex1.htm (downloaded on February 1, 2008).

United Nations Conference on Trade and Development (UNCTAD). 2004. "Environmental Requirements and Market Access for Developing Countries", Note by the UNCTAD Secretariat. Available online at http://www.unctad.org/trade_env/test1/meetings/rio/UNCTAD_DITC_TED_2004.7.pdf (downloaded on February 1, 2008).

World Bank, Development Committee. 2000. "Poverty Reduction and Global Public Goods: Issues for the World Bank in Support of Global Public Goods". Washington, DC: World Bank.

World Bank, Environment Department. 2007. "Warming up to Trade? Harnessing International Trade to Support Climate Change Objectives". Washington, DC: World Bank.

World Trade Organization. 1995. *Agreement Establishing the World Trade Organization*. Available online at http://www.wto.org/english/docs_elegal_e/04-wt.doc. (downloaded on July 15, 2008).

7

Effective Carbon Taxes and Public Policy Options

EHTISHAM AHMAD AND NICHOLAS STERN*

———— • ✦ • ————

I Introduction

During our work in the early 1980s on the applications of modern public finance methods to the context of developing countries, NIPFP under the leadership of Raja Chelliah and Amaresh Bagchi provided a home, friendship, and wise guidance. We use the intuition from our work from the early 1980s on the description and evaluation of indirect tax systems (Ahmad and Stern, 1984, 1991) to examine issues that have become prominent more recently, which relate to the design and implementation of environmental taxes. This involves designing the appropriate instruments for "carbon taxation" in terms of the carbon content of different goods and activities. It is also possible to evaluate the effects on people in different circumstances, and show possibilities for compensating the "losers". A further important issue in India concerns which level of government might be responsible for the administration of the tax. In this effort, we follow the distinguished tradition of Amaresh Bagchi, who was intimately involved in tax

* We are grateful to Junaid Ahmad, Giorgio Brosio, Vijay Kelkar, Arvind Subramaniam, and other participants at a seminar in Washington for the Indian Finance Commission for discussion, and to the NIPFP and Professors Chelliah and Bagchi for their support for the original research on the Indian tax system in the 1980s. All errors are ours.

policy design, including the political acceptability of options and in designing intergovernmental fiscal systems, for India and other developing countries.

In this chapter, we take as given the need for public action on climate change (Stern, 2007), and that carbon taxation is one of the key instruments for influencing both behavior of consumers and producers. The calculations also illustrate the eventual effects on prices of a scheme based, for example, at least in part on a quota-cum-trading scheme linked to upstream activities, such as electricity generation or steel production. Section II examines methods for designing and implementing effective carbon taxes. In Section III we ask whether the states/provinces or the Center should administer the tax. We also raise some political economy issues concerning gainers and losers, and possible compensation measures for poor people. Section IV provides the concluding remarks.

II Effective Carbon Taxes

The establishment of a carbon tax or excise for environmental purposes could be achieved by an import duty/excise on petroleum products or coal. This will work through the production structure and affect the prices of goods that use the inputs that are subjected to tax. In addition, whether the tax is administered by the Center on imports or/ and domestic production or by the states at the final stage, as would be required under the constitutional arrangements that prevail in the subcontinent, it would affect the revenue prospects not just of the level of government that levies the tax, but also of other levels of government. In this chapter, we build on the concept of "effective taxes" that we developed in order to assess cascading taxes that characterized the tax systems of India and Pakistan in the 1980s.

A Model of Effective Taxes

The structure for both taxes and subsidies is often complicated and they can apply to intermediate as well as final goods. As most carbon taxes involve the taxation of intermediate goods, such as petroleum, kerosene, gas, or coal, a full assessment requires the estimation of the effects of this taxation on the prices of all other goods, that is, the effective taxes that arise from any form of carbon tax. This not only permits an assessment of the different commodities on which the tax might be levied, but also permits an analysis of the incidence of the tax on households in different circumstances.

Studies of the incidence of indirect taxes and subsidies based on household consumption data requires the knowledge of the component of the price of a final good, which might be attributed to a change in the tax on any specific good or class of goods. Further, an evaluation of proposals for changes in taxes would also utilize, in principle, this information, since the government would need to know the consequences for revenue of changes in purchases of different goods resulting from the reforms being considered.

Let us review the model of effective taxes presented in Ahmad and Stern (1991). We begin with a simple closed economy Leontief model. All purchasers of a good pay are price inclusive of tax. We write the vector of prices faced by producers who are buying an input as "p" and the vector of prices received by a producer selling the good as "p^p" the difference is the tax incurred at the production stage. Consider a simple input-output model of production with fixed input-output matrix "A", gross output vector "x" and net output vector "z". The inputs are "Ax" and

$$z = x - Ax = (I - A)x \tag{1}$$

Competitive pricing conditions for this model are:

$$p^{p'} = p'A + y', \tag{2}$$

where primes denote row vectors and y is the vector of value-added by industry (which we assume for the moment to be fixed). If "t" is the tax vector, then

$$p' = p^{p'} + t', \tag{3}$$

from (2) and (3) we have

$$p' = t'(I - A)^{-1} + y'(I - A)^{-1}. \tag{4}$$

We define the effective tax vector 't^e' as

$$t^{e'} = t'(I - A)^{-1}, \tag{5}$$

and prices in the absence of taxes, the "basic" or shadow price vector $p^{b'}$ as

$$p^{b'} = y'(I - A)^{-1}. \tag{6}$$

The ith component of t^e is the amount government revenue would change, if there were a unit change in the final demand for a good. This is the formal definition of the effective tax: if the final demand vector is z and government revenue is R, then we have

$$t_i^e = \frac{\partial R}{\partial z_i} \text{ ; and}$$

$$t^{diff} = t^{e'} - t' \tag{7}$$

which measures the difference between the effective tax, t^e, and the nominal tax, t. Thus, t^{diff} indicates the extent to which inputs are taxed. The overall level of taxation of inputs in the economy is given by t^{diff} times the final demand vector z or

$$t^{diff}.z = t^{diff'}(I - A)x$$

$$= t^{e'}(I - A)x - t'(I - A)x$$

$$= t'(I - A)^{-1}(I - A)x - t'x + t'Ax$$

$$= t'Ax \tag{8}$$

Alternatively, we can see this last measure of the taxation of inputs as simply a decomposition of the total tax payment: into tax on final demand, t.z, and tax on intermediate goods, $t'Ax$:

$$t.x = t'(I - A)x + t'Ax$$

$$= t.z + t'Ax \tag{9}$$

While t^{diff} measures the extent to which inputs are taxed in the model, it does not indicate any costs associated with distortions of choice of technique resulting from taxation of inputs, since all coefficients are fixed. Further, changes in factor prices and pure profits have been assumed away, since we have a single factor and zero profits.

The assumption of fixed coefficients could be relaxed as follows. If we assume that each industry has a single output (no joint production) and there are constant returns to scale, we may write $c_i(p,w)$ as the minimum cost of producing good i, when input prices are p and the single factor has price w. If we choose the single factor as numeraire, we may write the vector of costs as a function $c(p)$ of p only. The most efficient way of producing each good can be defined simply in terms of the technique which gives the minimum quantity of the factor directly and indirectly required in production and these minimum costs, γ are the prices of the non-substitution theorem. We then have:

$$\gamma = c(\gamma) \tag{10}$$

and

$$\gamma' = y'(\gamma)(I - A(\gamma))^{-1} \tag{11}$$

where $y(\gamma)$ is the vector of factor requirements per unit of output for each industry and $A(\gamma)$ and the input-output matrix at prices γ. Notice that γ and A now depend on prices where they were previously fixed and that

$$(A(p))_{ij} = \frac{\partial c_i}{\partial p_j} \tag{12}$$

from the standard properties of the cost function.

When we have taxation of sales, producers receive a price p^p but pay p for inputs. Thus, in equilibrium, generalizing equation (2) above,

$$p^p = c(p) \tag{13}$$

The differences between prices with and without taxation is $p - \gamma$ which may be written using (3), (10) and (13)

$$p - \gamma = c(p) - c(\gamma) + t \tag{14}$$

$$\geq t'(I - A(p))^{-1} \tag{15}$$

Using the concavity of the cost function and (12). Thus,

$$p' - \gamma' \geq t'(I - A(p))^{-1} \tag{16}$$

Since $(I - A(p))^{-1}$ is we assume a non-negative matrix, the implication is that the effective tax estimated empirically using input–output tables at current prices, underestimates the price-raising effect of the taxes. The reason is that the fixed coefficients assumption ignores the rise in prices associated with the reorganization of inputs from those associated with $A(\gamma)$, which minimize resource costs to $A(p)$.

We can illustrate this point by writing a decomposition of the overall price rise as:

$$p'-\gamma'=t'(I-A(p))^{-1}+(p^{b'}-\gamma')\tag{17}$$

which comes from (4), (5), (6) remembering that A is now a function of p. Thus, the price rise is made up from the effective taxes, and the increase in the vector of resource costs of production, $p^{b'}-\gamma'$, which we know is non-negative from (16) or from the property that γ' is the vector of minimum resource costs. Similarly, the increase in the costs of production at market prices associated with the tax is:

$$p^{p'}-\gamma'=t^{diff'}+(p^{b'}-\gamma')\tag{18}$$

An obvious measure of the resource cost of the input taxation per unit of output is simply $(p^{b'}-\gamma')$ where:

$$p^{b'}=\gamma'(p)(I-A(p))^{-1}\tag{19}$$

And γ' is given by (11). This would be combined with a measure of output shifts in a calculation of overall losses.[1] For marginal changes, one would be interested in the rate of change of $p^{b'}$ with respect to taxes. This may be derived as follows: from (4), (5) and (6):

$$p^{b'}=p'-t^{e}\tag{20}$$

Thus,

$$\frac{\partial p^{b'}}{\partial t}=\frac{\partial p'}{\partial t}-\frac{\partial t^{e}}{\partial t}\tag{21}$$

where $\frac{\partial p'}{\partial t}$ is the matrix with the ij^{th} element $\frac{\partial p_j}{\partial t_i}$. From (3), (12) and (13) we have:

$$\frac{\partial p'}{\partial t}=(I-A)^{-1}\tag{22}$$

and from (5), (21) and (22) we have:

$$\frac{\partial p^{b'}}{\partial t}=-t'(\partial\overline{A})\overline{A}'\tag{23}$$

where $\bar{A}$ is $(I-A)^{-1}$ with ij^{th} element $\bar{q}_{ij}$, $\partial\bar{A}$ is the derivative of $\bar{A}$ with respect to prices p—it is a tensor with kjl^{th} element α_{kjl} equal to $\dfrac{\partial\bar{q}_{kj}}{\partial p_l}$, and the ij^{th} element of the rhs of (23) is $-\sum_{k,l} t_k \alpha_{kjl} \bar{q}_{li}$.

Flexible Coefficients

One of the objectives of the taxation of "carbon" is to induce both producer and consumer responses, and while the fixed co-efficient assumption is convenient for the estimation of effects on consumers, in terms of both welfare and shifts in demand patterns, it would be useful to incorporate more flexible assumptions concerning the production structure. Both $(p^{b'} - \gamma')$ and its marginal version (23) depend on the *change* in input-output coefficients, since it is the shift in these that is causing the resource cost. We know that the total loss $(p^{b'} - \gamma')$ is positive for each good, although this will not necessarily be true for the marginal. The calculation of these losses poses problems, however, since we observe $A(p)$ and not the input-output matrix $A(\gamma)$ and do not know the rate of change of A with respect to prices. One could compute $A(\gamma)$ or the derivative of A with a general equilibrium model of the production side which involved flexible coefficients, but then a large part of the answer would be from the assumption of functional forms and invention of parameters, and is unlikely to be available at the level of dis-aggregation of the standard input-output matrices.

We examine here the problem of calculating $\dfrac{\partial p_j}{\partial t_i}$ and $\dfrac{\partial w_k}{\partial t_i}$, where we have flexible coefficients in production. Again, we assume a competitive closed economy with constant returns to scale and no joint production. We could write the cost of production on good j as $c_j(p, \omega)$, where all purchasers of inputs buy at prices p, and ω_k is the purchasers' price of factor k—the seller's price $(w_k = \omega_k - \tau_k)$. The prices received by producers p^p differs from p through the vector of taxes t. Thus,

$$p = p^p + t$$

where,

$$p^p = c(p, \omega)$$

and

$$p = c(p, \omega) + t$$

Transposing and differentiating with respect to the tax t_i, we have,

$$\frac{\partial p_j}{\partial t_i} = \sum_k \frac{\partial c_j}{\partial p_k} \frac{\partial p_k}{\partial t_i} + \sum_m \frac{\partial c_j}{\partial \omega_m} \frac{\partial \omega_m}{\partial t_i} + \delta_{it} \quad (24)$$

In matrix form:

$$\Delta = \Delta A + WB + I \quad (25)$$

Where, $(\Delta)_{ij} = \dfrac{\partial p_j}{\partial t_i}$, $(A)_{kj} = \dfrac{\partial c_j}{\partial p_k}$, $(B)_{mj} = \dfrac{\partial c_j}{\partial \omega_m}$, and $(W)_{im} = \dfrac{\partial \omega_m}{\partial t_i}$.

Note that A is the familiar input-output matrix, since $\dfrac{\partial c_j}{\partial p_k}$ is simply the input of good k into industry j at unit production levels. Similarly, B is a matrix of factor requirements. Thus,

$$\Delta = (I - A)^{-1} + WB(I - A)^{-1} \quad (26)$$

Equation (25) establishes that the results for fixed coefficients extends to flexible coefficients. The effective tax t^e, calculated using the existing A, no longer reflects the price differential between the equilibrium with and without taxation, but the important feature is the rate of change of prices with respect to the tax, and that is given by $(I - A)^{-1}$, both with flexible and with fixed coefficients for intermediate goods.

Open Economy

We can extend the analysis to the open economy by distinguishing between domestically produced goods and their prices using superscript "d", and imported goods by the superscript "m"; as previously, the producer price has been indexed by the superscript "p". The buyer's price is the producer price plus the tax. Thus,

$$p^m = p^* + t^m$$

and

$$p^d = p^{pd} + t^d$$

where p^* is the exogenous world price of the import and t^m and t^d are taxes on imports and domestically produced goods, respectively. Thus,

$$p^d = c^d(p^d, p^m, \omega) + t^d \tag{27}$$

and

$$\Delta^d = \frac{\partial p_j^d}{\partial t_i^d} = \sum_l \frac{\partial c_j^d}{\partial p_l^d} \frac{\partial p_l^d}{\partial p_i^d} + \sum_f \frac{\partial c_j^d}{\partial \omega_f} \frac{\partial \omega^f}{\partial t_i^d} + \delta_{ij} \tag{28}$$

$$\Delta^m = \frac{\partial p_j^d}{\partial t_k^m} = \sum_r \frac{\partial c_j^d}{\partial p_r^d} \frac{\partial p_r^d}{\partial t_k^m} + \sum_f \frac{\partial c_j^d}{\partial \omega_f} \frac{\partial \omega^f}{\partial t_k^m} + \frac{\partial c_j^d}{\partial p_k^m} \tag{29}$$

where (28) and (29) are analogous to (24). And corresponding to (25):

$$\Delta^d = \Delta^d A^d + W^d B + I$$

and

$$\Delta^m = \Delta^m A^d + W^m B + A^m \tag{30}$$

where:

$A^d = \left(\dfrac{\partial c_j^d}{\partial p_l^d} \right)$ is the domestic input-output matrix, giving the coefficients of domestic goods into domestic production;

$A^m = \left(\dfrac{\partial c_j^d}{\partial p_k^m} \right)$ is the matrix of imported goods into domestic production;

W^d is the matrix of factor price responses to the taxation of domestic inputs; and

W^m is he corresponding factor price matrix for taxes on imported goods. Finally,

$$\Delta^d = (I - A^d)^{-1} + W^d B (I - A^d)^{-1}, \; and$$

$$\Delta^m = A^m (I - A^d)^{-1} + W^m B (I - A^d)^{-1} \tag{31}$$

Thus, in the fixed coefficients case, equations (31) reduce to give the overall effective tax:

$$t^{e} = t^{d'}(I - A^{d})^{-1} + t^{m'}A^{m}(I - A^{d})^{-1} \tag{32}$$

Simply put, the contribution of a domestic excise on carbon-related goods, which falls on domestic production alone, is given by the first term on the rhs of (32), and that of import duties on the vector of imports that feed into domestic production (second term on the rhs of [32]). The effects are additive. The effects of a sales tax levied regardless of origin are also given by (32) as these work in part by affecting prices of domestically produced goods and in part through imported inputs that feed into domestic production.

Directions of Reform

The effective taxes, resulting from the imposition of a carbon tax, need to be assessed. For a given revenue requirement, one could ask about the effects of the alternatives (for example, central excises on petroleum, gas, coal products; plus import duties/central sales tax; or final sales taxes or VAT imposed by the states/provinces) and mechanisms by which the choices might be made. The first step is to evaluate the effective taxes, as we have described previously. One of the key elements in the policy design is the effect on households in different circumstances. This is the second step, and we outline the methods below.

We use the concept of the welfare loss, associated with an increase in the ith tax, sufficient to raise Re 1 in revenue (Ahmad and Stern, 1984). This welfare loss, λ_{i}, is defined as:

$$\lambda_{i} = \frac{-\dfrac{\partial V}{\partial t_{i}}}{\dfrac{\partial R}{\partial t_{i}}} = \frac{\sum_{h} \beta^{h} x_{i}^{h}}{X_{i} + \sum_{j=1}^{n} t_{j}^{e} \dfrac{\partial X_{j}}{\partial p_{i}}} \tag{24}$$

Where the numerator $-\dfrac{\partial V}{\partial t_{i}}$ is the social loss associated with an increase in the price of the ith good, and is the money measure of the loss to household h, x_{i}^{h}, aggregated across households using welfare weights, β^{h}; where x_{i}^{h} is the consumption of commodity i by household h

($h = 1, 2,...H; i = 1,2,...n$). X_i is the total consumption of commodity i, $\dfrac{\partial X_j}{\partial p_i}$ is the matrix of demand derivatives, and t_j^e is the effective tax on good j.

One example of a structure for the welfare weights, β^h, would be to use a formula as follows:

$$\beta^h = \left(\frac{I^1}{I^h} \right)^e \tag{25}$$

Where I^1 and I^h are the expenditures per capita of the poorest household group and household h, respectively, and e can be interpreted as an inequality aversion parameter. For $e = 0$, we have all β^h equal to one or zero inequality aversion, and $e = 5$ begins to approach concern only for the poorest household group.

The effects of different assumptions concerning inequality aversion can change the desired options for reform. It is interesting that, in the empirical evaluation of the directions of reform in Pakistan (Ahmad and Stern, 1984,1991), as inequality aversion increases, the housing, fuel, and light category becomes the most attractive sector for additional taxation, given the relatively low (in proportional terms) expenditures of poor people on these items (see Table 7.1). In this case, both the theory of reform and environmental considerations point to higher taxation of carbon-intensive goods.

It should be noted that, in the Pakistan case for data from the 1980s, the category "housing, fuel and light" contains a composite grouping of commodities, dictated by the consideration that demands responses for a finer grouping were not available and that these may bear in different ways on the poorest households. The carbon-related components bore an effective tax of 0.35 for petroleum products, 0.21 for electricity, and 0.57 for gas—referring to the direct and indirect tax element, in the price of each good—covering all types and sources of taxation (duties, excises, and sales tax) that were levied at that time. In the Indian case, demand elasticity was available for the "fuel and light" grouping and the composite effective tax for this category was 0.27 for roughly the same period.

Interestingly, similar calculations for India showed that the λ_i for "fuel and light" remained high for all levels of inequality aversion (low ranks at all levels of ε—see Table 7.2). The differences in ranking, in relation to Pakistan, may be due to the fact that "housing" was not included in this category. While these numbers are used as illustrations of method, it is likely that changes in consumption patterns in India, with the greater use of automobiles by the middle and upper income groups, will likely have changed the rankings towards those in Pakistan.

It is not desirable for the tax rates on roughly similar items within a group of commodities to vary significantly; in order to prevent substitution effects and avoidance, however, tough one might wish to tax less heavily, for example, the types of fuel consumed more heavily by poor people. Thus, the issue of the impact of any tax measures relating to carbon taxation and identification of compensatory measures for the poorest is likely to be critical in any assessment of different options.

Table 7.1: Pakistan: Ranks for λ_i

ε	0	0.5	1.0	2.0	5.0
1. Wheat	10	4	1	1	1
2. Rice	7	7	6	6	7
3. Pulses	8	5	3	2	2
4. Meat, fish, eggs	13	13	13	13	13
5. Milk and products	11	11	10	10	11
6. Vegetables, fruits, and spices	12	12	11	11	9
7. Edible oils	1	1	4	4	4
8. Sugar	3	3	5	5	5
9. Tea	5	2	2	3	3
10. Housing, fuel, and light	2	6	8	9	10
11. Clothing	6	8	9	8	8
12. Other foods	9	9	7	7	6
13. Other non-foods	4	10	12	12	12

Source: Ahmad and Stern (1991).

Notes: The welfare loss for commodity *i*, λ_i represents the effects on all households (using Household Survey data on consumption and estimated demand responses) of an increase in the tax on the *i*th good sufficient to raise a rupee of government revenue. The β^h are welfare weights on households, and ε is the inequality aversion parameter, ranging from 0 to 5. Any good ranked 1 would be such that a switch of taxation from it to any other good would increase welfare at constant revenue.

$$\lambda_i = \frac{\sum_h \beta^h x_i^h}{X_i + \sum_j t_j^e \frac{\partial X_j}{\partial t_i}}$$

Table 7.2: India: Effective Taxes and Rankings of Welfare Losses, λ_i^t

Commodity	Effective tax, t_j^e	$\varepsilon = 0$	0.1	1	2	5
Cereals	0.052	8	7	2	2	2
Milk and dairy products	0.009	9	9	9	9	9
Edible oils	0.083	6	6	4	4	5
Meat, fish, eggs	0.014	7	8	6	5	4
Sugar and gur	0.069	5	5	5	5	6
Other foods	0.114	4	3	3	3	3
Clothing	0.242	1	1	7	7	8
Fuel and light	0.274	2	2	1	1	1
Other non-food	**0.133**	3	4	8	8	7

Source: Ahmad and Stern (1991).

Notes: The welfare loss for commodity i, λ_i represents the effects on all households (using Household Survey data on consumption and estimated demand responses) of an increase in the tax on the ith good sufficient to raise a rupee of government revenue. The β^h are welfare weights on households, and ε is the inequality aversion parameter, ranging from 0 to 5. Any good ranked 1 would be such that a switch of taxation from it to any other good would increase welfare at constant revenue.

$$\lambda_i = \frac{\sum_h \beta^h x_i^h}{X_i + \sum_j t_j^e \frac{\partial X_j}{\partial t_i}}$$

In order to evaluate in detail the impact on households in different circumstances, the model described previously could be used, together with the detailed household expenditure surveys, to work out the impacts on different groups of households. This could then be used as a mechanism to provide relief or a social safety net for the very poor, should that be deemed to be relevant. The method described previously has also been used to assess the effects of carbon taxes and welfare in New Zealand (Creedy and Sleeman, 2006).

III Who Should Administer a Carbon Tax?

The "carbon tax" could be designed as an excise or an import duty on a range of goods/sectors (petroleum, diesel, kerosene, and coal). If implemented by the Federal/Central government, it could be levied at the production stage. And if made operational by the states, it would most likely be implemented at the final sales point. One could then evaluate the welfare losses from each type of instrument by deciding which works best in relation to the relevant distributional considerations.

State and Federal Considerations

The model discussed earlier can be extended as follows. The main federal options for a carbon tax would be based on either excises on production or imports. The state provincial options relate to the sales or state VAT. The effective taxes associated with excises, imports, and the sales tax are given by:

Excises: $t_{(ex)}^{eC} = t^{C'}(I - A^d)^{-1}$ (26)

Imports: $t_{(m)}^{eC} = t^{m'}A^m(I - A^d)^{-1}$ (27)

Sales: $t^{eS} = t^{S'}(I - A^d)^{-1} + t^{S'}A^m(I - A^d)^{-1}$ (28)

Where t^C, t^m and t^S represent nominal per-unit rates of excise duties, imports, and sales taxes. As before, A^d is the coefficient matrix for domestic inputs to domestic production, and A^m is the coefficient matrix for imported inputs into domestic production. It is assumed that imported inputs are strict complements to domestic inputs and there are fixed coefficients (in this case for simplicity).

For given increases in taxes, one can calculate the changes in effective rates through equations (29) to (31).

Excises: $\lambda^{ex} = \dfrac{\sum_h \sum_i \beta^h x_i^h \Delta t_{i(ex)}^C}{\sum_i \left[X_i + \sum_j t_j^e \dfrac{\partial X_j}{\partial t_i^e} \right] \Delta t_{i(ex)}^{eC}}$ (29)

Imports: $$\lambda^m = \frac{\sum_h \sum_i \beta^h x_i^h \Delta t_{i(m)}^C}{\sum_i \left[X_i + \sum_i t_j^e \frac{\partial X_j}{\partial t_i^e} \right] \Delta t_{i(m)}^{eC}}$$ (30)

Sales taxes: $$\lambda^S = \frac{\sum_h \sum_i \beta^h x_i^h \Delta t_i^S}{\sum_i \left[X_i + \sum_i t_j^e \frac{\partial X_j}{\partial t_i^e} \right] \Delta t_i^{eS}}$$ (31)

Ahmad and Stern (1984, 1991) assessed the intergovernmental model, described earlier, for the evaluation of the welfare losses from the systems for India, using a Nasse modification of the linear expenditure system, household expenditure data using the NSS surveys, and a corresponding 89-group input-output matrix. They showed that at low levels of inequality aversion, $e = 0$ or 0.1, say, $\lambda^m > \lambda^{\alpha} > \lambda^S$. If one were not particularly concerned with the welfare of the poor, one might consider that a marginal increase in sales taxes would cause less social cost per marginal rupee of revenue than an increase in excise duties, and even less than an extra rupee generated through import duties. However, even with a moderate level of inequality aversion, $e = 1$, the rankings are reversed, states sales taxes would cause greater welfare losses than central taxes (including excises and import duties).

These are preliminary and general indications, and the exercise should be repeated with recent estimates and household and production data.

Administration and Political Economy Concerns

Concern with climate change and the externalities from greenhouse gases give a global perspective, and this is probably best seen as an issue for federal taxation. The excise/import duties route also is simple to administer and avoids the difficulties in the intra-state taxation of transactions that would arise if different states were to go for different rates of the VAT.

Moreover, it is not advisable to introduce differentiated VAT structures at the state level, as this is likely to generate potential for avoidance and difficulties in collection. Thus, administration considerations would also point to the advantages of a federal excise/import duty structure for the carbon tax.

The empirical assessment of the effective carbon taxes could then be used to help design any compensatory measures for the poorest people as might be deemed necessary by the federal or state governments. With federal collections, a sharing mechanism with states, that could be used to finance compensatory mechanisms at the state level, would greatly enhance the overall political-economy incentives for the central carbon tax.[2]

IV Concluding Remarks

We have pointed to the ways in which the concept of "effective taxes" and the theory of reform can be used to guide the design of carbon taxes. It can help identify the appropriate choice of commodities on which the taxes can be levied. This can then be used to identify the impact on households in different circumstances.

The methods can also be used to evaluate the design of inter-governmental responsibilities for carbon taxation. From our work on Indian taxation in the past, based at the NIPFP, and with the guidance and support of Raja Chelliah and Amaresh Bagchi, it would appear that a central excise might be the most appropriate course of action. In these cases, it is likely that administrative considerations, together with the political economy concerns, will predominate. In this case, a uniform treatment across states may be desirable. This could be achieved either by a central tax or harmonized state level taxes. In the Indian context, it would not, however, be desirable to introduce differentiation into state level VATs, and the appropriate instrument may well be a central excise.

Similar calculations would be relevant for a cap-and-trade scheme, where allocation of quotas were assigned to key upstream industries, and trading could then take place between enterprises. The eventual impact on prices could be calculated using similar methods. Auctioning of quotas would then provide the revenues.

The carbon tax or quota-trading scheme would, as suggested, need to be accompanied by compensatory measures for the poorest households that might be affected. These may have to be administered by state governments and partially financed by the carbon tax or revenues from auctioning of quotas, which could also be used to finance any needed restructuring of manufacturing or other activities.

In this chapter, the focus has been largely methodological, and the detailed policy assessments in the sub-continent should be based on more recent information on household consumptions and behavior, given that considerable structural changes have taken place since our work in the 1980s.

Notes

1   For very small taxes, the extra costs associated with taxes would be second order (essentially from the envelope theorem), but not necessarily for larger taxes.
2   For a survey of inter governmental transfer mechanisms (see Ahmad and Searle, 2006).

References

Ahmad, E. and N. Stern 1984. "The Theory of Tax Reform and Indian Indirect Taxes", *Journal of Public Economics*, 25 (3): 259–98.
———. 1991. *The Theory and Practice of Tax Reforms in Developing Countries*. Cambridge: Cambridge University Press.
Ahmad, E. and R. Searle. 2006. "On the Implementation of Transfers to Sub-national Levels of Administration", in Ehtisham Ahmad and Giorgio Brosio (eds), *Handbook of Fiscal Federalism*, pp. 381–404. Cheltenham: Edward Elgar.
Creedy, J. and C. Sleeman, 2006. "Carbon Taxation, Prices and Welfare in New Zealand", *Ecological Economics*, 57 (3): 333–45.
Stern, N.H. 2007. *Economics of Climate Change: The Stern Review*. Cambridge: Cambridge University Press.

8

Sustainable Economic Growth and Modeling for Resource and Income Accounting*

Ramprasad Sengupta

———— • ✦ • ————

I Introduction

The Indian economy is currently growing at a high rate in the range of 8 to 9 percent per annum for the last four years. China has also been a growing at an annual average rate of higher than 10 percent in the recent years. By the size of the population and the pace of growth, China and India rank as the top two nations in the world. By the size of the economy in terms of Gross Domestic Product (GDP) in purchasing power parity

* The author dedicates this paper to the memory of Dr Amaresh Bagchi who as a fiscal expert had deep concern for the sustainability of the development processes of the Indian economy and was a purist in his approach to the measurement of the indicators of development. This paper expands the notion of sustainability to take account of the feedback effects of the environment and resource system on the economy and the role of knowledge capital to ensure sustainability. It points to the need and the direction for the adjustment of the macroeconomic accounting for the correct estimation of the national income and wealth. The paper is, therefore, dedicated as a tribute to the memory of Dr Bagchi.

The author would further like to thank Dr Subrata Guha and Prof. Sugata Marjit for their comments and suggestions. He would also thank Shalini Saksena for providing very useful research assistance. The author alone is, however, responsible for all the assertions made in the paper.

unit, China is the second largest economy and India, the fourth largest one in the world. Both the size of population and that of the aggregate level of economic activities create pressure on the environment by way of demand for natural resources and that of the eco-system services of the natural environment for life support, supply of raw materials, and absorption of wastes generated by the processes of production and consumption. As significant incremental factor, there has developed a global concern regarding the high economic growth of India and China for their possible adverse effects in the forms of the global warming and climate change. At the national and local level, there has developed environmental concern regarding the sustainability of the growth and development process in the long run. Sustainability requires that such process of development should not deplete and degrade the natural environment, leading to the loss of regenerative ability of the nature, and to any counter-productive results of its diminishing capability of providing support to the human economy and society.

It is also a fact, on the other hand, that economic growth is a necessary condition for the removal of poverty and destitution in developing economies. In a civilized society, even if it is overpopulated, we have to provide a decent life to everyone and leave behind enough resources for those who are unborn. If there are limits to scale of support that nature's system can provide to an economy, due to the laws of the eco-systems governing their primary productivity, how do we meet the challenge of providing decent life to all the born and the unborn? The existence of limits of the physical system of the Earth for providing support to the economy by the supply of resources and absorption of wastes leads us to two basic issues. First, is it possible for an economy to grow indefinitely at a steady or non-steady state rate within Earth's fixed physical system? Or, is it possible that an appropriate social well-being indicator which captures the maximum attainable total value for a given physical system or steady state economy of Herman Daly's (Daly, 1973) can grow indefinitely? Second, if indefinite growth or sustained development is considered possible, remaining within the limits of the ecological system, does the existing system of national income accounts serve adequately the purpose of providing measures of changes in the level of sustainable well-being. If not so, how can we develop an environmentally oriented accounting system of macroeconomic income and assets which would appropriately monitor the changes in well-being and enable us to analyze them for the policy purposes of sustainable development.

This chapter addresses first the issues of feasibility of indefinite growth maintaining the ecological system in steady state equilibrium, and defines further the notion of sustainable development. Economic activity involves two-way interactions between nature and economy. The production of goods and services requires flow of material resources as well as other environmental services for the conversion of the former into products, which are either consumed or directly or indirectly used in the production system in an entropic matter. The wastes, which arise at the end of the life-cycle of material resources, flow back to the natural environment, which provides a sink service for the absorption of the wastes. The solar energy flow and the bio-geo-chemical cycles enable the natural environment to degrade these wastes and regenerate resources. However, since nature provides the supply of such an environmental service of resource regeneration and waste absorption at a fixed rate, there is a maximum rate of primary productivity of low entropy resources, and that of absorption of high entropy wastes, per unit of time. If the economic activities are organized in such a way that the rate of resource use exceeds the limits of resource supply and if the rate of waste generation exceeds the capacity level of waste absorption, the stock of natural resources would be depleted without replenishment, and the unabsorbed wastes would accumulate as pollutant stock in the environment. Such polluting stocks would degrade the environment, while the overuse of resources would lead to a situation of resource scarcity. The growing pollution would generate adverse externalities once it exceeds the environmental capacity of the eco-system, causing health injuries to humans and adversely affecting the primary productivity or regenerative ability of the natural eco-systems.

Economic growth has always had its environmental consequences over most of the period of economic history of the world, particularly since the invention of agriculture. Since industrial revolution, human society has invented and produced an endless stream of products and processes causing continuous creation of new wants. These processes have also led to the creation of shortages of resources and new types of pollution problems from time to time. However, this is also a fact that the constraints of environmental and natural resources have not led the historical process of growth into stagnation or any catastrophic changes. Neither the dismal prediction of Malthus made in the nineteenth century nor that of the Report of Club of Rome in 1970s (Meadows et al., 1972), based on the simulation model of limits to growth, has turned out to be true. While it is true that no new energy or material can be created by man, new human knowledge as created and embodied in the various forms of human skills, physical capital goods, infrastructure, technical know how, new energy and natural resources, and institutions and norms (social capital) has enabled the humans to overcome the constraints of environment and natural resources. It is the research and development (R&D) activities that create new ideas or inventions of different types which would have environmentally conserving effect to keep the ecosystems in equilibrium. Some of these R&D outputs would give ideas of energy and material conservation, some other would invent new resources and energy source and still some others would provide new technologies for abating pollution. There can also be development of ideas and technologies for adaptation which can reduce the impact of negative externalities of a given pollution or degradation on the aggregate production activities. These inventions or discoveries involve spending on R&D, and their outputs would be patented or non-patented ideas or technologies, depending on how intellectual property rights are defined on them. These are non-rivalrous goods having enormous spillover effects of externalities. Their use in production would mostly involve increasing returns to scale which would be realized in a regime of imperfectly competitive market environment. The application of inventions or ideas may, however, be effected only by follow-up investment in physical capital, infrastructure, or in manuals, documents, and software embodying or containing the ideas (Jones, 2006; Romer, 1990, 1993).

The interaction between such knowledge creation and natural resource and environment did not play any significant role in growth economics until recently, when the endogenous growth literature started incorporating environmental variables in the growth models, and the role of endogenous knowledge formation was recognized over growth (Jones, 2006; Smulders, 1999). This new growth theory while endogenizing the growth rate shows the knowledge creation to be the ultimate driving force behind long-run growth and shows how environmental variables and knowledge creation may interact with each other. Based on the idea and approach of such endogenous growth theory for addressing the environmental problem, we set up a simple dynamic model of resource use and capital accumulation in this chapter to define the concept of sustainable development and derive its operational implication in respect of development of a system of sustainable accounting of human well-being (Dasgupta, 2001; Dasgupta and Maler, 2000).

The interpretation of such model of sustainable development, as posed in this chapter, immediately leads to the necessity for enlarging the scope of coverage of the national accounts of income and wealth with some structural changes. It points to the importance of introduction of accounts of wealth, classified into human and man-made capital, knowledge capital, and natural capital, for understanding the dynamics of indicators of sustainable development and their interactions. The motivation behind the environmental adjustment of accounts has been ideally not only to capture the environmental consequences of economic activities of production and consumption in both physical and value terms, but also their feedback effect on the growth of knowledge. The latter would compensate partly for the environmental resource depletion or degradation in the estimation of genuine investment and true income. The classified components of asset account and their respective roles in the environmental adjustment of income would generate important data for the purpose of understanding the sustainability character of the growth process and that of policy use. With reference to operationalizing the ideas in the national accounts system, our construct of subsequent follow-up models, however, focuses mainly on environmental consequences of economic activities in the form of natural resource depletion and degradation and does not show the feedback of knowledge capital component in terms of creation of new ideas as results of Research and Development (R&D) activities which contribute towards sustainability. While the man-made capital account includes creation of new ideas and knowledge at their patent or royalty values, for the purposes of environmental conservation and other purposes, their separate classified treatment would obviously further contribute to understanding sustainability. It would be important to notice how far such knowledge formation can contribute to the experience of growth, remaining within the units of scale of Daly's steady state economy or the ecological system being in stationary equilibrium (Daly, 1973; Daly and Farley, 2003).

In any case, this chapter further describes in the above context the integration of the economic and environmental accounting as proposed by UN (UNSD, 1993) under the framework of a Satellite System of Environmental-Economic Accounting (SEEA) to reflect the environmental impact of the economic activities and economic defensive activities for environmental protection. It also describes the illustrative approach of a few countries, including India, to implement the SEEA and the state of development of sustainable accounting in India.

The conventional national accounts do not provide any deduction for depletion and degradation of the in-place natural resource stock for finding out the estimate of Net Domestic Product (NDP), while they allow for the deduction on account of the depreciation of the man-made capital. If man-made capital had been the only type of capital, which is scarce in availability, then the conventional NDP provides the level of maximum sustainable consumption, at some constant level over time, and we need not have bothered about the environmental adjustment of concepts and measures. In view of the growing scarcity of natural capital, the applicability of the Hicksian concept in National Income Accounting would require an explicit recognition of the use of the different types of environmental services and their valuation, to the extent possible, so that the accounts may reflect better the depletion and degradation of the environmental assets, and provide the estimates of true income in the Hicksian sense, and the true measure of net wealth formation as best as possible. However, all the environmental impacts of economic activities (particularly some of the ecosystem services like microclimate control or biodiversity conservation of forests) cannot always be assessed physically or monetarily. What is important is that we are able to make environmental impact assessment, as comprehensively as possible, and monetize at least some of them to the extent they can be made reliably. As we shall see, it may be desirable to take a physical-cum-monetary hybrid approach of sustainable accounting for obtaining reliable indicators of change and for policy guidance. This would be better than having a single scalar monetized measure involving wide sampling fluctuations due to factors of uncertainty involved in the formula of calculation.

II A Model of Sustainable Development

Let us begin by adopting the notion of the sustainability of development process, as conceived by the World Commission on Environment and Development, which is based on an ethical theory of inter-generational equity. A capital theoretic framework of the analysis of sustainable development, as developed in the literature (Dasgupta and Maler, 2000; Dasgupta, 2001; Dasgupta and Mitra, 2001; Maler, 1991; Hartwick, 1977; Weitzman, 1976), quite sharply points to the need for resource accounting as an essential condition for implementing any policy of sustainable development. This point is elaborated to emphasize the interdependence of different components of the stock of total capital of a nation and the importance of their accounting in determining the sustainability of the growth process, as would be evident from the following simple model.

The ethical theory of intergenerational equity, first of all, implies that the well-being of a society is to be defined not as current social well-being, but as social well-being over time (Dasgupta, 2001). Let the social well-being over time for the economy be represented by the discounted present equivalent of the intertemporal profile of instantaneous utilities, which depend positively on consumption and negatively on the level of pollution stock. A Ramsey-Koopmans type intertemporal social utility function, defined over an infinite time horizon, is used for an economy with stationary population in the next subsection.

Intertemporal Welfare Function

$$V(\tau)=\int_{\tau}^{\infty} u\{c(t),P(t)\}e^{-r(t-\tau)}dt \qquad (2.1)$$

where t is the time, c is the consumption of goods and services, $P(t)$ is the level of pollution stock, r is the time rate of discount, and u is the current utility out of consumption and environmental quality in terms of level of pollution.

With a view to examining the feasibility of steady growth within the fixed system of nature, we explicitly introduce technological change in the production function as typical in endogenous growth models. These technical changes would be conceived as production or creation of ideas regarding production of new commodities or new ways of production having impact on productivity and involving R&D investments. The technology or idea of production is, thus, produced by investment in research and development. In our model, technological changes would be classified into two broad types:

1. Change in total factor productivity arising from conservation of matter and energy, man-made and human capital, pollution abatement, and adaptation to environmental condition or pollution to enhance productivity. The level of such technology conceived as a composite one be denoted by $A(t)$. Let Z_A be the R&D investment for augmenting A.

2. Discovery of deposits of known or new source of energy and material resources in the form of established information. Let $B(t)$ be the level of knowledge regarding resources and $Z_B(t)$ be investment for new exploration of such resources.

Two points need to be noted here. First of all, we are not explicitly assuming anything regarding the definition of intellectual property rights. However, that would be important when we try to work out the microeconomic foundation of the current model. This has not been included in the scope of the current chapter and we stop at conceptualizing sustainability and its accounting implications for environmental sustainability.

Second, the technologies are all embodied in the man-made and human capital, and the production of these capitals in the concerned production or training sector. The production economy would use the ideas or technologies, which are outputs of the research sector as inputs to produce these capital goods. In view of the enormous spillover and non-rivalrous nature of use of knowledge or ideas, combined with the effects of positive externalities, there is likely to be enormous scope of economies of increasing returns to scale in these capital-goods sector which would be experiencing, as already mentioned, an imperfectly competitive situation (Jones, 2006).

In our model, the total social product (Y) would consist of (a) new technology or production of R&D, which may be classified into the two broad types as described above and (b) total production of non-R&D sector, which is an aggregate of consumption and all forms of capital goods, including the share of human capital formation. Let us further classify the natural resources into two types—renewable, which are regenerated by nature, and non-renewable, which cannot be regenerated by nature within human time scale. The R&D activities can, however, find alternative substitutes or discover more of the non-renewable resources that are lying underneath the earth. R&D requires only investment inputs involving the use of part of nations' savings.

The production of non-R&D goods and services, $Y(t)$, which constitutes that bulk of the production of the economy is obtained by transforming resources—both renewable (R_1) and non-renewable (R_2)—with the help of the services of the stock of composite of man-made and human capital and that of eco-service of the nature. The former service input can be denoted by K for keeping the model simple and the latter can be denoted by $e(t)$, that is, the emissions to be absorbed by the ecosystem as sink. However, the productivity of inputs in these general category of goods and services would be influenced by two factors: level of technology or $A(t)$ and the level of the stock of pollutants $P(t)$. We thus have the following formal presentation.

Production Function

$$Y(t) = f(A(t), K(t), \ R_1(t), \ R_2(t), \ e(t), \ P^\gamma(t))$$
$$= AK^\alpha \ R^\beta \ e^{1-\alpha-\beta} \ P. \tag{2.1}$$
$$\alpha > 0, \ \beta > 0, \ \alpha + \beta < 1, \ \gamma < 0$$

Accumulation of Man-made Capital

$$\overset{*}{K} = \overline{Y}(t) - C(t) - \delta K(t) - Z_A(t) - Z_B(t). \tag{2.2}$$

where $C(t)$ is consumption spending, δ is the depreciation factor, $Z_A(t)$ is the R&D investment in technological change and in the factor A and Z_B are the R&D investment for discovery of new resources.

Technological Changes

$$\overset{*}{A}(t) = m Z_A^{\rho_2}(t) = \overline{m} A(t)^{\rho_1} Z_A^{\rho_2} \tag{2.3}$$

where $m = \overline{m} A(t)^{\rho_1}$.

$$\overline{m} > 0, \ \rho_1 < 1, 0 < \rho_2 < 1$$

The productivity of R&D effort, however, depends on the pre-existing levels of technology development $A(t)$. While at the higher level of development of technology, the productivity of R&D effort would tend to be higher, due to cumulative knowledge on which it tends to build up, the discovery or innovation of a new technology becomes difficult at such a high level of technology development, as it is likely that low cost innovations or easy discoveries have already been mostly made. As a result, the impact of rise in $A(t)$ may be positive or negative. However, ρ_1, even if positive, is likely to be less than 1, as a net result of the two effects. Besides, the diminishing marginal productivity of R&D effort, Z_A, for any given level of technology A, would warrant $0 < \rho_2 < 1$.

Growth of Natural Resources

(i) Renewable resource

$$\overset{*}{N_1} = Q(N_1(t), P(t)) - R_1(t). \tag{2.4}$$

$\overset{*}{N_1}$ is the stock of renewable resource, where Q is the growth or regeneration of renewable resources by nature, and $R_1(t)$ is the renewable resource harvested and used in the production of Y. Q_1 is dependent on the pre-existing stock $N_1(t)$ and is also adversely affected by the stock of pollutant $P(t)$.

(ii) Non-renewable resource

$$\overset{*}{N_2} = \overset{*}{B}(t) - R_2(t) \tag{2.5}$$

Where $\overset{*}{N_2}$ is the stock of balance of non-renewable resources, B is the cumulative discovery of such resources, and $\overset{*}{B}(t)$ is the discovery of new resources in the concerned period to replenish the stock of non-renewable resources. $R_2(t)$ is the extraction of non-renewable resources for use in production.

Resource Discoveries

$$\overset{*}{B}(t) = n Z_B(t)^{\sigma_2} = \overline{n}.B^{\sigma_1}(t) Z_B^{\sigma_2}(t), \text{ where } n = \overline{n}\ B^{\sigma}(t) \tag{2.6}$$

$$n > 0, \sigma_1 < 1, 0 < \sigma_2 < 1$$

The productivity of R&D efforts for exploration and discovery of new deposits or substitute resource would depend on the cumulative level of discovery B(t) and not on the balance of stock N_2. The effect of experience of cumulative discovery is likely to have exactly analogous impact of productivity of R&D effort in new discovery of resources as in the case of R&D efforts for general technology development, that is, change in (t) for similar reason.

Growth of Stock of Pollution

$$\overset{*}{P}(t) = e(t) - \theta P(t) \tag{2.7}$$

where θ is the rate of degradation of the pollution stock by nature per unit of time.

Initial condition

$$K(\tau), N_1(\tau),\ N_2(\tau),\ P(\tau),\ A(\tau),\ B(\tau) \text{ are given.} \tag{2.8}$$

The dynamics of the various stocks, whose initial values are given, would yield an intertemporal utility profile as determined by the Resource Allocation Mechanism (RAM) of the society which is defined by the institutional arrangements of production and distribution. This allocation mechanism may not be perfect from the viewpoint of either competitiveness or that of attaining the first best social optimum (Dasgupta, 2001). The present equivalent value of the utility profile or the measure of social well-being over time thus generated by the RAM would, in fact, be equivalent to the aggregate value of all the initial capital stocks, technologies, and discovered resource base using the prices which are derived from the marginal value productivities of the different types of stocks of assets, including knowledge over time. The given initial configuration of $K(\tau),\ N_1(\tau), N_2(\tau), P(\tau), A(\tau), B(\tau)$

and the resource allocation mechanism, say α, would yield a time path of the variables $\{C(t), R_1(t), R_2(t), e(t), N_1(t), N_2(t), P(t), K(t), A(t) B(t)\}_\alpha$ and correspondingly, a utility time profile of $\{u(C(t), P(t))\}_\alpha$ and a value of $V_\alpha(\tau)$. The shadow rentals for the use of the stocks, as arising from the process, would yield the initial stock prices at the time τ as the discounted initial equivalent values. The aggregate value of these initial stocks of capital, natural resources, technology, and cumulative resource discoveries as per such accounting prices would be $V_\alpha(\tau)$. The sustainability of the development process would thus mean that the social well-being over time, or equivalently, the aggregate value of all the stocks of resources or wealth of the society, should be non-declining with the passage of time.

The sustainability condition would then imply:

$$\frac{dV^*(\tau)}{d(\tau)} = \frac{\partial V^*(\tau)}{\partial k(\tau)} \cdot \frac{dk(\tau)}{d\tau} + \frac{\partial V^*(\tau)}{\partial N(\tau)} \cdot \frac{dN(\tau)}{d\tau} + \frac{\partial V^*(\tau)}{\partial N_2(\tau)} \cdot \frac{dN_2(\tau)}{d\tau} + \frac{\partial V^*(\tau)}{\partial A(\tau)} \cdot$$

$$\frac{dA(\tau)}{d\tau} + \frac{\partial V^*(\tau)}{\partial B(\tau)} \cdot \frac{dB(\tau)}{d\tau}$$

$$= p(\tau) \frac{dK}{d\tau} + \pi_1(\tau) \frac{dN_1}{d\tau} + \pi_2(\tau) \frac{dN_2}{d\gamma} + \vartheta_A(\tau) \cdot \frac{dA(\tau)}{d\tilde{1}}$$

$$+ \vartheta_B^{(\gamma)} \frac{dB(\tau)}{d\tau} + \mu(\tau) \frac{dP}{d\tau}$$

$$= I_k(\tau) + I_{N_1}(\tau) + I_{N_2}(\gamma) + I_A(\tau) + I_B(\tau) + I_P(\tau)$$

$$= I(\tau) \geq 0$$

for all values τ as we move along the time axis, where $V^*(\tau)$ is the attainable value of $\vartheta(\tau)$ under the RAM; $p(\tau)$, $\pi_1(\tau)$, $\pi_2(\tau)$, $\mu(\tau)$, $\vartheta_A(\tau)$, $\vartheta_B(\tau)$ are the respective stock prices, and I_k, I_{N_1}, I_{N_2} and I_P are the respective investment values in man-made capital, natural capital, pollution stocks, technologies, and discoveries of resources. $I(\tau)$ is the aggregate true investment. The sustainability of development, thus, requires that true investment, which is the aggregate value of investments in all kinds of capital assets of a society, including knowledge or ideas regarding technology and discovered resources, should be non-negative.

The composition of this investment, thus, needs to be examined for understanding its precise implication, in respect of natural resource accounting, and for analyzing the sustainability character of the development process. One important implication of the condition

$I(\tau) \geq 0$ of the above model is that society's genuine or true measure of investment or accumulation of wealth, which would contribute to the progress of well-being, is not just the value of net accumulation of man-made and human capital, but the total value of net accumulation of man-made capital, natural capital of all kinds, and those of stock of knowledge and ideas, including discoveries of non-renewable resources, as adjusted for the net accumulation of the public bad of pollution stock. If there is an over-harvesting of the renewable resources of nature exceeding the limit of nature's ability to regenerate resources, depletion of non-renewable resources, exceeding new discoveries, and if the emission of pollutants exceed the ecosystem's ability to absorb them, then $\overset{*}{N_1}(\tau)<0$, $\overset{*}{N_2}(\tau)<0$, $\overset{*}{P}(\tau)>0$ leading to $I_{N_1}<0$, $I_{N_2}<0$, $I_P<0$ since $\pi_1(\tau), \pi_2(\tau)$ are expected to be positive and $\mu(\tau)$ negative. This would imply $I_E = I_{N_1} + I_{N_2} + I_P < 0$. I_E gives the aggregate measure of depletion of the environmental resource base of the economy, which includes the entire array of natural resources: fossil fuels, minerals, land and soil, water, forest and other vegetation and abiotic resources, atmosphere, ocean, lakes, rivers, and so forth. While the basic elementary contents of matter and energy of all these natural resource assets remain unchanged over time, the time rate of their human use often tends to exceed the scale of intervention that the nature can withstand, resulting in the dissipation of resources due to the entropy laws.

III Resource and Environmental Accounting

As the neo-classical production function allows substitutability between natural capital and man-made cum human capital, and admits growth of knowledge capital in our model, the sustainability of social well-being (in a weak sense) over time may be attainable by moderating the demand for the withdrawal of resources $R_1(t)$ and $R_2(t)$ from the stock of natural resources $N_1(t)$ and $N_2(t)$, or by reducing the pollution for the same production $Y(t)$. This can be achieved by investing in energy and material resource conservation and pollution abating technologies $A(t)$ and also in the substitution of $R_1(t)$ or $R_2(t)$ by $K(t)$. This would also have a beneficial effect on rising pollution because of the relation of material balance between the material resource flow and the return waste flow as per the entropy law. Besides, the spending on R&D for exploration of natural resources or the dynamics of B(t) is also of crucial importance in the sustenance of the growth and development process. The composition of knowledge capital, man-made and natural capital stocks, and the dynamics of their change, thus, need to be explicitly monitored and analyzed for guiding the policies and actions for sustainable development. A comprehensive asset accounting, including accounting for natural resources and knowledge capital with appropriate classification, thus, needs to be developed to monitor all such changes in both physical and value terms to the extent possible.

While the stock dynamics of $K(\tau)$, $N_1(\tau)$, $N_2(\tau)$ and $P(\tau)$ would indicate the pressure of the scale of the economy on the nature, the fact of the matter is that $A(\tau)$ and $B(\tau)$ are the main driving forces behind sustainability through the reduction of such pressures for de-linking of environment and development. One may in fact investigate the parametric condition in which $V(t)$ or $Y(t)$ may be allowed to grow indefinitely. While we do not enter into such investigation here, what appears to be clear from the model is that the endogenous knowledge capital formation in terms of innovations or technical changes and discoveries of new resources can enable the economy to grow without violating limits of the Earth's ecosystem and disturbing the ecological equilibrium under appropriate condition. Although we have not explicitly indicated separate accounting for the R&D sector's investment and output in this chapter, it would be important to compile and analyze such data for assessing the drive for sustainability of an economy. It is not only just the saving rate of the economy of the model, but its investment allocation, the formation of man-made capital, knowledge capital and new discoveries of resources which would have determining influence on both growth rate and its sustainability. Within technology development it would also be an important further enquiry to find out how the allocation for technology development for the alternative purposes of resource conservation, pollution abatement, and adaptation to environmental changes would matter in weakening the relationship between growth and environmental pressure. All these point to the necessity of developing a block of accounting for knowledge development as a part of the total system of sustainable resource accounting for monitoring changes and developing policies. In our following discussions on the models for resource and income accounting, we have not, however, explicitly shown separate treatment of the research sector due to the inadequate development of measures of various kinds of intangible knowledge formation, their sectoral allocation of use and costs because of the non-rivalrous public good nature of the knowledge as a good. The formation of aggregate knowledge capital has been, however, included in the composite man-made capital, mostly at cost price in our accounting models, although the discoveries or development of new resources would be separately shown at places.

What are the special or new dimensions of a national accounts system that would require to be developed in view of the model of the preceding section on sustainable development? First of all, there should be accounts showing clearly the quantitative or qualitative changes of all the major resource items: stock flow (both renewable and non-renewable separately) and fund flow resources like quality of air shed or water body as sink (see Daly and Farley, 2003). The conservation or protection of such resources may necessitate appropriate spending on current or capital accounts for the discovery of new resources or the upgradation of the existing resources or for the development of backstop resource and technology. Examples can be given of investment for the discovery of new oil deposits, or alternative energy resources, change in land use, forest development and management for promoting biotic growth or culture of biological resources, and so forth. Similarly, the spending on pollution abatement technologies on both current account and capital account would contribute to the reduction of pollution or to the cleaning up of the environment—particularly air, water bodies, and land—and to the conservation of the resource regenerating ability of the ecosystem.

Part of this spending on the primary and intermediate inputs for resource development or pollution abatement would be reflected in the changes in the man-made capital assets in the form of fixed non-residential or other structures and equipments, for example, rigs for oil exploration or pollution abatement equipments, in the macro asset account. The remaining part of the spending would be mainly reflected in the asset account as changes in the developed natural assets (or what may alternatively be called non-produced economic assets), which have been obtained by way of transfer of resources from the natural environment where they were lying in an undeveloped state, to the economic environment, in order to make them suitable for utilization in economic activities. These changes should be reflected, in most of the cases, in both the physical and monetary values of the concerned resources, for example, developed sub-soil assets, changes in land use, and so forth. Some of this spending may result in only qualitative changes like upgrading water quality or air quality indicators in terms of concentration of the pollutants in the concerned water body, air shed, and so forth, which may not be easily estimated in value terms because of the immediate non-marketability of the benefits. These values of developed or protected natural assets, whenever estimable, would, in fact, contain the scarcity value of the undeveloped *in situ* resource, or the natural environment as well as the costs of consumption of fixed capital assets and other primary and intermediate inputs, which were used for this transfer or protection, and which contributed to the augmentation of utilizable $N_2(t)$ or to the abatement of $P(t)$.

In any case, it is clear that the replenishment of the physical levels of depleted natural resource stock or the abatement of the pollutant stock would often raise the volume of economic activities and GDP, and also the gross value of capitalized assets or gross investment vis-à-vis a situation of neglect of environmental consideration in economic activities for sustainability. However, if such spending replenishes the depleted environmental stock, such additions of values to GDP or Gross Investment would offset the depreciation of natural assets, which were induced by the economic activities. The investment for replenishment or maintenance of such environmental resources should, therefore, be deducted when we have to work out the NDP or true investment. In fact, if in an economy, the actual replenishment or restoration of environmental assets is not adequate, the entire natural capital depreciation is to be provided for, for deriving the estimates of Hicksian income as well as the true investment of an economy.

An important outcome, of the earlier discussion on the conceptual theory of the sustainability of economic processes and its practical implication in accounting, is the recognition of the need for the following changes in our macro-economic accounting system:

1. To measure the opening physical resource stocks, their monetary values, and their changes with the compositional break-up during the concerned period, which are relevant to the sustainability of economic processes.
2. To restructure the wealth asset account of the economy, in order to take account of natural resource accounting in 1 and show the

linkage between man-made fixed capital with environmental resource development and protection.

3. To adjust the production, income, and expenditure accounts of the economy, in order to take account of resource accounting, and make it consistent with the changes in the wealth account in order to generate the estimates of true income or NDP at the macro level. The details of the re-oriented account should clarify the role of environment in production.

IV An Environmental Input-Output Framework of Analysis

While the model of Section II gave the condition for sustainable development and the rationale for resource accounting for monitoring and analyzing sustainability of the process of change of an economy, we now turn to a theoretical model for the integration of environmental accounting with that of national accounts for developing the sustainable accounting framework for the purpose. An extension of the input-output model as presented in the following pages incorporates the environment-economy interaction, and would be useful to understand not only the environmental consequences of economic activities and those of environmental protection or resource conservation on the sustainability of the economic system, but also to develop the schematic framework of the revised accounts and to derive the equations or formula for the environmental adjustments for the macro economic aggregates and national accounts.

The conventional input-output framework, first of all, needs to be reoriented for incorporating the flows between the economy and the natural environment in addition to the flows within the economy to capture the environmental consequences of the various sectoral economic activities. The flows between the environment and the economy would be captured in two ways: (a) flows of natural resources from the nature to economic activities and (b) flows of waste arising from the economic activities of production, as well as final use, to the natural environmental for their possible absorption (Ayres, 1978; Leontief, 1970; Pearson, 1989; Perman et al., 1996).

Both these types of flows can be conceived as input flows. The natural resources are obviously throughput to the economic system for either material processing for conversion into products or for providing energy or other services for such conversion. The waste arisings, unless immediately degraded, are by-products with negative external effects; the waste flows may be interpreted as throughput going into the sink of the nature as ecosystem. The latter would receive such waste flows in order to degrade or store them into itself. We do, however, allow that the production system contains waste or pollution abatement activities, which are external to the other different sectors defined, and reduces the pollution by treatment of wastewater, solid waste management, waste treatment, and so on. The products of such activities may be called environmental protection products, which would also use various types of resources. There are also some abatement measures, which are internal to an industrial sector and built into the basic technology of the concerned production activities. The waste arising from a sector as defined would obviously be net of such internal abatement.

In the extended framework of environmental input-output analysis, we thus can classify the input flows into four categories:

1. Intermediate inputs of produced goods and services
2. Primary inputs of labor and capital
3. Natural resource inputs
4. Waste-flow disposal service of the natural environment.

The producing sectors of the economy can be classified essentially into three categories:

1. Natural resource development and extraction activities like coal mining, iron ore mining, oil extraction, and so on. It is, in fact, the products of these activities that are used by the other economic sectors. The coal or oil as produced would, thus, for example, be intermediate goods, while the natural resource of coal as embodied in coal seams or crude oil, *in situ*, should be considered as inputs in the extraction activities as supplied by nature.
2. Environmental Protection activities which abate increase in pollution.
3. Other industrial activities.

We shall, however, club 1 and 3 together since a number of sectoral activities vertically combine the development of the natural resource with the use of energy, labor, and capital, the harvesting of the resource and its processing as it is the case in the sectors of agriculture, forestry, and fishery. These would, for example, include working on land and soil, forest biomass and biomass of fish stock, and so on, along with the activities of their development and use for yielding the sectoral marketed products of agricultural crops, forest, and aqua-cultural products.

Let $X=(X_j)$ be the vector of output of sectoral activities other than environmental protection. Let X^1_{ij} denote the flow of sectoral production from ith sector for intermediate input use in the jth conventional industrial sector (that is, other than environmental protection industries) and F_i denote its supply to the final user of the product.

Let Y^1_{kj} be the use of kth primary factors like labor, man-made capital, and so on, in the jth conventional industrial sector.

Let R^1_{lj} and W^1_{sj} be the flow of lth natural capital resource to the jth industrial sector and that of sth residual waste from the jth industrial sector to the natural environment, respectively.

Let $Z=(Z_s)$ be the vector of pollution abatement or environmental protection activities. Let X^2_{im}, Y^2_{km}, R^2_{lm} and W^2_{sm} be the flows of ith industrial good, k^{th} primary factor service, lth natural resource, and sth residual flows of waste to or from the mth environmental protection sector. Let W^f_s be the sth waste flow from the final use of the goods and services F_i for all i together. Let $\overline{W}_s$ be the unabated amount of sth waste flow in the concerned period.

We show the transaction flows of different products and input flows of the economy in Table 8.1. Each row of the table shows the flows of products or inputs or wastes to different using sectors. It may be noted that the total gross waste flows would be the total output of the abatement of the concerned waste plus the actual unabated amount. The columns, on the other hand, shows the spending by the different using sectors in real terms on different inputs, including the sink service of nature to obtain the output of the concerned producing sector or the benefit of final use.

Table 8.1: Transaction Flows

Users → Products or Inputs↓	Industries Other than Environmental Protection(s)	Environmental Protection or Pollution Abatement Sectors (m)	Final Users	Total
Industrial products other than Environmental protection ones	X^1_{ij}	X^2_{im}	F_i	X_i
Wastes	W^1_{sj}	W^2_{sm}	W^f_s	$Z_s + \bar{W}_s$
Primary factors	Y^1_{kj}	Y^2_{km}		b_k
Natural capital	R^1_{lj}	R^2_{lm}		r_l

Source: Prepared by the author.

If now p_i, t_s, v_k, π_l be the prices of the industrial product i, environmental protection product of abating s^{th} waste, primary factor k and natural resource l, we can derive easily a transaction table in value terms for our economy. However, given the assumption of linear technology of Leontief type, we may derive the following input-output model based on the above real transaction table. So far as the flows between the natural environment and the economy are concerned, the nature as resource supplier is supplying r_l and receiving as sink $\bar{W}_s s$, the unabated net waste. The entropy law and material balance condition would ensure the relationship,

$$\theta(r) = \theta_1(\bar{W}) + \theta_2$$

where θ is the total molecular weight of all the natural resource throughput represented by the vector $r = (r_l)$,

θ_1 is the total molecular weight of all unabated wastes represented by the vector $\bar{W} = (\bar{W}_s)$.

θ_2 is the total molecular weight of all durable material goods produced and accumulated for future use during the concerned period. θ_2 would depend on the composition of F_i's in terms of consumption, investment, export, and so on.

For the conventional input-output sectors, the demand-supply balance will yield the condition:

$$X = A_1 X + A_2 Z + F \tag{4.1}$$

where X, Z, and F are the column vectors $X = (X_j)$, $Z = (Z_m)$, $F = (F_i)$.

$A_1 = (a_{ij}^1)$ where $a_{ij}^1 = X_{ij}^1 / X_j$, A_1 is a square matrix

$A_2 = (a_{im}^2)$ where $a_{im}^2 = X_{im}^2 / Z_m$

For the environmental protection products of waste abatements, the supply-demand balance condition is found to be

$$Z = W_1X + W_2Z + W^f - \bar{W} \tag{4.2}$$

where matrix $W_1 = (w_{sj}^1)$ where $w_{sj}^1 = \dfrac{W_{sj}}{X_j}$

$W_2 = (w_{sm}^2)$ where $w_{sm}^2 = \dfrac{W_{sm}}{Z_m}$ and W_2 is a square matrix

For the primary factor inputs of labor and man-made capital, and the natural resources, supply-demand balance conditions would yield the following conditions:

$$b = B_1X + B_2Z, \tag{4.3}$$

$$r = R_1X + R_2Z \tag{4.4}$$

where $b = (b_k)$ and $r = (r_l)$ are the vectors of total primary factor use and natural resource uses, respectively

$B_1 = (b_{kj}^1)$ where $b_{kj}^1 = Y_{kj}^1 / X_j$

$B_2 = (b_{km}^2)$ where $b_{km}^2 = Y_{km}^2 / Z_m$

$R_1 = (r_{lj}^1)$ where $r_{lj}^1 = R_{lj}^1 / X_j$

$R_2 = (r_{lm}^2)$ where $r_{lm}^2 = R_{lm}^2 / Z_m$

The price-cost condition that will be satisfied under the technological assumptions of the model and the conditions of competition would be as follows:

$$p = pA_1 + vB_1 + \pi R_1 + tW_1 \tag{4.5}$$

$$t = pA_2 + vB_2 + \pi R_2 + tW_2 \tag{4.6}$$

where $p = (p_i)$, $v = (v_k)$, $\pi = (\pi_l)$, $t = (t_s)$ are the row price vectors of products and inputs.

In this economy for any given vector of final demand yielding an associated waste, arising from final uses of material goods, and given an unabated waste flow level (or net waste flow standard), equation (4.1) to (4.4) will solve for the gross level of outputs of the conventional industrial sectors and of various waste abatement activities, as well as for the total uses of primary factors and natural resource inputs. The supportive price system for the industrial goods and pollution abatement services will be solved by the equation (4.5) and (4.6) for given primary factor and natural resource prices.

The vectors p and t can be interpreted as marginal costs of production of the conventional industrial products and the marginal costs of abatement of pollution. The final demand F and the demand for environmental standard, as indicated by $\overline{W}$, should be consistent with p and t, and the generated total income as yielded by $vb + \pi r$ if the economy is in equilibrium. The theory of environmental economics would ensure that the marginal damage cost of unabated pollution waste from which the consumers or people of the society will suffer at the level $\overline{W}$ would be equal to the marginal cost of abatement of the various wastes as indicated by t. The environmental damage costs due to externalities from unabated wastes have not, however, been explicitly incorporated in the model. The vector t, as observed in an economy, can be conceived as a marginal defensive cost for environmental protection or equivalently as a measure of the valuation of marginal environmental degradation (marginal damage cost) for some assumed preference of the people for environmental quality, which warrants the actual unabated waste flow to be the social optimal. Once the technology, the conventional primary factor prices, and the natural capital prices are given, the marginal cost of abatement, which is independent of the scale of abatement in this model, would determine the environmental standard in terms of $\overline{W}$ where it is equated with the marginal damage cost. The t vector can in fact be treated as an environmental pollution tax, which the polluter will have to pay for disposing any unabated waste into the sink as a price of sink service of nature, for the control of the damages from wastes flow at the socially optimal level. If the actual unabated pollution W conforms to the standard, $\overline{W}$ can be interpreted to be the optimal level of pollution.

It is important here to note a common phenomenon that the environmental resource protection measures, including pollution abatement undertaken in a given period, is inadequate for maintaining the environmental resource capacity. It is also very often the situation that the natural environmental resource base and its capacity have been depleted over a long time due to neglect. It is often not only a question of replenishing the environmental resource stock as depreciated in a given year or period to maintain the level on a year to year basis, as at the beginning of the period, but also to restore the capacity to a benchmark level which corresponds to the environmental capacity in the base year period, and is considered normative for the sustainability of the functions of ecosystems (See Chapter 1 of SEEA, in UNSD 2000). For example, the Kyoto protocol targets to control the Green House Gas emission flow to a level marginally lower than that of 1990 levels for the protocol signatory nations. The sustainable capacity requirement would warrant investments to restore the capacity to the benchmark level. The standard or resource prices or pollution taxes may, thus, be required to be so fixed in a period that it may take care of restoration of the environmental capacity of the economy in a time frame to offset the depletion and degradation of the past and in the current period and make adjustments of wealth or income accounts accordingly.

The demand-supply balances of products and factor inputs and the competitive cost-price conditions, however, give us the following identity between the expenditure and factor income methods based estimates of GDP. This is obtained by pre-multiplying both sides of (4.1), (4.2), (4.3), and (4.4) by the respective vectors p, t, v, and π and post multiplying both sides of (4.5) and (4.6) by X and Z, respectively and setting at equality the alternative expressions of $pX + tZ$. We obtain the final result as:

$$pF + t(W^f - \overline{W}) = vb + \pi r \qquad (4.7a)$$

$$\text{or} \quad pF + tW^f = vb + \pi r + t\overline{W}. \qquad (4.7b)$$

The GDP would thus be $pF + tW^f$, the value of final expenditure on goods and services, including the share of waste disposal of such final uses. This is equivalent to the total factor incomes arising from the use of primary factors of labour and capital in the forms of wages and profits or return to man-made capital, the natural resources in the form of rent or royalty, and that of sink service of nature in the form of environmental taxes imposed for waste disposal at the rate of marginal abatement costs.

How much would the estimate of GDP vary, in our above formulation, because of the incorporation of environmental concerns? In the case of abundance of environmental capacity or neglect of environmental concerns, the actual or perceived environmental capacity is considered to be so large that the natural resources are treated as free goods, implying $\pi = 0$ and there is no need of restriction on the disposal of unabated polluting waste into the sink, that is, $\overline{W}$ can be any value with $Z = 0$ in (4.2), that is, $\overline{W} = W_1 X + W^f$.

In actual reality, the natural resources are not always intrinsically treated as free goods and the users often pay some rent or royalty, although such rent as charged is not always consistent with the sustainable patterns of use of the resources, as would be implied by the maintenance of the potential environmental capacity of an ecosystem over time. It is only in a situation of rational expectation behavior of the users of resources that the correct supporting sustainable or socially optimal prices π will be expected and actually be realized. This is not often the reality, and the political economy of resource use results in over-use of resources. For similar reasons, although the actual environmental protection measures undertaken by pollution abatement are positive, they fall short of the socially optimal level of abatement.

The comparative use of resources and waste flow, under the alternative conditions of abundant capacity, sustainable use of environmental capacity, and the actual situation of over-use of environmental capacity are depicted in the following two diagrams, that is, Figures 8.1 and 8.2 of natural resource use and pollution abatement.

In Figure 8.1, AS_2 shows the equilibrium use of a resource in the multi-sectoral macro-economy for the different resource price or resource rentals. If the sustainable price of the scarce resource be π_o, then OS_o will be the sustainable use of the resource, which is warranted by the optimal theory of resource use—renewable or non-renewable—over time. However, if the perceived resource scarcity is less than the true scarcity, as determined by the natural growth of a renewable resource or the cost price of use of the alternative resource and the associated backstop technology for an exhaustible resource, the resource rental may prevail at π_1, causing the use of OS_1, which is in excess of OS_o by the amount of $S_o S_1$. In a situation of resource abundance, the resource price should be zero and its use will go up to OS_2. The sustainable resource accounting will attempt to adjust the income and the total

Figure 8.1: Natural Resource Use

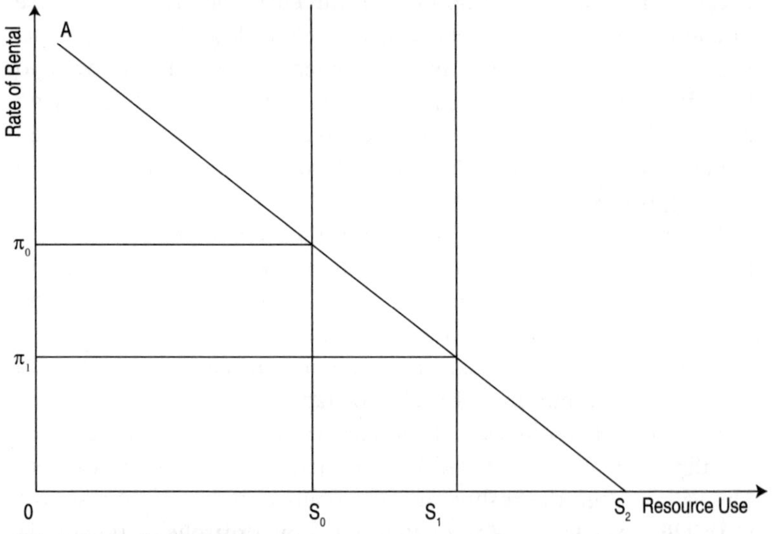

Source: Prepared by the author.

value added for the depletion of the resource, which is equivalent to $S_0 S_1$ in the diagram at the appropriate prices.

Similarly, in Figure 8.2, the waste flow in the macro-economy in the absence of any control of emission is given to be OW_2 and the marginal cost of abatement as $0t$. The curves $D_0 D_0$, $D_1 D_1$, and $D_2 D_2$ describe the marginal cost of environmental damage curves due to externalities for the respective situations of sustainable environmental capacity, the perceived environmental capacity (which is overestimated to be in excess of the sustainable level), and that of environmental capacity abundance for waste absorption. While the restoration to the truly sustainable environmental capacity will require an optimal abatement of $W_0 W_2$ with environmental standard $\bar{W} = OW_0$, the actual abatement would be $W_1 W_2$ with unabated emission $\bar{W} = OW_1$, causing under-abatement or environmental degradation beyond the sustainable level by an amount $W_0 W_1$. In a hypothetical situation of environmental capacity abundance, there would, however, be no abatement of pollution, and the waste flow will remain as OW_2. The sustainable environmental accounting will require adjustment of the income or net domestic product for the

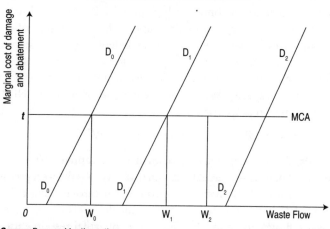

Figure 8.2: Pollution Flows and Abatement

Source: Prepared by the author.

environmental degradation to the extent of W_0W_1 at the marginal cost of abatement, that is, $0t$.

How should we, then, finally make environmental adjustment to GDP or National Income? In the conventional accounts, the environmental consequences are incorporated only to the extent the transactions are affected by the actual π_1, positive or zero, and the $\bar{W}_s$. Both π_1 and $\bar{W}_s$, as observed in actual transaction, often fall short of the sustainable price π_1^0 and exceeds the sustainable standard W_s^* respectively.

Thus, the environmental adjustment would require deduction of the value of the depletion of natural capital—non-renewable and renewable resources like minerals, fossil fuels, forest products, fish and other biota, water, and so on, beyond their sustainable level of use, and of the value of degradation of the natural environment, due to the unabated residual wastes of various kinds, beyond sustainable level affecting land, soil, air, water, and so on. While the conventional national income accounting adjusts for the depreciation of man-made capital which is included in v_k for k = man-made capital, it does not make any adjustment of income for the natural capital depletion or degradation for sustainability. If K be the physical stock of the primary factor man-made capital (u) and p_k be its price, then the gross return to capital $\Pi_k = (\delta+i)p_k K$, where δ is the rate of depreciation and i is the rate of interest or normal rate of return on man-made capital employed in the macro-economy. The

NDP is obtained from Gross Value Added or GDP by subtracting $\delta p_k K$. In order to obtain environmentally adjusted NDP, we need to work out, for each major type of natural capital, the counterpart of δ and p_k. In other words, we have to assess the extent of physical depletion or degradation, and the accounting prices to be used for assessing the depletion or degradation, with reference to the sustainable level of environmental capacity. With reference to equation 4.7b, the NDP can then be expressed as follows:

$$NDP = pF + tW^f - \delta\, p_k K - \pi(r - r^*) - t\,(\overline{W} - W^*) \qquad (4.8)$$

where $\delta p_k K$ is the depreciation of man-made capital, $\pi(r - r^*)$ the depletion of natural resource stocks and $t(\overline{W} - W^*)$ is the total provision for degradation of the natural environmental capacity due to waste flow; r^*, W^* being the vectors of sustainable levels of resource use and waste flows, and r and $\overline{W}$ the vectors of actual resource use and unabated waste flow.

The above adjustments necessitate the setting up of an asset account of a macro economy, including both man-made and natural capital with appropriate classification, showing the changes that occurred in the current year due to factors like capital formation, natural growth, their consumption or degradation in production, or other variations, and so on. It is the reduction in the values due to the production account which would only need to be adjusted for estimating national income as a sustainable flow of maximum possible consumption in the Hicksian sense. The integration of environment and economic accounting will require the careful linking of the two accounts to provide one integrated picture of income and wealth of a nation.

V Asset Accounts

The basic model of SEEA, however, focuses on how natural resources and ecosystem inputs flow into the economy, and the products and residuals are generated in the production. It essentially provides a schematic framework of presentation, juxtaposing the environmental and man-made asset account to the production and income account of the economy, with the sectoral break up of environmental protection and other economic activities and also that of total cost into environmental cost and economic cost (See Figure 8.3). As the sustainability condition ideally requires the total investment in all kinds of capital assets to be non-negative, sustainable accounting requires the development of an asset account of the economy, comprising the man-made capital assets, fixed capital, and inventory capital and the natural capital assets which are essential for the sustainability of economic processes. However, SNA 1993 delimited the scope of coverage of assets, including environmental ones, to the economic assets, which were required to satisfy two conditions:

1. Property rights should be defined on the asset at the level of individual, state, institution, or community.
2. Its value should be defined in terms of a flow of income or monetary benefit which it would generate over time.

These environmental assets are classified, first of all, into produced assets and non-produced asset. The produced environmental assets would consist of all cultivated biological assets like livestock, fish, fowl, orchards, plantations, standing agricultural crops, and so on. Although these are products of photosynthesis and solar energy flows through the food chain and cycles, there has been enormous human energy and capital subsidy in their regeneration and supply. These are, therefore, outputs of production activities of agriculture, fishery, forestry, and so on. These assets produced would be further classified into fixed assets and inventories. Fixed assets would be such cultivated assets, which are intended for repeated or continuous use in production, for example, vineyard, orchards, and plantations, livestock for breeding, diary, draught, and so on. On the other hand, agricultural standing crops for single use, livestock or fish for slaughter or catch, standing timber waiting to be felled, and so on, are natural inventory capital of cultivated products. It may be noted here that agricultural crops produced, harvested, and sold during a period would constitute a product flow, but not an economic asset.

Among the abiotic produced assets, land development should figure as a fixed capital formation. The produced fixed environmental assets also include some intangible asset like mineral exploration. This exploration with the capitalized value of all discovery expenses is an intangible knowledge, which has been a crucial causal factor for the resource function of this material asset.

Figure 8.3 SEEA: Flow and Stock Accounts with Environmental Assets

	OPENING STOCKS		Assets +		Rest of the World
	Industries	Households/Govt.	Economic assets	Environmental assets	
SUPPLY OF PRODUCTS	Domestic production				Imports of products
	thereof: for environmental protection				**thereof: for environmental protection**
USE OF PRODUCTS	Economic cost (intermediate consumption, consumption of fixed capital)	Final consumption	Gross capital formation, consumption of fixed capital		Exports
	thereof: for environmental protection				**thereof: for environmental protection**
USE OF NATURAL ASSETS	**Environmental cost of industries (imputed)**	**Environmental cost of households (imputed)**	**Natural capital consumption**		
OTHER CHANGES OF ASSETS			Other changes of economic assets	**Other changes of environmental assets**	
			=		
CLOSING STOCKS			Economic assets	**Environmental assets**	

Source: United Nations Statistics Division (2000).

Finally, all the produced natural assets are conventional products of economic activities having market values, and they already figure in the conventional national accounting system. However, a majority of environmental assets are non-produced assets where valuation is not immediately given by the market, but can be derived from the analysis of the environmental and economic data. These assets include land for various uses, fossil fuel reserves, metallic and non-metallic mineral reserves, other subsoil assets, non-cultivated biological resources (for example, wild fish in river-body or coastal water as growing in natural ecosystem without any human energy and capital subsidy), and water resources. Soil is an important resource, which was considered to be included in the land it covers, as per SNA 1993. However, it deserves to be treated as an asset by itself, which is associated with land, just as the surface water associated with it is treated. As the top-soil is removable and subject to erosion and soil erosion is a serious threat for sustainable agriculture, its explicit recognition in asset accounting, like that of water resource, has been recognized in the latest SEEA asset classification. The Ricardian rent of land is in fact attributable to its soil content, its quality and moisture. However, as already noted, land development cost as capitalized is to be considered as a man-made or produced fixed capital asset, and distinct from the value of land as an environmental asset.

Unlike SNA 1993, the latest update of SEEA includes ecosystems: terrestrial, aquatic, and atmospheric ecosystems to be environmental assets. Although they are not economic assets, as per SNA definition, since their measurement and valuation are difficult and the ownership right is not well-defined, it has been considered important to monitor the degradation of the quality of these ecosystems, particularly air, water, and land, due to the externalities of residual waste arising from the material flows between the economy and the environment. Such quality of ecosystem assets has been proposed to be quantified in terms of the residual flows, as received by the ecosystems—like air shed, water bodies, and landfill—and the value of their impact is to be imputed to the degradation of the concerned ecosystems. The accounting for such items has been limited to the changes in terms of quantities of residual flows only during a period without showing the opening and the closing stocks.

Finally, there are the intangible environmental economic assets which are related to the benefits of nature's ecosystems functioning. These are

Table 8.2: Natural Assets Classification

1	**Produced Assets**
1.1	*Fixed Assets*
1.1.1	Tangible man-made fixed assets
1.1.2	Cultivated Biological Assets—like livestock, plantation, and so on, for repeated use
1.2	*Intangible Fixed Assets*—mineral exploration
1.3.1	Inventories—Timber, crop and plant resources aquatic resources for harvest, livestock for slaughter
1.3.2	Work in progress of cultivated biological fixed assets
2	**Non-produced Assets**
2.1	*Tangible non-produced assets*
2.1.1	Land and surface water body for different uses
2.1.2	Natural resources
2.1.2.1	Subsoil Assets: Fossil fuels, metallic, and non-metallic mineral reserves, and so on
2.1.2.2	Soil
2.1.2.3	Water
2.1.2.4	Non-cultivated biological resources—wild aquatic resources, live fishes and other animals, natural forest resources.
2.1.3	Ecosystems
2.1.4	Intangible non-produced assets like lease for exploration right, tradable permits for emissions, and so on

Source: Prepared by the author.

the transferable licenses and concessions for the exploration of natural resources, permits for the emissions of residuals in the atmosphere, and so on.

Table 8.2 presents the asset classification with its SEEA updates as discussed above. While a common item like forest or aquatic resources may appear under more than one classification category depending on where it arises—cultivated or uncultivated source—or based on its use, such identity of classification would matter in respect of valuation and the sustainability benchmark for use.

Tables 8.3a and 8.3b provide illustrative asset accounts of produced and non-produced assets following the updated SEEA principle. Table 8.3a shows for a period the opening and closing stocks and the changes in

Table 8.3(a): Monetary Asset Accounts for Produced Assets
(Including Cultivated Natural Assets)

(monetary unit)

	Agriculture		Forestry		Other Industries	Total
	Cultivated Assets	Other	Cultivated Forest	Other		
Opening stock	3521	5139	1062	2352	701391	713465
Capital formation: Gross fixed capital formation*	274	633		215	86784	87906
Changes in inventories	47	41	128	32	−213	35
Consumption of fixed capital*	−48	−73		−39	−23765	−23925
Other volume changes	−21	−33	−11	−29	−174	−268
Revaluation	−83	106	−52	65	1266	1302
Closing stock	3690	5813	1127	2596	765289	778515

Source: UNSD (2000).
Note: *Including land improvement.

the produced assets due to investment or fixed capital formation (which will be acquisition less disposal in cultivated biological assets), inventory changes, including the changes in work-in-progress, depreciation, and losses due to natural disasters, political and other exogenous reasons not related with economic activities. For the non-produced assets, Table 8.3b shows illustrative figures of changes, which would consist of net effects of depletion due to economic use (like mineral extraction, fish catches, water abstraction, and so on), other accumulation and other volume changes in a given period. The category other accumulation would include discoveries of the resource, natural growth net of mortality, replenishment of resources like water due to natural cycle and reclassification of assets due to changes in functions or quality. The reclassification would include transfer of resources like land and other resources from the natural environment to economic use or land reclamation, and so on. Some of these variations would be measured by acquisition less disposal if it involves economic transactions as in the case of land, water body, and so on. These would also include reassessment and revaluation of mineral

Table 8.3(b): Monetary Asset Accounts for Non-produced Economic Assets

(monetary unit)

	Agricultural Land	Forest Land	Other Land (Including Built-up and Recreational Land)	Soil (Economic use)	Subsoil Assets Fossil Fuels	Forest (Economic use)	Fishery Resources	Groundwater	Other Freshwater
Opening stocks	440275	374784	2315578		262315	25261	20017	287	85
Gross fixed capital formation sustainable use	53	49	393			−1990	−2833	−97	−26
Depletion (including soil erosion)*	−3	−2	−19	432	−8004	−1807	−421	−21	
Other accumulation acquisition less disposal of non-financial assets	12354	−18804	6449						
Other	5362	−5001	107527		3802	1996	2905	102	33
Other volume changes	−1787	−625			−922	−393	−131	−8	−2
Revaluation	773	31715	38083		−16130	3727	2187	265	60
Closing stocks	457027	382116	2468010		243486	26791	21724	529	150

Source: UNSD (2000).

reserves, because of change in technology, prices, and new information about their qualitative character, which may make some resources an economic asset which had not been so earlier. The other volume changes, on the other hand, would mainly consist of changes due to natural calamity, political upheaval, and transfer of resource from the economic environment to the natural environment not connected with degradation attributed to economic activities.

The development of the asset account is important both in physical and monetary value terms. It is the physical quantities which would indicate the strength of the economy in terms of resource security, while the valuation is also important for integrating economic accounting with the environmental accounting and for estimating the change of the macro aggregate of the value of wealth of a nation. The physical asset account development requires the development of comprehensive resource, and environmental statistics and database, as well as the application of multi-disciplinary scientific knowledge to organize the statistics, and make them useful for sustainable accounting. The monetary valuation of the assets, on the other hand, as already discussed in a preceding section, would depend on the marketability of the resource, public good character of the asset, its renewability or non-renewability, and various scientific-technological specificities, which would be important in determining the precise formula of rent or royalty of the concerned resource depending on the end use.

VI Degradation of Assets

The development of asset account, as outlined above, confines only to the quantitative changes, but not the qualitative degradation which may occur as an environmental consequences of economic activities. It is difficult to measure and monitor the qualitative changes of all the assets regularly, although the residual waste arising or the concentration of pollution like CO_2, NO_x, SO_x, BOD, TSP, P, N, and so on, may be measurable or estimable. It is, therefore, the inventory of emissions and their damage valuation of flow which are proposed to be estimated, as per the scheme of SEEA for assessment of degradation of the natural assets—particularly, the ecosystem assets of air, water, and land—as already noted in Section V. The basis of valuation of degradation can be either defensive cost for environmental protection or willingness to pay by the beneficiary for the protection of such services. Broadly, the SEEA recommends the maintenance or defensive cost approach for evaluating the residual flows. As already noted, the maintenance cost comprises the cost of abatement of damage and restoration of environmental capacity, as per the marginal cost approach. There is one important difference between the accounting for depletion and degradation. The depletion of an asset is caused by the asset-using sectors, and its cost can be allocated among users, in proportion to the usage. The degradation of assets are caused due to externalities by sectors, who are generating the residuals, and may not directly be the user of the degraded asset, for example, energy industry causing NO_x emissions resulting in acidification and degradation of forest and aquatic ecosystem although the energy sector is not directly using these degraded assets. This has warranted the treatment and quantification of degradation in terms of the residuals and not the ultimate affected asset. The total damage cost is allocated across sectors, in proportion to the emissions arising, which are determined by their respective material usage and technology.

VII Environmental Adjustment to Flow Accounts

The macro level intersectoral flows of economic goods and services and those of environmental resources and wastes between the economy and the natural environments may often be developed initially as a hybrid account. While the flows of economic goods and services are expressed in value units, those of environmental resources and wastes are often expressed in physical units. The monetary conversion of the physical flows of the environmental materials and degradation due to residual flows would finally permit us to adjust the macro-aggregates of income, expenditure, and assets. It is true that it may not be possible to ensure adequate coverage of assets for accounting in physical and/ or value terms because of the inadequacy of the physical database for environmental impact assessment and difficulty in their reliable monetary valuation. The latter problem arises because of the non-marketability of many of the environmental resources, particularly the ones of eco-services. However, for the feasible extent of extension of asset boundary, we can derive the aggregate value of both the natural resource and ecosystem resource throughout to yield the estimate of consumption of natural capital—both produced and non-produced—with their allocation among producing sectors, final users, and the Rest of the World (ROW). The estimates of degradation value, on the other hand, can be assumed on the basis of the maintenance cost of environmental quality of the surrounding ecosystem, limited to the extent of provision for the reversal of the damage effect of the residual arising in excess of the sustainability standard. These maintenance costs would be allocated as per the distribution of actual maintenance or abatement costs incurred across sectors and various final uses.

We are now in a position to show how the national income and wealth accounts can be environmentally adjusted.

Let $\bar{X}$ = total gross value of output other than environmental control industry, that is, pX of section 4.

IC_0 = intermediate cost of production other than that of pollution abatement = pA_1x of section 4.

$\bar{Z} = \psi(W - \bar{W}) =$ total cost of abatement or maintenance/defensive cost.

ICz = intermediate cost for pollution abatement sector = pA_zZ of section 4.

CFC_0 = fixed capital consumption of industries other than environmental protection.

CFC_z = fixed capital consumption in environmental protection industry.

Dp = total value of depletion of natural resources and ecosystem inputs = $\pi(r-r^*)$ of section 4.

Dg = total value of degradation due to waste arising.

$dpNDP$ = depletion adjusted NDP.

$eaNDP$ = environmentally adjusted NDP.

If we assume that the current expenditures by the industry meet the environmental standard of the economy, then we end up with the following:

$$GDP_0 = \bar{X} - IC_0$$
$$GDP_z = \bar{Z} - IC_z$$
$$GDP = \bar{X} + \bar{Z} - IC_0 - IC_z$$
$$NDP_0 = GDP_0 - CFC_0 = \bar{X} - IC_0 - CFC_0$$

$$NDP_z = GDP_z - CFC_z = \overline{Z} - IC_z - CFC_z$$

$$NDP = \overline{X} + \overline{Z} - IC_0 - IC_z - CFC_0 - CFC_z$$

$$dpNDP = GDP - CFC_0 - CFC_z - D_p$$

$$= \overline{X} + \overline{Z} - IC_0 - IC_z - CFC_0 - CFC_z - D_p$$

$$= eaNDP \text{ (with environmental standard being met)}$$

If, however, the current spending on abatement falls short of the environmental standard, that is, $\overline{W} > W^*$, then $Dg = \left(t \times (\overline{W} - W^*)\right) + \psi(W - \overline{W})$ to be deducted from GDP for the consumption of the environmental capacity of the nature as sink due to inadequate abatement. We should thus have:

$$eaNDP = eaGDP - CFC - D_p - D_g$$

$$= eaNDP - D_g$$

$$= \overline{X} + \overline{Z} - IC_0 - IC_z - CFC_0 - CFC_z - D_p - D_g$$

If the economy had no spending on environmental maintenance, the gross savings or investment in the economy would have been S_0, where $S_0 = GDP_0 - \overline{C}$, where $\overline{C}$ is the total value of consumption. As per the actual expenditure, the estimates of gross savings S and that of genuine net savings S_g would be as follows:

$$S = GDP - \overline{C} = \overline{X} + \overline{Z} - IC_0 - IC_z - \overline{C}$$

$$S_g = GDP - CFC - D_p - D_g - \overline{C}$$

$$= \overline{X} + \overline{Z} - IC_0 - IC_z - CFC - D_p - D_g - \overline{C}$$

The ratio of S_g to GDP would represent the true saving rate of an economy. It is important to compare the time paths of GDP with eaNDP and that of S or S/GDP with S_g or S_g/GDP, respectively. We may refer to the Table 8.4, showing comparative estimates of genuine savings in various regions of the world, as worked out by the World Bank (2008), based on some crude assumptions. The calculation behind the estimates, however, considers educational expenditure as investment spending in human capital while working out the genuine savings. The last column of the table shows the genuine savings gross of educational expenses, which are part of savings utilized for educational investment, and correspond to the genuine savings as defined above.

Table 8.4: Region-wise Estimates of Genuine Savings, 2006

(as percent of GNI 2006)

	Gross Savings	Consumption of Fixed Capital	Net National Savings	Education Expenditure	Energy Depletion	Mineral Depletion	Net Forest Depletion	Carbon Dioxide Damage	Adjusted Net Savings
World	21.8	12.4	9.3	4.4	4.1	0.5	0	0.4	8.3
Low income	30.5	9	21.5	3.4	9.4	1.3	0.6	1	11.9
Middle income	30.5	10.9	19.6	3.5	12.8	1.6	0	0.9	7
High income	19.9	13	6.9	4.7	1.5	0.2	0	0.3	9.3
East Asia and Pacific	47.2	10.3	36.9	2.1	7.1	0.9	0	1.2	28.5
Europe and Central Asia	22.6	10.3	12.3	4.1	18.4	1.1	0	1.1	-4.9
Latin American and Caribbean	22.4	12.1	10.4	4.4	9.1	3	0	0.4	1.8
Middle East and North Africa	–	10.9	–	4.6	40	0.3	0.1	1.1	–
South Asia	32.1	8.9	23.2	3.5	4.5	0.9	0.5	1.1	18.8
India	33.7	9	24.7	3.9	4.3	1.2	0.5	1.3	20.6
Sub-saharan Africa	19.4	10.7	8.7	3.8	18.7	2.3	0.4	0.6	-10

Source: World Bank, 2008.

As the genuine savings and the genuine investment would be equal in expost accounting, it is the sign and magnitude of S_g, which is the indicator of sustainability of the macro-economy. The ratios D_p/GDP and D_g/GDP would be important indicators of depreciation of environmental capacity of a country while ($\bar{Z}$ – ICz)/GDP would indicate the environmental control effort of the economy for sustainability.

VIII Integrated Economic and Environmental Accounting: Empirical Work for India

In order to obtain an overview of the integration of economic and environmental accounting as discussed previously, we can bring the production-cum-income account and the asset account together by juxtaposing them to each other. The integrated accounts show the extension of the asset boundary to include various types of natural capital and restructuring of production account which may show environmental protection activities and products separately within the production account. This depicts the role of economy–environment interaction in determining true income, genuine savings, and wealth. While Figure 8.3 makes a schematic presentation of the overview of such integrated Production-cum-Asset Account, Table 8.5 makes a notational presentation of the integrated account in terms of matrix notations.

Despite the significance of accounting for natural resources in the National Accounts, Government sponsored effort in India to supplement or reform the National Accounts has remained restricted to only the compilation and presentation of environmental statistics in the "Compendium of Environmental Statistics" since 1997 (see Central Statistical Organisation, 1997, 2006, 2007). This document contains an inventory of environmental statistics under the six internationally recognized classified categories, that is, flora, fauna, atmosphere, water, land/soil, and human settlements, based on the United Nations framework for the development of environmental statistics. However, the database is compiled from several sources and in many cases, the data are not regularly collected and the statistics remain backdated for several resources. Due to lack of consistent

Table 8.5: Schematic Presentation (Notational) of Integrated Environmental and Economic Accounts

	Environmental Protection Industry	Other Industries	Imports	Exports	Consumption	Produced Assets	Natural Economic Assets	Environmental Assets
Opening stock						Ko	No	
Output	$\bar{Z}$	$\bar{X}$	$-\bar{M}$	$\bar{EX}$	$\bar{C}$	$\bar{I}$		
Intermediate cost	IC_z	IC_o						
Consumption of fixed capital	CFC_z	CFC_o				$-CFC$		
Resource depletion	Dp_z	Dp_o			Dp_c		Dp	
Degradation maintenance cost	Dg_z	Dg_o			Dg_c			Dg
GDP	GDP_z	GDP_o						
eaNDP	$eaNDP_z$	$eaNDP_o$						
Other accumulation							OA	
Other volume changes							OVC	
Revaluation							RV	
Closing stock						K_T	N_T	

Source: Author.

Notes: Dp_z, Dp_o and Dp_c are the sub-matrices of values of depletion of natural resources due to environmental protection activities, other conventional industries, and final consumption in the economy. Dg, Dg_o and Dg_c are the similar respective sectoral estimates of environmental degradation due to residual flows.

time series data, it is not possible at the current level and state of data collection to construct environmental-asset accounts as proposed under the SEEA.

Even though the data inventory exists for water and forest resources, no official attempt has been made to construct asset accounts for these resources. However, several academic endeavors of accounting for natural resources in India point to the feasibility of constructing integrated environmental and economic accounts. The Natural Resource Accounting involves substantive interdisciplinary research efforts, which would be quite country and ecosystem specific. In India, several research initiatives have taken place in the area of environmental impact analysis and valuation of environmental benefits and damages, although these initiatives have not been driven by the requirement of the SEEA implementation. The research results have, however, been important in developing both methodology and providing the building blocks of resource estimates in physical and value terms for the future implementation of the SEEA in India. We can refer here to the works like Parikh and Parikh (1997), Chopra and Kadekodi (1997), Chopra et al. (2001), Sankar (2004), Sengupta and Mandal (2005), Kadekodi (2004), Murty (2003), Murty et al. (2004), Haripriya (1998, 2000), TERI (1999), Sengupta and Saksena (2008), and GIST (2005) as important case studies of such environmental valuation of resources or environmentally adjusted sectoral income which would contribute ultimately to the development of data base for the integrated economic and environmental accounting of India.

While we do not enter here in the review of the works on individual resource accounting, we would like to make a special mention of the study of Green Indian States Trust (GIST) on the "Green Accounting for Indian States and Union Territories Project (GAISP)". This study has targeted setting up of economic models for state-wise annual estimates of *Adjusted* Gross State Domestic Product in order to capture and analyze the true value-addition at both state and national levels by economic activities. The first monograph (GIST, 2005) of this study incorporates forest resources into the National Accounts of India's states and union territories, using the satellite SEEA framework and accounts for timber, fuel wood, non-timber forest products, and carbon sequestration effects for each state. We present in Table 8.6 illustrative results of overall depletion-adjusted macro-economic income on account of accounts for timber, fuel wood, and carbon.

Table 8.6: GSDP, NSDP, and ESDP for Carbon for Different States (Million Rupees) for 2002/03

State/Union Territory	GSDP	NSDP	Forestry and Logging	Adjusted NSDP	Total Depletion	ESDP	ESDP/NSDP	Depletion of Timber as Percent of NDP	Depletion of Carbon as Percent of NDP	Depletion of NTFPs as Percent of NDP	Total Depletion as Percent of NDP
Andhra Pradesh	1607683.90	1439753.90	16992.80	1453730.86	−8094.07	1445636.80	0.99	0.55	0.52	0.17	0.56
Bihar	897150.20	787033.60	23133.80	803573.95	−37809.55	765764.40	0.95	4.82	0.64	0.41	4.71
Goa	77711.20	67356.90	136.80	70863.76	327.53	71191.30	1.00	−0.71	−0.46	−0.01	−0.46
Gujarat	1382850.30	1144047.60	5307.50	1271916.72	−4343.23	1267573.48	1.00	1.50	0.31	0.00	0.34
Haryana	658372.20	579374.90	1386.60	599546.21	−2187.86	597359.35	1.00	0.47	0.13	−0.06	0.36
Himachal Pradesh	159460.00	142024.30	7198.80	141338.51	−2809.31	138529.19	0.98	2.95	0.11	−0.85	1.99
J&K	147495.90	128052.00	4653.90	133391.52	1007.57	134399.09	1.01	−25.16	−0.76	−0.24	−0.76
UP	1796014.70	1568624.70	21802.20	1628485.29	−606.74	1627878.56	1.00	−0.13	0.08	−0.02	0.04
Karnataka	1139292.20	1004063.10	19120.90	1029435.50	698.00	1030133.50	1.00	−1.19	0.09	−0.04	−0.07
Kerala	761819.80	696021.20	13849.40	689093.27	−1943.65	687149.62	1.00	1.57	0.25	0.46	0.28
MP	1132756.60	974607.60	28846.70	1019420.99	3756.57	1023177.57	1.00	−0.77	−0.24	0.19	−0.37
Maharashtra	2951911.80	2632252.50	32471.10	2672291.73	−3732.03	2668559.71	1.00	−0.18	0.17	0.11	0.14
Orissa	446844.50	387373.00	11326.90	402749.10	570.51	403319.61	1.00	−0.94	0.19	0.23	−0.14

(Continued Table 8.6)

(Continued Table 8.6)

State/ Union Territory	GSDP	NSDP	Forestry and Logging	Adjusted NSDP	Total Depletion	ESDP	ESDP/ NSDP	Depletion of Timber as Percent of NDP	Depletion of Carbon as Percent of NDP	Depletion of NTFPs as Percent of NDP	Total Depletion as Percent of NDP
Punjab	707508.70	629677.50	2183.70	642935.52	−5700.36	637235.17	0.99	0.88	0.07	0.04	0.89
Rajasthan	873817.50	768878.00	11560.00	788085.83	−4956.45	783129.38	0.99	0.70	0.31	0.14	0.63
Sikkim	11527.30	10386.50	190.40	10407.554	−27.19	10380.35	1.00	61.95	−2.98	−0.60	0.26
Tamil Nadu	1537287.10	1367808.70	7177.20	1398966.56	−7602.77	1391363.79	0.99	0.41	0.56	0.02	0.54
West Bengal	1671370.80	1537807.20	10498.20	1515621.63	−12015.19	1503606.44	0.99	0.59	0.65	0.47	0.79
A&N	11563.90	10407.51	64.60	10673.13	3616.88	14290.01	1.34	−4.06	−77.11	0.02	−33.89
Arunachal Pradesh	19450.50	17395.10	806.00	19092.20	6134.84	25227.04	1.32	−240.93	−32.13	0.80	−32.13
Assam	354314.20	317208.00	5476.60	321714.02	−747.18	320966.84	1.00	−2.38	0.23	0.13	0.23
Manipur	35312.60	32047.80	628.30	32473.47	−565.00	31908.47	0.98	4.24	2.59	−2.80	1.74
Meghalaya	43429.20	38422.70	376.50	39927.60	−245.32	39682.28	0.99	8.11	0.53	0.62	0.61
Nagaland	36793.60	34272.00	1067.50	33308.47	5994.94	39303.41	1.18	−32.27	2.90	1.60	−18.00
Tripura	60616.90	56603.40	762.10	55594.42	−1921.26	53673.16	0.97	−0.65	3.80	1.70	3.46
Mizoram	17687.20	16346.10	167.20	16519.06	634.15	17153.21	1.04	−23.60	4.65	2.81	−3.84
Total	18539942.80	16387845.81	227185.70	16801156.88	−72549.05	16728607.83	1.00	−0.08	0.21	0.14	0.43

Source: GIST 2005.

IX Concluding Remarks

The development of the economics of natural resources and the environment has significantly contributed to the emergence of the concepts and methodology of measuring income, investment, and other variables of macro economic identities, which conform to the notion of sustainability of development and human well-being. Extensive empirical research has taken place in the area of valuation of natural assets and regulatory policies for environmental control in the recent decades and many important studies are ongoing in different countries. The problem of valuation, which involves the environmental impact assessment of economic activities, requires interdisciplinary research as the socio-ecological dimensions of the problem of environmental conservation has to be addressed in such enquiries. While important data are being generated for the purpose of valuation and measurement of the natural environment through such research more effort in this direction is required to get the results of estimates with higher reliability and robustness. However, the estimates of environmental valuation are likely to have high degree of variance, since the environmental valuation factors are specific to the socio-ecological context. As the environmental and the socio-ecological and economic factors are sometimes inextricably combined in their reflection in data, more research is required to obtain the pure effect of environmental changes on economic assets and income.

The above observation is important for the standardization of the methods of estimation of the environmental impacts in physical and value terms for the different regions or countries, and make them comparable after the purchasing power parity adjustment. We may like to comment here that the comparability and standardization of environmental statistics would require greater dependence of the methods on market or technology-based objective factors than on subjective factors (like stated preferences) for the valuation of the environmental benefits or damages. The defensive/maintenance cost approach would thus be preferable to the subjective willingness to pay approach for the valuation of environmental depreciation or environmental amenity services. All these point to the need for intensive and extensive research in the area, and greater exchange and sharing of research results and data among scholars and across countries in the interest of standardization and comparability.

While all these arguments provide a case for awarding greater priority to the support for environmental economic research on resource accounting and adjustment of the National Accounts System in India, it would, however, be prudent to make gradual progress towards the implementation of the SEEA in India at the present stage of data development. It is important to initiate now the development of physical asset accounts for important produced and non-produced environmental, assets, physical material flow account, and hybrid flow account for the development of environmental and resource use policies. The extent of coverage of monetization in the total scope of the physical asset and flow accounts should depend on the stage of development of database and on the standardization of the method of valuation of environmental resources and the robustness of the results of valuation. The UN system of Integration of Environmental and Economic Accounting has in fact cautioned against immediate variation of production boundary to include environmental services. The environmental adjustments of the macroeconomic aggregates may be attempted by stages, beginning by adjustments for only such items of depletion or degradation for which reliable physical data and monetary valuation are available.

Finally, our initial model of sustainable development of Section II, based on the concept of endogenous technical change, pointed to the crucial role that the R&D activities and the resulting knowledge formation and the development of human innovativeness and skill can play in delinking environment and development. As already observed, the sustainable accounting needs to cover more detailed accounting of both patented and non-patented knowledge and skill formation, and their use in the different sectors. It also requires classification of R&D investment and their outputs with reference to the different kinds of their effect on environmental resource bases like energy and resource conservation, pollution abatement, resource and technology discoveries, and adaptation to environmental changes. This would enable us to monitor and assess the growth of knowledge and human capital and their interaction with the resource and environment system. It is the creation of knowledge and ideas, as induced by the motivation of overcoming the constraints of earth's fixed ecological system and the human capability development, which are the most important driving factors for sustainable development. Further, extension of the work of sustainable accounting, in such direction would provide us better information and analysis for the purpose of development of better policies and planning for sustainable development.

Bibliography

Ayres, R.U. 1978. *Resources, Environment, and Economics: Applications of the Materials/Energy Balance Principle*. New York: John Wiley and Sons.

Ayres, R.U. and A.V. Kneese. 1969. "Production, Consumption, and Externalities", *American Economic Review*, 59 (June): 282–97.

CBS (Statistics Netherlands). 2006. *Present Status and Future Developments of the Dutch NAMEA*, Statistics Netherlands, Voorburg, Paper for the International Workshop for Interactive Analysis on Economy and Environment, March 4, 2006, Tokyo.

Central Statistical Organisation. 1997, 2006, 2007. *Compendium of Environmental Statistics*, Department of Statistics, M/o Planning & Programme Implementation, Government of India, New Delhi.

Chopra, K., B.B. Bhattacharya, and P. Kumar. 2001. "Contribution of Forestry Sector to Gross Domestic Product in India", draft, Institute of Economic Growth, New Delhi, Project sponsored by the Ministry of Environment and Forests, Government of India.

Chopra, K. and G. Kadekodi. 1997. *Natural Resource Accounting in Yamuna Basin: Accounting for Forest Resources*, (monograph). New Delhi: Institute of Economic Growth.

Cumberland J.H. 1966. "A Regional Inter-Industry Model for Analysis of Development Objectives", *Papers and Proceedings of the Regional Science Association*, 17: 61–75.

Daly, H.E. 1968. "On Economics as a Life Science", *Journal of Political Economy*, 76 (3): 392–406.

———. (ed.) 1973. *Economics, Ecology, Ethics: Towards a Steady State Economy*. San Francisco: Freeman.

———. 1991. "Elements of Environmental Macroeconomics", in R. Costanza (ed.) *Ecological Economics: The Science and Management of Sustainability*, New York, Columbia University Press.

Daly, H.E. and J. Farley. 2003. *Ecological Economics: Principles and Application*, Washington: Island Press.

Dasgupta, P. 2001. *Human Well-being and the Natural Environment*. New Delhi: Oxford University Press.

Dasgupta, P. and K.G. Mäler. 2000. "Net National Product, Wealth, and Social Well-Being', *Environment and Development Economics*, 5 (1): 69–93.

Dasgupta, S. and T. Mitra. 2001. "National Product, Income Accounts, and Sustainable Development", in Bose, A., D. Ray, and A. Sarkar (eds). *Contemporary Macroeconomics*, pp. 56–88. New Delhi: Oxford University Press.

El Serafy, S. 1994. "The Proper Calculation of Income from Depletable Natural Resources", in Ahmed Y.J., S. El Serafy, and Ernst Lutz (eds). *Environmental Accounting for Sustainable Development*. Washington DC: UNEP, World Bank Symposium.

Federal Statistical Office Germany. 2006. "The German System of Environmental–Economic Accounting Concept, Current State and Application", Paper presented at the Workshop on 'Rationale and Methods for Measuring Environmental Impact', 18–19 September 2006, New Delhi.

GIST. 2005. "The Value of Timber, Carbon, Fuel wood, and Non-Timber Forest Products in India's Forests", Monograph 1 of the Green Accounting for Indian States Project, Green Indian States Trust (GIST).

Hamilton, K. and G. Ruta. 2006. "From Curse to Blessing: Natural Resources and Institutional Quality", *Environment Matters* 2006, Annual Review: 24–27.

Hamilton, K. and M. Clemens. 1999. "Genuine Savings Rates in Developing Countries", *The World Bank Economic Review*, 13(2): 333–56.

Haripriya, G.S. 1998. "Forest Resource Accounting for the State of Maharashtra in India", *Development Policy Review*, 16 (2): 131–51.

———. 2000. "Integrating Forest Resources into the System of National Accounts in Maharashtra", *Environment and Development Economics*, 5 (1): 143–56.

Harris, M. and I. Fraser. 2002. "Natural Resource Accounting in Theory and Practice: A Critical Assessment", *Australian Journal of Agricultural and Resource Economics*, 46(2): 139–92.

Hartwick, J. 1977. "Intergenerational Equity and Investing of Rents from Exhaustible Resources", *American Economic Review*, 66: 291–304.

Hartwick, J. and A. Hageman. 1993. "Economic Depreciation of Mineral Stocks and The Contribution of El Serafy", in Ernst Lutz (ed.) *Toward Improved Accounting for the Environment*, pp. 211–35. Washington, DC: The World Bank.

Hotelling, H. 1931. "The Economics of Exhaustible Resources", *Journal of Political Economy*, 39 (2):137–75.

Isard, W., K. Bassett, C. Choguill, J. Furtado, R. Izumita, J. Kissin, E. Romanoff, R. Seyfarth, and R. Tatlock. 1967. "On the Linkage of Socio-Economic and Ecologic Systems", *Papers and Proceedings of the Regional Science Association*, 21: 79–99.

Jones, Charles I. 2006. *Introduction to Economic Growth*. London: W.W. Norton and Company.

Kadekodi, G. (ed.). 2004. *Environmental Economics in Practice*. New Delhi: Oxford University Press.

Leontief, W. 1970. "Environmental Repercussions and the Economic Structure: An Input-Output Approach", *Review of Economic Statistics*, 52 (3): 262–77.

Lutz, E. (ed.). 1993. *Toward Improved Accounting for the Environment*. Washington DC: UNSTAT–World Bank Symposium.

Mäler, K.G. 1991. "National Accounts and Environmental Resources", *Environmental and Resource Economics*, 1: 1–15.

Meadows, Donella H., Dennis L. Meadows, Jorgen Randers, and William W. Berhens III, 1972. *The Limits to Growth*. New York: Universe Books.

Murty, M.N. 2003. "Measuring Environmentally Corrected Net National Product: Case Studies of Industrial Water Pollution and Urban Air Pollution in India", Mimeo. Delhi: Institute of Economic Growth.

Murty, M.N. and S. Kumar. 2004. *Environmental and Economic Accounting for Industry*. New Delhi: Oxford University Press.

Parikh, K.S. and J. Parikh. 1997. *Accounting and Valuation of the Environment: Vol 1: A Premier for Developing Countries*. New York: United Nations.

Parikh, K.S., J. K. Parikh, V. K. Sharma, and J. P. Painuly. 1993. "Natural Resource Accounting: A Framework for India", Indira Gandhi Institute of Development Research, Report prepared for the Ministry of Environment & Forests, Government of India.

Pearson, D. 1989. *The Natural House Book*. New York: Simon and Schuster, Inc.

Perman, R., Yue Ma and G. James. Mc. 1996. *Natural Resource and Environmental Economics*. England: Addison Wesley Longman Limited.

Romer, P. 1990. "Engogenous Technical Changes", *Journal of Political Economy*, 1998 (October): S71–S102.

Romer, P. 1993. "Two Strategies for Economic Development: Using Ideas and Producing Ideas", *Proceedings of the World Bank Annual Conference on Development Economics 1992*. Washington, DC: World Bank.

————. 1993. "Idea Gaps and Object Gaps in Economic Development", *Journal of Monetary Economics*, 32 (December).

Sankar, U. 2004. "Pollution Control in Tanneries", in G. Kadekodi (ed.) *Environmental Economics in Practice*. New Delhi: Oxford University Press.

Sengupta, R. and S. Mandal. 2005. "Health Damage Cost of Automotive Air Pollution: Cost Benefit Analysis of Fuel Quality Upgradation for Indian Cities", Working Paper no. 37, National Institute of Public Finance and Policy, New Delhi.

Sengupta, Ramprasad and Shalini Saksena 2007. "Macroeconomics and Sustainable Accounting of Resources and Income", *India Macroeconomic Annual*: 39–103.

Smulders, Sjak. 1999. "Endogenous Growth Theory and the Environment" in Van den Bergh, J.C.J.M. (ed.), *Handbook of Environment and Resource Economics*, pp. 612–21. Cheltenham, UK: Edward Elgar.

TERI. 1999. *Pilot Project on Natural Resource Accounting in Goa (Phase I)*, prepared for Directorate of Planning and Statistics. Tata Energy Research Institute Project Report No. 99RD61, Goa.

UNSD.1993. *Integrated Environmental and National Accounting*, Interim Version, Handbook of National Accounting, Series F, No. 61, Department of Economic and Social Development, United Nations Statistical Division, New York.

————. 2000. *Integrated Environmental and Economic Accounting: An Operational Manual*, Handbook of National Accounting, Series F, No. 78, Department of Economic and Social Development, United Nations Statistical Division, New York.

————. 2003. *Integrated Environmental and Economic Accounting: An Operational Manual*, Handbook of National Accounting, Department of Economic and Social Development, United Nations Statistical Division, New York.

Victor, P.A. 1972. *Pollution: Economy and Environment*. London, UK: George Allen & Unwin Ltd.

Weitzman, M. 1976. "On the Welfare Significance of National Product in a Dynamic Economy", *Quarterly Journal of Economics*, 90 (1): 156–62.

World Bank. 1999. *World Development Indicators*. Washington, DC: The World Bank.

————. 2006. "Where is the Wealth of Nations? Measuring Capital for the 21st Century", The World Bank, Washington, DC Available online at http://go.worldbank.org/2QTH26ULQ0.

————2008. *World Bank Indicators*. Washington DC: World Bank.

9

Do Public Funds Increase Days of Instruction in Primary Schools? A Study of Three Districts in India*

ARNAB MUKHERJI AND ANJAN MUKHERJI

————— • ✦ • —————

I Introduction

Primary education has always been seen as a key ingredient to economic growth from both efficiency and equity considerations; consequently, its performance has been an important area of public policy debate (World Bank, 2001; Mehta, 2007). These debates are generally concerned with which methods to use to improve schooling outcomes and often, which schooling outcomes are the most important to improve.[1] In either instance, public funding has always been an important mechanism for improving schooling outcomes such as gross enrolment rates, literacy

---

* This paper is dedicated to the memory of Amaresh Bagchi who passed away in 2008. Professor Bagchi was to have participated in a course conducted by the first author at the IIM Bangalore just a few weeks before he passed away. Professor Bagchi was a friend, philosopher, and guide to a number of people and we both have been fortunate to be included in that select list. We are indebted to Professor M. Govinda Rao for providing us with an opportunity to pay this tribute. We are also grateful to A.C. Mehta and his team at the National University of Educational Planning and Administration (NUEPA) for creating such a detailed data set such as the DISE (District Information System for Education) data set, making it available to the public and promptly answering our queries.

rates, reduction in repetition rates, retention in school, and so on. A less frequently used, but no less important measure of schooling is the number of instructional days that a child potentially receives in school. The number of instructional days is known to be strongly related to the actual time a student spends on learning activities, and thus is of paramount importance from a supply of education perspective, as it determines the level of education which a child can potentially achieve.[2] This chapter looks at the impact of public funds and a number of other school-level attributes on the functioning of primary schools in terms of its instructional days.

For this analysis, we look at cross-sectional data from three neighboring and adjoining districts of India, namely, Nizamabad in Andhra Pradesh, Nanded in Maharashtra, and Bidar in Karnataka, to investigate the role of public funds on instructional days in three different bureaucratic and public school management settings. Using administrative school-level data from the District Information System for Education data for 2006–07, we look at the disbursal of funds from two key school funding programs that have been driving public funding under the Sarva Sikhsha Abhiyan (SSA).[3] In this chapter, we look at how provision of this kind of public funding translates into providing "adequate schooling", in terms of the number of instructional days.

A key concern in any study of cross-sectional data arises from the potential bias introduced by omitted variables that are co-related with both the possibly non-random allocation of public funds to a school as well as to the number of instructional days in a school. We address these concerns in two ways: first, given the richness of our administrative data set, we are able to control for a number of school, teacher, and school monitoring level attributes that are traditionally not available in socio-economic surveys; second, apart from detailed school level attributes, our dataset provides clear district, as well as block level identifiers that allow us to estimate a series of increasingly demanding regression models, which control for not only unobserved district level effects, but also for unobserved block level characteristics. Thus, we not only have a rich set of observed covariates in our regression model as controls for non-random assignment of public funds, we also have district (or block) level identifiers to control for unobserved covariates that affect the number of instructional days in a school in the same manner within a district (or block).

We begin our analysis by first showing that it is reasonable to discretize the number of instructional days into less than 201 days and more than 201 days of instruction based on the distribution of the number of instructional days in the sample. An obvious advantage of such a modeling strategy is that it allows us to estimate the inherently non-linear relationship between the instructional days and its various covariates.

Our regressions show that schools are heterogeneous not only across districts, but also within blocks; further, receiving any public funds, as opposed to receiving no public funds, has a statistically significant and substantially meaningful impact on a school being functional; thus, the first tranche of funds has a significant impact; however, incremental impacts of public funds when they are already receiving funds is not significant for this purpose; in addition, monitoring schools in the form of academic inspections, as well as visits by block and cluster coordinators, are important for primary schools being functional.[4] This chapter is organized as follows: Section II describes the primary schooling in India with a focus on the DISE program; Section III describes the sample, and presents summary statistics of key variables; Section IV discusses our estimation strategy; Section V discusses our findings, and concludes by placing our findings in the larger context of the primary education sector.

II Primary Schooling in India

Primary Schooling and Its Financing in India

Primary education in India has always been given a lot of policy importance since independence and is guided by provisions made for it under the Constitution of India. One of the more important mandates from the Constitution is the assurance of free education for all children under the age of 14 years. While initially, primary education was purely a state subject, it has been placed on the concurrent list since 1976 to enable national as well as state level focus. The financial burden for providing primary school has been with the state government, unless it is in the domain of a centrally sponsored scheme in which case the central government supports it independently, or in some sharing arrangement with the states, as, for example, in the case of the *Sarva Sikhsha Abhiyan* (SSA).[5]

The SSA is the flagship program of the Government of India that has a number of ambitious goals for primary (elementary) education in India. Specifically, the SSA documents report the following major aims:

1. All children are either in a school, or in one of Education Guarantee Centre, Alternate School, or a "Back-to-School" camp by 2003.
2. All children complete five years of primary schooling by 2007.
3. All children complete eight years of elementary schooling by 2010.
4. Focus on elementary education of satisfactory quality with emphasis on education for life.
5. Bridge all gender and social category gaps at primary stage by 2007 and at elementary education level by 2010.
6. Universal retention by 2010.

The SSA was initiated in 2001 with these extremely ambitious goals and has set in place a number of very detailed and innovative ways to allocate public funds to enhance schooling outcomes.[6] Thus, apart from specifying teacher–student ratios, the SSA makes teacher specific allowances within a school, and school infrastructure specific allocations every year (see Appendix for a current version of these norms). Sankar (2007) reviews trends in the education sector for the period 1986–87 to 2004–05 and finds that while significant improvements are seen in terms of access to schooling and getting children to enroll in school, particularly over the period 1999–2000 to 2004–05, which overlaps with the start of the SSA, there also remain alarming gaps. The hardest to reach children still remain out of school; rates for completing schooling remain very low, and while the role of private education in the sector has been increasing, states that had poor performances historically in enrolments, school infrastructure, and dropouts continue to have the most serious problems, even though they have made rapid progress. While much has been achieved, it is also clear that many of the proposed targets have not been and are not going to be met.

Impact of Number of Instructional Days on Schooling Outcomes

Lack of schooling in India has historically been a problem, both in terms of provision of it in terms of a lack of human and capital infrastructure, as well as a demand for it. The SSA shows that, within short periods of time, demand for schooling may be easily ramped up and infrastructural access may be improved, however, access to infrastructure alone is not sufficient if there is not enough instructional activity centered on the school. The total number of instructional days at school, or the length of school term, is known to be strongly associated with learning outcomes, as well as with later-on outcomes in life such as the return to education measured in terms of wages earned later on in life.[7] Pischke (2007) uses a policy change in Germany that reduced the school term from 37 weeks to 24 weeks over two years without changing curriculum, or the highest grade from which a student leaves school, to demonstrate that a decline in the school term led to statistically observable declines in grade repetition and reduction in the quality of education sought subsequently.[8] Similarly, in a developing country context, insufficient number of instructional days would dilute the impact of other schooling inputs (infrastructure, teacher training, and so on) on school outcomes. Lee and Barro (2001) developed a panel dataset to show that family input as well as various school level inputs including the length of the school year lead to improved schooling outcomes even in developing countries. Thus, the number of instructional days is an important school input, and any national program that seeks to provide education for all (*sarva sikhsha*) must necessarily ensure that adequate instructional school days are available to its students.

III Data and Sample Description

Sample Composition: Administrative data on approximately 7,000 schools from the districts of Nanded (Madhya Pradesh), Bidar (Karnataka), and Nizamabad (Andhra Pradesh) (see Figure 9.1.) were extracted from the DISE web-portal for this chapter. While these three districts are in close geographical proximity to each other, they in fact belong to three different states and have very different management types for

Figure 9.1: The Three Districts

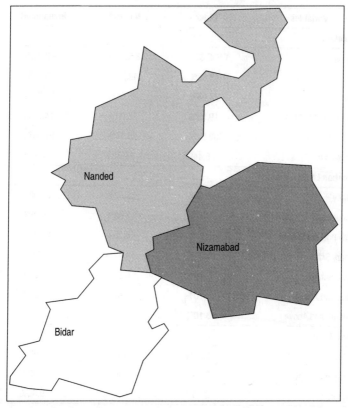

Source: These district lines are based on data from GeoCommunity (http://www.geocomm.com).

their primary school systems. Such variation in management structures within such a close geographical proximity allows us to compare and contrast our results. Table 9.1 provides details about each of these three districts from the 2001 census and we see that there are broad similarities in these three districts. Thus, broadly 75–80 percent of the population in each of these districts lives in rural areas, and each of these areas has seen a population growth rate of about 20 percent from their 1991 Census levels.[9] The fraction of the population that belongs to the scheduled caste and scheduled tribe categories ranges from 21.91 percent to 32.02 percent. In terms of literacy attainments, each of these districts is at the lower end in the country, with literacy rates

Table 9.1: Census Details for the Three Districts

Variables	Bidar	Nanded	Nizamabad
Population			
Persons	1,502,373	2,876,259	2,345,685
% Female	48.68%	48.50%	50.42%
Rural	77.04%	76.04%	81.89%
Growth (1991–2001)	19.56%	23.08%	14.98%
% SC or ST	32.02%	26.14%	21.91%
Area (sq. km.)	5,448	10,322	7,956
Education Level Attained			
Literacy	51.14%	56.52%	44.54%
Without Level	1.82%	2.49%	1.86%
Below Primary School	13.17%	18.25%	12.30%
Primary School	14.86%	14.47%	12.98%
Middle School	5.10%	6.64%	4.54%
Matric and Above	13.10%	11.48%	10.64%
Graduate and Above	3.10%	3.20%	2.21%
House Type			
Permanent	75.20%	49.40%	52.80%
Semi-permanent	22.50%	44%	37.60%
Temporary	2.30%	6.50%	9.60%

Source: Census of India 2001 and NIC website for each district for geographical area.

ranging from 44.54 percent to 56.52 percent (this is well below the national rate of 65 percent in the 2001 Census).

One dimension in which there is obvious variation is the geographical size of these districts, with Bidar being about half the size of Nanded, and two-thirds the size of Nizamabad, implying that fewer number of schools would be needed to span the entire state assuming any geographical placement of primary schools that ensures children do not need to travel too far for education. Another important dimension in which these states differ is in terms of income levels; while it is difficult to estimate district level income, a good proxy for income has usually been the quality of housing that people have access to and in this dimension, Bidar does considerably better than the other two districts, with almost 75 percent of its population living in permanent structures with the remaining distributed across semi-permanent and temporary housing; by way of comparison, only 50 percent of the population in Nizamabad and Nanded live in permanent structures. Finally, if we compare the population of these three districts with the other districts using the 2001 Census, we find that about 51 percent of all districts in India were smaller than Bidar, the smallest district in our sample. Nizamabad is the next largest district in the sample and it is smaller than 26 percent of the largest districts in India. Finally, Nanded is the largest district in the sample, and is smaller than about 16 percent of the largest districts.

Table 9.2 presents summary statistics of the variables we use in our analysis. About 17 percent of the sample consists of schools from Bidar, while the remaining 83 percent is split roughly evenly between Nanded (41 percent)) and Nizamabad (42 percent). Together in these three

Table 9.2: Summary Statistics of Sample

Variable	N	Mean	S.D.	Min	Max
District = Bidar	7006	0.168	0.374	0	1
District = Nanded	7006	0.408	0.492	0	1
District = Nizamabad	7006	0.424	0.494	0	1
Unique Block Identifier	7006	34.596	16.684	1	58
Public funds received by primary schools					
Does the school receive any public funds?	6980	0.782	0.413	0	1
SDG funds received (Rs Per 1,000)	6980	2.207	7.661	0	410
TLM Funds received TLM (Rs Per 1,000)	6980	1.610	2.178	0	50
Monitoring of primary schools					
# of visits by CRC coordinators	6980	7.126	6.614	0	73
# of visits by BRC coordinators	6980	2.630	3.891	0	70
# of Academic Inspections	6980	0.970	1.410	0	32

(Continued Table 9.2)

(Continued Table 9.2)

Variable	N	Mean	S.D.	Min	Max
Attributes of teachers in primary schools					
# of teachers in school	7006	5.479	4.497	0	71
Does the school have a head teacher?	6753	0.297	0.487	0	6
# of teachers who are college graduates	6753	2.778	3.374	0	41
# of days involved in non-teaching tasks	6753	5.907	43.241	0	1881
# of teachers reporting non-teaching tasks	6753	0.588	1.570	0	18
School infrastructure					
Age of the school	6951	29.88	20.51	1	127
Does the school run in shifts?	6953	0.128	0.334	0	1
School has common Toilets	6743	0.651	0.477	0	1
Total number of classrooms	6753	4.989	4.259	0	80
School is electrified	6750	0.523	0.500	0	1
School has a book bank	6751	0.743	0.437	0	1
School has a playground	6751	0.669	0.471	0	1
# of Blackboards	6753	5.886	4.777	0	88
Source of drinking water					
Tap	7006	0.297	0.457	0	1
No water	7006	0.293	0.455	0	1
Hand-pump	7006	0.239	0.426	0	1
Well	7006	0.029	0.168	0	1
Other school attributes					
% SC students in class 1	5926	0.221	0.256	0	1
% ST students in class 1	5926	0.157	0.284	0	1
% OBC students in class 1	5926	0.371	0.345	0	1
Total village enrolment	7006	399.560	1077.894	0	7197

Source: Data tabulated using school level data from DISE.
Notes: BRC stands for Block Resource Center and CRC for Cluster Resource Center. These are centers that make available to primary schools a head master or a graduate teacher, and high school teachers with B.Ed. training.

districts, there are 58 administrative blocks, with five from Bidar, 17 from Nanded, and 36 from Nizamabad.[10] 78.2 percent of all schools receive some public funding, either from the School Development Grant (SDG) or from the Teaching and Learning Material (TLM) grant, both of which are two major schemes under SSA to support primary schools in India. Schools on average tend to be about 30 years old in the sample; however, there is considerable variation in the age of schools across and within the three districts. Thus, schools in Nanded tend to be oldest on average, followed by Bidar, and then by Nizamabad. On average, Nizamabad's schools tend to be approximately 12–15 years younger than schools in the other two districts. A closer examination of the data (see Figure 9.2) shows that age of schools in these districts varies substantially; in Bidar and Nanded the distribution of the year of school establishment is bi-modal, suggesting that there have been

Figure 9.2: Distribution of the Year Schools were Established in Each District

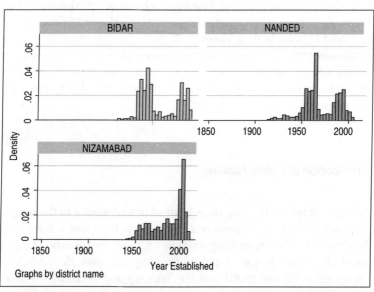

Graphs by district name

Source: Data tabulated using school level data from DISE.

Notes: Age of the school is the difference between 2007 and the year of establishment. In all districts the 1990s have been a period of primary school creation, presumably in response to the SSA. However, there was also an earlier wave of school construction in the decade immediately following independence that seems to have not existed for Nizamabad.

two major drives for building schools in these districts: one around the 1970s and another around the 1990s. In Nizamabad, however, there appears to have been a slow build up of schools, with the peak of school establishment being seen only in the 1990s.

Distribution of Alternative Management Structures

Table 9.3 provides the frequency distribution of the alternative school management types that are found in our sample, as well as the distribution of public funds under school development grant and the training and learning materials grant. The data identifies five predominant management categories uniquely; these are Department of Education, local bodies, private aided, private unaided, and social welfare department. Looking at the district-wise distributions, it is reasonably clear that the Department of Education schools are predominantly in Bidar, Karnataka, while most schools in Nanded and Nizamabad are managed by local bodies. There are likely to be important differences in schools, from different management types and uniformity in schools within any management category. One of the manifestations of this is the wide difference in mean allocation of both public funds across the three districts, as seen in Table 9.2.

Distribution of Public Funding

In terms of public funding there is lot of heterogeneity in the sample with approximately 78 percent of all schools receiving some public funding while the remaining manage on their own funds. The two most structured forms of public funding are through the School Development Grant (SDG) and the Training and Learning Materials grant (TLMs); officially the former provide support up to Rs. 2,000 per school per year for replacement of non-functional school equipment, while the later provides Rs 500 per teacher per year to each school and thus, they provide complimentary means of support to develop school infrastructure: capital and human. Not only is about 22 percent

Table 9.3: Distribution of Public Funds, by Type, District, and School Management

Managed by	Statistics	School Development Grant (Rs per '000)			Training and Learning Materials (Rs per '000)		
		Bidar	Nanded	Nizamabad	Bidar	Nanded	Nizamabad
Dept. of Education	*Mean*	4.17	NA	1.54	2.48	NA	1.39
	SD	14.95	NA	0.93	2.62	NA	1.21
	Obs.	1008	NA	57	1008	NA	57
Local Body	*Mean*	NA	2.53	2.08	NA	1.96	1.64
	SD	NA	1.08	3.68	NA	2.03	1.83
	Obs.	NA	2028	2107	NA	2028	2107
Social Welfare Depart.	*Mean*	0.50	1.11	NA	0.75	0.88	NA
	SD	1.24	1.39	NA	1.87	1.55	NA
	Obs.	12	94	NA	12	94	NA
Private Aided	*Mean*	NA	1.48	0.00	NA	1.83	0.00
	SD	NA	1.64	0.00	NA	3.32	0.00
	Obs.	NA	589	50	NA	589	50
Private Unaided	*Mean*	0.16	0.49	0.00	0.15	0.15	0.00
	SD	0.77	0.87	0.05	0.84	0.69	0.01
	Obs.	112	146	617	112	146	617
Others	*Mean*	0.28	2.00	4.74	0.05	2.25	0.05
	SD	1.42	0.00	35.92	0.26	3.18	0.22
	Obs.	47	2	111	47	2	111

Source: Data tabulated using school level data from DISE.

of primary schools in the sample completely dependent on their own funding (by and large all of these schools are managed by private institutions [mostly unaided], however, a small fraction of schools [20 percent] are publicly managed). We find that on average schools receive a statistically larger amount, by about Rs 765, of SDG than TLM. TLM allocations tend to depend on the number of teachers in the school, while SDG allocations are a lump-sum allocation, and thus, in the sample we find that SDG exceeds TLM in about 52 percent of the sample.

Table 9.4 reports the distribution of SDG and TLM in the sample, as well as the correlation between funds received and funds spent. Panel (A) looks at SDG and we see that while about 55 percent of the sample receives precisely Rs 2,000 per year, about 17 percent of the sample gets twice this amount, and the rest receive other amounts of funds. Similarly, Panel (B) looks at the distribution of the number of teachers in the sample, their predicted TLM that should have been received on the basis of Rs 500 per teacher rule, and the actually observed amount of public funds received. In both instances we note that there is a small but noticeable and presumably policy relevant discrepancy between how money is meant to be distributed and how it is distributed. Thus, under SDG an important fraction of the population has access to grants that are larger than the mandated Rs 2,000, and under the TLM it would appear that schools receive less money than what they should be receiving based on the number of teachers that they report. Additionally, the gap between actual and predicted TLM received is larger in schools with larger numbers of teachers. As with most public policy programs, it would appear that the operational criteria under which the SSA functions is a lot more complicated than what the policy documents intend them to be. Finally, as with most public funds allocation, it is important to know not only the allocation of funds, but also their expenditures. The DISE system not only report funds received, but also funds spent and here, most of the schools do very well, as seen in the high correlations between funds received and spent for both of these programs in Panel (C) of Table 9.4. For SDG, the correlation coefficient is very high at 0.95, while it is a bit lower but nevertheless very high at 0.83 for the TLM.

Table 9.4: Distribution Public Funds Received

Panel (A)

SDG Received (in Rs per 1,000)	Freq.	Cumulative
0	23.8	–
0.2–1.98	0.63	24.43
2	55.63	80.06
2.25–3.99	0.38	80.44
4	16.59	97.03
4.01–410	2.97	100.00

Panel (B)

# of Teachers	Freq.	TLM (in Rs per 1,000)		
		Predicted	Received	Gap
0	4.17	0	0.58	−0.6
1	2.95	0.5	0.38	0.12
2	24.94	1	0.86	0.14
3	11.1	1.5	1.13	0.37
4	8.21	2	1.49	0.51
5	6.29	2.5	1.63	0.87
6	7.02	3	2.14	0.86
7	7.41	3.5	2.64	0.86
8	8.89	4	2.75	1.25
9	5.87	4.5	3.15	1.35
10	3.6	5	3.11	1.89
11	1.93	5.5	3.82	1.68
12+	7.62	8.32	5.01	3.32
Total	100	2.6	1.83	0.76

Panel (C)

	SDG Received	SDG Spent	TLM Received	TLM Spent
SDG Received	1			
SDG Spent	0.953	1		
	0			
TLM Received	0.0813	0.072	1	
	0	0		
TLM Spent	0.0754	0.0765	0.8282	1
	0	0	0	

Source: Data tabulated using school level data from DISE.

Based on such high correlations, we decided to go with funds allocated rather than funds spent as that is more a reflection of the public systems functioning without being contaminated with any kind of idiosyncratic behavior from the school that determines the difference between funds allocated and funds spent.

Another dimension of interest is the level of supervision or monitoring that the schools report. In the entire sample, schools on average receive about seven visits a year from the Cluster Resources Center coordinators, more than two a year from the Block Resource Centre, as well as almost one academic inspection a year. Thus, on average, there are about 10 visitors per school year from outside the school, with whom the teaching staff can interact. Apart from monitoring of primary schools, we can also control for within school quality of teachers and teaching as we observe the number of teachers, if the school has a head teacher, and how many teachers the school has with graduate education, as well as the amount of non-teaching tasks that the school is engaged with. We find that on average there are more than five teachers to a school, only about 30 percent of the schools have a head teacher, just under three teachers tend to be college graduates, and collectively all teachers in a school tend to only spend six days on non-teaching activities. We also have a number of details about the school's infrastructure such as age, number of classrooms, availability of toilets, if it has a book-bank, number of blackboards, source of drinking water, and so on. Finally, we also observe that the fraction of students enrolled in Class I who are SC, ST, and OBCs are 22 percent, 15.7 percent, and 37.1 percent, respectively in the sample, and this broadly conforms to the SC or ST distribution in the 2001 Census in Table 9.1.

IV Estimation Strategy

Functionality of Primary Schools

We are interested in the relationship between public funds that are allocated to a school and the number of instructional days that the school has in the academic year. Two sets of concerns arise in trying to characterize such a relationship:

1. Identifying the impact of what would have happened if a school didn't have public funds—a credible counterfactual.

2. Modeling the relationship between public funds and the outcome, given the structural nature of our outcome variable—the instructional days.

This section discusses both these issues and presents our estimation strategy in the process.

Identifying a causal relationship in an observational setting is complicated because there is no *a priori* reason to believe that schools are allocated public funds randomly. Lacking randomness in allocation of public funds raises the possibility of schools with certain attributes being more likely to receive funds.[11] Thus, for example, an MLA for whom education in a specific block is important for electoral purposes may not only work hard to ensure that schools receive public funds, but may also visit schools to check on them, thereby ensuring more instructional days leading to an overestimate of the impact of public funds on instructional days.[12] Given the cross-sectional but grouped nature of our data (grouped at the district and at the block level), we can control for certain forms of omitted variable bias that may affect our estimates. Given that we have data on many schools in a block within a district, we can control for unobserved district level (or block level) factors that affect schools within a district (or a block) in an identical fashion with district (block) level fixed effects. We exploit variation in schools across districts as well as across blocks to estimate our coefficients. To reinforce this variation, we choose districts that are closely located to each other but are situated in different states to maximize variation across administrative boundaries. To account for possible non-independence and non-identical distribution within our sample, we cluster at the block level to ensure that our results are as robust as possible.

Our outcome of interest is the number of instructional days in the school year. This variable has a very natural upper limit of 365 calendar days as well as a minimum of zero days. The top panel of Figure 9.3 shows the histogram of the number of instructional days in the sample; this shows the bimodality of the number of instructional days, with about 10 percent of the sample with exactly zero instructional days and most other schools being close to around 230 instructional school days. We use this bimodality in the distribution of the instructional days to empirically motivate our definition for "functionality" or having an appropriate number of instructional days.[13] While about 12 percent of the entire sample has zero instructional school days, the subsample with more than 200 days of instruction (or about 8+ months at the rate of 24 instructional days in a month) has a median of 232 days of instruction (or slightly less than 10 months) with a standard deviation of 10 days (or about half a month). Thus, most schools, if they operate, tend to provide close to 10 months of instructions for their students and most of them have about eight to 12 months of instruction.

A plot of the quantiles of the number of instructional days greater than zero against the quantiles of a normal distribution suggests that the distribution of instructional days, given that it is positive, is approximately normal (see bottom panel of Figure 9.3). With a normal distribution, we know that roughly 99.7 percent of the distribution is within ±3 standard deviations of the mean, and so we identify a range of 231 ± 30 days, that is, (201, 261). For the analysis, we investigated other cut-offs as well, but the data between zero and 200 days is quite sparse, as seen in Figure 9.3, and hence the analysis is robust to other rules to identify schools that are functional. Thus, we use 201 instructional days, or a little over eight months as the cut-off for functionality for a primary school. For the sake of symmetry, we also drop observations with more than 261 days of observation for this investigation (this accounts for a mere 0.43 percent of the sample).

We treat schools with less than 201 days of instruction as being "not functional" (spanning about 14 percent of the sample) and rest as being "functional".[14] With a binary outcome ($y_i = 0$ indicating i is not a functional school and $y_i = 1$ indicating i is a functional school), a natural way to study the relationship between the flow of public funds and the school being functional is to impose a distributional assumption on the probability of a school being functional (i.e., $p_i = P(y_i=1)$). Specifically, we assume that the probability of being functional is a logistic function of a set of covariates x_i such that:

$$p_i = \frac{\exp(\beta x_i)}{1 + \exp(\beta x_i)}$$

where x_i is a vector of covariates for school i such as the amount of public funds it received, age of the school, number of academic inspections, certification of teachers, distance from block head quarters, and so forth.

Figure 9.3: Distribution of Number of Days of Instruction in Primary Schools

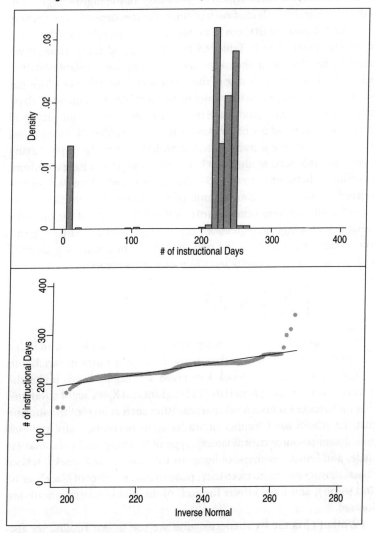

Source: Data tabulated using school level data from DISE.

Notes: The top panel shows the entire distribution of the number of instructional days while the bottom panel shows a Q–Q plot of the number of instructional days greater than 178 days against the quintiles of draws from a normal distribution.

In this context, the most important advantage of the logistic regression is that the marginal effect of each of the covariates depends upon where in the distribution of that covariate we calculate the effect at (thus, size of the effects reported in Table 9.5 are all calculated at the mean, if we calculate the effect of another academic visit, at say one standard deviation below the mean, then the size of the coefficient would change). This has two explicit advantages, with modeling the number of instructional days: first, schools simply cannot have more than 365 instructional days and thus, as the values of the covariates change, the number of instructional days cannot change linearly, since it would eventually imply having more than 365 days; secondly, schools do not appear to have a uniform distribution between zero and 232 days of instruction; thus, we are able to handle both issues of natural limits of the number of instructional days as well as the inherent non-linearity in the distribution of the outcome variable with a logistic regression. Expanding x_i, and collecting x_{ib} terms to one side, we model the log odds of being a functional school as an additive and linear in coefficients function of its covariates as:

$$\log\left(\frac{P_{ib}}{1-P_{ib}}\right) = \beta_0 + \beta_1 PF_{ib} + \beta X_{ib} + \mu_1 + \cdots + \mu_{56} \tag{1}$$

where i is an index for all primary schools in the sample, b is an index for the blocks from which data is used, PF_{ib} is a dummy variable to indicate if a school i in block b received any public funds under the Training and Learning Materials (TLM) grant and X_{ib} is a set of covariates that includes key school level characteristics such as level of monitoring that the school has (number of academic inspections, visits by block and cluster resource coordinators), type of teaching staff (headmaster, male, and female teachers, obligations to non-teaching work), school characteristics (access to electricity, playground, number of blackboards, and so on), and fixed effects for each of the blocks where schools are located.[15]

While (1) is the basic specification we use in our results, we also discuss alternative specifications, where instead of a dummy variable for receiving any funds, we look at the amount of SDG and TLM received, and there are some specifications where we look at district level fixed effects. For all except one model, we use clustered standard errors, where we cluster the data at the block level to account for potential non-independence and non-identical distribution at the block level.

The key coefficient of interest in Equation (1) is β_1, that is, the impact of receiving any public funds on the probability that the school is functional.

V Results

Table 9.5 presents results from our logit regressions, which look at the role that different covariates, particularly public funding, has on the probability that a school will be functional. Each of the columns report different specifications with the first model being the least demanding in terms of assuming Independent and Identical Distribution (IID) of

Table 9.5: Logistic Regression Models for P (Functional = 1 I X)

	est1	est2	est3	est4	est5	est6
Public funds received by primary schools						
Does school receive public funds? [v]	0.042*** [0.008]	0.042 [0.024]	0.049* [0.024]		0.097*** [0.024]	
Log of SGD received (Rs. Per 1,000)				0.004** [0.001]		0.005*** [0.001]
Log of TLM received (Rs. per 1,000)[iv]				0 [0.001]		0.001 [0.001]
Monitoring of primary schools						
# of visits by BRC coordinators	0.019*** [0.001]	0.019*** [0.003]	0.017*** [0.004]	0.016*** [0.004]	0.008*** [0.002]	0.008*** [0.002]
# of visits by CRC coordinators	0.004*** [0.001]	0.004*** [0.001]	0.004*** [0.001]	0.004*** [0.001]	0.004*** [0.001]	0.004*** [0.001]
# of Academic Inspections	0.025*** [0.003]	0.025** [0.008]	0.028*** [0.007]	0.027*** [0.007]	0.032*** [0.006]	0.032*** [0.006]
Teacher characteristics at school						
# of teachers in School	−0.001* [0.001]	−0.001 [0.001]	−0.001 [0.001]	−0.001 [0.001]	0.001 [0.001]	0 [0.001]
Does school have a head teacher?	0.014*** [0.004]	0.014** [0.005]	0.012** [0.004]	0.011** [0.004]	0.013** [0.004]	0.012** [0.004]

(Continued Table 9.5)

(Continued Table 9.5)

	est1	est2	est3	est4	est5	est6
# of college graduate teachers	0.007*** [0.001]	0.007** [0.002]	0.003** [0.001]	0.003** [0.001]	0.001 [0.001]	0.002 [0.001]
# of days of non-teaching tasks	0.001* [0.001]	0.001* [0.001]	0.001* [0.000]	0.001* [0.000]	0.001** [0.001]	0.001** [0.001]
# of teachers on non-teaching tasks	0.003 [0.004]	0.003 [0.004]	−0.004 [0.003]	−0.003 [0.003]	−0.007* [0.003]	−0.007* [0.004]
School infrastructure						
Age of the School	−0.001*** [0.000]	−0.001* [0.000]	0 [0.000]	−0.001 [0.000]	0 [0.000]	0 [0.000]
Square of age of the school	0.000* [0.000]	0 [0.000]	0 [0.000]	0 [0.000]	0 [0.000]	0 [0.000]
Does the school run in shifts?	−0.01 [0.006]	−0.01 [0.010]	0.003 [0.005]	0.002 [0.005]	0.003 [0.006]	0.003 [0.006]
School has common toilets?	0.008 [0.004]	0.008 [0.006]	0.002 [0.005]	0.001 [0.004]	0.008 [0.005]	0.007 [0.006]
Total number of classrooms	0 [0.001]	0 [0.001]	0 [0.001]	0 [0.001]	0 [0.001]	0 [0.001]
School is electrified?	−0.007 [0.004]	−0.007 [0.005]	−0.002 [0.004]	−0.003 [0.004]	−0.002 [0.005]	−0.004 [0.005]
School has a book bank?	0.005 [0.004]	0.005 [0.007]	0.009 [0.006]	0.007 [0.006]	0.013 [0.009]	0.011 [0.009]
School has a playground?	0.005 [0.004]	0.005 [0.005]	0.008 [0.005]	0.006 [0.005]	0.007 [0.007]	0.005 [0.007]
# of blackboards	−0.001 [0.001]	−0.001 [0.001]	0 [0.001]	0 [0.001]	0 [0.001]	0 [0.001]
Source of drinking water						
Tap	−0.01 [0.007]	−0.01 [0.009]	−0.006 [0.005]	−0.005 [0.006]	−0.002 [0.007]	−0.002 [0.007]
No water	−0.016* [0.007]	−0.016* [0.008]	−0.003 [0.006]	−0.002 [0.006]	−0.006 [0.008]	−0.004 [0.008]
Hand-pump	−0.004 [0.007]	−0.004 [0.006]	−0.002 [0.005]	−0.002 [0.005]	−0.003 [0.008]	−0.003 [0.008]
Well	−0.042* [0.017]	−0.042* [0.018]	−0.027* [0.013]	−0.029* [0.013]	−0.019 [0.013]	−0.022 [0.013]

(Continued Table 9.5)

(Continued Table 9.5)

	est1	est2	est3	est4	est5	est6
Total village enrollment	0.000*** [0.000]	0.000** [0.000]	0.000*** [0.000]	0.000*** [0.000]	0 [0.000]	0 [0.000]
Observations	5717	5717	5717	5685	5717	5621
R-Squared	0.3073	0.3073	0.3259	0.3192	0.4442	0.4278
Fixed Effects	None	None	District	District	Block	Block
Standard Error	iid	clustered	clustered	clustered	clustered	Clustered

Source: Data tabulated using school level data from DISE.

Notes:
(i) In all models the standard errors when clustered are clustered on the Block except for the model (1) where sampling is assumed to be clustered within blocks.
(ii) We report the marginal effect of each of the covariates on the probability scale and standard errors are reported below these marginal effects square brackets.
(iii) ***, **, and * indicates significance at > 0.001, > 0.05, and > 0.10 levels.
(iv) As TLM funds are dependent on the # of teachers in the school we standardize TLM across schools by dividing the TLM by the # of teachers.
(v) Schools which have missing data on SDG and TLM are assumed to receive no funding.

all schools across block and district lines. The second model improves on the first model by being more conservative on the standard errors by allowing within block non-independence of school outcomes. The third model tries to reduce bias in the model by improving on the second model with district fixed effects. Thus, unobserved district level influences such as the competency of the bureaucracy, weather, and so on, that would have the same impact across schools would be accounted for. The fourth model differs from the third in that it looks at the logarithm of the amount of money received under the SDG and TLM to investigate the semi-elasticity of public funds on school functionality. The fifth and sixth models are the counterparts of the third and the fourth model, except that we are much more conservative and use block fixed effects rather than district fixed effects.

Our estimate for β_1, the key coefficient of interest, varies substantially across our models from about two probability points[16] in model (1) to 9.7 probability points in model (5) suggesting that some of the corrections that we made to reduce bias are particularly relevant. The standard errors were also under-estimated, with the IID assumption, as once we cluster at the block level they are about four times larger. Thus, by granting public funds to a school that was not receiving any funds earlier we raise the probability of its becoming a functional school about 9.7 points on the probability scale. This is statistically significant and fundamentally important as well.

This increase in the probability is substantially smaller when we look at SDG, TLM, and their logarithms. We report models only for the logarithms since the impact of just SDG and TLM are both not significant.[17] The coefficient on logarithms should be interpreted as the change in the probability for a percentage growth in SDG (or TLM). The effect of TLM is positive but not statistically significant, while that of SDG is positive and statistically significant, but substantially very small; thus, a one percentage increase in SDG will lead to an increase in probability of a school becoming functional by 0.5 probability points. We reconcile these findings by suggesting that for school with no public funds, access to public funds has a strong impact on the school's becoming functional; however, subsequent incremental increases in public funding have little impact.

One set of covariates that are systematically significant across all models that we estimate is the number of academic, BRC coordinators, and CRC coordinators who visit a school. The coefficients on these covariates are always statistically significant and positive. An additional academic visit raises the probability of schools being functional by 3.2 probability points on our two most conservative models, while visits by BRC and CRC coordinators have a much smaller impact at 0.8 probability points and 0.4 probability points, respectively. In model (6) where we are looking at a continuous measure of public funds, the largest (and positive) coefficient is on the number of academic visits in schools which already receive funds. Thus, while the impact of public funding is large for schools not receiving any public funds (9.7 points), amongst schools receiving funds, an additional academic visit has a stronger impact on the school being functional than an additional one thousand rupees of public funds.[18]

Amongst the other coefficients that are statistically significant but have smaller coefficients are: the presence of a head teacher (1.2 probability points), the number of non-teaching days (0.1 probability points), and the number of teachers engaged in non-teaching tasks (−0.7 probability points). While the sign on the coefficients for the presence of a head teacher and the number of teachers engaged in non-teaching tasks is expected, that for non-teaching days is unexpected. We expected that the number of non-teaching days would have a negative influence on the probability of being functional, paralleling the effect we see on having another teacher engaged in non-teaching tasks; however, it is positive, though small in magnitude. A closer look at the summary statistics (Table 9.2) shows that schools on an average have about five teachers in a school, and cumulatively, they have about six days of non-teaching assignment per year, which is very modest. Thus, we interpret participating in non-teaching days as a sign of efficiency; schools which are not functional not only do not have any significant number of instructional days, but they also do not have teachers who report participating in non-teaching assignments.

In conclusion, we find evidence to suggest that schools that receive public funds are more likely to be functional in the sense of offering more than 201 instructional days to its students. However, the size of this effect does not have a relationship with the volume of funds that schools receive. A part of this could be because of the very nature of the public funding mechanism where schools receive a fixed amount for each school, under the SDG, or a fixed amount for each teacher, under the TLM. Thus, if there had been little variation from the institutional norms, then the only significant variation in receiving public funds in our sample would have come from schools who receive some or no funds. However, this is not the case, and we do find that there are operational differences between how the schools receive funding from what is stated. From a data perspective, these differences need greater documentation and understanding; however, we do see large and robust effects of receiving school funding on the length of the school term.

Apart from public funding, we also find strong evidence that schools which have greater number of visitors in the form of academic visitors, BRC and CRC coordinators, have a higher probability of being functional and this is an important, low-cost policy lever that may be used to enhance instructional days. Amongst teacher variables, one of the key variables that appear to be important is the presence of the head teacher in the school. Looking at our sample, only 29 percent of the sample reports having a head-teacher and thus, staffing schools with head teachers could potentially have large effects in the population.

We end with the caveat that generalizing these findings to the entire country is not a valid statistical exercise in so far as these districts are quite unique and our data only comes from these districts. We hope to confirm these by investigating this for other districts in India, as well as looking at how these trends have varied over time since the inception of the SSA.

Appendix

Norms for Financial Interventions under SSA

	INTERVENTION	NORM
1.	Teacher	• One teacher for every 40 children in primary and upper primary • At least two teachers in a primary school • One teacher for every class in the upper primary
2.	School/Alternative schooling facility	• Within one kilometre of every habitation • Provision for opening of new schools as per State norms or for setting up EGS like schools in unserved habitations
3.	Upper Primary schools/ Sector	• As per requirement based on the number of children completing primary education, up to a ceiling of one upper primary school/section for every two primary schools
4.	Classrooms	• A room for every teacher in primary & upper primary, with the provision that there would be two classrooms with verandah to every primary school with at least two teachers • A room for Head Master in upper primary school/section
5.	Free textbooks	• To all girls/SC/ST children at primary & upper primary level within an upper ceiling of Rs 150 per child • State to continue to fund free textbooks being currently provided from the State Plans
6.	Civil works	• Ceiling of 33 percent of SSA program funds • For improvement of school facilities, BRC/CRC construction • CRCs could also be used as an additional room • No expenditure to be incurred on construction of office buildings • Districts to prepare infrastructure plans
7.	Maintenance and repair of school buildings	• Only through school management committees/VECs • Upto Rs 5,000 per year as per specific proposal by the school committee • Must involve elements of community contribution

8.	Upgradation of EGS to regular school or setting up of a new Primary school as per State norm	• Provision for TLE @ Rs 10,000/- per school • TLE as per local context and need • Involvement of teachers and parents necessary in TLE selection and procurement • VEC/school-village level appropriate body to decide on best mode of procurement • Requirement of successful running of EGS center for two years before it is considered for upgradation • Provision for teacher & classrooms
9.	TLE for upper-primary	• @ Rs 50,000 per school for uncovered schools • As per local specific requirement to be determined by the teachers/school committee • School committee to decide on best mode of procurement, in consultation with teachers • School Committee may recommend district level procurement if there are advantages of scale
10.	Schools grant	• Rs 2,000 per year per primary/upper primary school for replacement of non-functional school equipment • Transparency in utilization • To be spent only by VEC/SMC
11.	Teacher grant	• Rs 500 per teacher per year in primary and upper primary • Transparency in utilization
12.	Teacher training	• Provision of 20 days In-service course for all teachers each year, 60 days refresher course for untrained teachers already employed as teachers, and 30 days orientation for freshly trained recruits @ Rs 70 per day • Unit cost is indicative; would be lower in non-residential training programs • Includes all training cost • Assessment of capacities for effective training during appraisal will determine extent of coverage • Support for SCERT/DIET under existing Teacher Education Scheme
13.	State Institute of Educational Management and Training (SIEMAT)	• One time assistance up to Rs 3 crore • States have to agree to sustain • Selection criteria for faculty to be rigorous

(Continued)

(Continued)

	INTERVENTION	NORM
14.	Training of community leaders	• For a maximum of eight persons in a village for two days in a year—preferably women • @ Rs. 30 per day
15.	Provision for disabled children	• Upto Rs 1,200 per child for integration of disabled children, as per specific proposal, per year • District Plan for children with special needs will be formulated within the Rs 1,200 per child norm • Involvement of resource institutions to be encouraged
16.	Research, evaluation, supervision, and monitoring	• Upto Rs 1,500 per school per year • Partnership with research and resource institutions, pool of resource teams with State specific focus • Priority to development of capacities for appraisal and supervision through resource/research institutions and on an effective EMIS • Provision for regular school mapping/micro planning for updating of household data • By creating pool of resource persons, providing travel grant and honorarium for monitoring, generation of community-based data, research studies, cost of assessment and appraisal terms and their field activities, classroom observation by resource persons • Funds to be spent at national, state, district, sub-district, school level out of the overall per school allocation • Rs 100 per school per year to be spent at national level • Expenditure at State/district/BRC/CRC/School level to be decided by State/UT, This would include expenditure on appraisal, supervision, MIS, classroom observation, and so on. Support to SCERT over and above the provision under the Teacher Education scheme may also be provided • Involvement of resource institutions willing to undertake state specific responsibilities
17.	Management cost	• Not to exceed 6 percent of the budget of a district plan • To include expenditure on office expenses, hiring of experts at various levels after assessment of existing manpower, POL, and so on • Priority to experts in MIS, community planning processes, civil works, gender, and so on. depending on capacity available in a particular district • Management costs should be used to develop effective teams at State/ District/Block/Cluster levels • Identification of personnel for BRC/CRC should be a priority in the pre-project phase itself so that a team is available for the intensive process based planning

18.	Innovative activity for girls' education, early childhood care and education, interventions for children belonging to SC/ST community, computer education, especially for upper primary level	• Upto to Rs 15 lakh for each innovative project and Rs 50 lakh for a district per year will apply for SSA • ECCE and girls education interventions to have unit costs already approved under other existing schemes
19.	Block Resource Centres/Cluster Resource Centres	• BRC/CRC to be located in school campus as far as possible • Rs 6 lakh ceiling for BRC building construction wherever required • Rs 2 lakh for CRC construction wherever required—should be used as an additional classroom in schools • Total cost of non-school (BRC and CRC) construction in any district should not exceed 5 percent of the overall projected expenditure under the program in any year • Deployment of up to 20 teacher in a block with more than 100 schools; 10 teachers in smaller Blocks in BRCs/CRCs • Provision of furniture, and so on @ Rs. 1 lakh for a BRC and Rs. 10,000 for a CRC • Contingency grant of Rs 12,500 for a BRC and Rs 2,500 for a CRC, per year • Identification of BRC/CRC personnel after intensive selection process in the preparatory phase itself
20.	Interventions for out of school children	• As per norms already approved under Education Guarantee Scheme and Alternative and Innovative Education, providing for the following kind of interventions • Setting up Education Guarantee Centers in unserved habitations • Setting up other alternative schooling models • Bridge Courses, remedial courses, Back-to-School Camps with a focus on mainstreaming out of school children into regular schools
21.	Preparatory activities for microplanning, household surveys, studies, community mobilization, school-based activities, office equipment, training and orientation at all levels, and so on	• As per specific proposal of a district, duly recommended by the state. Urban areas, within a district or metropolitan cities may be treated as a separate unit for planning as required

Source: SSA Framework Revised available at http://ssa.nic.in/page_portletlinks?foldername=ssa-framework (accessed October 21, 2008).

Notes

1 A number of studies document the current and historically changing state of primary education on the basis of many different schooling outcomes. For example, the PROBE report investigates attitudes about primary schooling, role of child labor, costs of primary education, and the role of local bodies (such as the Village Education Committee) in five north Indian states (PROBE Team, 1999). See Sankar (2008) to see an evaluation of primary schooling in terms of participation in schooling, role of private schooling as we well as school infrastructure across the country for the last two decades.

2 The relationship between time spent in school and student achievement is well documented. For a recent review of literature as well as a discussion of the state of time spent in primary school in a number of countries in the world, see Abadzi (2007a), Abadzi (2007b), and UNESCO Institute of Statistics (2008).

3 As a step towards universal primary education (UPE) in India, the District Primary Education Program (DPEP) was initiated in late 1994. The District Information System for Education (DISE) was set up in 1995 to evaluate the functioning of the DPEP and provides extensive details on a range of school attributes. See the Appendix for the details of financing available under SSA.

4 Throughout this chapter we use the word "functional" to imply that a school has 201 or more days of instruction. We discuss the choice of 201 days of instruction more carefully later on in the paper. This matches well with other estimates of the number of days of school functionality; UNESCO documents that about 90 percent of primary schools in India operate for 204 days in an academic year (UNESCO Institute of Statistics, 2008).

5 Section 1.8 details the financial norms and sharing ratios between the Center and state over the IXth and the Xth plan periods. See http://education.nic.in/ssa/ssa_1.asp.

6 See Banerji (2003) for a discussion of the original SSA norms and an optimistic but very clear discussion of the size of the problem that the SSA is dealing with.

7 Card and Kruger (1992), after controlling for cohort effects and location of birth effects, provide strong evidence to suggest that better school quality indicators, such as the average duration of the school term, amongst others, leads to improved individual earnings using data from the US.

8 Schooling in Germany follows different merit based tracks and the author presents evidence, after controlling for all other observable differences, to suggest that a reduction in school terms lead to a decline in people going for higher merit schooling later on. There was no impact on later life earnings due to this.

9 In our sample about 87 percent of all schools are in rural areas. The figures for the respective districts are 91 percent for Bidar, 84 percent for Nanded, and 89 percent for Nizamabad.

10 For our estimation, we drop one of the blocks from Nanded, Nanded CS, which has only 10 observations, so, in effect, there are 57 blocks for our analysis.

11 An example of this is the case of endogenous program placement, where interventions are made in districts where people are doing poorly. Thus, Angeles et al. (1998) discusses the case of fertility programs being targeted to areas where fertility is particularly high. After the intervention if we find that fertility is higher in intervention areas than in non-intervention areas then we need to be careful about what to infer; is the program dysfunctional or if a normally functioning program has led to declines but the high fertility area remains higher fertility even after the program. The appropriate counterfactual in

such a case is not necessarily the fertility in non-intervention areas, but a subset of it, and baseline levels of fertility in both program and non-program areas.

12 Let X^0 be the omitted variable (here progressive MLA) then the omitted variable bias in estimating the effect of X is given by $E(\hat{\beta}) = \beta + \beta^0 Cov(X, X^0)$ where $\hat{\beta}$ is the estimated coefficient for X when X^0 has been omitted from the regression, β is population parameter for X, β^0 is the population marginal effect of X^0 and Cov is the population covariance. In the story above we argued that both β^0 and Cov are positive for the progressive MLA and hence $E(\hat{\beta})$ would overestimate β.

13 A natural concern is that the sample tracks schools that have opened too recently or are too old, and hence, are not functional. Looking at the age distribution of schools, we find that median duration for which schools with zero functional days have been operating is about 28 years, with a minimum of one to a maximum of 106 years and thus spans the entire age distribution for schools that are functional and have positive number of instructional days. Additionally, the distribution of schools that have no zero instructional days are mostly in Bidar (20 percent) and Nanded (19 percent) and less so in Nizamabad (5 percent).

14 This appears to conform pretty well to international notions of a full academic school year. Thus, UNESCO Institute of Statistics (2008) reports that in India most students have a school year of 204; this is longer than school years in Argentina, Brazil, Malaysia, Paraguay, Peru, and Uruguay, but shorter than school years in Chile and Philippines.

15 Panel logit model with N units, each observed for T_i periods, is known to produce estimates of marginal effects that are not consistent when T_i is small and fixed. These fixed effects in non-linear models have been traditionally seen as problematic because T_i have been small and asymptotic arguments about the consistency of the estimators require large T_i and N. However, Heckman (1981) shows in a simulation study that with $T_i = 8$, and $N = 100$, that with the maximum likelihood fixed effects estimator, estimates of the regression coefficient can be arbitrarily close to its population values. In our study, $N = 57$ and the median $T_i = 86$ and thus, we have ample data to argue for large T_i and N. One of the blocks, Nanded M.C. has only ten schools—we remove these from the final estimation sample otherwise we'd have $N = 58$ in the sample. Also see Green (2001) for an updated discussion on this.

16 We use the term *probability points* to refer to values on the unit interval (i.e., between 0 and 1). Thus, if a variable increases the conditional probability of being functional by 10 percent we refer to this as an increase 10 probability points.

17 TLM and SDG have a statistically significant, but have a substantially small correlation coefficient of 0.08.

18 The confidents on log (SDG) and Number of Academic Visits are not only substantively different, they are also statistically different with a pvalue of 0.001 for a test of equality of coefficients.

References

Abadzi, Helen. 2007a. "Instructional Time Loss and Local Governance", *Prospects* 37(1): 3–16.

———. 2007b. "Absenteeism and Beyond: Instructional Time Loss and Consequences", World Bank Policy Research, Working Paper 4376. Available online at http://ssrn.com/abstract=1021370 (downloaded on November 11, 2008).

Angeles, Gustavo, David K. Guilkey, and Thomas A. Mroz. 1998. "Purposive Program Placement and the Estimation of Family Planning Program Effects in Tanzania", *Journal of the American Statistical Association*, 93 443): 884–99.

Banerji, Rukmini. 2003. "Sarva Shiksha Abhiyan: Every child in school and learning well", *Pratham*, July 7. Available online at http://www.pratham.org/readindia/shiksha_abhiyan. php.

Card, David and Alan B. Krueger. 1992. "Does School Quality Matter? Returns to Education and the Characteristics of Public Schools in the United States". *The Journal of Political Economy*, 100, (1): 1–40.

Green, W.H. 2001. "Estimating Econometric Models with Fixed Effects", Working Papers with number 01–10, Leonard N. Stern School of Business, Department of Economics, New York University.

Heckman, J. 1981. "The Incidental Parameters Problem and the Problem of Initial Conditions in Estimating a Discrete Time-Discrete Data Stochastic Process", in C. Manski and D. McFadden, (eds), *Structural Analysis of Discrete Data with Econometric Applications*, pp. 114–78. Cambridge: MIT Press.

Jong-wha, Lee and Robert J. Barro. 2001. "Schooling Quality in a Cross-section of Countries", *Economica*, 68: 465–88.

Mehta, A.C. 2007. *Elementary Education in India: Progress towards UEE*. Analytical Report for 2005–06. NUPA and MHRD. New Delhi.

Pischke, Jorn-Steffen. 2007. "The Impact of Length of School Year on Student Performance and Earnings: Evidence from the German Short School Years". *The Economic Journal* 117 (October): 1216–42.

PROBE Team. 1999. Public Report on Basic Education for India. New Delhi: Oxford University Press.

Sankar, Deepa. 2008. "What is the Progress in Elementary Education Participation in India During the Last Two Rounds? An Analysis Using NSS Education Rounds". Discussion Paper Series Report No. 24, South Asia Human Development Sector, The World Bank.

UNESCO Institute of Statistics. 2008. A View Inside Primary Schools: A World Education Indicators (WEI) Cross-National Study. Montreal, Quebec H3C 3J7, Canada. Available online at www.uis.unesco.org/template/pdf/wei/sps/Report.pdf.

World Bank 2001. *India: Expanding and Improving Upper Primary Education in India*, Report No. 20347-IN. Available online at http://go.worldbank.org/WLWP799PF1 (downloaded on November 11, 2008).

10

Neglected Topics in Public Economics Courses

Arindam Das-Gupta

—— • ✦ • ——

I Introduction

As its title implies, this chapter focuses on important gaps in the
coverage of typical undergraduate public economics courses if they are
to remain relevant in the face of the rapidly changing scope of public
sector activity during the past 50 odd years. The chapter takes as its
starting point topics not covered or inadequately covered in leading
undergraduate public finance and public economics textbooks.[1] Of the
various topics identified, the three topics discussed in relative detail are
now briefly introduced:

Economic Principles of the Government Budget

At best limited treatment in public economics text books of principles
applicable to what is arguably the most important fiscal policy
instrument, the government budget, is surprising.[2] The importance
of the budget stems, of course, from the overview it provides of the
role played by the government in the economy, via its integrated view
of revenue, expenditure, and debt policies. This makes it an essential

base from which to evaluate both past performance and announced future policies. As a result of this neglect, recent generations of undergraduate public economics students remain largely innocent of knowledge needed to adequately assess macro and micro fiscal policy in an integrated fashion. Section II of this chatper attempts to sketch the contours of a discussion of budget principles and practical tools to assess national budgets.

Non-tax Revenues

Most public economics texts cover tax finance in detail, but pay little if any attention to other sources of public finance, including debt, seigniorage, asset sales, and other revenue sources. "Other revenue sources" or non-tax revenues include all receipts other than taxes and seigniorage, and capital receipts from debt issues or asset sales. The absence of discussion of principles governing non-tax revenues makes coverage in these texts of limited use to economies, typically resource rich economies, with limited dependence on taxation. In fact, according to the World Bank's *World Development Indicators* (World Bank, 2003), in or around 2002, roughly 39 percent of revenues of the 166 countries covered there—not just resource rich economies—were from non-tax revenues.[3] If, as has been claimed in some recent writings,[4] increasing globalization erodes a country's ability to raise tax revenues, this percentage is likely to rise. The third section of this chapter provides a classification of non-tax revenue sources and attempts a preliminary discussion of the public finance theory of non-tax revenue.

International Tax Implications of the Global Fiscal Commons

Since Hardin (1968) coined the phrase "tragedy of the commons", common pool problems have been widely studied, and are known to arise with goods or resources over which property rights are either undefined or unenforceable. These features give rise to *non-excludability* even though consumption of the resource is *rival*. Common pool problems in the fiscal arena and the tendency to overexploitation have been studied in the context of federations and where problems of overlapping jurisdictions exist since at least Weingast, Shepsle, and Johnsen (1981). The global fiscal commons can be defined to consist of potentially taxable entities or transactions with at least some characteristic involving more than one jurisdiction: be it purchase, sale, trans-shipment, source, residence, or ownership. The rapidly expanding size of the global fiscal commons with increasing globalization and growing capital and skilled labor mobility poses potential risks to national fiscal capacities. This makes the topic both an important emerging area in the study of taxation as well as a vital area of concern for national policy makers. Aspects of the global fiscal commons and national policy are outlined in Section IV. In the concluding section of this chapter, some other less researched or possibly less important topics are identified which have attracted the attention of public economists or policy makers but which receive little attention in most public economics syllabi.

I first heard of most of the topics, including the three discussed here in depth or at any rate aspects of them, from the late Amaresh Bagchi, whom I look upon as my mentor and guide in the early days of my career as an applied public economist.[5] I believe the topics are illustrative of his wide ranging scholarship and forward looking approach to areas of public economics which are important for practical public policy. Despite this, the coverage topics is inevitably preliminary and incomplete and possibly lopsided.

II The Government Budget

Overview

The introductory discussion of the government budget here covers seven key areas beginning with its meaning, scope, and importance through a discussion of the optimal or efficient budget size, and the link between efficient budget rules and cost benefit analysis. The discussion then turns to important aspects of practical government budgeting, including problems with incomplete budget coverage, institutions for fiscal discipline and a medium term focus, and tools for assessing budget structure and performance. The coverage is selective and leaves out aspects such as budget formulation and its relation to macro and fiscal forecasts, budget accounting, and institutional aspects of monitoring and implementation.

Basics of Budget Economics

The meaning, scope, and importance of the budget

As Richard Musgrave put it, "a theory of public finance remains unsatisfactory unless it comprises both the revenue and expenditure sides of the fiscal process" (Musgrave, 1969 as quoted in Bird, 2005). This is perhaps the important reason for studying the government budget.

By examining commonly used definitions of the budget, two important features of real world budgets, their periodicity, and scope can be identified. As von Hagen (2006) puts it, "the government budget is a record of the revenues and expenditures of a government during a given period of time." The budget provides advance information, usually to obtain legislative approval, of "what the government intends to do during that period and how it intends to finance these activities. Ex post it shows what the govt actually did, who had to pay for it and in what form".

First, as the definition says, budgets are *periodic*—usually annual— statements of the entirety of government activity permitting or explicitly designed to enable oversight or control by citizens or the legislature. The period is artificial, and largely dictated by legislative convenience. To ensure continuity and a long-term perspective in government activity over time, annual budgets should ideally form part of a rolling, medium-term financial plan which, in turn, should derive from a long range plan of public sector activity and including financing plans.[6]

Second, budgets are statements recorded by *legally defined entities called governments* about their future plans and past activity. The entity may not include the entire public sector, excluding entities deliberately kept out of the legal purview of government, such as public sector enterprises or autonomous public agencies. Another situation is when multiple legal entities called governments serve overlapping constituencies though they each have their own budgets or are responsible to different legislatures, as in most federations.

Determination of the optimal or efficient budget size

As a starting point in discussion of economic principles, a static framework with one private good, one public good, and one productive factor available in fixed aggregate supply is useful. Furthermore, to abstract from differences in tastes or endowments a single representative consumer with convex preferences over both goods can be assumed. In such a world the optimal supply of the public good can be depicted, as is done in Figure 10.1.[7]

In Figure 10.1, the optimal budget size, measured in terms of its opportunity cost in terms of the private good, is aA and the amount of public good financed is Ob. However, if the extraction of resources causes private sector inefficiency, as can happen with distortionary taxes, or entails transactions costs, then Figure 10.1 will overstate the amount of public goods available from a given sacrifice of private goods. This situation is easily understood with respect to Figure 10.2. Conveniently,

Figure 10.1: Optimal Supply of Public Goods and Government Budget

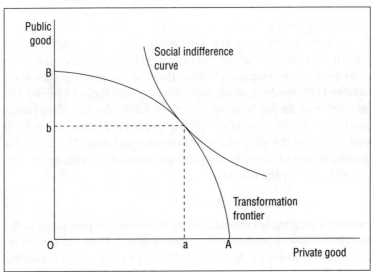

Source: Author.

Figure 10.2: Opportunity Cost of Public Goods with Leakages

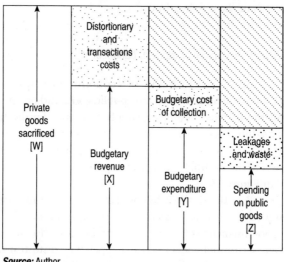

Source: Author.

Figure 10.2 also serves to intuitively motivate the marginal cost of funds (MCF) and the marginal benefit of public expenditure (MBP) which are key *measurable* tools for budget analysis linking revenue and expenditure.[8]

What Figure 10.2 shows is how different stages of the process of transforming private goods into public goods result in lost value compared to a costless world. Column heights measure their real value in terms of the private good.[9] Thus, the quantity of the private good sacrificed (W) results in actual expenditure of Z on the public good. For production of the public good to be worthwhile, the *value* of the public good measured in units of the private good, V(Z), must clearly be at least as great as the value of the private good sacrificed, W. In fact, for the *marginal* unit of expenditure on the public good, the efficient budget size is defined by the equality:

$$W = V(Z) \qquad (1)$$

(where all magnitudes should now be interpreted as pertaining to the marginal unit of expenditure on the public good). From this condition, the implications for the MCF and MBP can be easily seen by dividing both sides by the marginal budgetary expenditure (net of expenditure on revenue collection), Y, noting, from Figure 10.2 that Y = X − the budgetary cost of (revenue) collection, say X − A.

On doing this the following marginal condition for the efficient budget size is found to be:

$$\text{MCF} = \frac{W}{X-A} = \frac{V(Z)}{Y} = \text{MBP}. \tag{2}$$

This is, in fact, essentially the condition characterizing the efficient or optimal budget in Slemrod and Yitzhaki (2001).[10] From this condition, the MCF is seen to be the marginal sacrifice of private good (W) per rupee raised for budgetary expenditure (Y) or, equivalently, per rupee of public funds raised net of administrative expenditure on revenue collection. Similarly, the MBP is the benefit from the marginal unit of public good produced from the associated budgetary expenditure. Y. Slemrod and Yitzhaki (1996) break W up into gross government revenue raised (X) plus three types of costs: distortionary costs or the excess burden of the tax (or other revenue source), private sector compliance costs, and the deadweight loss associated with tax evasion or other forms of non-compliance. In similar fashion, on the expenditure side the difference between Y and Z captures any waste in government expenditure, loss due to a suboptimal allocation of the budget to different publicly provided services, and overheads not resulting directly in spending on the public good.[11] This condition and its implication for the optimum budget are illustrated in Figure 10.3. In the graph it is assumed that sources of finance can be arranged from least to most costly and similarly, public expenditure programs can be arranged in accordance with their marginal benefit from highest to lowest.

To obtain a deeper understanding of the MBP, the MCF, and optimal budget, several observations are needed. A few of the more important ones are now outlined.[12]

1. As Figure 10.2 makes clear, due to leakages in the transformation process, the MBP typically exceeds unity. *Given these leakages, an MBP or benefit-cost ratio of 1 or less for even the marginal public project can usually be taken to imply a budget that is larger than the efficient size.*[13]

2. Non-distortionary, lump-sum taxes that are costless to comply with and administer and impossible to avoid provide a hypothetical benchmark source of funds whose MCF is unity if, in addition, income effects of taxes are absent. Most existing estimates of the

Figure 10.3: The Optimal Government Budget Size is Where MCF = MBP

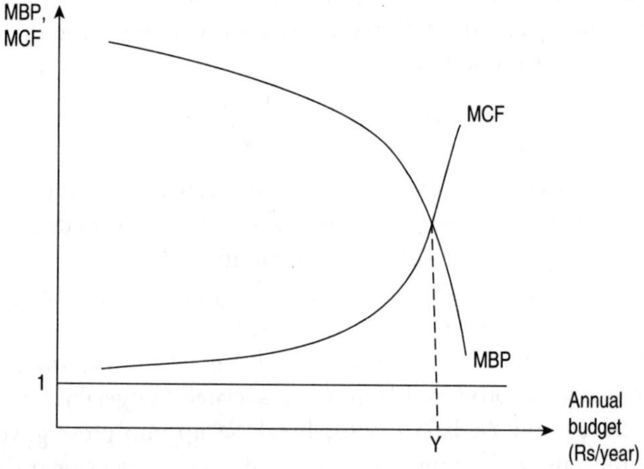

Source: Author.

MCF exceed unity (see Ballard and Fullerton, 1992; Bird, 2005). Nevertheless, examples of MCFs below unity can be constructed in a second best world or one in which existing policy is not optimal. An example of this is a Pigouvian tax to correct overproduction in the presence of a negative externality. Here, revenue can be raised while the tax, at the same time, improves resource allocation by correcting a market failure. Further, examples are discussed below when examining the mix of sources of public finance.

3. The previous observation shows that, in principle, it is possible though unlikely for the optimal budget to be characterized by an MBP below unity if all expenditures can be financed by sources of funds with MCFs below unity.[14]

4. As emphasized by Bird (2005), expenditure benefits and the cost of funds can affect each other, for example, when a public good is complementary or a substitute to a taxed commodity. So the MBP = MCF rule should, in principle, be applied in a general equilibrium framework to actually identify the optimal budget or, using a dynamic model, time path of the budget.[15]

5. The MBP = MCF rule cannot be held to imply that an annually balanced budget is optimal. This is in fact not generally true as discussed in the following sections.

Multiple sources of public finance and multiple publicly provided services

As should be obvious, when many revenue sources are available, their use in an optimal budget should normally follow the equal MCF Rule. This is familiar from the first order conditions that arise in multivariate optimization problems, and implies that financing sources should be exploited so that their MCFs are all equal. Similarly, for different public programs (health, education, power, roads), expenditure allocations should follow the equal MBP Rule which states that expenditure allocations across sectors should all have equal MBPs.

In discussing finance, consider taxes first. The equal MCF rule is generally agreed to apply to commodity taxes, though even here lumpiness of costs or, say, political constraints may make departures from this rule necessary in practice.[16] For income taxes, the MCF can initially be below unity if labor supply is backward bending, ignoring transactions, and administration costs. If so, other offsetting factors being absent, reliance on the income tax should take precedence over commodity taxes till the MCF exceeds unity.[17]

The equal MCF rule can also in principle be applied to the mix of tax, non-tax revenue, debt finance, and seigniorage. Seigniorage is taken here to be the government's purchase of real goods and services from monopoly issues of high powered money.[18] To illustrate its optimum use, consider a situation where money demand is described by a Quantity Theory of Money, one which implies money demand growing at the rate of real income in the absence of inflation. In such a situation, issuing high powered money so that it also grows at the rate of real income provides the government with revenue at zero private cost or MCF! According to this argument, inflationary money growth should, up to some level, have a lower MCF than further use of distortionary taxation.[19]

Turning to non-monetary deficit finance, the presumption created by the equal MCF rule is that some use of debt finance is efficient.[20] Click (1998) finds that the financing mix for taxes roughly equates their MCFs, but that this is not the case for other finance sources. Note that when viewed this way the equal MCF rule implies that budget deficits may be efficient. However, the optimal deficit (and both its cyclical and long term time paths) should ideally be determined in an intertemporal framework, which does not artificially limit the budgeting exercise to a single period. In such a framework, a realistic counter-example in which a budget surplus is optimal, is not difficult to devise. Consider the case of a country whose major income source is from exploiting a resource that is not expected to last indefinitely. For such a country, a budget surplus in the early years of resource exploitation to safeguard future resource availability can clearly be optimal. An additional important caveat is the incentive effects of budgets and legislative behavior, given different political institutions make rules derived from the neo-classical framework described here potentially too simplistic as a guide for designing practical budgeting institutions.

For the allocation of public expenditure, several institutional features can be identified which suggest that the equal MBP rule is not adhered to in practice.

The link between efficient budget rules and cost benefit analysis

This is the major focus of Bird (2005). The major point here is that the indirect cost of finance for a public project needs to be considered in cost-benefit analysis, particularly if projects are not infinitesimally small (as is more than likely). *In most text book treatments of cost benefit analysis, the cost of funds raised by distortionary taxes is not taken into account.* Instead, public projects are typically considered worthwhile, provided their benefit cost ratios (or MBPs) are at least one. This could be corrected either, as Bird (2005) suggests, by applying an appropriate shadow price to budgetary resources, or by setting a threshold MBP or cost benefit ratio for projects in line with that used for the optimal budget.[21] The application of this rule needs care in the presence of large projects or lumpy outlays.

Basic Issues of Budgeting Practice

Sources and problems of incomplete budget coverage

To the extent that the legal scope of government does not reflect all public sector activity, non-transparency results make it difficult to plan or analyze public sector efficiently. In particular, even a budget which satisfies the marginal optimality conditions, described earlier, will not provide evidence of an efficient public sector. Instead, the size of the public sector, the mix of financing sources and the intersectoral allocation of funds can all be suboptimal. This is the major argument for the desirability of a *comprehensive budget*.[22] Other arguments point to limited accountability to the legislature since off-budget receipts and outlays are typically less well documented than budgeted sums and to the limitations for macroeconomic analysis of budgetary data if public expenditure and deficits are not accurately reflected there. Major sources of deviation of real-world budgets from comprehensiveness include various *off-budget* items, and institutional restrictions that constrain feasible allocations of public resources. These are now listed.

Major sources of incomplete or constrained budgets include:[23]

Non-incorporation of budgets of autonomous agencies: including other (for example, sub-national) governments within the same economy. While autonomous agencies allow for greater operational autonomy, and federal systems allow greater flexibility in tailoring public services in line with public wants, their budgets are typically linked to the national budget only if there is a resource flow by way of grants or other transfers between the agency or sub-national government, and the national government.[24] Besides, limiting the scope for macroeconomic analysis with budgetary data, the existence of separate budgets hinders the identification of the MCF and MBP of the public sector—so that, for example, Figures 10.1 to 10.3 cannot serve as guides to efficient budgeting.

Extra-budgetary funds (EBFs): Allen and Radev (2006) identify seven types of EBFs, including revolving funds, sinking funds, and counterpart funds, and various special funds or special purpose vehicles. While these funds may have excellent justifications they do end up weakening the budget process. These authors reproduce the following illuminating quote on EBFs from the IMF's *Guidelines for Public Expenditure Management* (See Potter and Diamond, 1999).

> EBFs can result in a loss of aggregate expenditure control, because such expenditure may be outside the control of the ministry of finance; EBFs can distort the allocation of resources by circumventing the budget process and review of priorities; earmarked revenues can become entrenched so funding is no longer based on priority needs; less transparency may lead to inefficiency and/or misuse of funds; EBFs can facilitate rent-seeking and abuse of monopoly power; and EBFs are incompatible with good cash management practices. (Allen and Radev, 2006:18)

Earmarking of revenues: Earmarking ensures that funds are available for particular expenditures. The practice can often be justified as taxation and spending in line with the benefit principle.[25] Earmarking is often found in the financing schemes for EBFs or autonomous agencies. The problem from a budgeting perspective is that they potentially constrain budget allocation, both on the sources and the uses sides, causing the MCF = MBP rule to be violated.[26]

Invisible receipts and expenses includes:

1. *Quasi-fiscal expenses or receipts:* Such as interest subsidies, loan waivers or bailouts from retained funds and foreign exchange reserve growth of Central Banks if their accounts are not consolidated with the national government's budget.

2. *Tax expenditures:* Which include a variety of programs whereby revenues are foregone instead of explicit budgetary subsidies or transfers being given. An example is an investment allowance provided as a rebate from corporation taxes. Since they are a substitute for direct expenditure, tax expenditures should ideally be added to direct expenditures in the budget, with taxes being reported before providing for the tax expenditure. Ideally, the MCF of the tax before allowing for the tax rebate due to the investment allowance and the MBP of the implicit subsidy or transfer should both be reflected in the budget. Furthermore, both of these should be used to analyze changes in the quantum of expenditure given the implicit earmarking involved in tax expenditures. If only net tax collection is reported, this reduces the transparency of budget data and hides the real size of government.

3. *Contingent and implicit liabilities and assets:* Which the government does not provide for in the (*ex ante*) budget, including government guarantees that are taken up, relief provided in case of natural and economic disasters—including as the dramatic recent events suggest—financial market collapses. Once again marginal principles of budget allocation cannot be applied if these invisibles are present, and if adequate budgetary provision made on the basis of reasonably accurate expenditure forecasts is not made for them.

Budgetary institutions for fiscal discipline and medium term horizons

Public expenditure guides for practitioners identify three desirable features of budgets: operational efficiency, allocative efficiency, and aggregate fiscal discipline.[27]

Of these, operational efficiency is more commonly known as production efficiency in economic analysis, and corresponds to non-wasteful use of the minimum cost combination of productive inputs. This has been taken for granted in the discussion above. However, it has motivated a variety of "new public management" reforms in budgeting and expenditure management institutions, including (a) the move from compliance budgeting to performance budgeting systems and, more recently, output and outcome budgeting; (b) introduction of performance indicators which seek to measure the effectiveness and efficiency of public services and revenue administration and which, in some countries, forms the basis of formal performance agreements; and (c) moving from cash to accrual accounting and the introduction of capital budgets and balance sheets so that the economic value of resources used in providing government services is more accurately reflected in budget numbers.[28]

Allocative efficiency is reflected in the above discussion by the equal MCF and MBP rules. Few specific institutions appear to exist to achieve allocative efficiency, though accrual accounting helps to ensure that cash flows accurately reflect economic resources involved.[29]

Aggregate fiscal discipline can be linked to the MBP = MCF rule, for the optimum size of government. However, the rule is too difficult to operationalize, even if tractable economic models were available to guide medium-term budgeting. Instead, there are various types of budgetary laws and institutions to achieve prudent budgets, usually focussed on the budget deficit or the size of the public debt. These institutions are usually incorporated in what are known as *Organic Budget Laws* and *Fiscal Responsibility Laws*. Laws that earmark revenues for certain public expenditure are also fairly widespread to protect budgetary allocations to particular purposes that are deemed to be of sufficient importance.[30]

On the issue of off-budget funds, rules are advocated for their control and transparency. For example, Schiavo-Campo and Tommasi (1999) suggest four features of reporting requirements to enable effective legislative oversight. These are *no netting* or reporting of gross revenue and expenditures in the budget, even if some off-budget items do not need legislative authorization; *common classification* of items in off-budget funds and budgeted funds; *identical standards of scrutiny* and audit as budgeted funds even the legislature is not directly involved; and full *disclosure* in government financial reports of off-budget and budgeted funds.

Finally, recent policy advice from New Public Management specialists suggests the embedding of annual budgets within a rolling three to five year medium-term budget. In some countries (for example, Australia), medium-term frameworks are also subject to legislative scrutiny.[31]

Turning to empirical work on the effectiveness of budget institutions, considerable recent research exists from many parts of the world suggesting that well designed budgetary institutions are quite effective in curbing the fiscal Leviathan. An important caveat, however, is that fiscal institutions do not arise in a vacuum: they are themselves shaped by culture, history, and political power sharing.[32] This work also has had some success in explaining why large government and persistent budget deficits are a common tendency in most countries.[33]

Tools for assessing budget structure and performance

To enable students to put these principles to practical use, case studies of real-world budgets are essential to enable students to actually recognize them. In addition, they need to be introduced to toolkits which enable them to assess revenue, expenditure, fiscal discipline, and the adequacy of existing institutions to achieve these objectives. While textbook level presentations are not yet available, toolkits for practitioners, which can serve as source books, and also case studies exist, including World Bank (1998), PEFA (2006), Gill (2000), and possibly Das-Gupta (2002).

III Non-tax Revenue

Overview

To adequately discuss non-tax revenue, it must first be defined and its major components identified. Principles applying to different types of non-tax revenue can then be discussed.[34] Non-tax revenues are often incidental bi-products of government activity. In such cases, their revenue generation is not of primary importance, though scope for improvement may nonetheless exist. So to understand non-tax revenue a general discussion of different types of government activity and their financing is the starting point. Designing non-tax revenue instruments is the next important issue. As discussed below, design principles can be distilled from various branches of economic theory. The discussion of non-tax revenue closes with a discussion of practical problems in assessing non-tax revenue performance, and possible solutions where they exist.

Definition and Major Components of Non-tax Revenue

No explicit definition of the scope of non-tax revenue appears to be available.[35] I begin with a definition of taxes. According to the System of National Accounts 1993, "Taxes are compulsory, unrequited payments, in cash or kind made by institutional units to government units."[36] Taking this definition as a base, non-tax revenue includes payments made to the government that are compulsory and requited or voluntary whether requited or not. Five clarifications are needed to clearly delineate the scope of non-tax revenue.

First, a payment made to the government requited by future repayment or by a transfer of other assets is called a capital receipt, not non-tax revenue. Such receipts include government borrowing, money creation, and privatization proceeds.

Second, the boundaries of "government" need to be specified, which presents difficulties as the legal scope of government can be changed without affecting the mix of publicly provided service or resource flows. For example, a service provided by a government department can be transferred to a public sector corporation. This presents major difficulties in cross-jurisdictional and intertemporal comparability if public activities are reorganized. While this problem is being flagged here, no satisfactory solution appears to be available yet.

Third, the basis of accounting for receipts, cash or accrual, has a bearing on the volume of non-tax revenues. Those problems affect the reliability and comparability of all of a government's accounts, and not just non-tax revenue. No ready solution appears to be available other than requiring countries to adhere to particular conventions in presenting their public sector data. Such guidelines have been compiled by several international organizations, and are in use, by and large, in member states at least when making data available to these organizations.[37]

Fourth, while budget transparency generally requires that gross expenditures and receipts connected with a public activity be reported without netting, this may be misleading for certain activities undertaken purely to raise revenue, such as government lotteries. For lotteries accounted on a gross basis "expenditures" will include prize payouts and lottery administration expenses and "receipts" will include ticket sales. Rao (1981) distinguishes between commercial and non-commercial undertakings and suggests that the former be accounted for on a net basis.

Fifth, there is the problem of notional receipts, such as in the case of interest on capital works in irrigation in India. The notional return on these investments forms a large chunk of non-tax revenue in the budgets of many Indian states, this being matched by a contra-entry signifying notional expenditure. This problem suggests that transparency in presentation of non-tax revenue may require that whatever practice is adopted, supplementary statements accompanying a nation's budget are needed to make non-tax revenue figures comparable to that in other presentations.

Two other categories of non-tax revenue included in the International Monetary Fund's *Government Statistics Manual* (2001) are grants from other governments or international organizations and social contributions from employers or employees that "secure entitlements to social benefits for the contributors, their dependents, or their survivors". Both intergovernmental grants and social security are topics that are typically included in public economics curricula. So they are not further discussed here. Here non-tax revenue is taken to exclude capital receipts and notional receipts and expenditures. Where needed, a distinction is made between gross and net non-tax revenue associated with commercial activity. It should be noted that budget data presented to reflect this definition will not enable all questions to be readily answered without further research. For example, the rationale for excluding notional receipts matched by contra-expenditures is not clear cut. Estimating returns is essential in cost-benefit analysis of proposed investment projects, whether this return is recovered from users or not matter. Exclusion of returns means that government cash flows, as accounted, cannot be used to undertake ex post cost-benefit analysis of the investment. On the other hand, a notional cash flow cannot be used to finance government expenditure on any other good or service. So inclusion of notional receipts leads to incorrect estimation of government resources potentially available to finance other expenditures. It also leads to biased estimates of cash-based revenue-expenditure ratios, to assess the overall fiscal balance. To take another example, revenues are to an extent fungible. Increased user charge collection from an activity can be matched by decreased expenditure, releasing funds for other uses without changing the total outlay for an activity.

The two main examples of compulsory requited payments are earmarked taxes and fines or penalties.[38] The former are generally accounted for as tax receipts and are not discussed further here. Penalties and fines for tax non-compliance are also usually accounted as tax receipts. Otherwise they are accounted as non-tax receipts.

Voluntary, unrequited payments include voluntary contributions made to the government, and usually also unclaimed deposits with the government or unclaimed excess payments for services. No reporting problem arises in these cases.

From a revenue standpoint, the important non-tax revenue sources are all voluntary and requited. For most of these sources, revenue is a bi-product of goods, services, or resources the government provides. Included are revenue from assets, revenue from the sale of goods and services, new or used, and revenue from the sale of licenses and permits for regulated activities. In turn, assets from which the government derives revenue are of three types.

First are common property resources of which the government acts as a custodian (forests, wildernesses, marine, and riparian habitats, and wildlife as also historical monuments). From these resources, the government derives revenue by way of fees from the sale of usage rights including admissions fees, pollution permits, and fees or royalty payments from assigning the right to harvest and sell naturally occurring produce. An important recent example is the sale of licenses to use broadcasting bandwidth.

Second are exhaustible or renewable natural resources, to which private property rights are not assigned. Mineral deposits and mineral exploration rights are the most important examples of this. These provide the government with *royalty* and *rental* payments.

The third category includes assets created from government investments or which have earlier been nationalized. The most important examples of such assets are the capital of public sector undertakings (PSUs), infrastructure capital, equity investments in private concerns or public-private partnerships, and loans provided by the government. These assets potentially yield *dividends* and *interest* receipts. As pointed out, creation of a PSU to undertake an activity formerly carried out by a government department changes the scope of what is legally accounted for as "the government" since gross revenue is now substituted by (net) dividends paid to the government by the PSU and since the PSU's expenditure is no longer government expenditure.

Revenue from the sale of goods by the government yield is commonly termed *user charges*. *Tolls* for road usage and prices charged for, say, direct sale of forest produce or used goods and scrap are other examples.[39]

Revenue from licenses for regulated activity cover a wide array of sectors, and include business and shop licenses, construction and land use permits, examination and inspection fees, and so on. In Singapore, auction revenue from the sale of vehicle purchase permits (Certificates of Entitlement) are a major source of government revenue. In some cases, these fees and charges are mis-classified as a part of tax revenue, as with registration and related fees for property transfers in India, since they are a small amount relative to stamp duties which are collected with these fees. Given the diverse sources of non-tax revenue, different criteria must be adopted to assess non-tax revenue performance of different components. These are now briefly discussed.

Non-tax Revenue: Economic Principles

Principles for sources other than voluntary requited non-tax revenue

Fines and Penalties: Since by breaking laws citizens reveal that their private cost of doing so is below the cost to society, fines for breaking the law are similar to Pigouvian taxes levied on goods with negative external effects. The amount of the "tax" in the case of fines is the *ex ante*, expected value of the fine, in the event that the law breaker is caught and penalized. In designing fines, pure externality considerations must be tempered to take account of the incentive effect of fines on behavior and also the principle of natural justice which asserts that "the penalty should not exceed the crime". This is the subject of much ongoing research which, however, can already yield material suitable for undergraduate teaching.[40] To my knowledge no empirical assessment of whether fines are over- or under-used by the government has yet been made, though inadequate enforcement of laws in many developing countries makes it *a priori* likely that fines insufficiently penalize non-compliance.

A wide ranging discussion of penalty design is in Oldman (1965). As Bird puts it:

> Experience suggests that penalties should increase with (1) the potential revenue loss due to the tax offence; (2) the difficulty and cost of detecting the offence; (3) the effect of the offence on other taxpayers; (4) the offender's state of mind (a higher penalty should apply if the offence is deliberate and pre-planned); and (5) recidivism.

Other desirable design features of penalties require that: "Penalties for lesser degrees of non-compliance should follow the principle of marginal deterrence and be less than the marginal social loss so that citizens have the incentive to substitute away from higher levels of non-compliance"(Mookherjee and Png, 1994).

The *procedure* for levy of penalty should be transparent and not subject to administrative discretion. Penalties for corruption or inaction by bureaucrats and political representatives should be high enough to reduce opportunities for noncompliant citizens ("gainers") to compensate bureaucrats or representatives who are punished ("losers").

From a revenue standpoint, collection from well designed fines and penalties should increase with an increase in detected offences but decrease to the extent that non-compliance is deterred. So a monotonic relation between penalty revenue and compliance cannot be expected. Therefore, in evaluating penalties, both their design and implementation must be examined. In one case, penalties for non-payment of monetary dues, efficient penalties will translate into greater collection of these dues (but not necessarily penalty revenue). Unfortunately, systematic empirical studies of penalty design and implementation are hard to come by for any country.

Gifts and Donations: No general principles would appear to apply to these sources of revenue. In practice, it can be conjectured that gifts are more widespread in times of war and natural calamities. Nevertheless, to encourage gift giving, certain gifts are even made tax deductible or are the subject of appeals and publicity drives. There is some justification for this, since voluntary gifts have no distortionary costs and so, to the extent they can be relied on, are an efficient revenue source (but may have some transactions costs).

Similarly, no general principles would appear to apply to *unclaimed dues*. A key question is presumably to what extent rigidities in government procedures and red tape impede recovery of dues from the government by citizens. Sufficient red tape makes unclaimed dues no different from arbitrary taxes.

Principles for voluntary requited non-tax revenue sources

These sources require a three-part analysis before they can be assessed. The first plank is to identify the public activity that gives rise to the revenue source, and its economic characteristics. This provides one input for the "optimal" use of the revenue source to be specified to provide a benchmark to assess the performance of the revenue source.

The rationale for government provision is traditionally negatively derived in market economies from the inability of private institutions, market based or otherwise, to provide the good efficiently. To this is added a public role in achieving a desirable distribution of welfare which justifies additional interventions. While the discussion below adopts this perspective, three qualifications should be noted. Efficient government provision, given its second best rationale, may not be identical to that in an unconstrained, "first best" resource allocation. Second, the mix of goods which the government should provide depends on the extent of market imperfections and economic development, particularly capital market imperfections, the effectiveness and coverage of private non-market institutions, and the capacity of government. Thus, it is important to recognize inter-jurisdictional differences in efficient public provision of services as far as possible. Third, an acceptable rationale for government provision of a good, even if the private sector can provide the good efficiently, is if revenue from public provision is the least cost alternative for raising government revenue. This "nationalization" rationale does not carry much weight in practice.

Bearing these caveats in mind, at least seven characteristics of goods are generally discussed in welfare and public economics textbooks as important in determining if private markets or other non-government institutions, left to themselves, would supply the socially optimal quantity of the goods or not. Goods where government intervention is likely to be efficient include goods with (a) lower excludability, (b) greater non-rivalness in consumption,[41] (c) greater geographical coverage, (d) greater external or spill-over effects, (e) limited or asymmetric consumer information or bounded rationality,[42] (f) greater supply risk (for example, food crops)· and (g) greater lumpiness in production (such as public utilities). Pure merit goods (for example, public transport concessions for retired soldiers) are an additional category of goods where intervention can be justified. As the recent financial market events in the US dramatically illustrate, credit market imperfections may provide one more rationale for public provision, subsidies, or outright nationalization of private firms.

Besides intervention in goods markets, there are also good reasons for government intervention on occasion in asset markets. One is to secure a source of future revenue if current sources are not expected to last very far into the future. A key example in recent years is returns on government shares in private sector firms, such as through sovereign wealth funds. Pricing and sale of usage rights of publicly owned assets are other important reasons for government acting as a supplier in asset markets. As an illustration, the important example of auction of bandwidth is taken up below.

Given the existence of rationale for government intervention and so presumably a standard to judge the effectiveness of the intervention, the *second plank* in the analysis is to identify the selected mode of public provision of the good or service. That is, instead of completely private or direct government provision, a variety of institutional options exist. Table 10.1 provides some illustrations. Besides identifying institutional options, the table also identifies implications for revenue sources of these institutional arrangements in contrast to direct government provision of the good. A limitation for this analysis is that the conditions making different institutional options desirable have not yet been adequately studied. Even so, one general rule can be stated. The efficient institutional option is clearly that which enables provision to

Table 10.1: Institutional Alternatives to Direct State Government Management of Assets and Provision of Goods: Implications for Non-tax Revenue

Institution for Goods Supply or Asset Management	Examples	Revenue Sources Lost	Revenue Sources Gained	Remarks
Public undertaking	Road transport, forest development, power transmission corporations	User charges	Taxes; interest and dividends	Illustrates substitution of tax and non-tax revenue Expenditure saving
Private sector with subsidies	Schools receiving grants in aid Solar energy devices	User charges, sale prices	Tax; interest or dividend?	Interest or dividend if subsidy is through loan or equity Expenditure saving
Private ownership of assets	Privatization; Sale of mining concession	Dividend, interest, rent and royalty	Tax	One time or installment based asset transfer proceeds Expenditure saving
Outsourced to local or central government	Employment schemes; agricultural extension	Sale of goods and user charges if any	None	Inter-governmental transfers substitute direct expenditure
"Outsourced" to NGO or private sector association	Various social services Professional certification (Accountants, doctors)	Sale of goods and user charges if any	None	Transfers substitute direct expenditure
Outsourced to private sector	Contractual transport services; Hospitals; Zoos; Road maintenance; Bandwith auctions	User charges, sale of goods	Tax; contract payments	Contract payments affected by assignment mechanism Expenditure saving
Public–Private Partnership under a BOT (Build Own Transfer) contract	Roads, bridges, power plants	User charges, sale of goods	Tax; contract payments	Contract payments affected by assignment mechanism Expenditure saving
Exploitation permit or lease	Mining concession; Timber harvesting	Sale proceeds	Tax, Rents and royalties; contract payments	Expenditure saving
Community provision or management	Local irrigation: water users associations	User charges (partly)	None	Expenditure saving

Source: Das-Gupta (2005).

most closely approximate the efficient level while keeping provision costs low. Theoretical and empirical research on the relative social efficiency of different modes of provision of government services and asset management is limited and possibly still inconclusive.[43] Long-term evaluation of non-tax revenue should then take into account the progress of institutional reforms in government provision of goods and asset management.

The *third plank* in the analysis is to determine the optimal mix of financing sources of the planned interventions, given the institutional provision alternative selected. Here, analytic convenience suggests that the mix between, on the one hand, *direct finance* through user charges or benefits charges or, in the case of public-private partnerships, privately raised finance, and on the other hand, *general budgetary finance* be considered. That is, direct consideration of the debt-tax-direct finance mix need not be considered separately for each public intervention.

In examining direct finance through non-tax revenue a clear rationale is likely to be found in only some cases. For example, non-rival but excludible public goods may be more efficiently provided by the private sector. If this is the case, only government subsidies to private providers should optimally be provided. For private goods with external effects, tax, subsidy, or regulatory interventions rather than government supply are generally advocated. The rationale for full cost recovery from non-tax revenues is strongest for pure private goods for which government provision is socially desirable due to some characteristics leading to market failure other than from externalities or publicness. For impure public goods, at least partial budgetary finance will generally be desirable.

The growing literature on excludible public goods has several results concerning their finance. For example, greater reliance on user charges has been shown to be efficient for congestible public goods and for public goods which have negative external effects by Huber and Runkel (2004). An example for both cases is road user charges. These authors also show that increasing international tax competition and mobile factors make greater reliance on user charges desirable. Hellwig (2006) discusses efficient financing schemes where there are many excludible *and* non-excludible public goods. An important finding of his is that cross-subsidies can be part of an efficient financing scheme. The importance lies in the demonstration that *user fees that more than cover costs* and which can add to budget resources to finance other public goods can be efficient. On the other hand, depending on their characteristics user fees that achieve less than cost recovery may be optimal even for some excludible public goods. Tools to teach these results in undergraduate teaching are yet to be devised in most cases, but some simple graphs are given in the next section.

There are also some studies dealing with private goods which are publicly provided for distributional (poverty alleviation) reasons. These include goods such as food provided through a public distribution system and elementary education. Balestrino (1999) presents a model in which full cost recovery from user charges for goods provided to the poor, aid redistribution and welfare by causing richer citizens outside of target groups to opt out of public programs, thus, permitting superior targeting.[44]

For publicly-owned resources and assets, the rationale for non-tax revenue is more direct. In fact, if the government is otherwise resource constrained, it may be desirable for the government to exploit its monopoly power to raise revenue despite the negative effect on the use of the resource relative to the unconstrained case. The rationale for user charges to recover asset maintenance and debt amortization costs for publicly owned infrastructure is also relatively clear.

The fourth step in studying voluntary, requited non-tax revenue is then an examination of its design features, which is done in the theory of public sector pricing—an area that has seen many advances during the past 30 years.

Principles of design of voluntary, requited non-tax revenue instruments

For voluntary, requited non-tax revenue, it is easy to see that the design of revenue instruments is identical to the design of pricing strategies, and associated decisions related to production or provision of the good, service, or asset. Very often, because there is no private provision or because of public ownership of crucial resources, the government is also a monopoly provider of the good.[45] Therefore, design theory for voluntary, requited non-tax revenue instruments is identical to public sector pricing theory. Four important cases, in which pricing theory has been developed, are now briefly presented.

Increasing Cost Industries: (such as public utilities) providing either a single or multiple products.[46] As is well known, in such a case, marginal cost pricing is first best. When there is a revenue requirement (for example, if the industry is supposed to cover costs), then for the single product case, or multi-part tariffs along with price discrimination and constraints on the rate of return are generally advocated.[47] With multiple products, Ramsey-Boiteux pricing or multi-part tariffs incorporating this principle are optimal. Ramsey-Bioteux prices, according to which prices are set so that the percentage mark-ups over marginal cost are proportional to the inverse price elasticity of demand for the good (in the absence of cross-price effects), minimize deadweight loss. The total revenue required is set exogenously. Ramsey-Bioteux prices are easily illustrated in a demand cost diagram as is done in Figure 10.4.

The figure depicts two goods having the equal marginal costs of production per unit and quantity units per time period. If a common price, P, is chosen to meet revenue requirements then the deadweight loss from the good with the more elastic demand D_1, shown by the shaded area "$loss_1$", is greater than for good 2. The loss can be reduced while still meeting the revenue constraint by raising the price of good 2 above P, and lowering that of good 1. The loss is minimized when

Figure 10.4: Explaining Ramsey–Boiteux Pricing

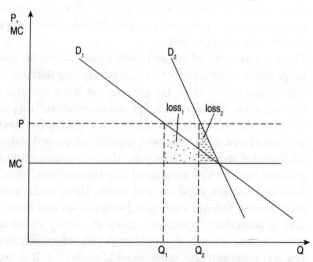

the ratio of the percentage mark-ups for the two goods is proportional to the inverse demand elasticities (provided the cross-price elasticity of demand is zero).

1. For multiple *excludible public goods* where the government is a monopolist (or where it can confer a monopoly) pricing rules similar to Ramsey-Boiteux prices, are also efficient under some restrictive conditions, as discussed in Hellwig (2006). Note that these prices are "admission" prices permitting usage of the goods rather than prices per unit of usage. However, as Hellwig (2006) also points out, mixed bundling schemes for public goods dominate Ramsey-Boiteux admission prices. Under such a scheme, bundles are priced lower than if admission fees for each good are considered separately. Intuitive examples of mixed bundling are a standard part of the basic microeconomic analysis of imperfect competitors. More complex situations have also been studied. For example, given buyer heterogeneity, Norman (2004) shows that third degree price discrimination in setting admissions fees by a monopoly provider of an excludible public good is asymptotically socially optimal.[48] As discussed earlier, discriminatory admissions prices can reflect distributional concerns even if an income tax is available (Hellwig, 2005).

   Hellwig (2005, 2006) also points to a major limitation of the theory in its current state since incentive effects of pricing strategies on consumers and, more importantly, producing agents, are yet to be incorporated.

2. The key examples of *excludible public resources* are radio spectrum usage rights, rights in airports to aircraft landing slots and mineral exploration rights. Here, the government is the resource owner but sells usage rights for a fixed period to private service providers who use this resource. The theory of auctions has developed extensively and, in fact, has been explicitly employed in designing auctions for spectrum use rights. The more successful of these auctions have yielded substantial non-tax revenues.[49]

3. Natural resource royalties and rents. These include income from forests, fishing, and mining concessions and licenses. The area is particularly important, given increasing environmental concerns, and is normally taught in specialized courses on natural resource economics and environmental economics. It is, however,

important that pricing of mineral and forest concessions, together with sustainable exploitation rates, figure in public economics courses, together with available instruments such as emissions trading schemes.

Several other examples of successful pricing, bundling, and quantity control in the public sector can be found. Three more examples are worth briefly mentioning. Discriminatory two-part tariffs incorporating cross-subsidies are in use in some state-run referral hospitals in India to benefit poor sections (Das-Gupta, 2005). However, targeting is poor as verification of poverty status is difficult. Improved targeting is possible, if this is combined with *quality* differences in facilities. These differences arise in the quality of such things as food, temperature control and furnishings, and ward privacy without compromising on the quality of medical care. In Singapore, (transferable) Certificates of Entitlement for ownership of motor vehicles are auctioned every fortnight and constitute a major source of government revenue (Chia, 1998). Liquor vends in some states in India are auctioned annually, instead of excise duty levies, thus allowing differential pricing of these rights (though the revenue is accounted for as part of state excise duty).

Problems with Assessing Non-tax Revenue Performance

What implications does the discussion above have for assessment of non-tax revenues? First, as has been mentioned, given their diversity, criteria need to be devised on a case by case basis. With the exception of state lotteries and some other commercial activities, which have a pure revenue motive, a common feature of all sources is, however, that revenue performance alone is never an appropriate yardstick to use; in fact, revenue performance may in some cases be entirely irrelevant. Three examples to illustrate this are below.

For *state lotteries* revenue performance relative to other states is the key parameter in terms of (a) net revenue raised and (b) the revenue-expenditure ratio. Institutionally, outsourcing to the private sector either wholly or for ticket vending has been used in some cases, as has management devolved to a public enterprise. Private contractors are normally chosen through open competitive bidding but subject to prequalification. In case of direct provision, lottery design features, distributor incentives, and other administration issues need examination to assess revenue performance.

For *penalties and fines*, as discussed, their structure and administration need to be analyzed as part of an overall enforcement system. Penalties are best assessed by (*a*) ascertaining if they are optimally included in enforcement policy design; (*b*) assessing if enforcement policy design is itself optimal; and (*c*) if the appropriate institutional implementation design is in place, and performing effectively. The appropriate benchmarks for the enforcement system are the compliance rate achieved per rupee of administrative outlay and the compliance rate itself.[50] Needless to say, much work needs to be done to operationalize these principles.

Third, take the case of *revenue from sale of exploitation rights for natural resources*. Key parameters in the design of non-tax revenue instruments are their perceived life or external effects or environmental damage arising from their exploitation. Both of these are also often subject to cross-border spillover, on the one hand, and uncertain demand and supply on the global market, on the other. The third concern that may influence assessment of these revenue sources is the claim in the literature that access to natural resource revenues can directly be linked to poor governance. So a satisfactory assessment framework for these revenues is hard to devise (see Gylafson et al., 1999; Collier and Hoeffler, 2005; Moore, 2007).

IV The Global Fiscal Commons

Overview and Outline

This section begins by describing the global fiscal commons including its impact on national tax capacity, and how technological developments and economic globalization as well as sophisticated avoidance opportunities compound this deterioration. This is followed by a discussion of principles of efficient international taxation. The third sub-section, in contrast, examines current and emerging institutions that seek to apportion rights to the commons. This motivates a discussion of some aspects of national strategy in this sphere given its vital importance in the face of a rapidly expanding fiscal commons. Of the neglected public finance issues discussed in this chapter, the subject of this section is perhaps the most serious omission.

The Global Fiscal Commons and Sovereign Fiscal Space

To use a geographical analogy applicable to a region full of game, the global "fiscal terrain" can be thought to consist of three types of economic activity. First, there are economic transactions, which no sovereign jurisdiction is able to tax, such as some "informal" transactions, especially those without a paper trail, barter transactions, private reciprocal transactions, and some types of e-commerce. Second, there is what may be termed *sovereign fiscal space* consisting of economic transactions that fall within and have connections to only a single jurisdiction which only that jurisdiction is able to tax. This includes income earned from a resident entity and spent on goods produced and sold within that country by a resident, goods produced and consumed, and factors originating from and used entirely within a jurisdiction. All other economic activity, potentially involving more than one jurisdiction, forms part of what may be termed "the fiscal commons".[51]

The global fiscal commons

As stated in the introduction, the global fiscal commons can be defined to consist of potentially taxable entities or transactions, with at least some characteristic involving more than one jurisdiction—be it purchase, sale, trans-shipment, source, residence, or ownership—henceforth abbreviated as *commons activity* and *commons entities*. Acceptable characteristics are those, according to Bird and Mintz (2003), that permit jurisdictions to claim what they term "economic allegiance" of an economic activity.[52] Since jurisdictions cannot claim economic allegiance over all economic activity in the world, the global commons is actually seen to be a set of several overlapping commons, each with its own club of non-excludible members. *Commons entities* include multinational business entities, "footloose" industries, cross-border investors that make international portfolio and FDI capital flows, and mobile skilled workers and professionals in scarce global supply. Of these, multinational business entities and cross-border investors include both legal entities engaged in legitimate activity and illegal entities engaged in illicit activities, including the drug trade, human and organ trafficking, and terrorism.[53]

The global fiscal commons is expanding rapidly with increasing globalization. A major reason is that a growing part of exclusive or commons tax bases are not immobile due to growing cross-border capital flows and skilled labor mobility. This gives rise to what Bird and Mintz (2003) term *fiscal externalities*, whereby exploitation of commons by a country causes it to shrink or expand, as mobile factors move out, simultaneously causing other national or commons bases to expand. This poses risks to national fiscal capacities whether forming part of the fiscal commons or not (see Asian Development Bank Institute, 2001). The lack of consensus regarding apportionment of property rights over the fiscal commons between sovereign nations and fears that sophisticated and quick moving rich countries are quickly claiming jurisdiction over large swathes of the global commons makes the topic both an important emerging area in the study of taxation as well as a vital area of concern for national policy makers, particularly in developing countries.

Globalization and decreasing national tax capacity

Limited work exists on studying the impact of globalization on tax revenues. Baunsgaard and Keen (2005) study the impact of trade liberalization on tax revenue of different groups of countries. They find that only high income countries—out of 111 countries in their sample—have benefited from trade liberalization, during the past 25 years. Of other countries, low income countries have fared the worst. They also find that the VAT or its absence does not affect their finding. On the VAT, Chang et al. (2001) present estimates of evasion in 10 EU member states for 1994–96 after the abolition of fiscal frontiers and physical checks in 1993. They find high levels of evasion (exceeding 5 percent and going up to 35 percent) by 1996 in eight of these states with evasion growing fastest in Germany and the United Kingdom.

Conceptually, according to Professor Lodin, the negative impact of globalization on national fiscal capacity is caused by "increased international financial flows, new communication technology, an explosion in cross-border investment opportunities, the increased importance of mobile production factors such as know-how and other intangibles, and the increased mobility of some types of labour and personnel" (see Asian Development Bank Institute, 2001). To this can be added new tax competition strategies of jurisdictions, the most important being jurisdictions that choose to become tax havens.

These factors interact with deficiencies in current international tax laws, including bilateral double taxation treaties, to decrease the effective of national tax systems. Four important global trends that illustrate the impact of factors identified by Professor Lodin, reported in the previous paragraph, are now presented.[54]

First, under existing international tax conventions and rules—made in less troublesome times—*residence or headquarters of multinational enterprises become hard to determine* though approximately half the world's trade now consists of intra-firm transactions. Certain transactions, such as payments for copyright and trade-mark use, headquarters services, and interest on intra-company loans all lend themselves to transfer pricing.

Second, there has been a *dramatic increase in cross-border portfolio investment* by individuals such as through retirement and other investment funds. It is increasingly becoming difficult to identify income from such investments, particularly due to the development of innovative financial products.

Third, there is the equally *dramatic increase in international trade in services.* Many professional services are "footloose" in the sense that the place where the service is performed need not be the place where the service is utilized.[55] This complicates determination of the jurisdiction having the right to tax. This ambiguity can also be exploited for tax avoidance. For example, if VAT is levied on a service input to an export good, intangible expenses such as R&D royalties can be used to "transfer-price" taxable value added to the lower tax jurisdiction (Mintz, 2001). Similarly, source countries for source based taxation of income become difficult to determine.

The fourth source of risk is the development of *e-commerce.* Businesses engaged in e-commerce transactions pose growing additional risks, since they can now have a virtual but not physical presence in a source country such as via a web page making residence hard to determine. Additionally, global business transactions are no longer the exclusive domain of multinationals since even small domestic businesses—and individuals—can have cross-border transactions such as on e-Bay.

The challenge of e-commerce

McLure (2006) points out that, first, e-commerce reduces the utility of bedrock concepts on which the current international taxation is system is based, such as for the determination of residence other than for natural persons like *permanent establishment*. This is because electronic entities are essentially footloose. Second, differentiating between royalties and income from providing services and selling goods will become more difficult. Third, "e-commerce will also make use of arms-length tests to identify transfer prices difficult if one of the jurisdictions involved is a tax haven." (McLure, 2006).

Three types of e-commerce transactions can be distinguished (ADBI, 2000).

1. For *remote selling of tangible goods* the issues are no different than for example goods sold through the post. Procedurally, in some countries, there may be a problem if electronic invoices are not valid.
2. For *remote delivery of services* the situation is similar. No new issues arise but there are practical administrative difficulties in insuring that the service delivery is verifiable.
3. For the third category of ecommerce sales, *electronic sale of digital products* (downloading) existing consumption tax laws will need to be modified to bring these transactions to tax. Furthermore, none of the existing taxation proposals is considered administratively attractive.[56]

For income taxes in all three cases, there may be disputes in identifying the source country of income, given the indeterminate geographical origin of internet communications.

Tax avoidance in the fiscal commons

Commons entities can engage in a variety of tax avoidance strategies to minimize their tax dues. Important among these activities, as discussed later, are routing financial flows through or acquiring legal residence in a tax haven, treaty shopping, transfer pricing, thin capitalization, double dipping, hybrid entities, and timing arbitrage.

For example, ADBI (2000) discusses three different methods of tax avoidance through arbitrage arrangements: *double-dipping* by taking advantage of different tax treatment of a transaction in two jurisdictions, cross-border differences in the treatment of tax entities to create a *hybrid entity*, and taking advantage of different tax accounting rules to enable *tax deferral*.

Following ADBI (2000), *double-dipping* can be illustrated through the tax treatment of a lease transaction. If properly structured, the lease can qualify for treatment as an *operating lease* so that lease payments would be treated as lease rentals in some countries. In other countries, the same lease could be considered a *finance lease* which would imply that lease payments would be treated as installment payments plus interest from a sale to the lessee. If the lessor could treat the lease as an operating lease in his country of residence, and the lessee could treat the lease as a finance lease, both would qualify for tax depreciation in their respective jurisdictions. More complicated tax dodges could also be conceived of whereby tax exempt could benefit by leasing through a taxable intermediary who could then take advantage of depreciation and share the gains with the tax free entity.

Similar tax arbitrage could be routed through *hybrid entities* with different classifications in each of two countries. For example, a firm could be treated as a pass-through entity such as a trust in one country and a separate entity such as a partnership firm in the other. Expense of this hybrid entity could then be deductible to the partnership in the source country, but to partnership members in the residence country.

Tax deferral arbitrage opportunities arise, for example, when tax accounting rules in source and residence countries differ as to when income receipt are accounted for and expenses are recognized.

The emergence of tax havens

The importance of tax havens in increasing the scope for tax avoidance has been extensively reviewed in recent literature.[57]

Tax havens are countries or autonomous jurisdictions having low tax regimes for non-residents. Low tax regimes are often coupled with secrecy laws or practices which result in no or limited information provision about non-residents to their fiscal and financial regulators, possibly opaque and discretionary tax and financial regulations, and lenient laws for incorporation of businesses by foreigners. Hines (2004) also points out that several tax havens actively advertise and promote these features about their tax regimes.

Desai, Foley, and Hines (2005) study recent US data to explore which firms are likely to have some economic allegiance, such as through affiliated firms, in tax havens. By inference, these are the firms with foreign economic activity which are most likely to engage in tax avoidance. They identify large firms with relatively large international exposure, especially in industries with high R&D spending or within firm transactions, as those most likely to have a tax haven connection. They relate this to the ability of haven affiliates from high tax countries to create a low cost channel to defer some of home country taxes on foreign source income. This advantage, they find, is particularly pronounced for affiliates in large tax haven countries, comprising seven havens in their sample with populations over 1 million. They predict that rising FDI and R&D spending along with increasing cross-border trade between connected firms will cause demand for tax havens to increase in future. Earlier research (Hines, 2004) also found that tax havens themselves benefit from being havens. "What is less clear is the impact of this avoidance on the economies of countries with high tax rates" (Desai, Foley, and Hines, 2005: 15).

McLure (2006) surveys familiar tax avoidance activities by commons entities paying particular attention to how low tax haven jurisdictions expand the scope of avoidance (and evasion) by firms.

Principles of Efficient International Taxation

To understand the impact of current and possibly future apportionment (or double taxation) of commons entities, it is useful to establish a benchmark by examining international tax principles that are consistent with allocative efficiency or what Musgrave and Musgrave (1989) term "inter-nation" equity. These principles were first developed looking at income and commodity taxes separately, and without taking account of interaction between taxing jurisdictions or responses by taxed entities.[58] The starting point for such coordination principles is the mutual recognition of the ability, and right of more than one sovereign nation, to tax commons entities.[59]

Let us begin with efficient taxation of capital.[60] This is identified in this literature as taxation that ensures *international tax neutrality*, that is, it ensures that taxes do not distort international capital flows by driving wedges between returns to investors. This is achieved by *capital-export neutrality* (CEN), whereby an investor receives the same marginal tax, regardless of which country the investment is made in. This requires, ultimately, for the residence country to credit foreign taxes against its own taxes and, if needed, suffer a revenue outflow via a refund. As Musgrave puts it, "Ensuring international tax neutrality is thus in the hands of the residence country" (Musgrave, 2004: 177).

A second principle of international tax neutrality is from the point of view of different investors rather than different jurisdictions, which requires that domestic and foreign savers receive the same marginal rate of return from investment in a jurisdiction. This principle translates to *capital import neutrality* (CIN), whereby only the *source* country taxes investment income.

Simultaneous achievement of CEN and CIN is clearly infeasible.

In contrast, "national tax neutrality" (NN) requires that foreign income net of costs, including tax costs be treated on par with domestic income net of costs for residents. This entails full taxation of net of foreign-tax foreign income (Desai and Hines, 2003).[61]

Given the growth in multi-country firms, Desai and Hines (2003) suggest that a more useful efficiency concept of worldwide efficiency is one which leaves investors free to maximize the productive returns to investment without being influenced by tax considerations. They explicitly take into account the possibility of differences in productivity of capital owned by investors from different jurisdictions. Tax regimes that achieve such *capital ownership neutrality* (CON) would, like CEN, have the residence country credit foreign taxes while taxing foreign income of residents. With this treatment all capital owners who would have invested in a jurisdiction would continue to receive the same return differentials from the same pattern of investment. A fifth efficiency concept is that of *national ownership neutrality*, whereby foreign income of residents is exempt from domestic tax.

Let us now turn to commodity taxes. Principles for efficient commodity taxation look at *origin* and *destination* based commodity taxes. It is usually assumed in older studies that taxation of intermediate goods is distortionary (partly justified by the Diamond and Mirrlees, 1971). Restricting attention, therefore, to the VAT a key result is the equivalence of origin and destination based commodity taxes if these are levied at a uniform rate in each jurisdiction (Ebrill et al., 2001). However, many other considerations enter in determining which of the two principles, origin-based taxes or destination-based taxes, are superior on efficiency grounds, especially if the extent of coordination between countries and administrative problems are taken account of. Consequently, no unambiguous support for either principle emerges, though the informal consensus favors destination-based consumption taxes.[62]

None of these neutrality principles discussed earlier necessarily result in *productive efficiency* given the Diamond and Mirrlees (1971) theorem that productive efficiency requires no taxation of inputs including capital inputs, domestic, or foreign. However, the Diamond-Mirrlees theorem is not strictly applicable in a world with many jurisdictions, each having governments with their own revenue requirements. A careful analysis of second best, efficient international taxation where there are many jurisdictions each with their own budget constraint is in Keen and Wildasin (2004). They conclude from their analysis that allocation of resources (and commodities) in line with international efficiency may not be necessarily desirable given the second best solution in the presence of government revenue needs which may make taxes that lead to production inefficiency to be superior to efficient taxes. In particular, "Second-best" international taxation may imply the use of commodity taxes which include both origin and destination taxes, and possibly the deployment of both domestic taxes and tariffs, and capital taxes based partly on the source and partly on the residence principle.

The unfortunate conclusion, resulting from this discussion, is that efficiency considerations provide very little guidance for the design of international taxes. Principles of equity or fairness can also be considered. However, in practice these end up being little more than application of reciprocity in granting of favorable tax treatment to other countries and, occasionally, poorer jurisdictions.[63]

Institutions to Establish Property Rights to the Commons

There are no accepted conventions that allocate rights to tax commons activity and entities across nations, not even in principle.[64] On the prospects of a fair and just global tax system emerging in due course, the following quote from Graetz (2001) is illuminating:

> It is a mistake to believe that the globalization of markets for goods, services, and capital signals the demise of national identy or national politics. Economic globalization does not imply global government. Modern developments, such as mobile capital and e-commerce, may limit the ability of any sovereign state to singlehandedly control its economic destiny, and therefore may usher in a new era of multinational cooperation but they do not mean the end of nationalism. (Graetz, 2001: 1373–74)

Cooperation between countries to counter such avoidance is hampered by a fundamental conflict which makes countries reluctant to cooperate in tax matters. The conflict arises from their need to compete to attract most commons entities to their jurisdictions to reap non-tax benefits.[65] Given this conflict, it is vital for countries to be able to engage in unilateral tax policy to protect their sovereign fiscal space and safeguard their commons exploitation ability, as this is the "fallback strategy", if bilateral or multilateral negotiations break down.

> With business operations integrated in various ways across borders, the untangling of profits and their assignment to different source jurisdictions becomes an artificial exercise, and rule of thumb measures often have to be adopted. Furthermore, this practice lends itself to profit shifting by the taxpayer to lower tax jurisdictions. Most fundamentally, rules are needed to assign equitable shares to the source countries in the income accruing to multinational corporations. Common source rules employing unitary combination and uniform formula apportionment are needed to avoid arbitrary and predatory practices for determining source. (Musgrave, 2004: 176)

The existing assignment of rights

What has, therefore, emerged piecemeal over time assigns rights to tax income in the laws of most countries roughly as follows (see ADBI 2000).

1. Source countries have the primary right to tax "active" (for example, labor) income.
2. Residence countries have the primary right to tax "passive" income (for example, capital income including dividends, interest, and royalties), and source country laws generally limit taxation of such income of non-residents.
3. Residence countries provide relief from international double taxation; this partly satisfies CEN.
4. Allocation of income in related party transactions follows the "the arm's length principle".

No widely accepted convention for origin/destination rights for commodity taxes exists though destination taxes are limited in practice, given administrative difficulties. Tax cooperation between countries tends to follow the path carved out by early movers, particularly OECD member countries, with other countries following their lead especially where OECD publications exist, such as their Model Tax Treaty, 2005. These principles often encompass reciprocal concessions.[66]

There are also several examples of institutions in which countries agree to cede what in "pre-globalization" times was considered part of sovereign fiscal space. Examples include the World Trade Organization and the right to tax trade in goods and services—even entirely domestic trade—to ensure non-discrimination; membership in free trade areas and customs unions; and the European Union's abolition of "fiscal frontiers", and tax related checks at national borders in 1993. Other examples, not directly related to taxation, include international commitments to non-inflationary finance, government budget balance; and balanced international payments flows.

Examples of cooperation to coordinate rights to commons exploitation include bilateral double tax avoidance tax treaties and guidelines produced by the OECD's Committee on Fiscal Affairs, especially its Harmful Tax Initiative, and International Accounting Standards. A possible though unlikely future possibility is a world tax organization. There also exist organizations that foster multi-country administrative cooperation including Centro Interamericano de Administraciones Tributarias (CIAT), Commonwealth Association of Tax Administrators (CATA), Intra-European Organization of Tax Administrations (IOTA), The World Customs Organization, and the European Union's VIES.

We now examine two leading examples of institutions to share the global fiscal commons, double tax avoidance tax treaties and the OECD's Harmful Tax Initiative.

Double tax avoidance tax treaties

As of 2008, about 600 comprehensive or limited treaties exist between pairs of countries from a possible maximum of around 80,000 treaties. These treaties are usually between countries with substantial trade or other economic relations. Most treaties are between pairs of developed countries while, of the balance, most are between developed and developing countries. As discussed above, these treaties (a) provide reciprocal concessions to ensure no double taxation; (b) assign taxation rights roughly in accordance with that "existing assignment of rights" described earlier; and (c) largely, though not rigidly, follow the OECD Model Treaty. Recent treaties contain new clauses, following the OECD Model Tax Treaty, 2005 which extends areas of cooperation to administrative and information issues and also provides for a Mutual Agreement Procedure for issues not covered in treaties.[67] While current treaties deal mainly with the right to tax incomes, the OECD's recent Model VAT Convention should expand the scope of bilateral treaties in future to also cover the VAT (Owens, 2002). Some further elaboration may help in gaining a clearer picture of treaties.

Bilateral treaties can result in inequitable treatment of treaty partners. For example, most source countries ordinarily tax business income on a net basis if it is earned by a "permanent establishment" in the country. They tax other capital incomes such as interest, dividends, and royalties on a gross basis often through withholding taxes, which can be at a lower rate than the normal rate on these types of income in that country (McLure, 2006). As Musgrave says, clearly, "the usual treaty requirements of non-discrimination in corporate income tax combined with reciprocity in withholding tax rates is unsatisfactory with respect to internation equity" (Musgrave, 2006: 176).

Tax avoidance opportunities also arise from the usual residence country tax provisions in treaties. The incentives arising from tax systems to shift income from high-tax to low-tax jurisdictions exist if the home country exempts foreign-source income. Only if income is repatriated by a firm resident in a country that taxes worldwide income which, furthermore, is unable to claim sufficient "foreign tax credits" will there be no incentive to shift income to low-tax jurisdictions.

The OECD's Harmful Tax Initiative

This initiative was initiated in 1998 in response to the large number of countries, whose rights to exploit the fiscal commons were not accepted by the OECD, that were making inroads into OECD member countries' tax bases using what they considered illegitimate means. Some commentators perceive this initiative as the use of "strong-arm" tactics by the rich and powerful members of the OECD to deprive smaller nations of their sovereign rights to tax. For example, the following quote from Langer (2000) is of interest.

> Mitchell says that this OECD effort…contradicts international norms and threatens the ability of sovereign countries to determine their own fiscal affairs. He adds that the OECD proposal …would create a cartel by eliminating or substantially reducing the competition these high-tax nations face from low-tax regimes. (Langer, 2000: 2)[68]

Or consider Christians (2008): "A defensive tone is evident throughout the OECD's harmful tax practices work—the authors seem aware of the need to justify their actions by framing them as in direct response to some wrongdoing" (Christians, 2008: 21).

Under this initiative, the OECD (see OECD, 1998) defined four key factors used in identifying tax havens and harmful preferential tax regimes in non-haven jurisdictions. Lack of transparency in tax laws and rules: low, nominal, or zero special tax rates for mobile income is the first criterion which, however, needs to be combined with one or more of the other three factors for a country's tax regime to be regarded as a "harmful" tax regime.[69]

The second criterion is existence of "ring-fencing", whereby the domestic economy is partially or fully isolated, insulated from the tax regime applicable to foreign taxable entities. In tax havens, with limited domestic economic activity, the ring-fencing is replaced by the criterion of "absence of substantial economic activity". A common example of ring fencing is a restriction of special tax benefits to non-residents.

The third criterion is lack of effective information exchange on taxpayers benefiting from low tax regimes in a jurisdiction.[70]

The fourth criterion is lack of transparency in legislative or administrative tax provisions conferring on tax administrations latitude in interpretation of tax laws, and room for negotiating tax dues from favored entities. Dharmapala and Hines (2006) discuss the current situation, following OECD efforts since 1998 to get jurisdictions to improve their transparency, and information exchange practices. They identify between 33 and 40 jurisdictions as tax havens though only five of these are on the current OECD HTP list. A possibly surprising finding of theirs is that tax havens are relatively affluent countries known for good governance.[71]

National Tax Policy and the Global Fiscal Commons

Given the complex structure and sophistication of the global fiscal commons, and yet its growing importance, it is important for countries to explicitly work out strategies to safeguard their interests. Ideally cooperation between countries is desirable through such things as tax treaties, formulary apportionment of the commons, and administrative cooperation. This is of major importance. Despite the "fundamental conflict" between cooperation and competition discussed earlier, without cooperation a competitive "race to the bottom" can result in seriously damaging national fiscal capacities. Besides formal and informal agreements, participation in multilateral forum to discuss international tax and tax administration issues, discussed earlier, is of importance. Key commons entities for national policy include resident and non-resident taxpayers in the home country, other jurisdictions involved in international transactions or that are the origin of taxable foreign entities.

Design of national strategy, needless to say, should look beyond the confines of taxes alone, and should assess all feasible current and future revenue sources including non-tax revenues, external and internal debt finance, and seigniorage. The focus below is limited to tax design issues.

First, to safeguard the interest of residents with foreign income, unilateral (tax sparing) measures to reduce tax on mobile capital and skilled labor are usually enacted despite the free tax benefits this confers on foreign jurisdictions.

Second, however, rules to plug loopholes by nationals and residents to prevent tax evasion and avoidance are usually enacted especially for resident entities dealing with low tax or haven jurisdictions. For example, to counteract the use of tax deferral by tax haven entities, some countries have *controlled foreign corporation* (CFC) rules, whereby certain income of foreign subsidiaries in low-tax jurisdictions is deemed to be currently repatriated and so liable to tax. A second example is *thin capitalization rules*, which restricts the extent of expensing of interest payments whereby net of interest profits can be "transferred" to a low tax jurisdiction.

Third, many recipients of foreign direct investment or countries where multinational corporations have operations also enact *transfer-pricing rules* to ensure that these businesses pay taxes on profits computed according to "arms-length" principles. Such rules include *arms length price rules* such the Comparable Uncontrolled Price (CUP) rule used in the United States; *profit-split rules* for apportioning global profits to the home country; *profit comparison methods* such as the Comparable Profit Method used in the US: and Advance Pricing Agreements, whereby the firm and fiscal authorities of the home and host countries agree on the method to establish arms-length prices in advance (McLure, 2006).

Most of the rules mentioned in the previous two paragraphs require a level of expertise in economic analysis unavailable in developing countries—a gap that these countries should make serious efforts to repair, especially if their participation in the global fiscal commons is increasing. As Vann (1998) puts it, "Because of the sophistication of international tax planning and its frequent combination of domestic law, tax havens, and tax treaties, the taxation of non-resident direct investors by developing and transition countries is not an easy task" (Vann, 1998: 797).

A fourth plank in national strategies to safeguard revenue includes various administrative measures enacted to prevent tax evasion by commons entities. These include withholding taxes on dividends, interest, and royalties especially if these are paid to beneficial owners benefiting from haven countries; enhanced reporting requirements for residents on transactions involving tax havens; and finally, though this is not yet widespread, there are exchange of information and mutual assistance clauses in tax treaties.

A final strategy a country should weigh is the costs and benefits of reforming its tax regime *to become a tax haven*. Costs arise mainly from denial of benefits and facilities or other sanctions by OECD subscribers to their Harmful Tax Initiative and possible loss of tax revenue. Benefits can arise from enhanced economic activity, and possibly inward capital inflows leading to higher growth. The decision to become a tax haven is not an all or nothing decision. Several "respectable" countries have discriminatory low tax regimes for some classes of foreign factors or firms, without attracting international sanctions.[72] Furthermore, according to Avi-Yonah (2000), countries that offer investment concessions for FDI—not just for financial flows without associated "real" activity—are also havens engaging in tax practices that ought to be recognized as harmful. If this proposal is an early warning of future encroachment of sovereign taxation powers by richer countries, discriminatory "tax haven" treatment of foreign entities should be weighed dispassionately focusing on national (or multilateral) benefits rather than the views of some powerful nations.

Other Neglected Areas

Choosing between Modes of Intervention for Public Service Delivery

The practical importance of the choice between different modes of public intervention has received much attention from policy makers and governments during the past three decades. Nevertheless, theoretical principles—which cover a multi-dimensional continuum from captive public production to complete non-intervention—have not been adequately researched and, as a consequence, are not adequately reflected in public economics texts.

The first column of Table 10.1 lists several options for provision or delivery of public services. The choice between these and other possible modes of provision rests on conceptually simple principles which, however, require operational content. An important principle that can be proposed is that the organizational and ownership form that is best suited to provide a public service is the one that can provide the service at the lowest social cost. The proposition, however, needs elaboration. For example, if the service can vary in quality and timeliness and not just raw quantity, then these must be taken into account in defining "service quantity". On the other hand, the cost of provision will be subject to risk and will also vary with the rate of time discount. Third, if resource constraints are binding for, say, direct government provision then use of public-private partnerships may be second best efficient. Unfortunately, no precise formulation and analysis of this proposition as yet appears to exist.[73]

The characteristics of organizations and their suitability for the provision of different public services is possibly best studied using the economic theory of organization behavior.[74] Nevertheless, since this literature has mostly a private sector origin, much work remains to be done. The other issue is the nature of public services that are candidates for provision other than directly by the government and, secondly, the extent of government involvement. Activities that have been provided by alternative means range from defense services, provision of justice and tax administration[75] to provision of education and health or road construction. Regarding the extent of government involvement, an illustrative example from the education sector is in Table 10.2. Principles to guide the choice between the five options in the table can, in principle, be distilled from the economic theory of organizations. This task remains to be undertaken.

Table 10.2: Options for Mixed Public-Private Provision

Asset (Building) Owner	Labor (Teacher) Employer	Producer of Education	Purchaser (Who Pays Producer)
Govt	Govt	Govt	Govt
A: Pure Public Provision			
Private	Govt	Govt	Govt
B: Public-Private partnership. Govt runs school in a private/community building			
Govt	Private	Private	Govt
C: Private school (govt may regulate), but govt provides building			
Private	Private	Private	Govt
D: Case of full scholarship or outsourcing (but govt may regulate)			
Private	Private	Private	Consumer, directly
E: Pure private provision (but govt may regulate)			

Source: Author. Based on discussion in Grout and Stevens (2003).

The Role of Government in the Information Sector

The changing role of government in the information age is another topic of obviously great current importance. This wide ranging area covers a variety of potential government roles.

First, there is the analysis of *government intervention in markets subject to information failures,* particularly asymmetric information. There is by now a vast literature on this, and the topic is a part of upper level or post-graduate courses in economics curricula.[76] In consequence, the advantages and disadvantages of several types of government intervention have been examined theoretically, econometrically, and in case studies. An important subset of markets that are subject to various failures but which are of central importance to the information sector are markets for scientific knowledge and R&D. Textbook examination of the role of government in these markets is usually limited, if at all, to the study of patents (for example, Stiglitz, 2000), though the actual scope of intervention is much wider (Hirschhorn et al., 2000). In particular, an important role may be that of standard setting or protocol construction in emerging areas of technology to enable coordination of private market activity and forestall battles over standards.[77]

A second area with an explicit connection to the information sector is the role of government as a provider of information infrastructure or regulator of private sector information goods, including such things as search engines (Google), web-based networks (Facebook), and on-line data repositories (Wikipedia). An example is the public provision of free internet access, as in several US cities and in Singapore. While standard principles apply, careful analysis of the properties of different information and information-related goods is needed to enable concrete discussion of these interventions. The third area encompasses consequences of advances in information technology for the scope of government activity. Two examples are the emergence of rapid government automation which has spawned the "e-governance" movement, and the growing recognition of citizen's rights to information regarding public activity. The economic rationale for these activities and rights, the scope and extent of government intervention, and pricing of information and e-services are some areas needing examination.

Public Financial Management and Administration

To adapt a well known saying, public policy is public financial management. In the context of tax policy, the great importance of tax administration and the economic analysis of tax administration are by now well recognized. So too is the economic assessment of private sector compliance costs.[78] Though much remains to be done, sufficient research exists by now to make it suitable for undergraduate syllabi.

Public financial management is the operational counterpart of public expenditure management and budgeting. Operational efficiency of budgetary allocations implies a proper assessment of economic costs of different services. This in turn leads to proper accounting of economic or resource costs. Proper implementation of budgeting requires sound cash flow and macro forecasting and treasury operations. It also requires proper financial supervision and institutions (e.g., for procurement) to avoid wastage and fraud.[79] The design and operation of such institutions such as supreme audit bodies, legislative review, and anti-corruption agencies is of great practical importance.[80] A third area of public financial management is the design and use of performance indicators for government operations for performance budgeting, and also for assessment of budget allocations and allocative efficiency. Incentive effects of such institutional structures are likely to have an important bearing on government performance itself, as well as the scope of government activity as the limited recent work available demonstrates.[81] Unfortunately, these issues too are seldom included in public economics syllabi.[82]

Notes

1   The texts examined include Musgrave (1959), Browning and Browning (1994), Boadway and Wildasin (1984), Cullis and Jones (1998), Musgrave and Musgrave (1984), Stiglitz (2000), Gruber (2004), Hindricks and Miles (2006), and Rosen and Gayer (2007). For a tabular comparison of coverage of topics in different texts see Eden and Shoup (1991).

2   Textbooks which do discuss government budget principles are the important early work of Musgrave (1959) in Part I of the text, and the later text by Musgrave and Musgrave (1989) in its Part Two. In fact, four of the five topics discussed in this chapter are recognized in these seminal public finance texts. While both normative and positive principles of

the government budget are discussed in them, the latter from a public choice theoretic perspective, their treatment stops short of what is needed for critical assessment of real world budgets. Stiglitz (2000) has a chapter on the relatively narrow topic of deficit finance and that too from the perspective of recent debate in the United States though, as with Cullis and Jones (1998), he briefly discusses the connection between optimal government expenditure and the economic cost of raising tax revenue.

3 As is discussed, the neglect of non-tax revenues makes the reliability and comparability of cross-country and even within country data on non-tax revenue suspect.

4 See, for example, Tanzi (2000) and Lodin (2002). Further references and some doubts about this hypothesis are in Andersen and Sorensen (2008).

5 In fact, aspects of three of these topics are discussed in Bagchi, Bird, and Das-Gupta (1995).

6 A review of existing institutions in different countries is beyond the scope of this chapter. Useful comparative information is available in Diamond (2006), Schiavo-Campo and Tommasi (1999) and such websites as that of the International Budget Partnership (www.internationalbudget.org) and the Public Expenditure and Financial Accountability (PEFA) Program of various multilateral organizations (www.pefa.org) and the Organization for Economic Cooperation and Development, Public Management Service (OECD, PUMA) (www.oecd.org).

7 This is a simplified version of the Figure 3.1 in Musgrave (1959) and Figures 5.3 and 5.4 in Musgrave and Musgrave (1989). The transformation frontier is similar to that in Figure 6.9 in Stiglitz (2000).

8 A presentation of basic theory is in Slemrod and Yitzhaki (2001). Bird (2005) contains an extensive and illuminating discussion of the MCF and its importance for the level of public expenditure, and also for cost-benefit analysis of individual projects. The basic intuition captured in Figure 10.2 is reflected in the "feasibility curve" in Figure 6.9 of Stiglitz (2000) who, however, limits the discussion to distortionary losses.

9 The unit of measurement, nominal or real, is not of importance to the discussion, so long as the same unit is used, for all magnitudes.

10 In the absence of real-world costs, waste and corruption is associated with public spending, for pure public goods would be identical to the sum of marginal rates of substitution across consumers familiar with the Samuelson rule for the optimal provision of public goods.

11 The expressions can be modified to incorporate unintended transfers from the government to the private sector via, say, evaded taxes and bribes.

12 Further discussion can be found in Ballard and Fullerton (1992), besides Slemrod and Yitzhaki (2001), and Bird (2005) and references cited there.

13 Further discussion of the link between efficient budget rules and cost-benefit analysis is below. It should be noted at this stage that the denominator of the MBP is budgetary cost.

14 See Gaube (2000). Also, ignoring transactions and administration costs the MCF of a wage tax will depend on whether labor supply is in the positively sloped or backward bending segments as pointed out by Ballard and Fullerton (1992). This would imply that a sufficiently high level of wages can be associated with an MCF below unity.

15 An example of a dynamic analysis is Corsetti and Roubini (1996). The importance of an intertemporal budget constraint in analyzing government budgets and the form such a constraint must take is discussed in Buiter (2007).

16 See Ballard and Fullerton (1992), Slemrod and Yitzhaki (2001), and Bird (2005). An additional issue is the extent to which intermediate goods should be taxed or not given

the Diamond-Mirlees theorem. See Diamond and Mirrlees (1971) but also Stiglitz and Dasgupta (1971).

17 Taxes must usually be described by a number of parameters. For example, a basic income tax can be described by a set of marginal tax rates and income thresholds from which each of the rates apply. In principle there is an MCF associated with each tax parameter. A similar statement can be made with respect to public expenditure program designs, which are associated with MBPs for each program design parameter. These nuances go beyond the basic discussion here.

18 This follows Buiter's (2007) terminology. See Buiter (1995, 2007) for careful definitions of seigniorage and related concepts and extensive discussion. The existence of a separate monetary authority with its own budget, which does not form a part of the government budget, is a source of budget non-comprehensiveness. However desirable autonomy may be (Buiter, 2007), this makes for a non-transparent public sector.

19 This analysis is potentially weakened by several considerations that depend on the costs of inflation and the general equilibrium effects associated with the expenditure financed out of the inflation tax. For example, if money is a universal intermediate good, then under the conditions required for the Diamond-Mirrlees theorem to hold, a zero inflation tax would be optimal. Note that a zero inflation tax still leaves the government with some seigniorage revenue if it is the monopoly provider of high powered money.

20 In practice both debt finance and seigniorage are seen to move pro-cyclically with taxation as the equal MCF rule would lead one to expect. See Trehan and Walsh (1990) for the United States but also the cross-section study of Click (1998).

21 That is, a program is worth financing through the budget provided the expenditure and financing requirement for the program have MBP − MCF ≥ 1 suitably reinterpreted! Note that the assessment of a program's benefits and costs using a modified discount rate is potentially unsatisfactory. In particular, for a program whose costs and benefits both arise during a single period the discount will have no role to play.

22 It should be noted that there are often excellent reasons for fragmented budgets that outweigh benefits from a comprehensive budget. Two examples are local autonomy with separate sub-national governments in federal states and autonomous agencies for particular public sector functions.

23 The discussion here largely follows Schiavo-Campo and Tommasi (1999).

24 For example, in the case of Singapore 50 autonomous "Statutory Boards" control a large part of public receipts and expenditures. Differences in the classification of these receipts and expenditures by the national government and the IMF have in the past resulted in one showing a budget deficit while the other shows a surplus.

25 Bird (1997), drawing on earlier work by Buchanan (1963) and others, points out that when earmarked taxes substitute for user charges, a benefit tax argument can be made for the optimality of earmarking. He identifies earmarked payroll taxes to fund social security systems, earmarked fuel taxes for roads, and earmarked pollution levies for environment preservation expenditure, as prominent examples. However, he also points out that earmarking when the tax base is unrelated to the earmarked use is not economically justifiable this may increase the political acceptability of additional taxation.

26 One type of implicit earmarking deserves mention. This is when user charges levied by autonomous agencies or government departments are retained by the agency or department and not reported as part of government receipts. Such *netting* makes it impossible to ascertain the real size of government revenue and expenditure. Further discussion of netting is below in connection with non-tax revenue.

27 See for example, World Bank (1998) and Schiavo-Campo and Tomassi (1999).

28 For further discussion see Potter and Diamond (1999) and Diamond (2006).

29 However, see the discussion of the efficiency dividend in Diamond (2006). Earlier attempts to achieve allocative and operational efficiency, for example, zero base budgeting, have also been tried unsuccessfully as discussed in World Bank (1998) and Schiavo-Campo and Tomassi (1999).

30 Economic theories point to a natural tendency for governments to grow stemming from the well known Leviathan hypothesis of Buchanan (introductory discussion is in Musgrave and Musgrave, 1989: Chapter 7). Other theories study the impact of voting institutions and special interest groups in shaping budgetary institutions, a recent example being Helpman and Grossman (2006).

31 The OECD has recently surveyed medium term budgeting practices in member countries. For a summary see Diamond (2006).

32 See, for example, Helpman and Grossman (2006) cited above and also Alesina and Perotti (1999).

33 See the studies in the volume edited by Poterba and von Hagen (1999). Also see the recent evidence on the impact of budgetary institutions on fiscal discipline in the US context in Auerbach (2008).

34 The discussion of non-tax revenue is based mainly on Das-Gupta (2005).

35 For the standard textbook classification of government revenues see, for example, Musgrave and Musgrave (1989). An earlier classification of government revenue sources is in Rao (1981). The implicit definition of non-tax revenue in the International Monetary Fund's *Government Statistics Manual*, 2001 follows approximately the same approach as is taken here.

36 "Institutional units" includes both individuals and other entities.

37 Examples are the United Nations System of National Accounts and the IMF's *Government Statistics Manual*, 2001.

38 Fines and penalties are "requited" in the negative sense that they are payments exacted for non-compliance with the law.

39 A detailed list of goods from which the government derives revenue is provided for the Indian case in Das-Gupta (2005).

40 Substitutes to fines, such as jail sentences, forfeitures, withdrawal of the right to carry on a business or profession, and even public shaming, must be taken into account in designing optimal fines. For an excellent review of the economic theory of enforcement see Polinsky and Shavell (2000). Several cases discussed there lend themselves to undergraduate teaching.

41 The growing recent literature on excludible (but non-rival) public goods is examined below. Norman (2004) discusses different examples:

> To the extent that copying can be prevented, electronic libraries, computer programs, and other goods that can be stored in digital format are almost perfect examples of such excludable public goods. Other examples include cable TV, parks, gyms, zoos, museums, trains (as long as there is excess capacity), innovations, and protection by a police or fire department. These examples may also be thought of as natural monopolies, and an excludable public good may in general be considered as a special case of a natural monopoly, with zero marginal cost.

42 Richard Musgrave termed goods with these problems merit goods, though not pure merit goods which are intrinsically private goods, not subject to market imperfections but which

have some desirable distributional characteristic. Examples where information is a factor include curative medical services, old age saving and insurance, and the "bads" alcohol and tobacco use.

43 On the option between Central versus local government provision, the standard public economics rationale relates to ensuring no spillovers or the internalization of all benefits and costs within a jurisdiction following the Oates Decentralization Theorem. More recently, on poverty alleviation interventions, there is evidence in Bardhan and Mookherjee (2004) for West Bengal surveyed along with other studies in Jutting et al. (2004). These studies do not permit a clear-cut conclusion that decentralized provision of poverty alleviation services is superior to direct provision by state governments. Provision by NGOs versus governments is studied by in Besley (1996) and Bardhan and Mookherjee (2004). Analysis and prescriptions of service delivery options by World Bank economists is reported in Devarajan and Shah (2004). On the UK and European Union experience with privatization and public-private partnerships (see Grout and Stevens 2003).

44 However, given differences in preferences of rich and poor and, in particular, a higher demand elasticity of the poor, Sepehri and Chernomas (2001) suggest that the opposite may, in fact, be the case.

45 Here, we abstract from institutional alternatives to direct government provision. Clearly actual provision can be outsourced or done in partnership with a private sector entity, for many items such as roads, education services, or even printing of government regulations.

46 An excellent discussion is to be found in Sankar (1992) which has been consulted extensively in writing this section. He reviews aspects of non-uniform pricing together with Indian applications to air passenger, electricity, and postal and telecommunications tariffs.

47 An excellent introduction to price discrimination, non-linear pricing, and for multiple products, bundling in the context of the private sector, is Besanko, Dranove, and Shanley (1996).

48 Examples could be internet or zoo admission for a fixed duration with differential admissions fees for different groups of buyers.

49 The UK auction in 2000 ended up garnering £22.5 billion according to Jehiel and Moldovanu (2003). This compares to a collection of about £150 billion in income taxes that year. An engaging and amusing discussion of the use of auctions for radio spectra is in Hartford (2006). He documents early mistakes and also later successes. A more serious and comprehensive discussion is in Jehiel and Moldovanu (2003) and also in the introductory section of Ockenfels, Reiley, and Sadrieh (2006). Auction theory as well as practical cases are the subject of Klemperer (2004).

50 More precisely the *shadow value* of the *marginal* compliance rate achieved from the *marginal* rupee of administrative outlay should be treated as the marginal benefit from such expenditure which should then be compared to other expenditure.

51 A reference to this commons is in Tanzi (2008). Besides this, the term does not appear to be in general use.

52 For a discussion of the concept of sovereignty which encompasses "tax sovereignty", a concept that possibly underlies "economic allegiance", see Christian (2008).

53 There are also non-governmental actors that shape *commons activity* such as multinational accounting firms.

54 These are taken from a presentation by Professor Lee Burns at the Asian Development Bank Institute. See Asian Development Bank Institute (2000).

55 To take an example, a doctor from Malaysia holidaying in Thailand may advise a team of Australian doctors about a surgical procedure being carried out in Indonesia. The payment may be sent from Australia to the Malaysian doctor's Singapore bank account.

56 The proposals include a "bit" tax, taxing payments to foreign sellers in the destination country and making sales by sellers other than "registered sellers" illegal.

57 See OECD (1998), Blum et al. (1998), Webb (2004), McLure (2006), and a series of related papers authored by one or more of Mihir Desai, C. Fritz Foley, James R. Hines, Jr., and Dhammika Dharmapala since 1998. In OECD (1998), the OECD Committee on Fiscal Affairs identifies 47 jurisdictions engaged in "harmful tax practices" (HTPs). HTPs are discussed later in the chapter.

58 As with other topics in this chapter, early treatment of international tax principles is in Musgrave and Musgrave (1989) drawing on pioneering earlier work of each of the authors. A good overview of this normative analysis is in Musgrave (2006). Alternative principles are discussed in Desai and Hines (2003). A critique of Musgrave's analysis as well as a wide-ranging survey of emerging issues in the domain of international taxation is in Graetz (2001).

59 The OECD's Harmful Tax Practices initiative is one case in which the right to tax of some havens is not recognized by other usually more powerful countries though ability to tax (or spare tax) is clearly present in these havens. This is discussed further.

60 A good discussion of the efficiency concepts presented here is in Desai and Hines (2003).

61 The international tax regime also has implications for tax harmonization of cooperating jurisdictions and tax competition. Razin and Sadka (1991) point out that tax harmonization is not needed even if countries engage in tax competition if they tax capital income in accordance with the residence principle. If not, countries end up in a "race to the bottom" whereby national taxation of only immobile factors results.

62 For a more detailed discussion and references to the literature, see Ebrill et al. (2001), Chapter 17.

63 Brief discussion is in Keen and Wildasin (2004) and also in Graetz (2001).

64 As Bird and Mintz (2003) put it, "Unfortunately, there do not appear to be principles that are both acceptable and feasible with respect to how to divide up such a complex and changing target as the international tax base in the multiplayer international tax game" (p. 422). They identify several possible principles that may be used in future and evaluate their relative merits.

65 According to Tanzi (2008), countries compete to attract foreign: financial and real capital, consumers, workers, high income individuals, and pensioners.

66 See Bird and Mintz (2003) who refer in their discussion to the implicit "OECD consensus".

67 Owens (2002) emphasizes the importance of Mutual Agreement Procedures in these treaties (DTAs) since there are inevitable gaps in the coverage of treaties.

68 "Commons capture" and apportionment are discussed in Langer (2000), Bird and Mintz (2003), and Rattsø (2003), the latter in the context of the European Union.

69 Avi-Yonah (2000) identifies production tax havens, countries offering production tax concessions. According to him, the definition of harmful tax competitor nations should be broadened to include those that offer any form of discriminatory concessional tax treatment to non-residents whether these result in no productive activity—covered in the current definition—or not.

70 Effective exchange of information has three dimensions: (*a*) relevant information must exist; (*b*) tax authorities need to have access to it; (*c*) the information needs to

be exchangeable. The judgmental, bullying tone of these requirements should be evident.

71 The discussion does not extend to "rogue nations" that act as financial havens for crime, terrorism, and individual tax evasion or money laundering. Such jurisdictions exist, but are by no means characteristic of a typical tax haven.

72 Including the USA, via certain interest concessions (Langer, 2000) and Singapore. On the latter, see Hines (2004).

73 On the choice between direct government and NGO provision, preliminary analysis may be found in Besley (1996).

74 Good texts on the economic analysis of organizations are Douma and Schreuder (1998) and Milgrom and Roberts (1992). An excellent assessment of British and EU experience with privatization and public-private partnerships is in Grout and Stevens (2003).

75 On tax administration see Johnson (2001), Yang (2005) and also Bagchi, Bird, and Das-Gupta (1995).

76 For example, information failures were the main subject area covered in a course by Robin Boadway at Queens University. See Boadway (2004).

77 As in the recent case of differing digital video disc technologies. For a discussion, see US Department of Commerce, IPV6 Task Force (2006).

78 For examples, see Bagchi, Bird, and Das-Gupta (1995) and McLaren (2003). On compliance costs, see Binh et al., (2000) and Evans (2003).

79 Examples are the exorbitant prices that are often paid for different goods by the US Pentagon during its Iraq operations and by the US Federal Emergency Management Administration (FEMA) during the aftermath of hurricane Katrina. An Indian episode is Telgi stamp scam whose costs to the government are still to be fully accounted. All of these cases have been widely reported in newspapers and are the subject of government reports.

80 These topics and various other topics in public financial management are the subject of several studies and reports from the International Monetary Fund, the Asian Development Bank, the OECD and various national governments. For a recent example, see Diamond (2006).

81 Examples in the context of tax administration are Kahn, Silva, Ziliak (2001), and Silva (2003). Such analysis forms part of the economic theory of organizations and a large literature exists for the private sector which can fruitfully be tapped.

82 However, the author taught an elective course for postgraduates in public financial management at the Lee Kuan Yew School of Public Policy during 2006 to 2008. The course was a parallel offering to one in public economics.

References

Alesina, Alberto and Roberto Perotti. 1999. "Budget Deficits and Budget Institutions" in James M. Poterba and Jürgen von Hagen (eds), *Fiscal Institutions and Fiscal Performance*, National Bureau of Economic Research conference report, pp. 85–101. Chicago: University of Chicago Press. Available online at http://www.nber.org/books/pote99-1 (accessed on October 3, 2008).

Allen, Richard and Dimitar Radev. 2006. "Managing and Controlling Extra Budgetary Funds", IMF Working Paper WP/06/286, Washington DC: Fiscal Affairs Department, International Monetary Fund.

Amacher, Gregory S., Richard J Brazee, and Meindert Witvliet. 2001. "Royalty Systems, Government Revenues, and Forest Conditions: An Application from Malaysia" *Land Economics*, 77 (2): 300–13.

Anderberg, Dan, Fredrik Andersson, and Alessandro Balestrino. 2000. "Time, Self Selection and User Charges for Public Goods", *FinanzArchiv*, 57 (2): 137–54.

Andersen, Torben M. and Allan Sørensen. 2008. "Globalisation Squeezes the Public Sector—Is It So Obvious?" Economics working paper 2008–8, School of Economics and Management, University of Aarhus, Aarhus, Denmark. Available online at http://ssrn.com/abstract=1261837 (accessed on October 18, 2008).

Arnold, Brian J. 2004. "Controlled Foreign Corporation Rules: Major Features, Recent Developments, and Practical Problems", paper presented at the 4th Annual World Tax Conference, Sydney, Australia, February 25–27.

Arnold, Brian J. and Patrick Dibout. 2001. "Limits on the Use of Low-Tax Regimes by Multinational Businesses: Current Measures and Emerging Trends: General Report", *Cahiers de Droit Fiscal International*, Vol. 86b, International Fiscal Association. The Hague: Kluwer Law International.

Asher, Mukul G. and Ramkishen S. Rajan. 2001. "Globalization and Tax Systems: Implications for Developing Countries with Particular Reference to Southeast Asia", *ASEAN Economic Bulletin*, 18 (1): 119–39.

Asian Development Bank Institute. 2000. "Tax Conference: 1999 Seminar on International Taxation, Tokyo" Executive Summary of Proceedings", Executive Summary Series, No S13/001, Tokyo: Asian Development Bank Institute. Available online at http://www.adbi.org/PDF/ess/ES13.pdf (downloaded on July 25, 2010).

———. 2001. "Millennium Tax Conference, 20–29 September 2000", Executive Summary Series, No S33/01, Tokyo: Asian Development Bank Institute. Available online at http://www.adbi.org/PDF/ess/ES33.pdf (downloaded on July 25, 2010).

Atkinson, Anthony and Nicholas Stem. 1974. "Pigou, Taxation, and Public Goods", *Review of Economic Studies*, 4(1): 119–28.

Auerbach, Alan J. 2008. "Federal Budget Rules: The US Experience", Working Paper No. W14288, National Bureau of Economic Research. Cambridge, Mass. Available online at http://www.nber.org/papers/w14288.

Avi-Yonah, Reuven S. 2000. "Globalization, Tax Competition, and the Fiscal Crisis of the Welfare State", *Harvard Law Review*, 113 (7): 1575–76.

Bagchi, Amaresh, Richard M. Bird, and Arindam Das-Gupta. 1995. "An Economic Approach to Tax Administration Reform" Discussion Paper No. 3. University of Toronto Faculty of Management, International Centre for Tax Studies.

Bailey, Stephen J. 1994. "User Charges for Urban Services", *Urban Studies*, 31 (4–5) 745–65.

Balestrino, Alessandro. 1999. "User Charges as Redistributive Devices", *Journal of Public Economic Theory*, 1 (4): 511–24.

Ballard, Charles L. and Don Fullerton. 1992. "Distortionary Taxes and the Provision of Public Goods", *Journal of Economic Perspectives*, 6(3): 117–31.

Bardhan, Pranab and Dilip Mookherjee. 2004. "Poverty Alleviation Efforts of Panchayats in West Bengal", *Economic and Political Weekly*, 39 (February 28): 965–74,

Baunsgaard, Thomas and Michael Keen. 2005. "Tax Revenue and (or?) Trade Liberalization", IMF Working Paper WP/05/112, Fiscal Affairs Department, Washington DC, International Monetary Fund.

Bentley, Duncan. 2003. "International Constraints on National Tax Policy", *Tax Notes International*, 30 (June 16): 1127–44.

Besanko, David, David Dranove and Mark Shanley. 1996. *Economics of Strategy*, New York: John Wiley.

Besley, Timothy. 1991. "Welfare Improving User Charges for Publicly Provided Private Goods", *Scandinavian Journal of Economics*, 93 (4): 495–510.

——. 1996. "Political Economy of Alleviating Poverty: Theory and Institutions", in *Proceedings of the World Bank Annual Conference on Development Economics*, pp. 117–48. Washington DC: The World Bank.

Bierhanzl, Edward J. 1999. "Incentives for Efficiency: User Charges and Municipal Spending", *Journal of Public Finance and Public Choice/Economia Delle Scelte Pubbliche*, 17 (1): 19–34.

Bierhanzl, Edward J. and Paul B. Downing. 1998. "User Charges and Bureaucratic Inefficiency", *Atlantic Economic Journal*, 26 (2): 175–89.

Binh, Tran-Nam, Chris Evans, Michael Walpole, and Katherine Ritchie. 2000. "Tax Compliance Research: Research Methodology and Empirical Evidence from Australia", *National Tax Journal*, 53 (2): 229–51.

Bird, Richard M. 1997. "Analysis of Earmarked Taxes", *Tax Notes International*, 14 (25): 2095–16.

——. 2001. "User Charges in Local Government Finance", in Mila Freire and Richard Stern, (eds), *The Challenge of Urban Government: Policies and Practices*. WBI Development Studies, Washington, DC: World Bank Institute.

——. 2005. "Evaluating Public Expenditures: Does it Matter How they are Financed?" ITP Paper 0506, University of Toronto Faculty of Management, International Centre for Tax Studies. Available online at http://www.rotman.utoronto.ca/iib/ (accessed on September 25, 2008).

Bird, Richard M. and Jack Mintz. 2003. "Sharing the International Tax Base in a Changing World", in Sijbren Cnossen and Hans-Werner Sinn (eds), *Public Finance and Public Policy in the New Century*, pp. 405–46.Cambridge: MIT Press.

Biswas, Rajiv (ed.). 2002. *International Tax Competition: Globalisation and Fiscal Sovereignty*. London: Commonwealth Secretariat.

Bjornstadt, David J. and Marylin A. Brown. 2004. "A Market Failures Framework for Defining the Government's Role in Energy Efficiency", Report Number: JIEE 2004–02, Knoxville, Tennessee: Oakridge National Laboratory, Joint Institute for Energy and Environment. Available online at http://www.ornl.gov/sci/mkt_trans/pdf/2004_02marketfail.pdf (accessed September 21, 2008).

Blum, Jack A., Michael Levi, R.Thomas Naylor, and Phil Williams. 1998. *Financial Havens, Banking Secrecy and Money Laundering*. New York: United Nations Office for Drug Control and Crime Prevention. Available online at: http://www.cf.ac.uk/socsi/whoswho/levi-laundering.pdf.

Boadway, Robin W. 2004. "Economics 442, Topics in Public Economics, Course Outline and Reading List". Available online at http://www.econ.queensu.ca/pub/undergrad/econ442.pdf, (accessed October 4, 2008).

Boadway, Robin and David Wildasin. 1984. *Public Sector Economics*, Second edition. Boston: Little, Brown and Co.

Brito, D.L. and W.H. Oakland. 1980. "On the Monopolistic Provision of Excludable Public Goods", *American Economic Review*, 70 (4): 269–304.

Browning, E.K and Browning, J.M. 1994. *Public Finance and the Price System*, 4th edition. New Jersey: Prentice-Hall.

Buchanan, James M. 1963. "The Economics of Earmarked Taxes", *Journal of Political Economy*, 71 (5): 457–69.

Buchanan, James M. 2002. "Fiscal Equalization Revisited" presented at the conference on 'Equalization: Welfare trap or helping hand?' organised by the Atlantic Institute for Market Studies, the Montreal Economic Institute and the Frontier Centre for Public Policy, Montreal, October, 2001.

Buiter, Willem H. 1983. "The Theory of Optimum Debt and Deficits", Working Paper No 1232, National Bureau of Economic Research, Cambridge, Mass. Available online at http://www.nber.org/papers/w1232.

———. 1995. "Macroeconomic Policy during a Transition to Monetary Union" Discussion Paper 261, Centre for Economic Performance, London School of Economics, Available online at http://cep.lse.ac.uk/pubs/download/dp0261.pdf (accessed October 7, 2008).

———. 2007. "Seigniorage", *Economics: The Open-Access, Open-Assessment E-Journal*, 1 (10). Available online at http://www.economics-ejournal.org/economics/journalarticles/2007-10 (downloaded on July 25, 2010).

Burgess, Philip. 2005. "Rendering unto other People's Caesars: Globalisation comes to Tax Collection", in Rodney Fisher and Michael Walpole (eds), *Global Challenges in Tax Administration*, pp. 58–66, Birmingham: Fiscal Publications.

Burns, M.E. and C. Walsh. 1981. "Market Provision of Price-Excludable Public Goods", *Journal of Political Economy* 71 (1): 166–91.

Chang Woon Nam, Rüdiger Parsche, and Barbara Schaden. 2001. "Measurement of Value Added Tax Evasion in Selected EU Countries on the Basis of National Accounts Data", CESifo Working Paper No. 431, Centre for Economic Studies & IFO Institute for Economic Research, Munich. Available online at http://www.cesifo-group.de/pls/guestci/download/CESifo%20Working%20Papers%202001/CESifo%20Working%20Papers%20March%202001/cesifo_wp431.pdf (downloaded on July 15, 2010).

Chia, Ngee-Choon. 1998. "Singapore: The Significance of Motor Vehicle Taxes in the Revenue System", *Asia-Pacific Tax Bulletin*, 4: 275–81.

Christians, Allison. 2008. "Sovereignty, Taxation, and Social Contract", Legal studies research paper series paper 1063, University of Wisconsin Law School, Wisconsin. Available online at http://ssrn.com/abstract=1259975 (accessed October 4, 2008).

Click, Reid W. 1998. "Seigniorage in a Cross-Section of Countries", *Journal of Money, Credit and Banking*, 30(2): 154–71.

Cockfield, Arthur. 2002. "Through the Looking Glass: Computer Servers and E-Commerce Profit Attribution", *Tax Notes International*, 25 (21): 269—75.

Collier, P. and A. Hoeffler, 2005. *Democracy and Natural Resource Rents*, Department of Economics, Oxford: Oxford University.

Corsetti, Giancarlo and Nouriel Roubini. 1996. "Optimal Government Spending and Taxation in Endogenous Growth Models", Cambridge, Mass: NBER Working Paper 5851.

Cremer, H. and J.J. Laffont. 2003. "Public Goods with Costly Access", *Journal of Public Economics* 87 (9): 1985–2012.

Cullis, John and Philip Jones. 1998. *Public Finance and Public Choice*, Second Edition. Oxford: Oxford University Press.

Das-Gupta, Arindam. 2002. "Central Tax and Administration Reform in the 1990s: An Assessment" in M. Govinda, Rao (ed.), *Development, Poverty and Fiscal Policy—Decentralization of Institutions* (Essays in Honour of Raja Chelliah), pp. 139–73. New Delhi: Oxford University Press.

———. 2005. "Non-Tax Revenues in Indian States: Principles and Case Studies", paper prepared for the Asian Development Bank. Available online at http://adb.org/Documents/Reports/Consultant/TAR-IND-4066/GovtBudget/dasgupta.pdf.

Desai, Mihir A. and James R. Hines. 2003. "Evaluating International Tax Reform", *National Tax Journal*, 56(3): 487–502.

Desai, Mihir A., C. Fritz Foley, and James R. Hines. 2005. "The Demand for Tax Haven Operations". Available online at http://papers.ssrn.com/sol3/papers.cfm?abstract_id=593546 (accessed October 4, 2008).

Devarajan, Shantayanan and Shekhar Shah. 2004. "Making Services Work for India's Poor", *Economic and Political Weekly*, 39 (February 28): 907–19.

Dharmapala, Dhammika and James R. Hines Jr. 2006. "Which Countries Become Tax Havens?" Working Paper 12802, National Bureau of Economic Research, Cambridge, Mass. Available at http://www.nber.org/papers/w12802.

Diamond, Jack. 2006. *Budget Systems Reform in Emerging Economies: Challenges and the Reform Agenda,* Occasional Paper 245, International Monetary Fund, Washington DC.

Diamond, Peter and James Mirrlees. 1971. "Optimal Taxation and Public Production I: Production Efficiency", *American Economic Review*, 61 (1): 8–27.

Dobbs, Ian M. 1991. "Litter and Waste Management: Disposal Taxes Versus User Charges", *Canadian Journal of Economics*, 24 (1): 221–27.

Douma, Sytse and Hein Schreuder. 1998. *Economic Approaches to Organizations*, second edition, Hempstead: Prentice-Hall Europe.

Downing, P.B. 1992. "The Revenue Potential of User Charges in Municipal Finance", *Public Finance Quarterly* 20 (4): 512–27.

Dwyer, Terry. 2002. "Harmful Tax Competition and the Future of Offshore Financial Centres", *Journal of Money Laundering Control*, 5(4): 302–17.

Easson, Alex. 2004a. "Harmful Tax Competition: An Evaluation of the OECD Initiative", *Tax Notes International*, 34 (June 7): 1037–77.

Ebrill, Liam, Michael Keen, Jean-Paul Bodin, and Victoria Summers. 2001. *The Modern VAT,* Washington DC: International Monetary Fund.

Eden, Lorraine and Carl S. Shoup. 1991. *Retrospectives on Public Finance*, Durham, North Carolina: Duke University Press.

Evans, Chris. 2003. "Studying the Studies: An Overview of Recent Research into Taxation Operating Costs", *eJournal of Tax Research*, 1 (1): 64–92.

Fraser, C.D. 1996. "On the Provision of Excludable Public Goods", *Journal of Public Economics* 60 (1): 111–30.

Fraser, Rob. 1999. "An Analysis of the Western Australian Gold Royalty", *Australian Journal of Agricultural and Resource Economics*, 43 (1): 35–50.

Gaube, Thomas. 2000. "When do Distortionary Taxes Reduce the Optimal Supply of Public Goods?", *Journal of Public Economics*, 76 (2): 151–80.

Gill, Jit B.S. 2000. "Diagnostic Framework for Revenue Administration", The World Bank. Available online at http://74.6.146.127/search/cache?ei=UTF-8&p=Gill+Diagnostic+Framework+for+Revenue+Administration&fr=yfp-t-704&u=www1.worldbank.org/publicsector/toolkitstax.pdf&w=gill+diagnostic+diagnostics+framework+%22frame+work%22+revenue+administration&d=F82G8LZfVFbN&icp=1&.intl=in&sig=kfRbUw9.KcUEm1m9ssr5HA (downloaded on July 25, 2010).

Government of India. 1992. *Report of the Committee on Pricing of Irrigation Water*, New Delhi: Planning Commission.

Graetz, Michael J. 2001. "Taxing International Income: Inadequate Principles, Outdated Concepts and Unsatisfactory Policies", *Tax Law Review*, 54, reprinted in *The Brookings Journal of International Law*, 24(4): 1357–448.

Gregor, Martin. 2004. "Governing Fiscal Commons in the Enlarged EU", Working Paper IES56, Faculty of Social Sciences, Institute of Economic Studies, Charles University Prague. Available online at http://ies.fsv.cuni.cz/default/file/download/id/1277 (accessed September 26, 2008).

Gronau, Reuben. 1994. "Fuel Taxes and Road User Charges in LDC's: Some Lessons from Sub Saharan Africa", in Yoshitsugu Hayashi, Kenneth Button and Peter Nijkamp, (eds), *The Environment and Transport,* Cheltenham, UK and Northampton, Mass.: Edward Elgar.

Grout, Paul A. and Margaret Stevens. 2003. "The Assessment: Financing and Managing Public Services", *Oxford Review of Economic Policy,* 19(2): 215–34.

Gruber, Jonathan. 2004. "14.41 *Public Economics*, MIT Open Courseware". Available online at http://ocw.mit.edu/OcwWeb/Economics/14-41Fall-2004/CourseHome/index.htm (accessed October 4, 2008).

Gwilliam, Ken and Zmarak Shalizi. 1999. "Road Funds, User Charges and Taxes", *World Bank Research Observer,* 14 (2): 159–85.

Gylfason, Thorvaldur, Tryggvi Thor Herbertsson, and Gylfi Zoega. 1999. "A Mixed Blessing: Natural resources and Economic Growth", *Macroeconomic Dynamics,* 3 (June): 204–25.

Hardin, Garrett. 1968. "The Tragedy of the Commons", *Science,* 162 (3859): 1243–48.

Hartford, Tim. 2006. *The Undercover Economist,* London: Little, Brown and Có.

Hellwig, Martin. 2005. "Public Goods and Welfare Economics", Research programme outline, Max Planck Institute for Research on Collective Goods. Available online at http://www.coll.mpg.de/pdf_dat/Report2005/ReportCI.pdf (downloaded on October 7, 2008).

————. 2005 "Public Goods and Welfare Economics: Incentive Mechanisms, Finance and Governance", Online publication, Max Planck Institute for Research on Collective Goods, available at http://www.coll.mpg.de/pdf_dat/Report2005/ReportCI.pdf (downloaded on October 10, 2008).

————. 2006. "The Provision and Pricing of Excludable Public Goods: Ramsey–Boiteux Pricing versus Bundling", Preprints of the Max Planck Institute for Research on Collective Goods Bonn 2006/21. Available online at http://www.coll.mpg.de/pdf_dat/2006_21online. pdf (downloaded on July, 25, 2010).

Helpman Elhanan and Gene M. Grossman. 2006. "Separation of Powers and the Budget Process", Working Paper No. 4-2006, University of Tel Aviv, Tel Aviv; Israel: The Foerder Institute for Economic Research and The Sackler Institute of Economic Studies.

Hindriks, Jean and Gareth D. Myles. 2006. *Intermediate Public Economics.* Cambridge, Mass: MIT Press.

Hines, James R. Jr. 2004. "Do Tax Havens Flourish?" Working Paper 10936, Cambridge, Mass: National Bureau of Economic Research. Available online at http://www.nber.org/papers/w10936 (downloaded on July, 25, 2010).

Hines James R. Jr. and Eric M. Rice. 2004. "Fiscal Paradise: Foreign Tax Havens and American Business", *Quarterly Journal of Economics,* 109 (1): 149–82.

Hirshhorn, Ronald, Serge Nadeau, and Someshwar Rao. 2000. "Innovation in a Knowledge-Based Economy: The Role of Government", University of British Columbia. Available online at http://pacific.commerce.ubc.ca/kbe/rao.pdf (downloaded on September 21, 2008).

Holland, David and Richard J. Vann. 1998. "Income Tax Incentives for Investment", in Victor Thuronyi, (ed.), *Tax Law and Drafting,* 986–1020. Washington DC: IMF.

Holmström, Bengt. 1999. "Managerial Incentive Problems: A Dynamic Perspective", *Review of Economic Studies,* 66 (1): 169–82.

Huber, Bernd and Marco Runkel. 2004. "Tax Competition, Excludable Public Goods and User Charges", CesIfo Working Paper No. 1172, Ludwig Maximilian University, Center for Economic Studies (CES), Munich and Munich University, Institute for Economic Research University (Ifo).

International Monetary Fund. 2001. *Government Finance Statistics Manual*. Washington DC: International Monetary Fund.

Jehiel, Philippe and Benny Moldovanu. 2003. "An Economic Perspective on Auctions", *Economic Policy*, 18 (36, April) , 269–308.

Johnson, Noel. 2001. "Committing to Civil Service Reform: The Performance of Pre-shipment Inspection under Different Institutional Regimes", Working paper No. 2594, The World Bank, Washington DC.

Jütting, Johannes, Céline Kauffmann, Ida Mc Donnell, Holger Osterrieder, Nicolas Pinaud, and Lucia Weg. 2004. "Decentralization and Poverty in Developing Countries: Exploring the Impact", Working Paper No. 236,OECD Development Centre, Paris.

Kahn, Charles, Emilson C.D. Silva, and James Ziliak. 2001. "Performance-Based Wages in Tax Collection: The Brazilian Tax Collection Reform and Its Effects", *Economic Journal*, 111 (468): 118–205.

Keen, M. and D. Wildasin. 2004. "Pareto-Efficient International Taxation", *American Economic Review*, 94 (1): 259–75.

Klemperer, Paul. 2004. *Auctions: Theory and Practice*. Princeton: Princeton University Press.

Langer, Marshall J. 2000. "Who are the Real Tax Havens?", *Tax Notes International*, December 18: pp. 1–9. Available online at http://www.freedomandprosperity.org/Articles/tni12-18-00.pdf (downloaded on October 7, 2008).

Lienert, Ian and Moo-Kyung Jung. 2004. "The Legal Framework for Budgeting: An International Comparison", *OECD Journal of Budgeting*: Special Issue, 4(3): 23–479. http://www.oecd.org/dataoecd/48/48/35933542.pdf.

Lodin, Sven-Olaf. 2002. "What Ought to be Taxed and What Can be Taxed: A New International Dilemma", in M. Govinda Rao (ed.), *Development, Poverty, and Fiscal Policy: Decentralization of Institutions* (Essays in honour of Raja J. Chelliah), pp. 85–101. New Delhi: Oxford University Press.

McAfee, R Preston and John McMillan. 1996. "Analyzing the Airwaves Auction", *Journal of Economic Perspectives*, 10 (1): 159–75.

McLaren, John, (ed.). 2003. "Institutional Elements of Tax Design and Reform", Technical Paper No. 539, The World Bank, Washington DC.

McLure, Charles E., Jr. 2001. "Globalization, Tax Rules and National Sovereignty", *Bulletin for International Fiscal Documentation*, 55(8): 328–41.

———. 2002. "Replacing Separate Entity Accounting and the Arm's Length Standard with Formulary Apportionment", *Bulletin for International Fiscal Documentation*, 56(December 12): 586–99.

———. 2003. "Taxation of Electronic Commerce in Developing Countries", in James Robert Alm and Jorge Martinez, (eds), *Public Finance in Developing and Transition Countries: Essays in Honor of Richard Bird*, pp. 283–323. Cheltenham: Edward Elgar.

———. 2006. "Transfer Pricing and Tax Havens: Mending the LDC Revenue Net", in James Alm, Jorge Martinez, and Mark Rider (eds), *The Challenges of Tax Reform in the Global Economy*, pp. 77–136. Berlin: Springer Verlag.

McMillan, John. 1994. "Selling Spectrum Rights", *Journal of Economic Perspectives*, 8 (3): 145–62.

Mehrotra, Santosh. 2004. "Reforming Public Spending on Education and Mobilizing Resources: Lessons from International Experience", *Economic and Political Weekly*, 39 (February 28): 987–97.

Milgrom, Paul and John Roberts. 1992. *Economics, Organization and Management*. Upper Saddle River, New Jersey: Prentice-Hall Inc.

Mintz, Jack. 2001. "National Tax Policy and Global Competition", *Brookings Journal of International Law*, 26 (4): 1285–302.

Mookherjee, Dilip and Ivan P.L. Png. 1994. "Marginal Deterrence in Enforcement of Law", *Journal of Political Economy*, 102 (5): 1039–66.

Moore, Mick. 2007. "How Does Taxation Affect the Quality of Governance?" IDS Working Paper 280, Institute of Development Studies, Sussex.

Moynihan, Donald P. 2003. *Performance-based Budgeting: Beyond Rhetoric*. Washington DC: The World Bank.

Musgrave, Peggy B. 2006. "National Taxation in a Globalizing World" in Inge Kaul and Pedro Conciecao (eds), *The New Public Finance*, pp. 167–93. New York and Oxford: UNDP and Oxford University Press.

Musgrave, Richard A. 1959. *The Theory of Public Finance: A Study in Public Economy*, (International Student Edition), Tokyo: McGraw-Hill Kogakusha, Ltd.

———. 1969. "Cost-Benefit Analyses and the Theory of Public Finance" *Journal of Economic Literature*, 7 (3): 797–806.

Musgrave, Richard A. and Peggy B. Musgrave. 1984. *Public Finance in Theory and Practice*, 5th edition, McGraw-Hill International Editions. Singapore: McGraw-Hill.

Muten, Leif. 2002. "Fiscal Relations between Rich and Poor Countries", in M. Govinda Rao (ed.), *Development, Poverty, and Fiscal Policy: Decentralization of Institutions* (Essays in honour of Raja J. Chelliah), pp. 102–17. New Delhi: Oxford University Press.

Myles, Gareth D. 1995. *Public Economics*, Cambridge: Cambridge University Press.

Nellor, David C.L. and Emil M. Sunley. 1994. "Fiscal Regimes for Natural Resource Producing Developing Countries", International Monetary Fund Papers on Policy Analysis and Assessment, Number 9424.

Newbery, D. 1986. "On the Desirability of Input Taxes", *Economics Letters*, 20 (1): 267–70.

Newbery, David M. and Georgina Santos. 1999. "Road Taxes, Road User Charges and Earmarking", *Fiscal Studies*, 20 (2): 103–32.

Norman, P. 2004. "Efficient Mechanisms for Public Goods with Use Exclusions", *Review of Economic Studies*, 71(4): 1163–88.

Oakland, W.H. 1987. "Theory of Public Goods", in A.J. Auerbach and M. Feldstein (eds), *Handbook of Public Economics*, pp. 485–536. Amsterdam: North-Holland.

Ockenfels, Axel, David Reiley, and Abdolkarim Sadrieh. 2006. "Online Auctions", Working Paper 12785, National Bureau of Economic Research, Cambridge, Mass. Available online at http://www.nber.org/papers/w12785 (accessed October 8, 2008).

Oldman, Oliver. 1965. "Controlling Income Tax Evasion", in Joint Tax Program, *Problems of Tax Administration in Latin America*. Baltimore: Johns Hopkins University Press.

OECD. 1998. *Harmful Tax Competition: An Emerging Global Issue*. Paris: OECD Committee on Fiscal Affairs, available at http://www.oecd.org/dataoecd/33/1/1904184.pdf (downloaded on July 25, 2010).

———. 2004. *Changes to the Model Tax Convention* (articles 25 to 27) approved by the Committee on Fiscal Affairs on 1 June 2004. Available at http://www.oecd.org/dataoecd/28/4/33614065.pdf (downloaded on July 25, 2010).

OECD. 2005. *Articles of the Model Convention with Respect to Taxes on Income and on Capital*, as they read on 15 July 2005. Available at http://www.oecd.org/dataoecd/50/49/35363840.pdf (downloaded on July 25, 2010).

———. 2006. *Tax Administration in OECD and Selected Non-OECD Countries*, Comparative Information Series. Available at http://www.oecd.org/LongAbstract/0,3425,en_2649_33749_380 93383_119656_1_1_37427,00.html (downloaded on July 25, 2010).

Osmundsen, Petter. 1998. "Dynamic Taxation of Non-Renewable Natural Resources Under Asymmetric Information About Reserves", *Canadian Journal of Economics*, 31 (4): 933–51.

Owens, Jeffrey. 2002. "Tax Administration in the New Millennium" , *Intertax*, 30(4): 125–30.

PEFA Secretariat. 2006. *Public Financial Management (PFM) Performance Measurement Framework*. Washington DC: PEFA Secretariat, The World Bank. Available online at http://www.pefa.org/about_test.htm.

Polinsky A.M. and S. Shavell. 2000. "The Economic Theory of Public Enforcement of Law", *Journal of Economic Literature*, 38 (1): 45–76.

Poterba, James M. and Jiirgen von Hagen (eds). 1999. *Fiscal Institutions and Fiscal Performance*, National Bureau of Economic Research conference report, Chicago: University of Chicago Press. Available online at http://www.nber.org/books/pote99-1 (downloaded on October 3, 2008).

Potter, Barry H. and Jack Diamond. 1999. *Guidelines for Public Expenditure Management*. Washington DC: International Monetary Fund.

Rao, M. Govinda. 1981. *Political Economy of Tax and Expenditure Determination*. New Delhi: Allied Publishers.

Rattsø, John. 2003. "Fiscal Federation or Confederation in the European Union: The Challenge of the Common Pool Problem", Working paper, Department of Economics, Norwegian University of Science and Technology. Available at http://www.svt.ntnu.no/iso/Jorn. Rattso/Papers/jrffieurev.pdf (accessed September 18, 2008).

Razin, Assaf and Efraim Sadka. 1991. "International Tax Competition and Gains from Tax Harmonization", *Economics Letters*, 37(August): 69–76.

Rosen, Harvey S. and Ted Gayer. 2007. *Public Finance*, 8th edition. Boston: McGraw-Hill.

Sankar, U.1992. *Public Sector Pricing: Theory and Applications*. New Delhi: Indian Economic Association Trust for Research and Development.

Sawyer, Adrian. 2005. "Is the International Tax Organisation and Appropriate Forum for Administering Binding Rulings and APA's?", in Rodney Fisher and Michael Walpole (eds), *Global Challenges in Tax Administration*, pp. 67–97. Birmingham: Fiscal Publications.

Schantz, Radford Jr. 1994. "Purpose and Effects of a Royalty on Public Land Minerals", *Resources Policy*, 20 (1): 35–48.

Schiavo-Campo, S. and Daniel Tommasi. 1999. *Managing Government Expenditure*, Manila: Asian Development Bank. Available online at http://www.adb.org/documents/manuals/govt_expenditure/default.asp (downloaded on July 25, 2010).

Schmitz, P.W. 1997. "Monopolistic Provision of Excludable Public Goods under Private Information", *Public Finance*, 52 (1): 89–101.

Sepehri, Ardeshir and Robert Chernomas. 2001. "Are User Charges Efficiency and Equity Enhancing? A Critical Review of Economic Literature with Particular Reference to Experience from Developing Countries", *Journal of International Development*, 13 (2) 183–209.

Shah, Anwar. (ed.). 2006. *Budgeting and Budgetary Institutions*, Washington DC: The World Bank. Available online athttp://siteresources.worldbank.org/PSGLP/Resources/BudgetingandBudgetaryInstitutions.pdf (downloaded on July 25, 2010).

Shah, Tushaar, Mark Giordano, and Jinxia Wang. 2004. "Irrigation Institutions in a Dynamic Economy", *Economic and Political Weekly*, 39(July 31): 3452–61.

Silva, Emilson C.D. 2003. "Incentive Effects of Performance-Based Rewards in Tax Administration", in John McLaren (ed.), *Institutional Elements of Tax Design and Reform*, Technical paper no. 539, pp. 135–52. Washington DC: The World Bank.

Slemrod, Joel and Shlomo Yitzhaki. 1996. "The Social Cost of Taxation and the Marginal Cost of Funds", *International Monetary Fund Staff Papers*, 43 (1): 172–98.

————. 2001. "Integrating Expenditure and Tax Decisions: The Marginal Cost of Funds and the Marginal Benefit of Projects", *National Tax Journal*, 54(2): 189–201.

Stiglitz Joseph E. and Partha Dasgupta. 1971. "Differential Taxation, Public Goods and Economic Efficiency", *Review of Economic Studies*, 38 (2); 151–74.

Stiglitz, Joseph E. 2000. *Economics of Public Sector*, 3rd edition. New York and London: WW Norton.

Tanzi, Vito. 1999. "Is There a Need for a World Tax Organization?", in Assaf Razin and Ephriam Sadka (eds), *The Economics of Globalization: Policy Perspectives from Public Economics*, pp. 173-87. Cambridge and New York: Cambridge University Press.

————. 2000. "Globalization, Technological Developments, and the Work of Fiscal Termites", Working paper WP/00/181, Washington DC: International Monetary Fund.

————. 2008. "Theory and Practice of Tax Policy and Reform in a Globalizing Era", Presentation made at the Conference on Tax Reform in Globalization Era, Tokyo, February 23, 2008. Available online at http://www.hit-u.ac.jp/IPP/pep (downloaded on July 25, 2010).

Trehan, B. and C.E. Walsh. 1990. "Seigniorage and Tax Smoothing in the United States. 1914-1986", *Journal of Monetary Economics*, 25 (1): 97–112.

United Nations. 1993. *System of National Accounts 1993*, New York: United Nations and other organizations.

US Department of Commerce, IPV6 Task Force. 2006. *Technical and Economic Assessment of Internet Protocol, Version 6 (IPv6)*, Washington DC: National Telecommunications and Information Administration, National Institute of Standards and Technology. Available online at http://www.ntia.doc.gov/ntiahome/ntiageneral/ipv6/final/IPv6finalTOC.htm (downloaded on July 25, 2010).

Vann, Richard J. 1998. "International Aspects of Income Tax", in Victor Thuronyi (ed.), *Tax Law and Drafting*, pp. 718–810. Washington: International Monetary Fund.

von Hagen, Jürgen. 2006. "Budgeting Institutions for Better Fiscal Performance", in Anwar Shah (ed.), *Budgeting and Budgetary Institutions*, pp. 27–88. Washington DC: The World Bank. Available at http://siteresources.worldbank.org/PSGLP/Resources/BudgetingandBudgetaryInstitutions.pdf.

Wagner, Richard E. (ed.) 1991. *Charging for Government: User Charges and Earmarked Taxes in Principle and Practice*, London and New York: Routledge.

Webb, Michael C. 2004. "Defining the Boundaries of Legitimate State Practice: Norms, Transnational Actors, and the OECD's Project on Harmful Tax Competition". *Review of International Political Economy*, 11 (4): 787–827.

Weingast, B., K. Shepsle, and C. Johnsen. 1981. "The Political Economy of Benefits and Costs: A Neoclassical Approach to Redistributive Politics", *Journal of Political Economy*, 89 (4): 642–64.

Wilson, J.Q. 1989. *Bureaucracy: What Government Agencies Do and Why They Do It*. New York: Basic Books.

World Bank. 1998. *Public Expenditure Management Handbook*, Washington, DC: World Bank. Available online at http://www1.worldbank.org/publicsector/pe/handbook/pem98.pdf (downloaded on July 25, 2010).

World Bank. 2003. *World Development Indicators*. Washington DC: World Bank.

Wrede, Matthias. 1999. "Tragedy of the Fiscal Common? Fiscal Stock Externalities in a Leviathan Model of Federalism", *Public Choice*, 101 (3): 177–93.

Yang, Dean. 2005. "Integrity for Hire: An Analysis of a Widespread Program for Combating Customs Corruption", Ford School of Public Policy Working Paper Series No. 2005–001, University of Michigan, Ann Arbor. Available online at http://papers.ssrn.com/paper. taf?abstract_id=649095 (downloaded on July 25, 2010).

Zagaris, Bruce. 2001. "Tax Havens Beware, Fiscal Transparency, and What Else? The Rules are Changing and it's Crazy Out There!", *Journal of International Banking Regulation*, 3(2): 111–44.

———. 2003. "Increasing Cooperation of International Tax Enforcement and Anti-Money-Laundering Enforcement", *Tax Notes International*, 32 (November 17): 649–63.

Zee, Howell H. 1998. "Taxation of Financial Capital in a Globalized Environment: The Role of Withholding Taxes", *National Tax Journal*, 51(3): 587–99.

Zee, Howell H., Janet G. Stotsky, and Eduardo Ley. 2002. "Tax Incentives for Business Investment: A Primer for Policy Makers in Developing Countries", *World Development*, 30 (September): 1497–516.

Reminiscences

A Teacher Remembers

TAPAS MAJUMDAR

I have been greatly fortunate in having had a string of highly talented students spread over all my years of teaching. Of many of these, I can truthfully say, I eventually extracted very much more from them than whatever little I could have given them in the first place. Amaresh Bagchi was a late-comer in this illustrious group and also the senior-most. I found it a matter of extra pride that he chose me for his Ph.D. supervisor; after all, he was only two years my junior at college. But it is not for this I wanted to sit down and write this today. I wanted to tell people instead of the success story he made of his own life. He turned from what he considered only humdrum to what, to him, was *meaningful*. He boldly took action before it was too late for he already had reached middle age! I write this wanting to pay my departed old student, friend, and mentor a small tribute I could not pay before. Amaresh Bagchi's example should not go unrecorded though, as you will see, his recipe for changing to a life of meaningful work that he had boldly followed without any fanfare was a difficult one even in our times (his and mine). Today people, running after ready fixes, might even call such effort absolute madness. I don't know whose judgment you will take.

It was in 1967 I think, Amaresh Bagchi one day turned up in my den at Presidency College and announced he was preparing for the life of a teacher and researcher. Would I help him? Once that end was achieved, he would be ready to give up his steady government job as an income tax officer in the IRS. He had appeared at the IAS examinations only because he could not afford a waiting time before starting a career. He had tried but found no job in the academic line. So he had entered the "babudom". But he had gone on with his own studies and private research. I showed some interest possibly because he was an old friend and he had enjoyed a good reputation at college. Moreover, Panchanan Chakrabartty and Bhabatosh Datta, both our teachers held a high opinion of his abilities. Panchanan Babu once even spoke to me of his disappointment when he found Amaresh had to go and join the IRS. I was also thrilled a bit by the idea itself of throwing up a safe job almost at middle age for the sake of the kind of work one hankered for. Amaresh actually wanted to use me as a sounding board, and gave me some of the things he had written for my candid opinion. I had to spend a few days reading it all through. My surprise increased as I proceeded. I increasingly realized I did not even recognize most of the literature in Public Finance he was referring to and I was then teaching Public Finance in the Economics Honours classes at college! A bit of Musgrave and others I had picked up on my own but this was much much more—spreading out from economics into constitutional law and political science! Amaresh was getting interested in the working of federal systems while the usual basically addressed the simpler model of the unitary state. Already, he was far in advance of my knowledge in these areas.

Recalling all this after nearly forty years—I have to admit we used to be very poorly trained in Public Finance at university in our days at the hands of even eminent economists—was difficultt. For example, we knew next to nothing about the crucial problems and constraints that a federal state had to address in coordinating the fiscal powers between the Center and the states as laid down in the Constitution or in actual practice responding to the perceived interests of the different constituent states of India.

To continue my story, I wasted no time and consulted Bhabatosh Babu. Our Centre at Presidency had a Research Fellow's post to offer. Could we have Amaresh for this for a start? His advice was very positive. My colleagues Mihir Rakshit and Dipak Banerjee supported the proposal enthusiastically. The Principal agreed and made Amaresh the offer. Amaresh took this to his superiors, and was granted something like a study leave for him tenable at Presidency, within an amazingly short period of time. We all felt triumphant and happily Amaresh joined us.

That was the beginning of his year of misery! Amaresh did not get his salary for most part of the year. First, AG West Bengal kept returning the bill on one pretext or other. We patiently went on meeting the objections. We learnt on inquiry all this was only preliminary; the main blow was coming. It came. The section under which the Board of Direct Taxes had passed the other did not apply to moving an officer from the Central to a state government. The Board had failed to recognize that Presidency College was part of a state government. Both Amaresh and Ratna, his brave wife, bore this stoically. You can imagine how the rest of us at Presidency felt. The revised order came at some point. Amaresh happily went back to his parent office in Delhi after the stint, quite satisfied with his own progress and totally unperturbed.

After I came over to Jawaharlal Nehru University (JNU) in 1972, Amaresh told me he was now ready to do his Ph.D. with me. The subject? Federal Tax policy. This was acceptable to my new Centre for Educational Studies at JNU too, for Education has been always a disputed terrain between the Centre and the states. When he finished, the two greatest luminaries of that period, Lakdawalla and K.N. Raj were appointed the external examiners. When it was all over, both told me they had never seen a better dissertation. Both said his long experience was not really meaningless after all, for it had given an authentic finish to the body of the dissertation. Amaresh Bagchi never had to look back after that. But IRS would not let go of him so easily. That is another story.

The happy ending came when the newly founded National Institute of Public Finance and Policy made him first its Professor, then Director, and finally Emeritus. I have not given you in this account the murkier details of his brave struggle for a life of academic freedom and creativity that he won at last. His sixty-page introduction to the Readings in Public Finance (2005) that he edited also contains his updated review article on two contrasting visions of the state (one of Buchanan and the other of Musgrave). These will remain definitive. These late writings will show he had won.

Very few knew of another struggle Amaresh was calmly waging inside his body. Only two evenings before the end, he and Ratna had come to visit us after I had been recently released from hospital. He looked no different—a fighter and victor to the end.

My Friend Amaresh*

Shankar Acharya

On the morning of February 20th, a good man passed away in Delhi. He may not have been famous. But he was well-known and greatly respected and loved amongst the community of public finance scholars and practitioners. Above all, he was a gem of a human being, one in a million. Amaresh Bagchi finally succumbed to the blood cancer ailment he had so valiantly fought for the last 12 years. Few knew of his ailment. He bore its tribulations with characteristic grace and stoicism. Understated and self-effacing as ever, this outstanding scholar-cum-public-servant continued to serve the cause of rational and humane public policy to his last day. His demise leaves a gaping void among the handful of top-notch public finance specialists who have served the country so well in the last few decades.

Born in Malda, Bengal in 1930, Amaresh-da (as he was widely known) lived a rather unusual life. After graduating from Presidency College, Kolkata and acquiring a master's degree in economics, he joined the Income Tax Service in the early 1950s. For the next 15 years he followed his chosen vocation with vigor and dedication. It included his tenacious pursuit of tax evasion cases relating to some prominent politicians of eastern India. In at least one famous case his tenacity won the grudging respect of his quarry. But the administration of income tax was too confining an activity for the breadth of his interests, especially in economics and public policy. In 1967 he took a year's study leave and returned to Presidency College as a senior fellow at its Centre for Economic Study. The following year he was transferred to Delhi to serve

---

* An earlier version of this chapter was published in Business Standard, February 25, 2008.

at the Ministry of Finance, initially in Revenue, then Banking and later in the Department of Economic Affairs (DEA).

The DEA became his professional home for most of the next 18 years, with occasional forays into academics: a couple of years in the early 1970s, writing his rigorous and thoughtful doctoral thesis on the "Concept of Income in Taxation" at JNU under Professor Tapas Majumdar; and later, another couple of years in the early 1980s as RBI Chair Professor at the National Institute of Public Finance and Policy (NIPFP). During 1975–80 he directed the DEA's Fiscal Policy Unit with unmatched distinction. From 1985 onwards Amaresh-da was the jewel in the crown of NIPFP, the first 10 years as its Director and the last 13 as Emeritus Professor.

During his 40 years in Delhi, Amaresh Bagchi was an invaluable resource to all those engaged in the conduct and reform of Indian public finance, especially tax policy, tax administration, and fiscal federalism. Perhaps uniquely among public finance specialists, he knew and understood the nitty gritty of tax administration. He could bridge the great divides between the "practical men" and the economists. And among economists he was equally respected by the academics of Delhi School of Economics and JNU and the policy types in government. Almost every serious government report on tax reform owes some debt to Amaresh-da, ranging as far back as the 1972 K.N. Raj report on taxation of agricultural income and wealth. More recently, he was the key member of the hugely influential Raja Chelliah Tax Reforms Committee, whose reports (1991–93) guided the far-reaching tax reforms of the 1990s. In 1998–2000, he was the specialist Member and guiding light of the Eleventh Finance Commission. At the time of his death he was serving as a Member of the Commission on Center–state relations.

Amaresh Bagchi's scholarly output on public finance topics was prolific and diverse, especially during his 25 year association with NIPFP. Perhaps, his single most influential contribution was the classic study (authored by him and his NIPFP team in 1994) on "Reform of Domestic Trade Taxes in India". This was the key document guiding the subsequent reform of state sales taxes (into state level VATs) and exploring the options available for an integrated national VAT, which has finally culminated in the government's commitment to an integrated GST. Over the last three decades he published frequently in the *Economic and Political Weekly*, not just in his own name but often through un-attributed editorials and commentary. Aside from his own writings, Amaresh-da also contributed enormously through his unstinting support and guidance to dozens of young scholars at NIPFP, and to numerous civil servants with academic aspirations. He was a true institution builder at NIPFP, toiling unceasingly to attract the best available talent, giving them the requisite freedom and flexibility, and striving to maintain high standards.

Like most Presidency graduates and Bengali *bhadroloks* of his generation, Amaresh-da's politics were left off-centre. Unlike many of them, his intellectual integrity and honesty rejected the cant and hypocrisy which often accompanied the Left's monopoly of political power in Bengal for the last three decades. Especially in recent years, he was forthright and fearless in his trenchant critiques of West Bengal's weak economic and social performance. Amaresh-da's humility and politeness were legendary. They were matched only by his steely adherence to what he believed to be right and true. Characteristically, when I conveyed the news of Bagchi's demise to Governor Reddy of RBI, his instant reaction was "a warm-hearted, humble man but utterly fearless...and with great intellectual integrity".

Amaresh Bagchi's lifestyle was simple and frugal. He was uncomfortable with the growing consumerism and widening disparities of Indian society and bemoaned the failure of the government sector in providing decent education and health services to the vast majority of the country's citizens. In our semi-feudal, class-ridden society, he was a natural democrat. Coupled with his innate warmth and humanity, he had authentic empathy for the weak and poor. Perhaps, it was this warmth and humanity which was Amaresh's most endearing feature. A small anecdote: in the mid-1990s the Bagchis lived in our current flat in Delhi for a couple of years. They employed a part-time cleaning lady, who has continued to work in our building since then. When we informed her of Amaresh-da's death, she spontaneously burst into tears remembering her kind and good-hearted employer of a decade ago. I wonder how many of Delhi's luminaries would trigger such grief from their household help of yesteryears.

At the personal level, I feel immensely privileged to have been counted among Amaresh-da's friends. Although he was some 15 years older and we lived different lives, it didn't seem to detract from our mutual affection and respect. When I first returned to India in 1982 to join NIPFP, Amaresh-da was there to help smooth my transition back to Delhi, after 23 years abroad. Three years later, he was there again to induct me into the Finance Ministry. I learned much about India and her economic problems from him. Most of all, I am grateful for the opportunity to be friends with one of the most truly civilized and kind human beings to cross my path. They say that when a good man passes away, the whole world feels a little diminished. I used to think that was just a turn of phrase. Unfortunately, now I know what it means.

About the Editors and Contributors

————— • ✦ • —————

The Editors

M. Govinda Rao is the Director of National Institute of Public Finance and Policy. He is also a Member of Economic Advisory Council to the Prime Minister. His past positions include Director, Institute for Social and Economic Change, Bangalore (1998–2002) and Fellow, Research School of Pacific and Asian Studies, Australian National University, Canberra, Australia (1995–98). Besides being a Member of the Economic Advisory Council to the Prime Minister, he has served on several advisory panels such as Member, International Advisory Panel on Governance; Member, Expert Committee on Multilevel Planning, Planning Commission, Government of India; Chairman, Expert Group on Taxation of Services (2000–01); Chairman, Technical Experts Committee on VAT; and Member, Consultative Group of Interstate Council, Government of India. He is also a Member of the Taxation Policy Group in the Initiative for Policy Dialogue led by Professor Joseph Stiglitz of Columbia University.

Dr Rao's research interests include public finance and fiscal policy, fiscal federalism, and state and local finance. He has been a consultant to the World Bank, International Monetary Fund, Asian Development Bank, and the UNDP on issues relating to tax policy and reforms, public expenditure management and fiscal decentralization in Cambodia, China, Laos, Pakistan, and Vietnam. His recent books include *Political Economy of Federalism in India* (2005); *Sustainable Fiscal Policy for India: An International Perspective* (edited with Peter Heller, 2006); and *Development, Poverty and Fiscal Policy* (2005).

Mihir Rakshit is the Director of Monetary Research Project at ICRA Ltd., Kolkata. He is the President of Annual Econometric Society. He is also the Editor-in-Chief of the journal *Money and Finance*. Dr Rakshit received his Doctorate from London School of Economics and went on to serve as Professor and Head of the Department of Economics at Presidency College, Kolkata. He chaired the Economics Research Unit of the Indian Statistical Institute, Kolkata. He also served as faculty in the Delhi School of Economics, Delhi, India and the Erasmus University, Rotterdam, Netherlands. He has been an advisor to the Indian Government as well as on the Board of Directors of the Reserve Bank of India (RBI). Dr Rakshit's field of expertise includes money and finance, transnational macroeconomics, and crises and recovery in developing economies.

Some of his publications include *Trade, Mercantile Capital, and Economic Development* (1993); *The East Asian Currency Crisis* (2001); *Macroeconomics of Post-reform India* (2008); *Money and Finance in the Indian Economy* (2008); *Studies in the Macroeconomics of Developing Countries* (1989); *Issues in Economic Theory and Public Policy* (co-edited with A. Bose and A. Sinha, 1997); *Planning and Economic Policy in India: Evaluation and Lessons for the Future* (co-edited with M. Chattopadhyay and Pradip Maiti, 1996); and *Essays on Public Intervention, Institutional Arrangements and Economic Efficiency* (co-edited with M. Chattopadhyay and Pradip Maiti, 1999).

The Contributors

Shankar Acharya is Honorary Professor and Member, Board of Governors at the Indian Council for Research on International Economic Relations (ICRIER) and former Chief Economic Advisor to the Government of India.

Ehtisham Ahmad is Division Chief of Fiscal Affairs Department, International Monetary Fund, Washington DC.

Richard M. Bird is Faculty at Business Economics, Rotman School of Management, University of Toronto.

Arindam Das-Gupta is Senior Professor and Head, Centre for Economic Research at the Goa Institute of Management, Raibandar, Goa.

Tapas Majumdar is Professor Emeritus at Academic Staff College, Jawaharlal Nehru University (JNU), New Delhi.

Anjan Mukherji is RBI Chair Professor at Centre for Economic Studies and Planning, JNU, New Delhi.

Arnab Mukherji is Assistant Professor at Center for Public Policy at Indian Institute of Management, Bangalore.

Sudipto Mundle is Professor Emeritus at National Institute of Public Finance and Policy, New Delhi.

Satya Poddar is Partner, Ernst & Young Pvt. Ltd

U. Sankar is Honorary Professor at Madras School of Economics, Chennai.

Ramprasad Sengupta is Professor at Centre for Economic Studies and Planning, JNU, New Delhi.

Nicholas Stern is IG Patel Chair and Director, Asia Research Centre, London School of Economics.

Index

Japan, 73
  levy tax, 87
  tax rate, 73, 89

land, and real property, 92–94
liberalization of trade in services,
  151
liberal open economy, 5
literacy, 27, 228, 233
loan forgiveness programs, 40
low entropy resources, 182
low income states, 136

macro-economic income, 181,
  220
  depletion adjusted, 220–22
macro-economy, 26
  indicator of sustainability of,
    218
  multi-sectoral, 203
  return on man-made capital
    employed in, 205
  waste flow in, 204
marginal benefit of public
  expenditure (MBP), 264
marginal productivity, 19
market-based instruments, 134
market-based liberalization, 134
market-oriented decentralized
  systems, 137
maximum retail price (MRP), 66
Millennium Development Goals
  (MDGs), 146
  as global public goods, 148
Ministry of Finance (MF), 5, 6,
  7, 12
modern property tax system,
  133
modern VAT system, 93

monetary asset accounts
  for non-produced economic
    assets, 212
  for produced assets, 211
multiple VAT rates, 73
municipal finances, 6
municipalities, 6

national GST, 81–83, 89
National Highway Development
  Programme (NHDP), 30
national income, 23, 113, 180,
  181, 185, 205, 206, 215
National Institute of Public
  Finance and Policy (NIPFP), 6,
  7, 9, 64, 163, 325, 327
national ownership neutrality,
  293
national tax, 74, 289
  policy, 299–301
national tax neutrality (NN),
  293
National University of
  Educational Planning and
  Administration (NUEPA), 228
national VAT, 82
natural assets classification, 210
natural environment, 181, 182
  for life support, 181
neoclassical economy, debt in,
  18–21
Net Domestic Product (NDP),
  185
New Zealand
  effects of carbon taxes and
    welfare in, 175
  Goods and Services Tax (GST)
    supplies taxable under, 96
  yield revenues, 113

public financial management,
304
public funding, 228, 229, 238,
247, 250, 251
public investment, 18, 23, 30,
31, 127
publicly-funded capital stock,
18
public sector, 4, 29, 30, 49, 96,
124, 132, 136, 262, 268, 269
public service delivery, 301
mixed public–private
provision, options for, 302
provision/delivery, options
for, 301
pure global public goods
(GPGs), 145, 149, 158, 159

Quebec Sales Tax (QST), 111

reform, directions of
welfare loss, 172, 174, 175
India, rankings of, 175
Pakistan, ranking of, 174
welfare weights, 173
Reform of Domestic Trade Taxes
in India, 327
regional development, balanced,
135–37
regional equity, 135
rent control act, 132
research and development (R&D)
activities, 183, 184
Reserve Bank of India (RBI), 6,
12
foreign exchange reserves, 13
regulations, 4
residential rentals, exemption
from taxes, 93

resources
allocations, 135
and environmental
accounting, 192–96
additions of values to GDP/
Gross Investment, 195
conservation/protection of
resources, 194
depleted natural resource
stock, 195
dimensions of national
accounts system, 194
macro-economic
accounting system,
changes, 195
non-produced economic
assets, 194
for the R&D sector's
investment, 193
stock dynamics, 193
regeneration, 182
supply of, 181
revenue, 52
balances, 17
deficit, 13, 14, 15–17
conventional estimates of,
24
definition and uses, 24–25
measures, 24, 25
raising, 51
surplus, 14
from taxing capital income,
41
Revenue Department, Ministry of
Finance, 4
revenue neutral rate (RNR), 88
reverse-charge mechanism,
105
Rio principle, 149, 153–55